The 1984 Election
and the Future of American Politics

The 1984 Election
and the Future of American Politics

Edited by

Peter W. Schramm
Dennis J. Mahoney

Carolina Academic Press
and
The Claremont Institute for the Study of
Statesmanship and Political Philosophy

Library of Congress Catalog Card Number 86-71002

International Standard Book Number   0-89089-311-X

Printed in the United States of America

Carolina Academic Press
Post Office Box 8795
Durham, North Carolina 27707

Contents

Preface   vii

Introduction   ix

Foreign Policy in the 1984 Campaign: A Retreat from the
Brink?
Patrick J. Garrity   3

Reaganomics Manqué, Realignment Manqué
Thomas B. Silver   25

The 1984 Democratic Primary Election: Issues and Image
Glen E. Thurow   37

A Political Party in Search of Itself: Republican Realignment
and the Dallas Platform of 1984
Douglas A. Jeffrey and Dennis Teti   53

The General Election Campaign: Going for the Gold
Dennis J. Mahoney   73

Demography of 1984's National Majorities
John Adams Wettergreen   89

The Campaign Strategy of the 1984 Election: Partisan
Realignment or Minority Party Victory?
Thomas F. Payne   109

Party Rules
Josiah Lee Auspitz   133

Money in Politics: Campaign Finance Reform and the 1984
Election
John Marini   183

The Teflon Media
Steven Hayward   211

Ethnicity and Politics: Citizens as "the mutual guardians of
their mutual happiness" and the Politics of Realignment
Ken Masugi   223

The Reagan Revolution and the Legacy of the New Deal:
Obstacles to Party Realignment
Charles R. Kesler   245

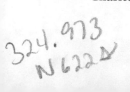

Incumbency and Nonpartisanship in the Congressional
   Elections
      Peter W. Schramm   265

The 1984 Election: Entitlements Versus Opportunity
      Harvey C. Mansfield, Jr.   277

Appendix   289

Contributors   297

Index   299

Preface

We intend that this book, although written by several hands, should present a coherent and comprehensive account of the events and procedures involved in the 1984 election. Each chapter describes and analyzes some key element of the electoral process or of the 1984 election. This book differs from other standard works on recent elections in focusing on the issues dividing the candidates and the parties. We intend that the book should show why it makes a difference whether Ronald Reagan or Walter Mondale was successful in the election, and should examine how the American people went about deciding which would prevail. We hope that this book will be a useful reference for citizens interested in the electoral process in general and in the 1984 election in particular. But the special audience of the book comprises students in college courses in parties, politics, and elections.

It has become fashionable in recent years for political scientists' books about American politics and elections to overwhelm the reader with statistics and with "behavioral" analysis. Under a veneer of mathematical symbols suggesting scientific precision, there is generally a mass of unwarranted assumptions and untested hypotheses. Very often the authors do not respect politics as the distinctly human activity, but treat political things as quantitative data, much like those of physics or chemistry. The approach tends to put readers—including students—at a distance from the phenomena of political life.

This is not, however, the way we experience politics. As citizens and as participants in campaigns and elections, we are excited: the events of the campaign and the results of the election elate or distress us. The quadrennial exercise of choosing a President dominates the news reports and enlivens our private conversations. All this is so because we are engaged in determining how we shall be governed, and because we believe that the results of the elections will really make a difference.

A book—and especially a textbook—about the election should convey that excitement and that involvement. Too often the events and results of electoral campaigns are presented as sterile data, without significance except such as the political scientist imposes by virtue of his technique. We believe that a textbook is needed which conveys to the student the importance of the electoral process as well as imparting information about technical aspects of the party structure or of campaign strategy.

The structure of the book is intended to form a convenient outline for the study of the election. We begin with discussions of the issues, foreign and domestic, that were to be decided by the election, we then tell the story of the campaign from the early days before the Iowa caucuses and the New Hampshire primary right through election night, next we examine various structural or institutional aspects of the campaign, after which we look at special constituencies or complexes of issues. Finally, we look at the congressional elections. Within each section, and within each chapter, we consider a number of questions bearing on the issues, the candidates, the campaign, and the electoral process itself.

One young professor, recently assigned to teach a course on politics and elections, remarked of the available texts that one could read them all and still not know anything important about the American political system. We hope that he will not be able to say this about the present book.

Introduction

A collection of essays about a presidential election that is over is perforce a work on the past of American politics. Indeed, nearly a year had elapsed between the 1984 election and the preparation of the final draft of many of the essays in this book. The emphasis in each of the essays is on the issues, events, and personalities of the 1984 election campaign; none of the essays ventures to make a prediction as to what issues, events, or personalities may predominate in 1988 or beyond. How, then, can this be said to be a book about the *future* of American politics?

In the first place, an election is a prospective event. More and more, in commentary on American politics, both journalists and political scientists treat elections as retrospective. Public officeholders are said to be always running for reelection, and the results of any election are subject to interpretation in terms of their approving or disapproving of the conduct of the officeholder during the term then ending. Because such commentators regard running for reelection as the primary activity of officeholders, one who is constitutionally debarred from reelection or who declines to seek reelection is frequently regarded as politically irrelevant. Hence even pundits who should know better (such as John McLaughlin) began referring to President Reagan as a "lame duck" as soon as his reelection seemed assured (although the term "lame duck" properly applies to an officeholder who has *lost* his bid for reelection and is therefore without a prospective mandate from the people). Such analyses, to the extent to which the public pays them any attention, may even be said to foster retrospective voting.

Nevertheless, nothing could be clearer than that the result of an election is to invest the winner with the powers, and to charge the winner with the duties, of a particular officer for a term not yet begun. Properly understood, a candidate's previous performance in an office to which he seeks reelection, is relevant to the electors only as one indicator of how he will perform in the future. It is certainly no safe predictor of future performance; well may the candidate for reelection say, "You ain't seen nothin' yet."

An election, then, represents the people's opportunity to make choices about their future governance. Such choices may not always be wisely made. Autonomously under the guidance of journalists and political scientists, the people may prodigally use this opportunity to indicate their sentiments concerning the immediate political past. Even if that is so, however, the election serves to determine the direction of the political future.

Therefore, a book about the 1984 election, to the extent that it takes seriously the phenomenon of the election as an exercise of the people's choice, is a book about the future of American politics. It is a book about how the people have chosen to be governed during the period 1985-1989.

But the 1984 election may prove to have a bearing on the future of American politics extending well beyond the term of office of those elected in that year. Throughout the campaign one heard, from the lips of politicians, of commentators, and even of the candidates themselves, the word "realignment." There was a sense among the electorate that more was at stake in 1984 than a four-year lease on the White House.

The term "realignment," once a bit of technical jargon used by political scientists and political historians, became part of the working vocabulary of reporters, columnists, and voters. Behind the term is the history of party emergence and party decline, of political crisis, and, consequently, of critical elections. From time to time, throughout the two hundred years of America's history as an independent federal Republic, an election has proved to be the end of a political era and the beginning of a new era. This happens when the voters take the reins of government out of the hands of a party that has held them for some time and gives them to a new, or newly reorganized, party.

In critical elections, the public is faced with a clear alternative between divergent views of America as a nation, of the Constitution as the frame of government for that nation, and of the principles by which that nation is to be governed. Between critical elections, the choice is between parties and candidates who offer alternative courses of action within the context of a shared understanding of the most important questions.

A consideration of the future of American politics must begin with the possibility that the 1984 election was, or might have been, such a watershed. As will transpire, it is the consensus of the political scientists who have contributed to this volume that there was no realignment in 1984, although many of the authors believe that 1984 offered an opportunity for realignment, and some believe that the election results amount to a partial or incipient realignment.

The consensus among the authors comprises an understanding of realignment that is somewhat at odds with the majority of political scientists. We think of realignment as a phenomenon essentially related to political conviction rather than, for example, to demographics. That is, if (or when) realignment occurs, the most important fact about it will be the emergence of a new national consensus concerning the regime. No doubt it will also be true that political power will have shifted to a new coalition of regional, economic, ethnic, and religious interests, but that fact will be of secondary importance.

The dominant political conviction of the United States from the early 1930s to the late 1960s was the New Deal synthesis of the social welfare state at home and interventionism abroad. Shortly after it was introduced by the Democratic Party, the same theme was adopted by the Republican Party, albeit in a less robust form; the Republican Party, which had dominated American national politics since the beginning of the Civil War became the party of "me too," as the Democrats established themselves in all three branches of the national government. By the end of Lyndon Johnson's presidency, however, the broad base of support for the New Deal consensus had eroded. During its brief revival in the Carter-Mondale administration, interest-group liberalism was transformed into the ideology of the entitlement state, and American politics bade fair to become little more than an auction.

The process of realignment began with the success of the Goldwater movement in 1964 in making the Republican Party the vehicle of active opposition to the New Deal consensus. Paradoxically, the process was interrupted by another success, namely that of Richard M. Nixon. The debacle of the Watergate election of 1974, which erased all the gains the new Republicans had made, temporarily diverted public attention from the main political question to matters of housekeeping. The Democratic Party seized the opportunity thus provided to entrench itself in the legislative branch through reapportionment.

The future of American politics, at least in the short term, depends upon the progress of the realignment that 1984 did not bring to fruition. The realignment process may have reached a peak, from which American politics will descend again to the squalid competition between the beneficiaries of rival entitlement programs. Or the Reagan Revolution may have so "dealigned" American politics that interest group liberalism has become a thing of the past, but, by so doing may merely have opened a window of vulnerability to a new realignment to leftward. Or the 1980 and 1984 elections may prove to have been incidents in a rolling realignment that, by 1988 or 1992, may transform American politics for the next half century.

To consider the presidential election of 1984 is to consider the future of American politics, whether in the short or the long term. Each of the essays in this collection was written with that in mind. Some of the essays concentrate on the election itself, while others explicitly take the longer view. But the essays are all part of an attempt to understand the future of American politics by understanding the election of 1984.

The 1984 Election
and the Future of American Politics

Foreign and Defense Policy in the 1984 Campaign:
A Retreat from the Brink

Patrick J. Garrity

To have some understanding of the role that national security issues played in the 1984 presidential campaign, it is first essential to recall the election four years previously. The Republican challenger, Ronald Reagan, based his campaign on the theme of restoring America's greatness, both at home and abroad—implying, and often explicitly stating, that the incumbent, Jimmy Carter, had led the nation into economic ruin and grave international danger. The rhetoric of the 1980 Republican party platform was stark:

> The Republican Party convenes, presents this platform, and selects its nominees at a time of crisis. Our country moves agonizingly, aimlessly, almost helplessly into one of the most dangerous and disorderly periods in history.

The platform was particularly unstinting in its criticism of Carter's failures as diplomat and Commander-in-Chief. An explicit comparison was drawn between Britain's strategic blindness in the late 1930s and the United States' alleged global pusillanimity in the late 1970s—with Jimmy Carter playing the role of a latter-day Neville Chamberlain.

> At the start of the 1980s, the United States faces the most serious challenge to its survival in the two centuries of its existence.... The Administration's neglect of America's defense posture in the face of overwhelming evidence of a threatening military buildup is without parallel since the 1930s.... Mired in incompetence, bereft of strategic vision and purpose, the President's failure to shoulder the burden of leadership in the Atlantic Alliance has placed America in danger without parallel since December 7, 1941.

The bill of particulars charged against the Carter Administration included reducing the size and capacity of U.S. nuclear forces despite an ominous Soviet buildup; undermining of friendly governments besieged by Soviet and Soviet-bloc military forces; ignoring the increased Soviet military threat to Western Europe, the Middle East, Southern Africa, and vital shipping lanes; and failing to respond to terrorist assaults on American citizens and diplomats abroad. The Carter Administration's strategic follies were epitomized by the "fundamentally flawed" SALT II Treaty, which was the focus of Republican and conservative attacks in 1979 and throughout the 1980 campaign, even after President Carter withdrew the Treaty from Senate consideration. SALT II was portrayed in the platform as a technical, and even more importantly a political, admission by the President that he was "content to passively accept the gradual but inexorable decline of America."

Strong words indeed from a party that, only four years previously, had embraced (however narrowly) the policies of an administration and a secretary of state (Henry Kissinger) that were based on Soviet-American detente and arms control. Ronald Reagan had unsuccessfully challenged President Ford in 1976 precisely on the grounds that those policies had failed and that their continuance (under a Republican or Democratic administration) would lead to grave international danger for the United States. But when Henry Kissinger mounted the rostrum of the 1980 Republican Convention he did so to assure the delegates that his policies and goals (what Richard Nixon had come to call "hard-headed detente") were not at all incompatible with the "Russians are coming" theme of the Reagan campaign. Kissinger's rhetoric clearly indicated that the center of gravity in the Republican Party had moved significantly to the right, at least on foreign and defense issues—i.e., more concern with the possibility of Soviet aggression, more emphasis on military spending and a satisfactory military balance, more focus on defending unilateral American interests.

The Republican party of 1980 self-consciously sought to redefine American foreign policy by turning back the clock, by rejecting the anti-interventionist consensus that obtained in the United States for most of the previous decade. The party preferred to return to an earlier way of approaching international affairs—unremitting opposition to Soviet expansionism—that had been largely discarded because of the American experience in Vietnam. There were even inclinations to challenge the Soviet empire along its marches, if not to attack the legitimacy of the Soviet regime itself. The party's tone was harsh, in the expectation that only strong and immediate action would prevent geopolitical catastrophe without war, and possibly even war itself. This was the stuff of 1950, of the period of anti-Soviet internationalism (known to some as the Cold War), vastly different from the retrenchment of the 1970s.

Significantly, the Carter administration (if not the Democratic Party as a whole) had also moved to the right from the time of the 1976 campaign and from many of its original policies—although not nearly so far as the Republicans. Candidate Jimmy Carter had pledged in 1976 to cut defense spending by $7 billion, and defense spending fell to a post-Korean War low as a percentage of the gross national product in the late 1970s; but the last five-year defense budget projections of the Carter administration were not significantly different from what President Reagan would eventually seek. Carter's early infatuation with a minimum nuclear deterrence policy was replaced with an endorsement of the "countervailing strategy" that continued the trend toward more flexible and militarily useful nuclear options. Prominent advocates of a radical "human rights" policy (e.g., U.N. Ambassador Andrew Young and Assistant Secretary of State Patricia Derian) were replaced or became less prominent. The 1980 Democratic party platform actually chided the "Nixon-

Ford Administration" for presiding over "a steady decline of 33 percent in real U.S. military spending between 1968 and 1976."

> Our fourth major objective is to strengthen the military security of the United States at a time when trends in the military balance have become increasingly adverse. America is now, and will continue to be, the strongest power on earth. It was the Democratic Party's greatest hope that we could, in fact, reduce our military effort. But realities of the world situation, including the unremitting buildup of Soviet military forces, required that we begin early to reduce the decade-long decline in American defense efforts.

A series of major foreign policy setbacks—including Soviet/Cuban operations in Ethiopia, the controversy over a Soviet "combat brigade" in Cuba, the fall of the Shah and the Iranian hostage crisis, and the Soviet invasion of Afghanistan—was apparently sufficient to persuade a majority of American voters that President Carter was not competent to deal with an increasingly dangerous international environment. It was not clear, however, whether the popular rejection of Carter could be completely equated with support for the rather revolutionary world view of Ronald Reagan.

This brief review of the major themes and events of 1980 is important because it provides the baseline from which the major themes and events of 1984 are best judged. The two critical questions arise from this approach. Was President Reagan able to devise and create political support for the radical national security approach—a return to a policy of anti-Soviet internationalism—that he had articulated as a candidate? Did the Democratic party respond to the defeat of Carter by moving to the left or to the right on defense and foreign policy issues?

Toward 1984: The Reagan Administration

The national security policies advocated by candidate Reagan were "revolutionary" and "radical." These terms are not used to indicate the correctness or incorrectness of these views, but rather their degree of departure from the general consensus about U.S. foreign policy that was dominant throughout most of the 1970s. This "post-Vietnam" consensus might generally by characterized as follows: the Soviet Union was not the sole, and perhaps not even the major, threat to international stability and American security; the United States had overextended its commitments abroad and therefore needed to reduce those commitments by distinguishing between vital and peripheral interests; the use of American military power in the Third World was as a rule futile and counterproductive; defense spending should decline relative to social spending; and the existence of large numbers of nuclear weapons had so fundamentally altered the nature of war and international politics that both superpowers were compelled to avoid direct conflict and to seek negotiated agreements to control these weapons.

In 1980 Reagan rejected each of these familiar post-Vietnam era tenets. The Soviet Union was, for rhetorical purposes at least, the source of all evil in the world. The United States should be willing to use force to protect its allies and interests abroad. A substantial five-year defense buildup was necessary, as the nation had significantly undervalued the relative importance of defense spending in the federal budget during the 1970s. Arms control had become the end rather than one of the means of national security policy, a misapprehension which the Soviets had successfully manipulated through a series of one-sided or unverifiable agreements, culminating in the SALT II Treaty. If there was any point of convergence between the post-Vietnam consensus and the Reagan program, it probably existed in the belief that the United States ought to redefine its priorities overseas. But while the Carter administration had attempted (at least until 1979) to shift U.S. defense emphasis toward Europe and away from Third World commitments (and hence was viewed as "anti-Navy"), the Reagan campaign and early presidency tended to be somewhat "anti-European" and strongly in favor of a naval buildup.

The most striking element of the late 1970s critique of the post-Vietnam foreign policy was the notion of a "window of vulnerability." The Soviet Union, it was feared, would soon obtain potentially decisive advantages in military power which might be translated into political gains if not victory in war. The growth in Soviet strategic nuclear power, and particularly in land-based ICBMs, suggested that the USSR was seeking more than to simply assure a balance of terror. The Soviet Union would shortly reach the point—partly sanctioned by favorable arms control agreements, partly by American unilateral restraint—where it could theoretically destroy in a first or preemptive strike virtually all of the U.S. land-based ICBM force, roughly two-thirds of the bomber force, and about one-half of the ballistic missile submarine force. If the Soviets executed such an attack but did not simultaneously strike at U.S. cities, an American president would face a cruel dilemma: retaliate against Soviet cities (because the surviving U.S. nuclear forces would not be very effective against Soviet military targets) and thus trigger a devastating Soviet counter-city blow, or reach a bargain on Soviet terms.

Those who raised the "window of vulnerability" issue did not necessarily predict this "nuclear Pearl Harbor" or any other particular scenario. There was rather a general concern that newfound Soviet advantages in nuclear capability (however theoretical), combined with traditional Soviet conventional superiority and increased power-projection forces, would encourage the USSR to become much more aggressive and expansionist. Soviet direct and indirect (proxy) activities in Angola, Vietnam, Ethiopia, Libya, South Yemen, Mozambique, Nicaragua, and elsewhere were cited as evidence that Moscow was indeed feeling its oats. Simultaneously, according to these conservative strategists, American allies and neutral states had begun adjusting their policies to conform to a balance of political and military power which now favored the Soviet Union.

Of course, the concept of a "window of vulnerability" was not unique in post-World War II American foreign policy. In 1950, the critical factors suggesting a period of maximum danger ahead were the loss of U.S. nuclear monopoly and the outbreak of the Korean War. In the late 1950s, public awareness of the Soviet ICBM program and the apparent vulnerability of existing U.S. nuclear forces spawned the "missile gap." But in both these instances, the resulting surge in American defense spending fit relatively comfortably into the existing internationalist consensus concerning the primary necessity to contain Soviet expansionism. The proposed Reagan defense buildup, however, went exactly counter to the post-Vietnam consensus with its reduced emphasis on the Soviet threat and on the utility of military force. Rather than being somewhat ahead of the tide of elite opinion, then, the newly elected President was proposing to reverse course completely.

The precise course that the "Reagan revolution" would take in national security was never spelled out authoritatively. Reagan's supporters called for significant increases in American military capability on virtually every level— low-intensity conflict and antiterrorism (including supporting intelligence), Third-World and NATO conventional contingencies, naval warfare, and various nuclear forces. The last category received the most attention, and was probably the intellectual linchpin of Reagan's design to create a new consensus, because its most prominent advocates rejected the premise that U.S.-Soviet relations depended upon the reality of nuclear parity. The Soviets, according to Richard Pipes (a leading critic of SALT II and a National Security Council staff member in 1981 and 1982), believed that a nuclear war could indeed be fought and won, and were building a strategic arsenal designed (if not intended) to do exactly that.

These conclusions led conservative Republicans and their supporters to urge that the adverse trend in the nuclear balance be halted and completely reversed before a serious attempt was made to deal politically with the Soviets. Numerous suggestions from 1978 to 1980 were made for "quick fixes" of U.S. strategic nuclear forces to mitigate the worst effects of the window of vulnerability—e.g., reopening of the Minuteman III production line; deployment of Minuteman in a multiple vertical silo protective shelter mode; rebasing of B-52 bombers inland and increase their alert rate; and production and deployment of sea-launched cruise missiles (SLCMs) on submarines and surface vessels. The 1980 Republican party platform set the goal of achieving "overall military and technological superiority over the Soviet Union"—given the geopolitical situation of the United States, this strongly implied the necessity for some kind of meaningful nuclear superiority. The first five-year defense guidance produced by the administration reportedly sought capabilities to "prevail" in the event of nuclear war—although there was considerable controversy over the meaning of "prevail," and the Reagan administration quickly denied that it was intended to be synonymous with "win."

As the administration's policies developed over time, however, it became increasingly unlikely that there would be a truly radical departure from the basic national security framework developed over the previous decade. Six weeks after the 1984 election, Henry Kissinger wrote in the *Washington Post*:

> For more than a decade the phrase detente polarized the American domestic debate. The Reagan administration has so far muted this controversy by a skillful balancing act, which combined the rhetoric of the opponents of detente with many of the policies of its advocates...
>
> The beginning of wisdom is to admit—however painful this may be in the light of previous pronouncements—that the administration is now involved in an essentially irrevocable process indistinguishable in substance from what used to be called detente.

Some of this "skillful balancing act" can be attributed to a shrewd calculus on the part of the administration as to what Congress and public opinion would ultimately bear. After all, the United States demonstrated "flexibility" in the nuclear arms control negotiations, and yet no "bad" agreement (and indeed no agreement at all) resulted. But as Strobe Talbott detailed in his book *Deadly Gambits*, the administration was racked by severe internal disagreements about the future course of U.S. foreign policy.

On the one side were those who represented the intellectual core of the previously described anti-SALT, anti-detente sentiment—e.g., Jeanne Kirkpatrick, Richard Perle, Richard Allen, Fred Iklé, Eugene Rostow, and (to some extent) Paul Nitze. But Reagan, who had identified himself closely with the ideas and many of the individuals associated with this group, was unable (or unwilling) to find enough of these "hard liners" to fill the key foreign and defense policy positions in his administration. Instead, he turned in part to the "pragmatic" wing of the Republican party—which Reagan had opposed so vehemently in 1976—for such officials as George Shultz, Richard Burt, James Baker, Lawrence Eagleburger, Robert McFarlane, and (to some extent) Alexander Haig. As a rule, these officials—although concerned about Soviet expansionism—did not believe that a return to purely anti-Soviet rhetoric or policies was politically or strategically realistic. By and large, they believed that detente and arms control had failed not because of inherent deficiencies, but because American domestic weakness created by Vietnam and Watergate had not allowed the U.S. sufficient international leverage to conduct those policies realistically. The Reagan victory, however, might well create a domestic consensus sufficient to provide both the incentives and disincentives ("carrots and sticks") necessary to manage U.S.-Soviet relations over the long term. The United States, in their opinion, must learn that its security did not rest on simplistic analogies to the situation of Britain in the late 1930s. Rather than rejecting the post-Vietnam consensus, the "pragmatists" were very much a part of its political universe.

The first sign that the "hard liners" would not dominate the new administration was the decision in early 1981 that the United States would continue to abide by (not undercut) the SALT II Treaty as long as the Soviet Union also observed the treaty. This might be seen as a shocking change of heart for a man who had been SALT II's principal political critic. But Reagan was apparently persuaded that the principal objection to SALT II was political in character, and not military or technical. In other words, if the United States formally ratified the treaty, it would send a dangerous political signal to the American public and U.S. allies that Soviet-American relations were once more "normal"—and that substantial increases in defense spending were thus unnecessary. But in military and technical terms, the United States was better off with the constraints of SALT II than without them—i.e., the USSR was in a better position to run an open-ended nuclear arms race than was the United States. Also, if the U.S. held out any hopes for future progress (or even the appearance thereof) in arms control negotiations, SALT II provided the only foundation on which to seek the administration's goal of substantial reductions. The solution to this dilemma—one that was challenged by some "hard liners"—was to abide by, but not to seek ratification of, SALT II.

The "no undercut" policy thus freed the administration to pursue negotiations over nuclear weapons with the Soviet Union. In the case of the planned deployment of 572 U.S. intermediate range nuclear force (INF) systems in Western Europe, the United States decided to enter into negotiations with the Soviets two years before the first Pershing II and ground-launched cruise missiles were scheduled to be activated. The Reagan administration could argue that such negotiations were essential in the short run to maintain the cohesion of the NATO alliance, since the United States had in December 1979 agreed to the "two track" approach (negotiations and deployment) at the request of the West Europeans. But the administration also resumed strategic nuclear talks with the USSR (renamed START, or Strategic Arms Reduction Talks) in 1982, and a year later introduced substantial negotiating flexibility—including a version of the "build down" formula promoted by moderate and liberal Congressional members and outside experts.

Renewed arms control negotiations effectively precluded many of the "quick fixes" that had been advocated to close the window of vulnerability. Indeed, the administration quickly abandoned this concept that had been so central to the conservative critique of American defense policies in the late 1970s. The administration did revive the B-1 bomber and propose the deployment of SLCMs, but it cut in half the number of MX missiles that had been planned by the Carter administration (from 200 to 100). Even more importantly, the Reagan administration seemed relatively unconcerned about enhancing the short term survivability of U.S. strategic nuclear forces. It eventually settled upon a compromise worked out by the bipartisan Scowcroft Commission (President's Commission on Strategic Forces), which rejected the window of vulnerability argument because of the overall retaliatory capability of the strategic triad and because of timing difficulties confronting Soviet attack planners. As part of a political compromise, the Reagan administration would receive the MX missile—based, to be sure, in vulnerable fixed silos—

in return for its commitment to introduce a new START proposal and to develop and deploy small, single-warhead ICBMs in the early 1990s.

This pattern was repeated along a broad front as the administration adapted to what it perceived to be political necessity. Thus, the United States abandoned its attempt to block West European assistance for and dependence on the new natural gas pipeline from Siberia, in exchange for greater (if less tangible) European cooperation on restricting high-technology experts to the Soviet Union. The much publicized Reagan commitment never to abandon Taiwan gradually evolved into a serious effort to improve strategic relations with the People's Republic of China. When congressional and public support for the deployment of the U.S. peacekeeping force in Lebanon waned following the bombing of the Marine compound in Beirut, the administration withdrew the troops. The large projected increase in defense spending proved impossible to maintain fully as the political climate changed in 1982 and 1983, although Defense Secretary Caspar Weinberger was much more reluctant to compromise than the White House staff and the Office of Management and Budget.

Certainly, on many matters the administration remained considerably at odds with Republican and Democratic moderates—its Central American policy perhaps being the major example. As 1984 began, the balance of policy within the administration was still being maintained between the "hard line ideologues" and the "pragmatists." The President's campaign for reelection was expected to result in one faction or the other gaining ascendency; the outcome of the internal struggle for intellectual, bureaucratic, and political control of the campaign's themes was believed likely to play a decisive role in determining the foreign and defense policies of a second Reagan term.

There was one major exception to the general tendency of the Reagan administration to move toward "pragmatic" national security policies: the March 1983 "Star Wars" speech of the President. In this address, Reagan caught most of official Washington off guard with his challenge to the scientific community that it devise the means to make nuclear weapons impotent and obsolete. This indeed was a radical departure, even more radical than a return to anti-Soviet internationalism, because American foreign and defense policy of whatever stripe since 1945 had ultimately depended on the deterrent effect of nuclear weapons. If the President (or his Democratic challenger) were to make the proposed Strategic Defense Initiative program a major campaign issue, the 1984 election could have consequences even more important than those implicit in 1980.

Toward 1984: The Democratic Party

The defeat of Jimmy Carter in 1980 was in some ways less traumatic to the Democratic party than might have been expected. Carter, after all, had prided himself on being an outsider—a politician beholden neither to the Democratic Party leadership nor to the Washington establishment. His loss to Ronald Reagan, then, could be rationalized by party leaders as a personal failure rather than as a popular rejection of Democratic foreign and defense policies. It was also somewhat difficult to identify precisely which set of national security policies failed, since the Carter administration had moved from the left to the center of the party over time.

As a result, there was never overwhelming pressure on the Democratic Party as a whole to arrive at a coherent alternative to the national security policy of the Reagan administration. Instead, most of the party's attention, at least at the presidential level, was focused on creating (or recreating) an electoral co-alition sufficient to recapture the White House. Until the dramatic economic recovery of 1983, recession and unemployment seemed to be the principal is-sues on which the Democratic party could most plausibly attack the President.

There was one important exception to the general Democratic neglect of national security policy in the three years leading up to the 1984 election: the nuclear freeze movement. The rhetoric of Reagan and his associates was seized upon by critics of U.S. nuclear deterrence policy as evidence that the United States was planning to fight and win a nuclear war—the most prominent ex-ample being Robert Scheer's *With Enough Shovels: Reagan, Bush, and Nu-clear War*. Drawing heavily from the antinuclear campaign in Europe, books such as Jonathan Schell's *Fate of the Earth* ignored the various controversies over the means of nuclear deterrence and focused instead on the existential terrors created by the mere existence of weapons for mass destruction. Posses-sion of nuclear weapons, for whatever purpose, was by definition immoral.

The antinuclear movement seemingly had the potential to become the 1980s equivalent of the anti-Vietnam War movement. In the 1960s and early 1970s, the antiwar movement had coalesced around the simple demand that the United States withdraw its military forces from Vietnam. The antinuclear movement had a similar rallying point: a mutual and verifiable freeze on the production, development, and testing of nuclear weapons by both the United States and the Soviet Union.

The nuclear freeze campaign became so powerful politically that all of the major Democratic candidates endorsed it in one form or another. Senator Alan Cranston of California conducted what was, in effect, a single issue cam-paign around the nuclear freeze, hoping to parlay the enthusiasm of antinu-clear activists into momentum toward the Democratic nomination, much as George McGovern had emerged from nowhere a decade earlier on the strength of the antiwar movement. Cranston wrote in January 1984:

> The primary moral and political challenge of our time is to change our way of thinking in order to cope with the threat nuclear weapons pose each day to our survival. That requires not just a small adjustment in our rhetoric. It requires a fundamental change in our view of the world. It requires a fundamental change in our national commitment to nuclear arms reductions...
>
> We cannot rely on routine negotiations to reverse the vicious cycle of the arms race and end our hair-trigger relationship. The next President of the United States

must not leave negotiations to the bureaucrats who have failed us in the past and are failing us now. The next President must put his whole mind and energy into the effort. It will require a supreme undertaking. It can only be carried through successfully by a President who is truly dedicated to ending the arms race, and who is determined to concentrate the full power of the Presidency on that task. We have never had such a President.

The world has never had an American or Soviet leader who made nuclear peace his number one priority. Once in a lifetime—while there is still time—we need that kind of President.

The early demise of Cranston's campaign did not necessarily indicate any lack of political clout by the antinuclear movement within the Democratic party. Other candidates, including front runners Walter Mondale and subsequently Gary Hart, had stronger organizations or broader appeals to complement their impeccable credentials on arms control. The fact that the nuclear freeze issue did not dominate the Democratic nomination race can be explained at least partly by the apparent negotiating flexibility in Geneva demonstrated by the Reagan administration, and the eventual Soviet withdrawal from the INF and START talks at the end of the year. As George McGovern discovered in 1972, an incumbent President has tremendous political leverage if he can control or take advantage of domestic and international events. (Jimmy Carter had discovered in 1980 the political peril of losing control of such conditions, notably the Iranian hostage situation.)

The general acceptance of the philosophy of the antinuclear movement within the Democratic party did raise questions about the future direction of that party's approach to foreign and defense policy issues. The McGovern-led antiwar movement that captured the Democratic party in 1972 represented much more than opposition to one particular policy—it constituted rejection of the entire anti-Soviet containment strategy that had formed the core of the postwar internationalist foreign policy consensus. The antithesis of containment was born out of the reaction against the Vietnam war, and that antithesis—in moderate or radical form—dominated American foreign policy for the remainder of the 1970s. The nuclear freeze movement in the early 1980s can be seen as the most visible manifestation of resistance to Reagan's apparent revival of anti–Soviet containment, very much in the spirit of the original critique of U.S. Cold War policy. That is why Democratic candidates of varying stripes could accept membership (more or less comfortably) in the antinuclear movement, because each one (more or less comfortably) embraced that critique. Had the circumstances been more propitious—e.g., a collapse of the NATO alliance directly attributed to a failure of American policy relative to the "two-track" INF decision—the nuclear freeze movement might well have generated an entirely new thesis relative to U.S. national strategy. Even the post-Vietnam consensus admitted to some interests overseas (e.g., Western Europe) that were vital to American security and hence liable to protection—at least theoretically—by the U.S. nuclear deterrent. But acceptance of the most radical thesis of the antinuclear movement—that no interest was so vital that it was worth risking Armageddon—could have led to pressures for a U.S. global withdrawal far beyond that advocated even in the 1970s. The fact that the foreign policy debate did not take place in these terms, either in the Democratic primaries or in the general campaign, is one of the most significant events (or nonevents) in the 1984 election.

The Democratic Presidential Race

The contest for the Democratic party's presidential nomination did not in fact reveal a major schism over foreign and defense policy. No significant faction sought to argue that the President's commitment to a pre-Vietnam understanding of U.S. foreign policy was correct, or that the Democrats had a more effective policy of anti-Soviet containment. (This was the form that the 1960 election had taken.) No significant faction sought to abandon America's position as a global and military superpower to lessen substantially the risks of nuclear war. Within the broad Democratic agreement over the post-Vietnam pattern of U.S. diplomacy, though, there was a considerable fragmentation of opinion. Four particular schools of thought seemed to emerge during the primaries but because a Democrat was not elected as chief executive in 1984, no one particular view can be said to have emerged as definitive for the party. That question, though deferred, remains.

The eventual nominee, Walter Mondale, represented what may be fairly characterized as the center of the contemporary Democratic party on national security issues. As a senator, Mondale went through the same disillusionment over Vietnam as did most of the party's leaders, and this experience left a considerable reluctance to repeat that same strategic error. The centrist Democrats remain attached to some overseas involvement, although they are reluctant to specify the nature of those commitments beyond Western Europe and possibly Japan and Israel. Detente with the Soviet Union is seen as the best way to secure those (and other) interests at a reasonable cost and risk; the mutual fear of nuclear holocaust is presumed to be the unavoidable condition which mandates reasonable and predictable U.S.-Soviet relations. These centrists have always placed great emphasis on arms control, but Mondale's attempt to identify himself rather closely with the antinuclear movement indicates that the party as a whole has moved considerably to the left on the entire deterrence question. Mondale did call for positive growth in defense spending (four percent increase per year), with most of the expansion presumably being applied to conventional force improvements.

Two factions seemed to be competing for control of the national security agenda of the left wing of the Democratic party. It may not quite be accurate to place Gary Hart in this category—in the campaign, Hart proposed that real defense spending grow annually at four and one-half to five percent, a figure slightly higher than that suggested by Walter Mondale. But Hart was probably the most isolationist (or perhaps, more precisely, anti–interventionist) of the candidates who survived the initial round of primaries and caucuses. He supposedly represented the young, urban, professional people (known in the media as the "yuppies") whose foreign policy consciousness was formed during the Vietnam war and not the anti-Soviet containment period. American intervention in Vietnam and elsewhere in the Third World was, for Hart, not merely a miscalculation or misapplication of U.S. power; the war was wrongly entered and immorally fought. Hart opposed the deployment of the Marines in Lebanon from the beginning and criticized those Democrats (e.g., Mondale) who had not unequivocally done so. Hart claimed to be "solid" in his support for Israel, but did not want "American boys to die unnecessarily . . . for Persian Gulf oil."

Hart's anti-interventionism was most apparent in his position on Central America. He advocated the immediate and unconditional withdrawal of all U.S. troops and advisers from El Salvador and Honduras. When Mondale indicated his reluctance to go quite that far, Hart issued a series of television commercials that suggested his opponent would lead the United States into more Vietnams. "Our sons as bargaining chips—will we never learn," said a voiceover in a commercial depicting a slowly burning fuse. (Mondale, in turn, had a television ad that showed a red telephone ringing, with the question raised whether Americans really wanted an untried man in charge of the hotline to Moscow.) Hart condemned the bipartisan Kissinger Commission report as recommending "a continued policy of war" in Central America "on a blind search for the wrong enemy." The real enemy "is not communism, but poverty." Rather than conduct a military struggle against the Soviet Union, Hart proposed to emphasize the political and economic competition, to "challenge the Soviets to a crusade to eliminate hunger for every child on this planet in the 1980s." Instead of being "the arsenal of the world . . . the United States should be the university of the world [and] the granary of the world."

Hart's major attractiveness as a candidate appeared to rest primarily on "new ideas" to get the country moving again. His theme was not dissimilar to that of George McGovern in 1972 ("Come home, America") as an appeal to repair internal wounds before solving the world's problems. An incident during the New York primary is perhaps revealing in this regard: Hart criticized the current tax laws because they were "Europeanizing" the United States by encouraging disrespect for the law and the government. Hart elaborated on this point by describing Richard Nixon as America's "first European president" for his interjection of cynicism into public life.

Jesse Jackson's campaign for the nomination is generally assessed in terms of its impact on the domestic agenda of the Democratic party, the future of blacks in American politics, and so on. Jackson's few well-publicized ventures into foreign affairs—e.g., his visits to Syria and Cuba to secure the release of American prisoners—were not often taken seriously. Nevertheless, Jackson did offer a distinct (if not always clear) view on foreign policy that represented a potential interventionist competitor to the left-wing isolationism often implicit in Gary Hart's campaign.

According to Jackson, his object as president would have been literally to reverse the course of American foreign policy. "What happens all the time is that those who struggle for self–determination are resisted by us and we join our pals who are in power. Somoza was on the wrong side of history and the Sandinistas are on the right side of history," Jackson observed during an interview published in April 1984. To that extent, Jackson seems in agreement with the critique of postwar U.S. foreign policy offered by Hart. But while the latter seemed inclined to let historical forces work their way in the Third World without any American involvement or attempt at direction, the former appeared much more inclined to intervene directly and personally on behalf of history. This sentiment, which had been particularly strong during the early years of the Carter administration, grew out of the experience of the domestic civil rights movement. "Some views come from my understanding of the Third World. I've had a Third World experience right here in America," Jackson explained. "When we started out, we were resisted. Dr. King was accused of being a Communist. It wasn't true." Jackson told audiences that he "grew up under apartheid in South Carolina," and that "I know how to negotiate with a superpower. I've been negotiating with a superpower all my life." Rather than turning inward to discover (or rediscover) a new American spirit and creativity, as Hart would have it, Jackson was eager rather to internationalize the American experience, or perhaps more precisely to expose Americans to the global struggle for human liberation.

The fourth, and in some ways the weakest of the four major Democratic factions, was the conservative, prodefense wing that used to be associated with the late Senator Henry Jackson. This weakness became apparent when none of the three candidates who might be said to represent this faction— John Glenn, Ernest Hollings, and Reuben Askew—survived past the first primaries and caucuses. In some sense, this lack of influence by the conservative wing of the party had been apparent for more than a decade, a period in which the Democrats attempted to come to grips with the failure in Vietnam. Henry Jackson himself ran and was defeated for the nomination in 1972 and 1976. Conservative Democratic Congressmen and Senators from the south had retired over time and were being replaced by more liberal party members or by Republicans. Some former Democratic officials and intellectuals fled the party in the late 1970s because of disagreement over the "soft" foreign and defense policies of the Carter administration. Organized labor, which traditionally was associated with prodefense and anticommunist policies, had for other reasons thrown in its lot quite early with Mondale. In short, the conservative elements in the party had been drawn down to the point where they even failed to influence substantially the choice of a presidential candidate or the contents of the party's platform.

Walter Mondale's eventual nomination signalled that the Democrats would not veer far to the left or the right from the party's cautious noninterventionist inclinations of the 1970s. Although the language of the platform itself made several significant concessions to the Hart position, particularly on the limits of U.S. force abroad, Mondale avoided platform commitments to reduce defense spending and to pledge no first use of nuclear weapons. Mondale's stance assumed that the post-Vietnam consensus remained intellectually intact and politically viable, and that the results of the 1980 election were an aberration in terms of American foreign policy. The goal of the new nominee was hence to ensure that President Reagan and his policies were perceived as being outside the legitimate bounds of that consensus.

The General Election: No Surprises

The role that foreign and defense issues played in the 1984 campaign from the time of the party conventions (in July and August) onward was decisively conditioned by the logic of public opinion polls. National polls showed Reagan maintaining a lead of from 15 to 25 percentage points, a figure that narrowed noticeably (and briefly) only after the Democratic convention and the first televised presidential debate. This lead provided the President with a sufficient margin to absorb all but the most damning gaffe, or to strike out into politically dangerous waters. The challenger, in turn, would be forced to gamble and to develop a theme which could somehow circumvent the "Teflon coating" allegedly protecting the President's personal popularity despite his disastrous policies. Given the strength of the incumbent, the campaign went pretty much according to form: no major gaffes or controversial initiatives by Reagan, and no major breakthroughs by Mondale.

On the surface, facing a strong economy and a popular rival, Mondale's best hope for an issue that would turn the campaign in his favor was in the area of foreign and defense policy. In 1980, President Carter had unsuccessfully sought to portray Reagan as a "madman" who might conceivably involve the United States in a war—possibly nuclear—because of his reflexive belligerence. With four years of empirical evidence weighing against a repetition of this particular charge in 1984, Mondale shifted the accusation into a question of the President's competence. By raising doubts about the Reagan's grasp of the essential details of arms control, nuclear deterrence, and U.S.-Soviet relations, Mondale hoped to emphasize the President's specific political vulnerabilities on these issues, to undermine the widely held favorable view of Reagan's qualities as a leader, and to suggest indirectly that the President might be too old for high office. In their second televised debate, Mondale attempted to make his case by recalling several supposed mistakes by the President:

> The bottom line of national strength is that the president must be in command, he must lead. And when a president doesn't know that submarine missiles are recallable [sic], says that 70 percent of our strategic forces are conventional, discovers three years into his administration that our arms control efforts have

failed, because he didn't know that most Soviet missiles were on land, these are things a president must know to command.

The Reagan campaign, as a rule, preferred to deflect questions about the President's competence rather than meet them head on. Reagan's statement about the recallability of submarine-launched ballistic missiles, for example, was said to be an error of syntax (he meant to say that the submarines could be recalled) and not one of understanding. And of course, the President's joke during the debate about his opponent's youth and inexperience is widely credited with defusing the age issue. But above all, the Republicans sought to take the offensive against Mondale by raising the "wimp" issue. The Democratic candidate's weakness on Soviet expansionism and his opposition to a strong defense, it was alleged, would lead to a repetition of the strategic defeats of the Carter years. Reagan campaign spokesmen cited Mondale's record of Senate opposition to the F-14 fighter, *Nimitz*-class aircraft carriers, the C-5A cargo plane, the Harrier jet, the Minuteman III missile, the Poseidon submarine missile, the cruise missile, the B-1 bomber, the Trident submarine, and earlier versions of an anti-ballistic missile system. Mondale's votes for withdrawal of one-half of U.S. forces from NATO (1971), and for a 40 percent reduction in U.S. troop strength worldwide (1973), were also criticized. This "frightening" record and Mondale's stated "hostility to a strong, secure America" meant that his election would "send a signal of decline, lessened will and weakness to friends and adversaries alike." Reagan contrasted this prospect with his own record: "Since 1980, not a single nation has fallen to Communist aggression and the people of one nation, Grenada, have been set free."

The President, who in 1980 was portrayed as a radical right-winger on national security issues, tried to turn the tables in 1984 by proclaiming that the Democrats had gone so far to the left that they had left America. This expression fit nicely into Reagan's vision of a realigning election that would make his party the new majority, and foreign policy seemed to be an attractive means to lure conservative Democrats:

> But it can be a very wrenching thing, I found, to change parties. You feel as though you're abandoning your past. But I tell you, the only abandoning I see is that the Democratic leadership has abandoned the good and decent Democrats of the JFK, FDR, and Harry Truman tradition—people who believe in the interests of working people, who are not ashamed or afraid of America standing up for freedom in the world.

President John F. Kennedy was a Democratic figure frequently cited by Reagan: "Were he [Kennedy] alive today, I believe he would be ashamed of those in the liberal Democratic leadership who would weaken our defense, endanger our security and sell out the cause of freedom in Latin America." This led Senator Edward M. Kennedy to note that Reagan had supported Richard Nixon over John Kennedy in 1960. The Mondale campaign also uncovered a letter from Reagan to Nixon that same year which compared Kennedy's domestic programs to the ideas of Karl Marx and Adolf Hitler.

The sharpest issue between the two candidates was, predictably, over arms control and nuclear deterrence. "This is arms control year," Democratic Congressman Les Aspin predicted in June. "Everybody is for arms control. We have more arms control amendments on this [military authorization] bill than defense amendments. There is a very, very strong interest in arms control." Democratic Vice Presidential candidate Geraldine Ferraro declared that all other questions "pale by comparison" to "the war and peace issue." Ferraro's advisers—perhaps more out of wishful thinking than studied analysis—were said to believe that presidential elections are decided by global concerns rather than domestic issues. For his part, Mondale pledged to seek a summit meeting with the Soviet leadership to negotiate a nuclear freeze within six months of his election. In the interim, as an incentive for the Soviets to rejoin the Geneva arms control talks, Mondale would unilaterally declare "temporary moratoriums" on testing of all nuclear weapons and testing and deployment of all weapons in space. The Democratic candidate also proposed to alter U.S. military strategy by augmenting conventional forces to reduce dependence on various nuclear options.

President Reagan's Strategic Defense Initiative ("Star Wars") predictably drew harsh criticism from Mondale and served as the foil of the Democratic television commercial theme "draw the line at the heavens." According to Mondale:

> When Mr. Reagan explains Star Wars, it is as comforting as listening to a bed-time story. Once upon a time, there was an evil empire that threatened us with terrible weapons. But then one day, our side discovered a magic invisible shield. When we stretched it across our country, no missiles could penetrate it. From that day on, we stopped worrying about nuclear war—and lived happily ever after.
>
> I can think of only one reason to support Star Wars; fairy tales are often more appealing than reality.

Significantly, the Reagan campaign studiously avoided the "Star Wars" issue whenever possible. The President himself did not formally speak to his proposal from March 1983 until September 1984, and then only in very general terms. The Republicans rather sought to claim the issues of arms control and deterrence as their own. In late September, the President gave what his aides described as a conciliatory address toward the Soviet Union at the United Nations General Assembly, proposing what became known as the "umbrella talks." Several days later, Mr. Reagan met with Soviet Minister Andrei Gromyko after the United States delayed publication of a report that charged the USSR with numerous violations of arms control treaties. Talk about an evil empire had long been superceded in the President's rhetoric by more traditional language of the imperatives of nuclear deterrence:

We must and will engage the Soviets in a dialogue as serious and constructive as possible, a dialogue that will serve to promote peace in the troubled regions of the world, reduce the level of arms and build a constructive working relationship.

Neither we nor the Soviet Union can wish away the differences between our two societies and our philosophies, but we should always remember we do have common interests. And foremost among them is to avoid war and reduce the level of arms.

There is no rational alternative but to steer a course which I would call credible deterrence and peaceful competition. And if we do so, we might find areas in which we could engage in constructive cooperation.

Reagan claimed that the United States was in far better position to negotiate seriously with the Soviets in 1984 than it had been when he entered office:

I believe that 1984 finds the United States in the strongest position in years to establish a constructive and realistic working relationship with the Soviet Union. We've come a long way since the decade of the 70s, years when the United States seemed filled with self-doubt and neglected its defenses while the Soviet Union increased its military might and sought to expand its influence by armed forces and threat.... America's deterrence is more credible, and it is making the world a safer place. Safer because now there is less danger that the Soviet leadership will underestimate our strength or question our resolve.

This address ended with the President imagining that "an Ivan and an Anya" happened to meet "a Jim and a Sally," with the moral that governments, and not people, make wars.

Mondale noted after the President's U.N. address that this was hardly the rhetoric or logic that Reagan had used during the previous campaign and or much of his term of office: "For four years . . . he talked like [former SAC Commander General] Curtis LeMay. This morning he tried to talk like Walter Mondale. Why this change now, 42 days before the election? Has he really been born again? Has he been converted? Is it a new Nixon?" (Mondale corrected himself to say, "a new Reagan?") Mondale recalled that his father, a Methodist minister, had once told him to be skeptical of deathbed conversions "because sometimes they get well on you."

Most other foreign policy issues did not reach this level of relatively detailed debate. The most controversial regional question involved Central America, where the United States supported the government of El Salvador against Marxist rebels, and "covertly" aided the antigovernment *contras* against the pro-Soviet, pro-Cuban government of Nicaragua. Since coming into office, the Reagan administration had struggled to maintain even a modest level of military aid for El Salvador because of congressional suspicion about that government's human rights record. Congressional funding for the *contras* in Nicaragua was at least temporarily cut off in 1984.

Mondale had been a critic of the Administration's policies during the primary season, although not nearly as vocal in that opposition as Gary Hart. In general, Mondale accused the Reagan Administration of wrongly stressing the East-West rather than the North-South dimensions of the conflicts in Central America; of favoring military force over diplomatic solutions; of siding with the forces of reaction rather than those of reform. The logical outcome of Reagan's policies, according to Mondale, was the introduction of American troops into the region. This implicitly raised the question of the "Vietnam syndrome" (i.e., U.S. military involvement in a civil war because of the failure to understand the underlying causes of conflict). Late in the campaign, Mondale sought to reestablish "human rights as a foreign policy priority," as a standard by which to avoid future miscalculations. The President had sold arms to "dictatorships" in Guatemala and Haiti, sent top diplomats to Chile to "clink glasses with the thugs that run that country," and make the United States the sole dissenter from a U.N. Security Council resolution condemning mass arrests in South Africa.

> America must not only stand tall. We must stand for something; we must stand for something as America. In our [foreign policy] debate ... the president said that the choice was between our tyrants and communism. Shame on you, Mr. President. That's not the issue at all. I don't want the peoples of the world who yearn for freedom to turn to the Soviets. I want them to turn to the United States as the symbol of leadership and decency in the world.

Speaking specifically of the United States' support of antigovernment forces in Nicaragua, Mondale declared:

> I object to the covert action in Nicaragua. That's a classic example of a strategy that's embarrassed us, strengthened our opposition and undermined the moral authority of our people and our country in the region. Strength requires knowledge, command.

Mondale stressed that he, like Reagan, would not accept the establishment of Soviet or Cuban military bases in Nicaragua, but that the Administration had "not pursued the diplomatic opportunities, either within El Salvador or as between the countries, and have lost time during which we might have been able to achieve peace."

The President was somewhat on the defensive about Central America during the campaign because of allegations concerning CIA misbehavior (e.g., a training manual supposedly advocating assassination). He responded to Mondale's charges by observing that the Soviets and Cubans, and not the Americans, had introduced the East-West dimension into the conflict; that the United States did support a diplomatic solution, while recognizing that negotiations would not succeed as long as Marxist forces enjoyed an effective monopoly on military power; and that the United States had correctly aligned itself with the forces of democracy and against those of tyranny. It was Reagan's contention that his opponent's policy of weakness would inevitably lead to the unpalatable choice between direct U.S. intervention and the loss of a strategically vital area to Soviet or Cuban control.

The Middle East received even less detailed attention, and here again Reagan was somewhat on the defensive because of the bombing of the U.S. Marine compound in Beirut. Rather than debating the premises of American policy in the region, the two candidates squared off over the issue of presidential competence. Mondale, having suffered through the Iranian hostage crisis during the 1980 campaign, was no doubt happy to turn the tables on the present incumbent.

> The Joint Chiefs urged the President not to put our troops in that barracks, because they were indefensible. They went to him five days before they were killed and said, "Please take them out of there." . . . The report following the explosion in the barracks disclosed that we had not taken any of the steps that we should have taken. . . . The terrorists have won each time. The president told the terrorists that he was going to retaliate. He didn't. They called their [sic] bluff. And the bottom line is, the United States left in humiliation, and our enemies are stronger.

For his part, the President denied that the United States had been humiliated in Lebanon. Indeed, it was precisely the success of the Marine peacekeeping mission "as a stabilizing force" in allowing the Beirut government to establish its sovereignty, that forced the terrorists to take drastic action. Reagan denied that he had "order[ed] the Marines into the barracks. That was a command decision made by the commanders on the spot"—although of course he had to assume ultimate responsibility. In regard to U.S. retaliation:

> I'm tempted to ask you [Mondale] what you would do. These are unidentified people. . . . We are going to, as you say, we are busy trying to find the centers where these operations stem from, and retaliation will be taken. But we are not going to simply kill some people to say, "Oh, look. We got even." We want to know when we retaliate that we're retaliating with those who are responsible for terrorist acts.

Conclusion

At least in reference to foreign and defense policy issues, the 1984 presidential campaign is best analyzed not in terms of the dynamics of Republican versus Democrat—i.e., whether Reagan or Mondale "won" on any particular issue—but rather in terms of how the campaign affected each particular party and the factions therein.

This is not to minimize the policy differences that existed between the two candidates and their respective parties. But in retrospect, the President's overwhelming margin of victory meant that the Republicans were free to articulate their own perspective on national security without having to tailor the campaign solely to score points or minimize damage vis-a-vis the Democrats. The Democrats, in turn, were not under pressure to trim their sails solely to sway uncommitted voters who might otherwise be crucial. The issue was then not so much winning or losing as the grounds on which victory or defeat would take place.

The Republican party, under Reagan's leadership, decided to accept victory by moving markedly toward the center on most defense and foreign policy questions. Indeed, a good case can be made that the President abandoned any pretense of reinstitutionalizing a national strategy similar to those of the 1950s and early 1960s (which are described above for convenience as the anti-Soviet internationalist consensus). To be sure, his tentative embrace of an admittedly very conservative version of the post-Vietnam war view began taking place from almost the beginning of the first term. There was certainly an indication in his March 1983 "Star Wars" speech, however, that a radical rejection of the post-Vietnam consensus was still a possibility. But from the evidence of the 1984 campaign, the second Reagan administration will in all likelihood be more moderate in tone and policy than the first. (This assumes, of course, that unexpected international events do not themselves force a major alteration in tone or substance, as happened during the Carter administration.)

One could argue that the 1984 Republican campaign's move to the center represented a tactical ploy rather than a strategic reversal. After all, prospective landslides can be turned into squeakers and even defeat if mistakes are made. But the President's own pollster conducted daily tracking surveys that reportedly showed Reagan's lead to be never less than eight percentage points, and indeed an almost consistent 17 to 20 points advantage. Had the President chosen to repeat the "Russians are coming" theme of 1980—admittedly more difficult as an incumbent than as a challenger—it is almost certain that he would still have won, although perhaps with a reduced margin.

The "pragmatic" wing of the administration succeeded in using its tactical control of the campaign as a mechanism to define the substantive agenda for the second term—in some cases by ignoring altogether the proposals of the "ideologues." The Strategic Defense Initiative is a case in point. Almost neglected altogether during the campaign, the Strategic Defense Initiative faces a difficult road in the Congressional funding process because the administration has failed to articulate a strategically convincing or politically persuasive rationale. Such a rationale was never made by the Republicans (assuming that they had one to begin with) because Reagan's "pragmatic" advisers argued that the controversial nature of the program might harm the President politically in 1984.

The critical element in the administration's prospective moderation is Reagan's stated conviction that his programs have already restored American strength to the point where any window of political or military vulnerability is closed. In addition, the President has taken a much less ideologically hostile view of the Soviet Union—either because he has changed his mind, or because the U.S. military buildup has altered the Kremlin's behavior.

Although they are careful not to be critical of Reagan personally, the "ideological" wing of the Republican party, both inside and outside the administration, clearly disagrees with these assessments. In its latest report—deliberately released only after the election—the conservative Committee on the Present Danger (which was candidate Reagan's principal brain trust on defense issues in 1980) asserted:

> A major effort to restore survivability to U.S. strategic nuclear forces is essential to a credible national security policy. To date, the lack of such a priority program is the most striking deficiency—with the most potentially dangerous consequences—of the Administration's defense program.
>
> Our analysis concludes that the United States is still second best to the Soviet Union in overall military power. Can America catch up? Yes, but not at the present and projected rate of increase in the overall defense effort.
>
> There is no more urgent task for America than restoring the military balance. Only then can we again feel confidence in America's ability to preserve peace with freedom.[1]

If the "pragmatists" have gained the upper hand in the administration partly as a result of the 1984 campaign, the political weight in the Republican party as a whole is still sharply to the right. The 1984 party convention was dominated by staunch conservatives on foreign and defense policies, who openly expressed their distaste for the "moderates." The President's direct intervention was reportedly necessary to avoid major platform fights over a pledge to gain U.S. military superiority (which the 1984 platform, unlike that of 1980, did not call for) and to build (as opposed to achieve) a space-based ballistic missile defense.

Under Reagan's genial leadership, then, the Republican party is badly divided on foreign and defense policy—indeed, the party has traditionally been split over international affairs. The President was able to manage this division, artfully or otherwise, at least well enough to be reelected by landslide proportions. Whatever his success or failure in a second term, the 1988 Republican primary campaign will probably be critical in defining the party's future views on foreign and defense policies: Reagan will then no longer play a dominant role in the party and, unlike in 1968 and in 1980, there will not be an unpopular Democratic administration to run against.

The Democratic party, without the responsibilities of the White House, will likely avoid any major decision on its foreign and defense policies for some time. The experience of 1984 revealed that leftward pressures in the party e.g., Hart and Jackson—were somewhat offset by pressure toward the center created by the immediate necessities of electoral politics, and the memory of the disasters in 1972 and 1980, when the Democratic candidate was perceived to be too weak on international issues. Despite a defeat of similar proportions in 1984, however, the Democratic party may remain wedded to the left of the post–Vietnam consensus because its conservative wing no longer has signifi-

---

1. "Can America Catch Up?" (Washington, D.C.: Committee on the Present Danger, November 1984), p. v.

cant influence over policy and candidate selection. This leftward tendency will probably prevent the establishment of any broad political consensus in support of major foreign policy initiatives by the Reagan administration, even as that administration moves closer to the center.

Reaganomics Manqué, Realignment Manqué

Thomas B. Silver

Reagan and Roosevelt

In his speech accepting the 1984 Republican nomination, President Reagan said that America was facing its clearest political choice in fifty years. The President then related how he himself, fifty years ago, had made that clear choice: he voted Democratic! In 1932, he voted for Franklin Roosevelt, who promised sharp cuts in government spending, a balanced budget, and a reduction in the number of unemployed. He then voted to re-elect Roosevelt, despite FDR's failure to redeem any of these promises that had won the young Mr. Reagan's vote.

It was an apt story. In 1980, Ronald Reagan promised reduced federal spending, a balanced budget, and a reduction in the number of unemployed. Ever consistent, he then voted to re-elect himself, notwithstanding his failure to deliver on a single one of those promises.

Walter Mondale and Alf Landon were not remiss in bringing such unfulfilled promises to the attention of the electorate, but—to say the very least—neither man was campaigning from the economic high ground, and the voters knew it. Reagan's 1984 sweep of all but one state and the District of Columbia was on the scale of FDR's sweep of all but two states in 1936.

To hear the Republicans tell it, 1984 was 1936, Ronald Reagan is Franklin Roosevelt, and an epochal realignment is taking place in American politics. Unfortunately for the Republicans, there is one massive objection to this thesis: Tip O'Neill. Past realignments have been marked by the destruction or disappearance of one of the major political parties, namely the Federalists after 1800, the Democrats after 1860, and the Republicans after 1932.

These decisive political changes were followed by decisive policy changes. However, despite Reagan's extraordinary sweep in 1984, neither a decisive political nor a decisive policy change has occurred. The defeat of Fritz Mondale was not the death knell of the Democratic Party, and the victory of Ronald Reagan was not the herald of an emerging, let alone an emerged, Republican majority.

The central issue of the 1984 campaign was the budget crisis. From that issue radiated many of the major prudential choices that the country faced: greater or lesser military expenditures; reformist or radical reductions in the rate of growth of the welfare state; higher taxes or lower spending.

Walter Mondale, heir of Roosevelt, was badly defeated. Alas for those who believe that 1984 was 1936, Speaker O'Neill and his congressional army were

25

not. They remain on the field of battle, rather effectively resisting the "trend of history," which, according to President Reagan in his acceptance speech, is on the side of the Republicans.

With Reagan at the head of one branch and O'Neill at the head of another, the federal government has become an Irish Janus, and the result has been the kind of comity and cooperation for which Irish politics are so renowned. What we have, instead of a realignment, is a deadlock of democracy, whose chief symptom is the federal budget crisis. The President will not abide a tax increase; the Speaker will not abide lower spending. Until the President can break that deadlock, there will be no realignment, and displacement of the New Deal/Great Society welfare state will remain an unaccomplished goal of Reagan conservatism. The thesis of this essay is that the President has not taken the harsh course necessary to break the deadlock, assuming that it is breakable. No doubt his optimism, his sense that the "trend of history" is with him, is an element of his caution. Nevertheless, we must remember in judging Reagan by the standard of realignment, that despite his immense political success as governor of California, his legacy was higher taxes and spending, and the "trend of history" after Reagan in California led to domination of the legislative, executive, and judicial branches by Willie Brown, Jerry Brown, and Rose Bird.

The "Failure" of Reaganomics

It has been said that the Reagan Administration began with a determination to restore America's defenses but with no coherent plan to achieve that goal; and indeed, the confusion over, e.g., the MX basing mode lends credence to that view. The same, however, cannot be said of economic policy. President Reagan knew precisely what he wanted to do in fiscal and monetary policy, viz., (1) reduce federal spending as a percentage of gross national product; (2) reduce the tax burden; (3) produce slow, steady growth of the money supply.

These policies were to form the solid and unshakeable tripod upon which sustained economic recovery would rest. Tax cuts, spending restraint, and disciplined money growth were to produce, respectively, strong economic growth, a balanced budget, and an end to inflation.

In fiscal 1985, however, well into the Reagan presidency, the United States was in a growth recession. Economic growth was limping along at about two percent. Unemployment during the year following the 1984 election averaged 7.2%. In all the years between the Great Depression and 1980, there were only two that had an unemployment rate that high. The federal budget deficit was $200 billion, and the rate of inflation was 4%—high by historical standards, low only in contrast to its level in the seventies.

It would not be correct to say that Reaganomics had failed to achieve its intended goals. Reaganomics was never tried. Federal spending during Reagan's first term, far from falling, increased sharply as a percentage of the gross national product, until it reached a historic high: one fourth of national income. Monetary growth, far from being slow and steady, was as rapid as it was in the seventies and much more volatile. Tax revenues—which averaged 19% of GNP in the years 1970 through 1980, averaged 19% of GNP in 1985—though, to be sure, this figure was down sharply from the peak of 20.8% in 1981. Again, Reagan looks good only in contrast to Jimmy Carter.

Paradoxically, Reagan's 1984 landslide victory, which was predicated on the 1983-84 economic recovery, was caused not by Reaganomics but by the failure of the Reagan Administration to implement it. This paradox will take some explaining. On July 1, 1984, the American economy had just completed the strongest four quarters of growth in a generation, while inflation had fallen dramatically from its rate under Carter. This coincidence of factors gave Reagan his 49 state sweep. What lay behind this coincidence was a monetary policy that was the exact reverse of the one Reagan proposed in his first budget message.

Between April of 1980 and April of 1981, growth of M_1 (currency plus demand deposits) was in double digits—an unprecedented peacetime rate. This excessive monetary growth produced double digit inflation and interest rates. In April of 1981, shortly after Reagan took office, money growth went from double digits to zero. The money supply was smaller in the fall of 1981 than it had been in the spring, and thereafter grew only modestly until August of 1982. It had been the intention of the administration to lower money growth gradually and smoothly, by perhaps a percentage point a year, as one might smoothly decelerate a speeding automobile from 90 m.p.h. to 30 m.p.h. Instead, the Federal Reserve Board jammed the monetary brakes to the floor. Two consequences followed, one immediately and one after a lag. The economy quickly suffered its worst downturn since the thirties; but by 1983, inflation was below 4%.

Beginning in August of 1982, monetary policy reversed course, and returned for more than a year to the extraordinary excesses of Carter's final year. It was this burst of money growth (at a moment when the tax cuts were beginning to take full effect) that created the surge of economic activity that carried through to the midpoint of election year 1984.

A moderation of monetary policy in late 1983 then caused the growth recession that began in mid 1984. Fortunately for Reagan, the impending growth recession was largely invisible at election time. What the public saw, as a result of Paul Volcker's erratic mismanagement of the money supply, was low inflation and high growth. It forgot, or at least forgave, the severity of the 1982 contraction; it could not divine the 1984-85 growth recession, which, in any event, would likely only have reduced the President's margin of victory. That a revival of Carteresque money growth might someday lead to a revival of Carteresque inflation was less tangible than the very real fact of lower inflation as voters went to the polls in November of 1984 to choose between Ronald Reagan and Jimmy Carter's Vice-President.

Mondale

In the midst of the most powerful economic recovery in thirty years, President Reagan's only vulnerability was the federal budget deficit, which the Congressional budget office in 1984 was estimating would grow to $263 billion in 1989. Walter Mondale hammered away at this weakness throughout the campaign, beginning in his acceptance speech:

> Here is the truth about the future: we are living on borrowed money and borrowed time. These deficits hike interest rates, clobber exports, stunt investment, kill jobs, undermine growth, cheat our kids and shrink our future.
> Whoever is inaugurated in January will have to pay Mr. Reagan's bills.

When one looks at Mondale's proposed solution to the evil of the Reagan deficits, one is struck by the inertia of the budget process and by the modesty of the differences between the proposed budgets of the two parties. In rhetoric—and in principle—there are significant differences between the parties; but these are expressed in policy as differences of emphasis. For example, in the Reagan Administration's first three fiscal years (1982-1984), the President's budget requests entailed spending of $2.34 trillion dollars. Congress actually spent $2.37 trillion ... the difference accounted for only a fraction of the half trillion dollars added to the federal debt during those three years.

Likewise, Mondale's proposed spending revisions would have represented only a minor departure from the Reagan projections. Mondale, to begin with, did not promise a balanced budget. Instead, he promised to reduce the deficit to "only" $86 billion by the end of his first term in 1989. This was hardly the rallying cry that was going to move millions of voters back into the Democratic column in 1984. Deficit reduction was to be accomplished through spending cuts and tax increases, in nearly equal measures—$75 billion in spending cuts, $85 billion in tax increases.

The spending cuts were designed to offend no one, especially the interest groups that form the backbone of the Democratic Party. Two-thirds of the $75 million spending reduction was to be achieved through lower interest payments on the national debt! Nearly all the rest was to be achieved through vaguely defined efficiencies in managing government programs.

The main difference between Reagan and Mondale was in the composition of the budget. Mondale proposed to restore a net $22 billion of Reagan's cuts in social programs. This was to be offset by a $25 billion reduction in defense spending from Reagan's projected budget, which would still allow defense spending to increase at a real rate of four percent. "I refuse," said Mondale, "to cut Social Security, Medicare, education, student loans and other things essential for a decent life. ... " Mondale, in short, refused to cut anything.

In campaigning for these spending priorities, Mondale was not enlarging his electoral base, he was appealing primarily to the Great Society constituencies that depend upon federal largesse. Had President Reagan been more radical in his attacks on the Great Society, the broad middle of the electorate would have been more open to the Mondale candidacy. As it was, many voters perceived Mondale as a reactionary candidate, fighting to preserve the excesses of the welfare state, and asking them to continue paying for them through tax increases.

"What we have is government of the rich, by the rich, and for the rich," Mondale said, as he attempted to counter that perception by portraying his tax increases as retribution upon the wealthy. And indeed, many of his proposals were aimed at the rich: surtaxes on incomes over $100,000, elimination of tax shelters, a minimum tax on corporations, and repeal of the third year of the tax cuts for people making more than $60,000 a year.

However, $25 to $30 billion of the additional revenue (coincidentally, the amount of money that Mondale wanted to put back into social programs) was to come from the repeal of indexing, and this would have come directly out of the pockets of middle class taxpayers. True to his liberalism, Mondale's theme during the 1984 campaign was that the voters—at their own expense—should rectify the injustices that Reagan had inflicted upon the welfare state. The voters, however, were disinclined to employ such distasteful means in pursuit of such a debatable end.

Deficit Reduction

One way or another, sooner or later, the deficit will be reduced, because there is no alternative. President and Congress will find a way—even if that way is something as extreme as a balanced budget amendment—because otherwise a federal debt that grows faster than GNP will necessarily in time become an insupportable burden on the budget and on the economy.

Consider the following hypothetical trends. If the American economy grew at a steady rate of three percent over the next quarter of a century, we would at that time have an economy of more that eight trillion dollars, in today's money. If the national debt meanwhile doubled every five years (it doubled from 1981 to 1985), it would in the same period grow to 64 trillion dollars! Obviously, that's not going to happen.

If the debt, however, were allowed to grow at the rate of four percent of GNP per year, it would over three decades approach the size of the entire annual national output. At that point it would be as though the national debt, instead of being two trillion dollars today, were four trillion dollars. The interest payments on that debt would consume 28 percent of the budget instead of the current 14 percent or so. That would imply either a massive crowding out of other programs (as when a profligate family must severely curtail its standard of living in order to honor past obligations), or a deficit-driven budget deficit that was totally out of control because no programs had been cut to make room for the increased debt service.

The question is not whether there will be deficit reduction, the question is the character of that reduction. Will it involve a tax increase? If so, then the heart will have to be cut out of Reaganomics. To the extent that it involves reductions in spending, how will those reductions be apportioned between defense and domestic programs? The vaunted Reagan military buildup (which the Republicans in 1984 praised as having restored America's security) has in fact corresponded more closely to Jimmy Carter's defense spending projections (which the Republicans in 1980 denounced as inadequate to America's security) than to Ronald Reagan's. Yet it is impossible to imagine the House of Representatives allowing domestic spending programs to be cut by hundreds of billions of dollars in the coming decade, without reductions of similar magnitude in defense spending.

Until the Democratic majority in the House is broken, the budget is not going to be balanced on Ronald Reagan's terms. The President therefore will spend much if not all his second term wrestling with a dilemma. To the extent that he is compelled to compromise with his congressional opponents so as to narrow the deficit, will he sacrifice defense spending and national security, or will he sacrifice the tax cuts upon which, in his understanding, economic recovery and national security depend?

What Might Have Been

To say that Ronald Reagan has not wrought a realignment in American politics is not necessarily to criticize him. Realignments are not to be had just for the asking. Politics is not malleable, like clay or plastic. What statesman has had greater vision, courage, determination, and eloquence than Winston Churchill in the thirties—or less success?

Miracles are not the work of men, however great. Not even the vision and eloquence of a Churchill could inspire the blind to see or the deaf to hear. The case against Ronald Reagan is not that he could have done so much more had he been more skillful politically. The argument is that he failed to do what he could have, and did not try to do what he might have. His political skills were not insufficient but unused.

Realignment means fundamental changes of policy and opinion. Reagan has succeeded in changing neither. In the one important area of economic policy that was within his sphere of influence—monetary policy—he has without any question failed to promote slow, steady growth of the money supply. In the area that was only partly within his sphere of influence—spending—he has witnessed a miserable failure of policy to conform to his expectations.

The actual course of monetary policy during the Reagan presidency has deviated greatly from its intended course. On the whole since mid-1982 money has been easy. Reagan, the political beneficiary of this policy (even as the Democrats were the beneficiary of restrained money growth in 1982), has made no effort to get it to conform to his original intent. On the contrary, he reappointed Paul Volcker, the man who has piloted money supply on its capricious course.

The relationship between Volcker and Reagan has been that of the leader and the end man in a game of crack-the-whip. The economy of the eighties has been whipping back and forth, flung one way and then the other by the monetary policies of Volcker: the worst recession since World War II, followed by the strongest recovery in thirty years, followed by a growth recession, followed by what I predict will be another boom. At times the game has been painful, as in 1982; more often, it has been exhilarating. But one thing is certain: Reagan has been controlled by events, he has not controlled them.

Reagan has been much more aggressive in his attempts to cut federal spending than he has been in his attempts to influence monetary policy. Nevertheless, spending has continued to increase, absolutely and relative to the economy. The real increase in spending during Reagan's first term was almost identical to the real spending increase during Carter's term. We are reminded, when we hear such figures, that the state budget in California has increased by 50% during the administration of each of the past four governors—Republican and Democrat, liberal and conservative—including Ronald Reagan. To change spending policy, Congress would have to be changed; to change Congress, public opinion would have to be changed; to change public opinion would entail giving the public a reason to change its opinion. Realignments typically result from national crises, when public opinion is molten, ready to be poured into new forms. Yet the rhetoric of Ronald Reagan is in no sense the hot and fiery rhetoric of crisis, notwithstanding spending and tax burdens that are greater than those of the seventies. Indeed, Reagan's mute acquiescence in a monetary policy that dissipated the quasicrisis atmosphere of 1980 made such a rhetoric impossible. To the extent that this monetary policy artificially created the illusion of recovery, Ronald Reagan in 1984 was a proud cock, crowing at a false dawn.

Deadlock of Democracy: Camelot Revisited

If 1984 was not 1936, it was in some ways like 1964: a hapless challenge to an adjustment, rather than a realignment, in American politics. In 1980, as in 1960, a tall, handsome, rich, glamorous, successful politician promised to get America moving again after a period of malaise and stagnation. In both elections, there was a sense that America must be more vigorous in responding to the Soviet military challenge, whether symbolized by Sputnik, the missile gap and Cuba, or by the SS-18, the SS-20, and Afghanistan. In both elections, there was a sense that the full potential of the American economy had yet to be unlocked.

Of course, the state of our economy and defenses was worse in 1980 than in 1960—and the anti-hero Carter was by no means equal in stature to Eisenhower—so that Reagan's margin of victory was correspondingly greater than John F. Kennedy's. Yet Reagan, no more than Kennedy, could carry with him a working majority for his domestic program as a whole.

Both Kennedy and Reagan did in fact bring a renewed spirit of optimism and progress to the country, and through policies that in many respects are parallel: a military buildup, tax cuts, free trade, and accommodative monetary policy. Like 1984, 1964 was a time of economic growth, relatively low inflation, and rallies in the stock and bond markets. Yet both men had trouble moving the most essential parts of their domestic programs through Congress: Kennedy a significant extension of the New Deal, Reagan, a significant reduction.

In 1963, troubled by Kennedy's inability to move his program through Congress, Professor James MacGregor Burns wrote *The Deadlock of Democracy*, in which he criticized the "Madisonian" plan of Congressional government, with its frustrating scheme of checks and balances. Burns contrasted it with what he called "the great competing scheme of Jefferson," namely, strong presidential and party leadership.

Burns knew that American political opinion was moderate in character—a bell shaped curve if you will—and he had no desire to replace moderate politics with highly ideologized politics. In fact, he thought that a competitive two-party system was the best guarantee of moderation. However, Burns did wish to change the expression of political opinion. Through strong presidential and party leadership, Burns hoped to invert the bell-shaped curve, to force the expression of opinion more toward the political extremes, albeit within the confines of moderates politics. As he put it, "The two presidential parties are the motors of national realignment, polarizing the electorate everywhere around their national doctrines."

Of course, Burns knew of the thesis that history progresses through alternating periods of conservative and liberal sentiment, and that many of his fellow liberals were content to abide by the regular and rhythmic undulations of history: two steps forward... pause... two steps forward.

He believed, however, that history had accelerated; that in our fast-paced world we had lost our "cushion of time"; that drift produces crisis; that our political system produces a lag—sometimes a "near fatal lag"—between events and our reaction to them. These new circumstances required parties with convictions, and the ability to carry out those convictions decisively. Burns thought that the time had come to harness the American political system to history.

Among the institutional reforms that he proposed, to nudge the American political system in the direction of presidential parties, were elimination of midterm elections, repeal of the two-term restriction on the president, and de-gerrymandering of Congressional districts. These, however, were secondary. Burns's most important point—and the peroration of the book—was a call for presidential leadership:

> Madisonian politics has a place for leadership, of course, but it is essentially brokerage. The leader responds to the amalgam of pressures working on him. He is

a manipulator, a mediator, a master bargainer among the group pressures and fragmentized forces that the Madisonian model glorifies. At most the leader may point out a direction, enunciate principles and policies, and exert influences through persuasion, bargaining, and narrow forms of pressure.

The Jeffersonian leader must be much more than this. He must gain leadership of a big national party and guide it in seizing and holding majority status. He must publicize his and his party's program and goals with such clarity and conviction that he can help convert latent and amorphous popular attitudes into a powerful public opinion bolstering his cause. He must build structural support in his personal following by merging it with his national party organization or by creating new political units ... he must be willing to narrow his personal popularity if by so doing he can intensify and consolidate a working majority in Congress or the electorate.

In the typology of James MacGregor Burns, Ronald Reagan is a Madisonian leader. His election was an epiphenomenon of the conservative revival, and his success as president has consisted of his personal popularity and his legislative victories, rather than his ability to "reshape to some degree the constellation of political forces in which he operates."

The argument is now made, by optimists, that Reagan will work his magic on a Congress facing the necessity for deficit reduction. The suggestion is made that the Democrats will be persuaded to approve a mix of defense and domestic spending congenial to Reagan. If so, then the Democratic Party will have made itself the vehicle of a Republican realignment. Such obliging conduct would save Reagan the trouble of destroying the Democrats as a prelude to realignment.

This kind of wishful thinking reminds one of those during the 1960s who argued that the deadlocked war in Vietnam would be resolved in due course through North Vietnamese concessions, i.e., that the Vietnamese would weary of stalemate on the battlefield and would, in effect, concede defeat. The question, "What if they don't?" was never much discussed, because the answer was one nobody wanted to hear: if they did not act reasonably, then a favorable outcome would depend on destroying the enemy forces in battle.

If the Democrats in Congress do not act "reasonably," if they refuse to swerve in their game of political chicken with Reagan, then there would seem to be two possibilities. Either defense and domestic spending must be cut deeply, or taxes will rise, perhaps to 21 or 22 percent of GNP, while defense and domestic expenditures stagnate or decline. Such would be the shriveled and sour fruits of the Reagan Revolution.

In order to break the back of Congressional resistance, Reagan would have had to transform public opinion against Congress in 1984. To do so would have required that runaway federal spending be kept before the public as the paramount domestic crisis of 1984. The plausibility of such an argument and the harsh rhetoric that would necessarily have accompanied it, could only have arisen from prior confrontations between President and Congress, in which the President vetoed every Congressional spending bill in excess of his proposed budget. Just as Harry Truman lacerated the do-nothing 80th Congress, so Reagan could have attacked the spend-too-much 98th Congress incessantly in 1984, as a prelude to putting the Democratic Party on trial in the fall of 1984.

Reagan's only real hope of realignment lay in making the Congressional elections, rather than his own reelection, the focus of the campaign. But he used the veto only sparingly, did not emphasize the importance of Congress, and did not make any attempt to destroy the legitimacy of the Democrats and drive them beyond the pale of the American political tradition, as witness his invocations of Franklin Roosevelt and John Kennedy.

This brings up an interesting point. Reagan is known for his affability and graciousness, and is universally liked by friends and opponents both. His manner is disarming, not confrontational. The words hardness and hatred are misplaced in any discussion of him. Yet the presidents who have been identified with past realignments have all provoked hatred, loathing, and fury. People hate when they are convinced that they have been done a serious injustice or injury. Their passions run high when they believe that much is at stake, and they are in danger of suffering irreparable losses. Is it not then instructive that no one hates Ronald Reagan?

If Reagan had savaged the Democratic opposition, cast them out of American politics, and literally attempted to destroy them, he would have earned the hatred of his opponents and part of the electorate. He would possibly have sacrificed his personal popularity and his margin of victory in 1984. It would have been a risky strategy, but he would have had the satisfaction of knowing that he had done everything possible to bring about a genuine realignment in American politics. In short, a serious attack on the Democratic Party was the necessary condition of political realignment. Whether it would have been a sufficient condition is another question.

Epilogue

Ronald Reagan and other conservatives presented the seventies as a period of crisis of the kind that could presage a national realignment. In domestic affairs, the crisis was said to the inevitable consequence of the New Deal's departure from sound economic principles. The new president was very clear and specific about what needed to be done. It has not been done. Nevertheless, Reagan is pleased with the course of events and believes that the crisis has passed because of his leadership.

In truth what we have is a regathering economic storm, but no Churchill to warn of the unseen impending fury. It will become visible only when it breaks upon us. And only then will we realize that the Reagan administration was nothing more than the eye of a hurricane.

Let us attempt to plot the probable course of events as it might be expected to unfold by the neoclassical economics that Reagan embraces. 1986 will be a boom year because of the year-long explosion in M_1 throughout 1985. The consensus forecast, which projects modest growth, points to two facts, first, that M_1 has been overstated, and second, that velocity has fallen in recent years relative to its secular trend line. It is certainly true that the growth of M_1, which is generally within one percentage point of the growth of the monetary base, year over year, ran several points above the base in 1985. Still, even though the base did not grow at a double digit-rate, as M_1 did, it did grow at a very fast pace of 8%. This strong stimulant is confirmed by the extraordinary behavior of the capital markets, which parallels monetary developments and precedes the general economy.

Velocity is procyclical, not in the short term but over the course of an economic cycle. That is, when money supply (M) goes up, velocity (V) goes up, and when M falls, V falls. Velocity took what many regarded as a surprising fall in 1982, but its behavior was consistent with an abnormally sharp decline in money growth. Likewise—and this is not so widely realized—velocity rose above its secular trend during the most powerful phase of the Reagan recovery. Precise predictions of economic behavior are impossible, but any surprise in 1986 is likely to be on the upside.

Inflation, which used to horrify people when it bumped up against its four percent ceiling, now soothes when it bumps along its four percent floor. Strong money growth over many years, from the middle of 1982 to the end of 1985, will rekindle inflation. The pyromaniacal monetary policies of Volcker, abetted by a falling dollar, will reignite the fires of inflation.

Stronger than expected economic growth should reduce the projected budget deficit for fiscal 1986. In due course, however, higher growth and inflation should cause a more restrictive Federal Reserve policy. The stronger the growth, the more restrictive the Fed is likely to be. If the Fed overreacts—as it always does—a severe tightening of money could plunge the capital markets into panic and the United States into a recession in 1987. The prospective budget deficit would soar. Stagflation, rising unemployment, and deficits on such a scale as to blot out any hope of more tax cuts as far as the eye can see might well produce a consensus that Reaganomics has not worked.

The 1980s—like the 1920s—would then come to be understood as an illusion, an interlude, an island in the stream of history. And left alone on that island would be America's own Prospero, the Great Communicator, lamenting:

> Now I want
> Spirits to enforce, art to enchant,
> And my ending is despair

In retrospect the 1984 election would resemble even more closely the election of 1964, whose real winner was Barry Goldwater. Goldwater's victory consisted of shifting the Republican Party to the right, and laying the ground-work for the conservative movement to emerge as a force in national politics.

If the Reagan Administration in 1985 is in fact at its peak, just as the New Frontier/Great Society was in 1965, then the Democratic Party—contrary to every appearance and expectation—could be on its way back after four Republican victories in the past five presidential elections. Should "Reaganomics" lead us full circle to the stagflation of the seventies, a candidate could then arise from within the Democratic Party with "new ideas" to meet the emergency: massive tax increases and man-sized cuts in defense spending. Should such a candidate capture the presidency, he would arrive in Washington, D.C., in January of 1989, to find awaiting him a Democratic Congress, which, having survived realignment, would be ready to do his bidding.

The 1984 Democratic Primary Election: Issues and Image

Glen E. Thurow

Between 1968 and 1984 the presidential nominees of the Democratic Party were men initially without widespread support among party officials and office holders. Both George McGovern and Jimmy Carter won the party's endorsement over the opposition or indifference of these leaders by winning primary victories. But in 1984, as in 1968, the Democratic nominee did not storm the party from without, but was the clear choice of party insiders. Walter Mondale was backed by most of the party's prominent leaders and influential groups and benefitted from new rules designed to strengthen the hand of the party's elect. The course of the nomination fight, and the choice of Mondale, provides a portrait of a party as well as a man. The united party presented to the electorate at the end of the San Francisco convention was mirrored in the man who united it. The bridge that Mondale, the protégé of Hubert Humphrey, seemed to make to 1968 was overshadowed in both party and man by the radical changes that had occurred in the intervening years.

A generation ago, in 1960, the Democratic Party recaptured the Presidency after being temporarily eclipsed by a popular war hero. Yet its eclipse had not caused it to doubt its cause. In his Inaugural Address, the youthful Kennedy reflected the optimism and confidence of his party by proclaiming his determination to eliminate poverty from the land and to "bear any burden" to advance the cause of liberty in the world. Even after the shock of Kennedy's assassination, the party set about creating a "great society." The party was proud of its New Deal past, confident of its ability to govern, sure that it knew how to appeal to its fellow citizens, and moved by the better America, freed of poverty and segregation, it wished to build.

This confidence, and the liberalism upon which it rested, was shattered by the bitter battle within the Democratic Party over the Vietnam War during the election of 1968. In the wake of this battle and the consequent defeat of its nominee, Hubert Humphrey, the party reformed the rules governing selection of delegates to its convention in an effort to prevent a repeat of 1968. The result of these reforms was not the restoration of harmony within the party, however. Their initial effect, at least, was to broaden and deepen the conflict within the party by allowing increased representation for those who most wished to change the course of the party. On the two great issues of the day, the party of Johnson and Humphrey had stood for the foreign policy of containment and the protection of civil rights for all. The new voices called for a lessening of the use of American force abroad and a movement away from impartially protecting civil rights to compensating disadvantaged groups for the injustices they had suffered in the past. These policies formed a coherent whole through the contention that America in the past had used its might to oppress other people abroad and large elements of its own population at home. Profiting from changes in nomination procedures, these views captured the nomination in 1972 with the selection of George McGovern. But they did not wholly capture the party, and large elements of the party either sat out the election or supported the Democrats' long-time arch-enemy, Richard Nixon, for President.

Until 1984 the Democratic Party was deeply torn between the old liberalism and the new, more radical liberalism championed by McGovern. Although the convention of 1976 ended in relative harmony, this was due more to the ability of Jimmy Carter rhetorically to straddle the party's divisions than it was to any genuine agreement within. That artificial harmony broke down in the disputes and failures of the Carter presidency and erupted into another bitter campaign within the party in 1980 to unseat the Democrats' own President. The convention of 1980 ended with a televised snub of the party's nominee, the President of the United States, by the second most prominent man in the party.

The primary campaign of 1984 ended in a way which suggested that the division of the party had been mended. Despite a contest for the nomination protracted beyond what nearly all contemplated at the start of the delegate selection season, the convention displayed a unity unknown to the Democrats for the past two decades. Walter Mondale, unlike Jimmy Carter and George McGovern, had the backing, if not the complete enthusiasm of the party. In selecting Geraldine Ferraro as his running mate, Mondale sought less to balance the ticket than to give a clear indication to Americans of the character of the party. The genuine cheers which greeted her selection suggested that the party did indeed share a common direction.

The new-found unity of the 1984 convention rested upon questionable foundations, however. It was made possible by a significant shift to the left within the party and by the absence from the convention of what had previously been the center and right of the party—the old liberalism. This posed not only the immediate problem of whether the party could attract a sufficient number of voters in November, but also the longer range question of whether the party was any longer capable of tapping those deep currents in the American political tradition which had been the basis of the old liberalism's long ascendance. This shift was accompanied by a style of political bargaining which conceded as much as possible to the particular groups and interests comprising the party without demanding their subordination to the party's aspirations in return. This style would not only make Walter Mondale appear to be a weak leader to the voters in the general election, but obscured the higher principles of the party. Finally unity was made possible only by the hope held out to the 1984 losers that they would have a better chance of being winners another year. This was done not by pointing out that Mondale might not be in their way another time, but by promising further leftward reform of the party, thus tending to undermine the legitimacy of its present state.

The 1984 Democratic nomination battle reveals the major elements of the party and how they were forged into a particular kind of unity by the time of the convention. We will focus on several of the most significant elements of the nomination process: the rules of selecting delegates to the convention and the inability of the party to reach consensus on the proper rules; the collapse of the candidates of the old Democratic center and right in the early primaries; the character of the challenges to Mondale's nomination by Gary Hart and Jesse Jackson and his response to them; and the decisions of the victorious Mondale in choosing Geraldine Ferraro as the Vice Presidential nominee and in shaping the platform of the party.

Delegate Selection Rules

Few matters are as important to the success or failure of a Presidential candidate as the rules determining how delegates to the conventions are to be selected. But if these rules are important for the immediate outcome of an election, they also reflect a party's understanding of the principles of representative democracy. After every election since 1968 the Democratic Party has established a commission to reform the rules for selecting delegates to the party convention. Potential candidates in upcoming elections have sought to influence this reform for their own advantage. But the continual change of these rules by the party has also reflected the deep dispute within the party concerning the proper principles of representation and the practical effects of various reforms. It is necessary to see the rules for 1984 against the background of the reforms of the past decade and a half.

In 1968 the delegates had been selected according to a pattern that had prevailed since the advent of primaries in 1912. This pattern, sometimes known as the "mixed system," combined primaries with party-run and controlled caucuses. In a typical year somewhat more than a third of the delegates would be chosen in primaries. Although it was useful to win primaries, a candidate could not secure the nomination by means of primary victories alone. Primaries were chiefly useful as an argument with which to approach the party leaders who controlled the caucuses and the delegations chosen by them. In 1960, John Kennedy ran in only four contested primary elections. By winning in West Virginia where the issue of his Catholicism was faced head on, he gained an argument with party leaders that Catholicism needed no longer to be a barrier to one's becoming President. But he still had to convince party leaders that he was the best man to be the standard bearer. In 1968, on the eve of the reform movement, Hubert Humphrey received the Democratic nomination without entering a single primary.

In the wake of the disaffection of the anti-Vietnam War Democrats caused by the nomination of Hubert Humphrey, the party established a reform commission to change the nominating process. The commission, chaired by Senator McGovern, set about rewriting the party's rules in order to bring the disaffected back into the fold and to hasten the entry of new groups into the Democratic Party. There were two main paths taken to accomplish this goal: One was to open the nomination process to wider sections of the electorate. Rules were fashioned to diminish the control of party "bosses," whether the selection of delegates was done by primaries or by caucuses. The second path was to ensure that the results of the selection process would be representation at the convention on the part of various groups--women, young people, and racial and other minorities. This was to be accomplished either by outright quotas (in the case of women) or by rules which had the same effect as quotas but allowed the appearance that the party had rejected quotas. These changes looked to practical benefits for the party in attracting women, minorities, and others to the party, but they were also viewed by many elements within the party as based on principles more just and fair than the previous procedures. They were, it was thought, more democratic and they were required to right the wrongs done by prior exclusion of women, blacks, and others from the political process.

The new rules of the party led in turn to reforms in state laws, particularly since the courts upheld the right of the party to enforce its rules even if they conflicted with state laws. The result was a transformed nomination procedure, dominated by primaries. The percentage of delegates chosen by primaries rose from 38 percent in 1968 to 61 percent in 1972. By 1980 there were binding primaries in 29 states and 72 percent of the delegates were chosen by them. The old system was reversed. Instead of primary victories being useful to persuade party leaders, the support of party leaders became useful only for the aid they could give in winning primaries (and usually that was not as important as other factors). In 1972 and 1976 the nominees were selected either in opposition to party leaders (McGovern) or without their support (Carter). The dominance of primaries and the new rules of the party led to changed behavior in the caucus states as well. Because the outcome of the race was likely to be decided before the convention, caucuses no longer chose uncommitted delegates. By banning the unit rule—the rule that all of a state's delegates must vote for the candidate preferred by the majority of the delegation—and requiring proportional representation, the rules for the 1980 Democratic Convention effectively undercut the power of state leaders. Finally, by requiring delegates to follow their pledges for the first few ballots, delegate discretion was effectively removed. There has not been a second ballot at a major political convention since 1952. Courtship of voters, in primaries or caucuses, took the place of courtship of powerful leaders or even of individual delegates.

One result of these reforms was that the character of the delegates changed significantly. There was increased representation of minorities and disadvantaged groups in the convention, and decreased representation of party and elected officials. Only eight Democratic Senators and 37 Democratic House members attended the 1980 Democratic Convention. Because fewer of the delegates were regulars of state and local party organizations, most delegates had little stake in the party's future. Less attention was given to the general and long-range interests of the party and more to the immediate advancement of the particular political positions of the delegates. Although delegates to Democratic conventions have always been more liberal than the voters as a whole, liberal opinions were given greater sway by the absence of non-ideological considerations.

Once again for the 1984 election the Democrats formed a commission to reform the selection rules of the party. But this time the commission, chaired by Governor Jim Hunt of North Carolina, swam against the tides of the three previous commissions. The commission moved to increase the influence of party leaders and officials, to increase the discretion allowed the delegates, to lessen the volatility of primary results and the length of the primary season. The direction of these changes was due in part to the particular political configuration which existed at the time the commission was formed and did its work. Following the Democratic loss in 1980, there were two prominent candidates for the nomination in 1984, Edward Kennedy and Walter Mondale. Because both had strength within the party and were well-known to the electorate at large, they shared an interest in strengthening the hands of party regulars and decreasing the chances of an outsider winning the primaries. At the same time this interest coincided with a more generalized critique of the results of the previous reforms. To reintroduce party officials at the convention, it was thought, would give it a significant element willing to moderate its views in order to achieve victory in the November elections and to consider the longer range interests of the party. The chance of the selection of a person whose impact upon party fortunes could not be carefully assessed would be further reduced by shortening the primary season (thus making it harder for unknowns to become known during the primary season itself). That assessment would be made possible by not binding the delegates to their pledged candidates, thus allowing the deliberation of the convention itself to influence the decision.

To accomplish these goals, new rules were devised. Of the 3933 delegates to the convention, 568 were to be officially unpledged party and elected officials. (These delegates quickly became known as "super-delegates.") Out of the unpledged total, the Democratic Caucus of the House of Representatives and the Democratic Conference of the Senate were allowed to select up to three fifths of their members. The remaining were to be selected by the individual states in the number allocated to each. In addition another 305 seats were reserved for party and elected officials pledged to particular candidates.

To help concentrate the vote on major candidates, the party dropped the requirement for proportional representation it had in 1980. Instead it allowed the states to follow either the rule of proportional representation or one of two other options. States could award a bonus of one delegate in each congressional district, or they could award the winner all of the delegates from that district. Twelve states adopted one of these two alternatives instead of proportional representation.

The new rules also sought to confine delegate selection to a three and a half month period in the spring, prohibiting the selection process from beginning before the second Tuesday in March or after the second Tuesday in June. Two exceptions were allowed. The New Hampshire primary was permitted to be the first Tuesday in March and the Iowa caucuses the week before that.

Finally, to allow assessment of the results of the primary and caucus season, delegates to the convention were not mandated by party rules to vote for the candidate to which they were pledged, as they had been in 1980. Instead they were only bound to "in all good conscience reflect the sentiments of those who elected them."

The Effect of the Rules on the Campaign

With Senator Kennedy deciding not to run for the nomination, the new rules significantly aided Walter Mondale's quest for the nomination. However, they did not fundamentally change the nature of the nominating procedure, much less the direction of the Democratic Party. Nor did they open the Democratic Convention to greater deliberation or concern for the long-range fate of the party.

At the beginning of the primary season, it seemed as if the new rules might backfire against Mondale. The shortening of the primary season, combined with the desire of many states to have early primaries in order to maximize their influence, created the possibility of a decisive blow at the beginning of the process. Mondale organized early to take advantage of this possibility. By January of 1984 *Newsweek* reported that he had the biggest, best organized, and most sophisticated campaign organization in American history. He had raised $9.5 million in private donations and another $4.3 million in federal matching grants, more than all the other candidates combined. Yet the vagaries of the electorate, the influence of the media, and the concentration of early primaries almost gave the knock-out blow to Gary Hart.

Gary Hart received only 14 percent of the vote in the first selection contest, the Iowa caucuses, compared to Mondale's 44 percent. However, that was enough to put him in second place in the balloting. Particularly because the third place candidate, George McGovern with 12 percent of the vote, was not taken as a serious candidate, Hart received great attention in the following week before the New Hampshire primary. At the start of the week polls had indicated voters in New Hampshire favoring Mondale over Hart by a 37-13 margin. Yet Hart won, 40-29 percent. When told who of the other six candidates was the realistic alternative to Mondale, New Hampshire voters flocked to him. The momentum of the campaign went with Hart. He appeared on the cover of national news magazines and appeared nightly on the evening news.

Gary Hart was news, Walter Mondale was not. From the New Hampshire primary on, the contest was between Mondale and Hart. After New Hampshire Hart won all of the caucuses and the remaining primaries held before March 13. By then Hart had gathered 51 percent of the primary vote to 25 percent for Mondale, and Mondale was widely regarded as in trouble.

However, Mondale was saved by the scheduling of the primaries, his superior organization, and a shift in media coverage. On March 13, "super-Tuesday," five primaries were held. Hart had little organization in some of them, and this quick onslaught of a large number of states gave him little time to develop the organization needed. Still, Hart won three of the primaries, in Florida, Massachusetts, and Rhode Island, while Mondale managed to salvage Georgia by a narrow margin and Alabama by a substantial one. Because Mondale had succeeded in convincing the media that he only needed to hold Hart to a draw on super-Tuesday, this turned the media and primary tide. The media began to take a more critical stance towards Hart, and had a new appreciation of Mondale's toughness and skill.

Super-Tuesday was followed by a series of primaries largely in the industrial North where Mondale was strongest. Between March 13 and May 8, Hart won only the March 27th primary in Connecticut and the non-binding primary in Wisconsin, while Mondale won delegate-rich victories in Illinois, New York, Pennsylvania, Puerto Rico, and Tennessee, and caucuses in Michigan, Arkansas, Minnesota, and other states. It was not until May 8 that Hart won significant victories in the midwest, in Indiana and Ohio. He again picked up a string of victories as the location of the primaries moved mostly west of the Mississippi after May 8. Mondale, in fact, won no primaries in the West. The primary season ended with Mondale's receiving approximately 39 percent of the vote, Hart 36 percent, and Jackson 18 percent. Hart had won more primaries, 16 to Mondale's 11. But the early concentration of primaries and caucuses, and the scheduling of the northern industrial states at a critical juncture, were decisive aids to Mondale's eventual victory.

Mondale benefitted from the scheduling of the primaries. He also benefitted from other rule changes. Despite the closeness of the popular vote in the primaries, Mondale emerged with a decisive lead at the convention, receiving nearly a thousand votes more than Hart in the balloting. The creation of the super-delegates was a substantial aid to Mondale. He received support from more than 500 of the 568 super-delegates. These delegates did not act as the Hunt Commission had imagined. Instead of remaining a block of uncommitted delegates who could assess matters at convention time, most committed themselves to candidates early in the process—even before the primary occurred. Partly for this reason, Mondale never trailed in the delegate count. This support among party leaders not only netted Mondale the bulk of the super-delegates, but gave him important support throughout the caucus process. Although Hart won a 51-44 percent victory in the initial Maine caucuses, for example, he wound up with only one more delegate than Mondale (13-12) because of Mondale's support from state leaders.

Because the allocation of delegates was weighted toward traditionally Democratic districts and because the new rules abandoned the requirement for proportional representation, Mondale tended to pick up more convention delegates for the same number of primary votes. Mondale appealed more to the traditional Democratic voter, while Hart tended to appeal to independent voters. Hence, Mondale's wins in congressional districts tended to net him more delegates than Hart's wins in less heavily Democratic districts. In the industrial north the most heavily Democratic districts had seven, eight, or nine delegates apiece whereas districts which were independent or Republican, in which Hart ran best, had as few as three delegates. Furthermore many of the states in which Mondale did well had adopted either the winner-take-all or the winner's bonus system for awarding the district delegates. Hart's wins, on the other hand, tended to come in states which determined delegates by proportional representation. Mondale's 40-35 percent win in Illinois netted him 95 pledged delegates to Hart's 41, a margin further increased by his support among uncommitted party delegates. Conversely Hart's win in Indiana by 42-41 percent gave him 38 votes to Mondale's 37. With the addition of the super-delegates, Mondale actually had more delegate support in Indiana than Hart.

It must be added that Mondale had developed the superior organization and strategy which allowed him to take advantage of the new rules. Beginning early, with a strategy of trying to achieve victory in every state, Mondale was well-prepared for the early primary onslaught. His organization allowed him to gain votes even when Hart won the primary. Hart won the Florida primary with 40 percent of the vote to 32 percent for Mondale. Yet, because Hart's campaign had full delegate slates in only 5 of the 19 congressional districts in the state, Mondale wound up with 50 percent of the delegates to Hart's 40 percent.

The new rules helped to assure the victory of the candidate supported by party leaders, Mondale. However, they did not achieve many of the other objectives of the Hunt Commission. They did not significantly reduce the volatility of the primary campaign, particularly in its early stages, as we have described. In fact, were it not for accidents of scheduling, the shortening of the campaign might have increased it. Iowa and New Hampshire retained their inordinate influence over the nomination, as did the media in its crucial early role of designating Hart as the challenger to Mondale.

The creation of super-delegates only superficially recreated what the party had lost through the reform movement. There was no greater deliberation at the convention than four years earlier, because there was no uncommitted block remaining when San Francisco rolled around. In the final stages of the campaign, Hart tried to use the primary results to argue that he could win in November while Mondale could not. Yet in fact there was no large group at the convention open to such an argument. While the pre-reform uncommitted delegates constituted state blocks that could be directed by party leaders, the super-delegates, spread across the states, were not a block led by anyone. Each was on his own, and his interest was to choose up sides lest a candidate win while he was still sitting on the fence. Instead of the super-delegates representing the concerns of the party, each represented no one but himself.

The "Fairness Commission"

The rules themselves became an issue in the campaign. Both Hart and Jackson objected that the rules were unfair, because they favored the party-backed candidate. As part of the effort to achieve harmony at the convention, Mondale agreed to the establishment of yet another reform commission, dubbed the "Fairness Commission."

In establishing the "Fairness Commission," the convention also passed a number of non-binding resolutions which showed clearly the direction in which the convention wished the new reforms to go. These resolutions called for cutting the number of super-delegates in half, deferring their selection until after the first primary or caucus, lowering the threshold needed to win a share of delegates, and requiring proportional representation in the first half of the primary season. Furthermore the resolutions called for strengthening the representation of "Blacks, Hispanics, native Americans, Asian/Pacifics, women and persons of all sexual preference consistent with their proportional representation in the party." And the new commission was directed to "examine the question of assured percentages of various disadvantaged groups in the composition of state delegations by racial, ethnic, and other categories with the objective of making allocations similar to those now accorded on the basis of gender." (The allocations based on gender are strict quotas—50 percent women.) In short the resolutions called for continuing the direction of the three prior reform commissions rather than that charted by the rules for 1984. Perhaps most significant for revealing the view of the San Francisco delegates was the title of the reform commission, the "Fairness Commission." It seemed to say that whatever reasons of expediency there might have been for the direction of the 1984 rules, justice required quotas or something like them, and little, if any, weight for party leaders.

The Collapse of the Center and Right

The 1984 convention ended in harmony in part because there was considerable agreement in opinion and outlook among the delegates. Those who favored the traditional combination of the welfare state, equal protection of civil rights, and the foreign policy of containment, not to mention the old conservative Southern wing of the party, were virtually absent from the convention. The candidacy of those from the old center and right of the party had collapsed early in the nomination procedure. The results of the Iowa caucuses and the New Hampshire primary were devastating to those who might have continued the legacy of the Scoop Jackson wing of the party. In the Iowa precinct caucuses, Askew, Glenn, and Hollings combined received less than 10 percent of the vote. Immediately after the New Hampshire primary, in which the three did scarcely better, Hollings and Askew dropped from the race. Glenn dropped two weeks later.

The poor showing of these candidates was due in part to the difficulty any middle-of-the-road or right-of-center candidate faces in the Democratic primaries. The more liberal Democrats are the ones most likely to come out for primary or caucus voting. In addition the campaigns of Glenn and Hollings were poorly managed. Not only was this true of the day-to-day organizing of the campaign, but it was also true of the overall strategy of the candidates. Although Glenn tried to picture himself as the centrist candidate, he wavered from this strategy, sometimes moving to a more conservative stance and sometimes trying to picture himself as a "peace" candidate, by means of his support of the nuclear freeze. He also tried to make his appeal chiefly through television rather than organization and cultivation of supporting groups; however, he turned out to have only minimal appeal in personal appearances.

The result was that the remainder of the campaign was fought between candidates on the left wing of the party. When Walter Mondale was chosen by Jimmy Carter to be his running mate in 1976, it was in part because Mondale represented the more liberal wing of the party, useful for balancing Carter's Southern and more conservative image. But among the remaining candidates in 1984, Mondale was the most "conservative," with the clearest ties to the old liberalism. During the bulk of the primary season, the collapse of opposition to the right did not push Mondale to the left; indeed, he appeared to become more moderate, defending at least some uses of American force abroad and opposing quotas at home. However, in the final stages of the nomination season, when Mondale's main goal became unity within the party at the San Francisco convention, it was people to his left who were the candidates and delegates he had to placate. Yet the bulk of American voters were to his right. Mondale's strategy in this dilemma seemed to be to speak to people on his right, while yielding on issues to people on his left. He gave the most moderate speech at the Democratic Convention. Yet he adopted the candidate of NOW as his running mate, yielded to Hart on a plank barring the use of American force under almost all circumstances except an invasion, acceded to Jackson on quotas, and to both Jackson and Hart on the "Fairness Commission." The moderate rhetoric, combined with his concessions to the left, made him look simply weak to many voters.

The Challenge by Hart

We have already described the ups and downs of Gary Hart's challenge to Mondale's nomination. It remains to consider the substance of this challenge. What did Hart stand for that differentiated him from Mondale?

Hart ran a campaign of themes or moods, rather than issues. He sought to portray himself as the candidate of new ideas, unbeholden to special interests, and focused upon the future. These themes were in part developed to play upon Mondale's weaknesses—his ties to organized labor and other special groups, and the perception that he represented an older, partially discredited politics. However, Hart found it difficult to justify himself as the candidate of new ideas under Mondale's constant questioning, "Where's the beef?" And Mondale sought, with some success, to throw the issue back on Hart, charging that Hart was too inexperienced to be President. What seemed to appeal most to voters was Hart's anti-Washington, anti-establishment theme. His greatest success was among younger voters and to those with weaker ties to the Democratic Party. A new term, Yuppie, was coined to indicate the type of voter who found Hart appealing. This affluent voter differed from the traditional New Deal voter above all in being concerned with the excessive demands placed upon him by Washington. While Mondale's backing from labor and his inability to distinguish his beliefs in any way from those of organized labor made him appear the very representative of the post-New Deal establishment, Hart, like McGovern and Carter before him, ran against the political and economic establishment of the country.

On the major issues facing the country, Hart positioned himself clearly to the left of Mondale. He was explicitly in favor of quotas. But he was most concerned with foreign policy. He vigorously opposed any use of American force either in the Middle East or in Central America. He advocated cutting off aid to the Nicaraguan rebels and to El Salvador, and withdrawing U.S. forces from Honduras. He vehemently assailed the President for his Central American policy, and accused Mondale of complicity with this policy when Mondale suggested some conditions on withdrawal from Honduras. The "new ideas" and the "future," according to Hart, belonged to a further leftward movement.

Hart thus combined the anti-establishment tone of Jimmy Carter with clearer new left views on foreign and domestic policy. Hart had first risen to national prominence as the campaign manager for George McGovern. In the intervening years he had tried to distance himself from McGovern by arguing for a stronger military, not through increased defense spending but through reform of military practices and the building of smaller and simpler weapons. However, Hart did not differ at all from McGovern's position on when American forces ought to be used—only if the United States were directly attacked.

In preferring Mondale over Hart it is not clear that the party rejected the ideas of Hart. Not only were Mondale's views not that far distant from Hart's, but at the convention the party adopted resolutions on both quotas and foreign policy that were closer to Hart's original views than to Mondale's.

The Candidacy of Jesse Jackson

Jesse Jackson's candidacy was the first major try for the Democratic or Republican nomination by a black candidate. Jackson decided to make the his-

48 / Glen E. Thurow

toric run for the nomination even though he faced an apparently difficult situation. He and his allies had little experience in Presidential politics, and he faced wide opposition among the country's black leadership. Nevertheless he ran. Although he professed throughout the campaign that his aim was to achieve the nomination, he remained in the race long after there was any hope of victory. It may be surmised, therefore, that he had other ends in view as well.

Jesse Jackson sought to create a "rainbow coalition" of all those who were in some way at the bottom of the ladder or were allies of those at the bottom—blacks, Hispanics, women, poor, homosexuals, liberal activists. He did not succeed in developing such a coalition during the campaign. One large stumbling block to this goal occurred over two incidents involving his attitude toward Jews. The first was when, speaking off the record, he called Jews Hymies and New York Hymietown. The word got out and Jackson was slow to apologize. The second was when it took months for him to repudiate the comments of his supporter, Louis Farrakhan of the Nation of Islam. Farrakhan had denounced Jews and threatened to harm anyone hindering Jackson's campaign. Although the Jackson campaign spoke of a "rainbow coalition," it concentrated its efforts upon the black vote. Jackson won 77 percent of the black votes in the primaries, and only five percent of the white vote.

Jackson's policy views were at the left end of the Democratic spectrum. He favored quotas. He made an issue out of run-off primaries, arguing that they diluted the votes of minorities. He, like Hart, opposed aid to the Nicaraguan rebels and to the government of El Salvador. He believed that U.S. foreign policy had centered too much on the threat from the Soviet Union and had not focused sufficiently on the problems of the third world. In all these stands, Jackson's views were widely shared on the left of the party.

Although the policies suggested by Jackson were not strange in Democratic circles, the boldness of the underlying rhetoric supporting them was for a major Presidential candidate. His rhetoric has sometimes been described as third world. In the 1950s and 1960s Martin Luther King had forged a multi-racial coalition of both blacks and whites to combat segregation in the name of the nation's fundamental commitment to equality. Jackson, on the other hand, appealed not to the claim that all men are created equal, but to the rhetoric of class and racial grievance. At the Democratic convention, Jackson said that he spoke for "the damned, disinherited, disrespected, despised. . . ." Where King had believed that American principles were good, but not followed in practice, Jackson argued that there was a sickness at America's heart. Nicaragua, he said, was "on the right side of history" and the U.S. "on the wrong." Given that his appeal was largely to blacks, it might be said that Jackson professed class politics and practiced racial politics.

The differences that existed between Jackson and the other two major candidates were not drawn sharply. In part this was due to the desire of both Hart and Mondale not to alienate the most cohesive block of voters within the party. The movement of the party to the left meant that electoral victory in November depended upon securing a large turnout of black voters, and Jackson was seen as the key to that effort. But in refusing to draw the issues between them, Hart and Mondale also helped to undercut the more moderate black leadership. Jackson became accepted, both by the media and the party leadership, as well as by a considerable number of black voters, as the leader of black America. This was due in part to his own boldness and abilities, but it was also due to the failure of others to present an alternative to his vision. Although Mondale resisted some of Jackson's suggestions, he never met them on the level of principle. The result was not only that Jackson was not challenged for leadership among blacks, but that Jackson could portray himself as, and could in measure become, the conscience of the party. At the convention the reception given Jackson's address suggested that he spoke for the heart of the party, albeit it had in practice to accommodate itself to electoral realities.

The Victorious Mondale

On June 11, the final day of the primary season, the Mondale forces saw that their man had lost California but won New Jersey. Mondale moved quickly to get public pledges from uncommitted delegates in order to put his delegate number over the top. He succeeded. Having sewn up the nomination, Mondale from this point on sought to achieve two goals: unity within the party and a stance that would provide the strongest possible starting point for the fall election. As the center and right of the party had been thoroughly routed with the withdrawal of Askew, Hollings, and Glenn, the danger to party unity came from Mondale's left. Mondale dealt with those on his left not by threatening them with Ronald Reagan, but by preempting the left, at least symbolically, in the choice of a vice presidential nominee and by appeasing the left by granting those platform and other demands that did not seem to jeopardize the fall election. At the same time he sought to foster a more moderate image for the party to reach out to the general electorate on his right by means of his own rhetoric and portrayals of his own and Ferraro's character.

In his choice of a vice presidential nominee, it became immediately apparent that Mondale was not going to use the position to reach out to the center and right, but to bring in the left and highlight the direction of the party and his candidacy. Mondale conducted a series of interviews with potential vice presidential nominees, much publicized in the press. Of the seven people interviewed, only the choice of Senator Bentsen of Texas would have been designed primarily to reach out towards the center. All of the other six were either women or minorities. Of these, only Governor Martha Lane Collins of Kentucky was from the party's center. In the event Mondale chose Geraldine Ferraro, a congresswoman from Brooklyn.

The drama of the selection of a major party's first woman vice presidential nominee was designed to create new enthusiasm for the Mondale campaign, to counter the charge that Mondale lacked boldness or leadership, and to publicize the direction of the party. By choosing Ferraro, Mondale made it difficult for those on his left to object to the ticket. In fact Gary Hart was forced to say that should he be nominated, he, too, would choose Ferraro as his vice presidential running mate.

The selection of Ferraro was also meant to reach out to Catholic and ethnic voters who were showing signs of discontent at the direction of the Democratic Party. But this latter strategy depended upon the voters' not considering Geraldine Ferraro's opinions. In the end it turned out to be less important that Mondale had chosen a woman vice presidential candidate than that he had chosen a particular kind of woman: a feminist who was endorsed at the convention by Gloria Steinem with the words, "It doesn't help to have them look like us and act like them."

Besides the selection of the vice presidential candidate, the formation of the platform was the other major task in which the hand of Mondale could be seen. Not much attention is paid in the general election to party platforms, and that was true of 1984. Platforms tend to be long and to be lists of suggestions on many matters, rather than enunciations of bold themes which can be used effectively in campaign oratory. Yet platforms in the past have been fairly reliable indications of the intentions of the party should it attain office. While the platform is not terribly important as a campaign document, it is an important source of information about the party.

The 1984 platform, unlike that of 1980, was written in relative harmony. Mondale supporters were in firm control. Of the 184 members of the full Platform Committee, 90 were pledged to Mondale, 58 to Hart, and 16 to Jackson, with the remainder unpledged. The harmony arose not only because Mondale had pretty clearly won the nomination by the time the committee met in mid-June, but also because there were not great differences of opinion on the issues between Mondale and Hart, and because Mondale followed a policy of giving as much to Jackson as he could.

Three or four of the main planks of the platform indicate its general direction. On economic policy, the platform, unlike those of 1976 or 1980, did not call for any major new social spending program. It alleged that Reagan's program favored the few, while the Democratic favored fairness. It promised to reduce budget deficits by reassessing defense expenditures, controlling health costs, and creating an "adequate and fair" tax system. On defense the platform called for reducing the rate of increase in defense spending. It did not call for reducing defense spending. A minority plank backed by Jackson supporters calling for major reductions in defense spending received enough support to be sent to the convention floor but was defeated there 2590.6 to 1127.6 (some delegates casting fractional votes). The platform also called for ending production of the MX missile and the B-1 bomber, and called for steps leading to "a comprehensive, mutual and verifiable nuclear weapons freeze." A Jackson proposal calling for no first use of nuclear weapons was sent to the floor of the convention where it was defeated 2216.3 to 1405.7.

On two issues, however, more moderate planks drafted by the Platform Committee were replaced by more left-wing planks by the full convention. At the platform hearings Mondale delegates rejected planks submitted by Hart delegates to restrict the use of force abroad. An amendment sent to the floor was accepted by Mondale before it came to a vote and passed 3271.8 to 351.2. Known as the "Persian Gulf-Central American plank" it specified that troops not be sent to these regions unless American objectives were clear and diplomatic efforts had been exhausted. Although Mondale accepted the amendment, it was unclear in any event that he had the votes to stop it on the floor. In effect the delegates endorsed the Hart, rather than the original Mondale foreign policy position.

The original plank on civil rights by the platform committee pledged that a Democratic administration would use affirmative action goals and timetables, but specifically rejected the use of quotas. Jackson supporters, however, presented an amendment which would have allowed quotas to end discrimination in hiring, promotion, and education and stating that "the Democratic Party opposes quotas which are inconsistent with the principles of our country." The wording, of course, implied that some quotas were not inconsistent with those principles. Mondale worked out a compromise with Jackson supporters leaving out the explicit rejection of quotas and endorsing the "use of affirmative action goals, timetables, and other verifiable measures." Each side was free to interpret whether "other verifiable measures" meant quotas.

We have already noted the third major concession at the convention to the left, the establishment of the "Fairness Commission" to rewrite once again the party's delegate selection rules. Because the resolutions accompanying its establishment called for a decline in the number of super-delegates and stricter delegate quotas for minority groups, its establishment implied a rejection of the direction taken by the Hunt Commission. The new apportionment of delegates was meant to be "fair" in contrast to the "unfair" 1984 apportionment.

The bold action in making the vice presidential nomination, and the concessions on the platform and the "Fairness Commission" did succeed in uniting the convention in San Francisco, but they created two further problems. The succession of concessions did not look much like leadership, for Mondale got support for himself in return but no concessions on any substantive issue to parallel the concessions he made. Even the selection of Ferraro could appear to many voters as less a sign of strength than as caving in to a public threat made by NOW shortly before the convention. And all of these actions pointed the party away from the center of the political spectrum.

Mondale sought to address these problems through his rhetoric. We have already noted the moderate tone of his acceptance speech in comparison to many other speeches at the convention. In presenting the Democratic policy positions he strikingly began by stressing the importance of "a strong defense, and a sober view of the Soviets," the need for government to be "as well-managed as it is well-meaning," and the virtues of "a healthy, growing private economy." He defensively conceded something to the Republican position before presenting the differing Democratic one.

But the clearest way in which the speech tried to present the Democrats as moderate was through a description of the party and of its candidates for President and Vice President. Mondale presented the party not through the focus of its stand on issues, but through its pluralistic racial, ethnic, age, and sexual makeup: "Just look at us here tonight: Black and white, Asian and Hispanic, native and immigrant, young and old, urban and rural, male and female--from yuppie to lunchpail, from sea to shining sea." And he presented himself by means of a brief biography designed to show that his roots were midwestern and that his story was the classic American one of pulling oneself up through hard work. And Geraldine Ferraro's story was the same, demonstrating belief in "Doing your work. Earning your way. Paying your dues. Rising on merit."

The most dramatic policy proposal of the speech was the announcement that he would raise taxes if elected. This proposal was designed in part to indicate the responsible character of the Democrats. But the fact that it was not accompanied by any discussion of how the government might save money so as not to raise taxes too much or any showing that the government could not save money revealed that the proposal was meant not only—or even primarily—as a policy stand but as a revelation of the difference between Mondale's and Reagan's character. Mondale said that Reagan, too, would raise taxes if elected, but that the difference between them was that he, Mondale, was honest with the American people while Reagan was not. In spite of his proclamation that the election presented a decisive choice for the future of the country, Mondale's speech presented that choice most dramatically in personal terms—the decent and moderate Mondale versus the dishonest and rich-loving Reagan.

But this rhetorical strategy was deeply flawed. It made the major issue between the parties the question of whether taxes should be increased, and it tried to pitch the campaign on the level of personality and character—a level on which Reagan did not seem particularly vulnerable. These rhetorical flaws were partly avoidable, but underlying them lay the deeper problem faced by the Democrats, that they had endorsed a view of America and a consequent series of policies that were not shared by the majority of Americans and that could not be presented to them in a straight-forward and open manner.

A Political Party In Search of Itself: Republican Realignment and the Dallas Platform of 1984

Douglas A. Jeffrey and Dennis Teti

The presidential primary selection system came into its own in the years after 1956. Powerful elected and nonelected party officials with statewide and local constituencies found themselves increasingly unable to strike agreements behind closed doors to determine party candidates at so-called brokered political conventions. One consequence of the less structured primary process has been the increased unlikelihood of an incumbent president receiving his party's blessing without having to face some sort of serious factional challenge. No Republican president has been lucky enough to escape such a challenge since 1956, and for an instance of a convention in which *neither* he nor his vice-presidential choice was challenged, one would have to search back decades. Yet just such an extraordinary event occurred in the Republican nominating process of 1984—perhaps the quietest in sixty years. The appearance was of a rare consensus within the party, reflecting consensus across the whole country as demonstrated in the November outcome—a 49 state sweep by the Reagan-Bush ticket. Talk of realignment blossomed even before the election results were in.

A precondition of political realignment—such as those of 1800, 1860, or 1932—is an aligned, or disciplined and principled, political party to which public loyalty can attach itself and through which public opinion can express itself in government and public policy. Do the events of 1984 suggest that it is appropriate to speak of a new Republican realignment?

It is an illusion that no battles took place on the Republican front in 1984. The illusion is fostered in part by the preponderance of attention afforded the character of President Reagan, who was protected against intrapartisan attack by the deep affection felt for him by the American people. The illusion was also fostered by the directors of the President's campaign, who thought it would be in the best interest of the candidate for the party and the nation to seem to be devoid of any serious political division. The illusion survived, due largely to a perhaps understandable disinterest among the voters regarding party platforms—a disinterest that was never dispelled by the media's superficial platform analysis.

A word must be said about the significance of platforms: for if this essay has anything to teach, certain ordinary beliefs regarding these statements of principle will need to be suspended.

It is a commonplace that political conventions in our time are nothing more than media hoopla and delegate circuses, the outcomes of which have been more or less "packaged" and predetermined beforehand. Given that the identity of the presidential nominee has been settled in twenty or thirty primary contests from coast to coast, the nominating convention story on which public attention used to be concentrated has, to use a journalistic expression, grown whiskers. As a result of that commonplace, party public relations experts do their best to commercialize and trivialize the whole event, while the electronic media scramble for ratings with celebrity interviews, instant pressure group analyses, and other activities which distract the audience from the real political significance of what is taking place. To say no more, the nature of the electronic media makes them resistant to phenomena such as the drafting of party platforms whose essential characteristic is not the depiction of actions but the writing of words.

It is useful to consider what the modern political convention retains from its older counterpart which was unencumbered by these distractions. For the quadrennial conventions are the only regularly scheduled occasions when national, state, and grassroots level political leaders of each of the great parties, in the nation which bears the burden of the world's freedom, "convene" or assemble together in one meeting hall to nominate potential national leaders and to state the principles and policies for which they stand. If we believe that politics depends on and is guided, at least to some degree, by reason or human deliberation, then we as "democrats" cannot dismiss such events as insignificant. It is in a sense ironic that in the era of advanced technology and open doors, the essence of the political convention is more concealed from the electorate than in the much maligned days of the smoke filled room.

And just as conventions are misconceived as meaningless, so the party platforms adopted by the party's delegates are often wrongly dismissed—though not wrongly described—as "symbolic." For a symbol is as significant or insignificant as that which it symbolizes: if there is to be *a* party (and this, as we shall see, is the question of great moment for the Republicans), then its platform cannot be dismissed as if it were no more than the latest scribbling of some best-selling fiction writer.

Let us take one example of the importance of symbols. After the British House of Commons was destroyed by German bombs in the Second World War, there was much discussion of rebuilding the parliamentary chamber on a model which was different from the original. Winston Churchill ended that discussion with arguments demonstrating the importance of political symbols. The chamber, he said, should be just what it had been—oblong with benches opposite to and facing one another—because this plan reflected a political system characterized by open and deliberate confrontation between two unified parties. But he suggested that it helps sustain that system as well; for instance, the plan discourages a member of either party from taking lightly a decision to vote with the opposition. Properly understood, a symbol not only reflects and illuminates that which it symbolizes, but it has real, sometimes great consequences.

The importance of symbols for political practice is often underestimated. We believe this is the case today regarding political party platforms in general. In symbolizing the party—insofar as the party is a unified body—the platform can serve to realign partisan loyalties by attracting new members to its ranks and by propelling defectors. The platform is indicative of the state of present debate, but also, and in some years more importantly, it can be indicative of future direction. In 1976 the Republican platform not only pointed in the direction of the party's future drift but it also *ensured* a future in the short term for the party itself. President Ford defeated Mr. Reagan that year in an often divisive nomination struggle, but the platform itself was clearly a "Reaganite" document. After the ex-governor's nomination defeat, much talk ensued among conservatives about forming a third party. Reagan's successful opposition to a schism that would have rendered the Republican Party moribund relied heavily on the victory his supporters had scored in adopting their platform. Thus the 1976 platform symbolized the future direction of the party and Reagan's eventual triumph.

It is not a singular phenomenon for a platform to become more consequential for public policy than the immediately important nomination. The Republican Party, after all, was born in 1856 with a platform whose significance far outlasted the nominee's of that year—John C. Frémont's. The platform centerpiece was a "social issues" plank opposing "the twin pillars of barbarism ... polygamy and slavery." Every American schoolboy knows the terrible but glorious consequences of that platform over the course of the decade that followed; indeed that platform foreshadowed the general direction of American politics and policy for the next 72 years. Similarly, it is possible that historians will conclude in years to come that the most important political debate of 1984 was not the one between Reagan and Mondale, but rather the debate of the days leading up to the convention, at the party platform hearings in Dallas.

The contest between Reagan and Mondale had, for all practical purposes, been decided by the voters in 1980, and perhaps at four year intervals after and including 1968. It is easy to forget that Republicans held the Executive mansion for twelve of the sixteen years since Lyndon Johnson's Administration. Still, many young Republican leaders arrived in Dallas believing that the people, having repeatedly petitioned for more representative government and less bureaucracy, had been thwarted in their purposes by virtually *all* who had received their trust. These leaders were not to be satisfied by less than a complete partisan exchange of the reins of government, and they forced the platform committee to confront what they perceived to be critical questions that might otherwise, for the sake of a show of unity, have been ignored or swept under the rug. At stake for these men and women—and they were to carry the day in Dallas—was whether their party would act as advocate for the American people, and in so doing would redefine the terms of a political dialogue that they saw as having become narrowed and corrupted. Thinking beyond the task at hand—that of reforming the Republican Party—they regarded themselves as architects of a radical change of direction in American politics. But the task at hand—designing a platform—came first, and in that they were hardly unopposed.

In the pages below we will consider the division within the Republican Party as it became manifest in the struggle over one particular issue at the 1984 platform hearings. After this, we will survey the platform as a whole to discover its governing principle, under the assumption that it was intended as a consistent document. Finally we will briefly discuss the party's health, and its possible future direction, in the light of our findings.

Having said that the outcome of platform disputes can determine the direction of a party for years to come, we will show that the single most hotly contested battle in the drafting of the 1984 Republican platform took place over the inclusion of a solitary comma in one sentence of a document the length of a short novel. In the end the comma survived, and therein hangs a tale of the party's past.

The New Deal primarily signified a new *economic* deal for the American people. It legitimized a role by government in the nation's economic affairs which government had never previously enjoyed. Even so, over a quarter of a century passed before the barriers to *bona fide* interventionism were effectively removed. With the influx of social science experts to Washington and the creation of the redistributive and regulatory Great Society programs in the 1960s, a bureaucracy blossomed in the national capital and the public sector began to grow at an astonishing rate. By 1980 over half the population of the United States were being sustained in whole or in part by programs of public support. The painful economic results of this trend, such as ever rising taxes, high interest rates, and above all increasing inflation, in turn generated a flood tide of dissatisfaction around the country which crested with Ronald Reagan's first election to the White House that year. This popular unhappiness with the results of redistributionist policies was, to be sure, no secret to most commentators of the time. But we cannot sufficiently understand these events by tracing causes and effects in the realm of public policy. We must look behind those policies for their animating principle.

The great policy debates in American politics prior to the so-called progressive era were *political* ones. They aimed at establishing policies proper to the maintenance and strengthening of democratic government, and therefore at defining what that form of government is in its essence. They tended to revolve around the proper understanding of America's democratic principles of equality and liberty. But the early advocates of progressivism like Woodrow Wilson began to argue that the idea of democracy was simple, its maintenance no longer greatly threatened, and so that the political question was obsolete. What was now needed, they argued, was a rational method of conducting democracy's daily affairs, to be guided by an *administrative science*. In adopting this outlook, subsequent generations of New Deal politicians and the even more candid Great Society bureaucrats afforded a new character to political discourse. It no longer recurred in any regular or serious way during policy deliberations to the principles of the Founders nor to the meaning of democracy itself. The New Deal-Great Society progressive outlook, concerned with the nonpolitical science of administration, took its bearings from an image of the future rather than from the thought of the past.

Except for the civil rights movement, which culminated in the passage of the Voting Rights Act of 1965, and whose leaders such as Rev. Martin Luther King, Jr. invoked the principle of equality and the idea of liberty in the Lincolnian fashion of an older politics, these concepts were taken for granted when not simply forgotten. (We note that the civil rights movement was conceived not in Washington but in the rural churches of America.) The primary task of those who govern, argued Wilson in *The New Freedom*, was not recurrence to principle, but "perfect adjustments of human interests and human activity and human energies." The language of political discourse reconciling liberty and equality gradually gave way to that of balancing capitalism and socialism (although in America, unlike Europe, most advocates of socialist policy avoided the socialist label like the plague, preferring to be known as liberals). These ideological concepts, considered in themselves irrelevant by older-fashioned politicians, became the substance of our politics. And the arbiter among the concerns represented by these concepts became government itself.

While the Democratic Party was the party of FDR and became the New Deal's political womb, its electoral success meant that it set the terms of debate in the whole political arena. Republican opposition came to be characterized, not without justification, as the view of the "country club" set, that is, of a particular narrow interest group whose special interest was the preservation of their capital. The core of mainstream Republican rhetoric in the decades leading up to the Reagan years had become opposition to encroachment of the public into the private sector. Republicans argued for years against higher taxes and deficit spending. So this was nothing new in their 1984 platform or, for that matter, in the platform of 1980. But as to the *character* of this opposition and as to the proper grounds on which to base its rhetoric, "new" schools of thought were arising by 1980. In the American context, however, we shall see that the "old" is actually much newer than the "new," so-called.

The Three Factions

There were three identifiable Republican factions which converged on Dallas to hammer out a platform in the week before the convention was gavelled into session. We will, for the moment, refer to them in the vernacular of the media pundits of the day.

First, to be mentioned only once and no more, were the "liberals." Descended from the Rockefeller wing of the party, and with Senator Lowell

Weicker as its most prominent spokesman in Dallas, this faction sought primarily to effect a retreat from 1980 platform positions which opposed the Equal Rights Amendment and supported legislation of morality, for instance restrictive abortion laws. The liberals held pre-convention public hearings over which much printer's ink was spilled, yet in the end they received no support from attending delegates. There were embarrassing cases when not one delegate could be cajoled into seconding the motions the liberals proposed; indicative of the low state of their fortunes was the final platform committee vote of 76 to 15 against an ERA plank. It is not controversial to state the obvious: this faction, insofar as it stands apart from the next to be introduced below, was annihilated in 1984 as a force in the Republican Party.

The "pragmatists" or traditional Republicans made up the second faction, personified by Senator Robert Dole, President Ford's 1976 running mate and one of those said to be a possible successor to Reagan. This faction is characterized by its moderation in the context of New Deal perimeters on political debate. Unquestioned defenders of capitalism, their greatest concern in 1984, as for decades past, was the national debt.

The third faction was the "young Turks" of the party's right wing. Generally speaking younger than the pragmatists, Congressmen Jack Kemp and Newt Gingrich were their leading lights. The password to their ranks was "opportunity," and their vision was of an "opportunity society." The young Turks were to square off with the old guard traditional Republicans over the party's position to be taken in regard to taxes—which is where the episode of the controversial comma comes in.

Since the end of the 1970s, Congressman Kemp of New York had been the leading Republican spokesman for "supply side" economics, the central tenet of which is the reduction of marginal tax rates as an incentive to economic expansion. Kemp's plan for long-term prosperity, which he was determined to write into the platform, represented the "opportunity agenda" and had four tiers: an absolute stand against tax increases of any sort must be taken; a flat rate tax should replace the progressive model, eliminating high marginal rates to enhance incentives for creative investment; the nation should return to a modernized gold standard in order to cement control of inflation and to prevent deflation; (the adoption of a version of this proposal into the platform was, typically, hailed as revolutionary although the gold standard had only been entirely abandoned in 1971); and programs of assistance for poverty-stricken urban areas should be implemented, the chief of which would be enterprise zones—tax relieved and deregulated areas where risk-taking investment and job opportunities would be encouraged. Ultimately, however, everything in a sense hinged on acceptance of unconditional opposition to higher taxes: for Kemp's vision of economic recovery took its departure from a belief that individual enterprise would in time generate enough new wealth to pay off the national debt—or that America was not necessarily, in the language of the Carter Administration, a "zero sum" society with limited productive capabilities, wherein austerity was the order of the day. There was an alternative to simply diminished expectations as to what government could do, the young Turks insisted, which was to *expand* expectations of what independent self-reliance could accomplish.

While the pragmatists embraced in theory the desirability of lower taxes, they pleaded for an open-ended platform position regarding them, arguing that tax hikes may become needed to curb the deficit "as a last resort." (Most in this faction were being coy in an election year, and in fact thought the "last resort" would be inevitable. In this they were in agreement with Democratic candidate Walter Mondale who, however, chose the politically disastrous course of being candid.) At one level the traditional argument ran thus: we live in a democracy whose citizens have petitioned the representative government to provide them with certain services. Whether or not they were prudent in doing so, it is right that they pay the price for those services, so as not to leave the burden unfairly on their children. This probably will mean higher taxes. In the context of Republican politics theirs was not an easily controverted argument.

It should be recognized that *both* factions opposed any notion that the debt could be used as an economic stimulus, which is to say that they agreed on the baneful effects of a debt at any level. Where their arguments diverged can be spoken of on two levels—one regarding the means of eliminating the debt, and the other, perhaps finally more important, regarding the root cause of the debt and its attendant effects. At *either* level one can see that the young Turks, but not the traditionals, fundamentally challenged the New Deal understanding. Underlying the policy dispute was the assumption by traditional Republicans that the political question of who should rule was not at issue in the battle over taxes—that properly democratic practices had been followed in the past and that democracy was safe for the future. But the young Turks seems to be suggesting by their arguments—which we will elaborate hereafter—that the survival of democratic government in America was in fact *the* issue at stake.

In the weeks before the convention, Mondale's pledge to raise taxes dashed any hope of the traditional Republicans that their platform could be silent on the subject. Thus a sentence proposed as a compromise platform position in the midst of the debate ran as follows: "We therefore oppose any attempts to increase taxes which would harm the recovery and reverse the trend to restoring control of the economy to individual Americans." In that form, of course, the sentence left open the possibility of raising those kinds of taxes which would *not* harm the recovery. The controversial comma, offered by Congressman Tom Loeffler, elegantly did away with the ambiguity of the sentiment expressed: "We therefore oppose any attempts to increase taxes, which would harm the recovery. . . ." As corrected, the sentence clearly stated that *all* tax increases would be harmful to economic recovery.

President Reagan seemed to throw his weight behind the pragmatists on this issue only a week before the hearings, when he applied to tax policy a maxim he had used before about remaining free to meet foreign policy contingencies: "A president should never say 'never'." Yet, to illustrate the ambiguous message that emanated from the president, on the Saturday prior to the hearings he sent a symbolic message in his weekly radio address by speaking for an "opportunity society." The administration's representative to the hearings, former Transportation Secretary Drew Lewis, in accord with the election strategy followed by the president's campaign directors the entire year, threw his weight unambiguously behind any compromise which would avoid the appearance of intra-party rift. But the young Turks were uncompromising, and aided by the adroit maneuverings of platform chairman Congressman Trent Lott, a closet sympathizer, and before the White House knew what was happening, the comma was adopted. All tax hikes were now forbidden fruit, and the revolutionaries had, by all accounts, bushwhacked the proceedings of what appeared to be a staid political convention.

What the Victory Means

Let us now consider whether this revolution, continuing trends begun in 1976 and 1980, portends the possibility of a bold new world in American politics, or whether, like some (but not all) revolutions, it has the character less of progress than of return.

The victors at Dallas had historically been more adamant in their support for Ronald Reagan than the vanquished had been. Yet it was a common charge against the president that he represented a simpler bygone age, rather than that he posed any new revolutionary threat to the polity. In this light we will argue that it was not just symbolic of Reagan's tenure, but even more that he portended his party's drift in 1984, when he moved Calvin Coolidge's portrait to the Cabinet Room of the White House upon his arrival.

Coolidge, in his autobiography, recalled an occasion of his economic education in a childhood episode when his father bade him walk to town, taking on the wagon in young Calvin's place a hired hand needing a ride. On that day, he wrote, he discovered the superiority of labor to capital. What would become a basic tenet of the "supply side" school of the 1980s was no novelty to the Republican Party; in fact it antedated the prominence of the language of economic science in politics. In 1859 Lincoln himself had addressed the topic of labor's role in the movement toward material progress, in a speech at the Wisconsin State Fair. He expressed the view that "capital is the fruit of labor, and could never have existed if labor had not *first* existed," and thus that "labor is the superior—greatly the superior—of capital." Indeed most free men, he argued, neither hire nor are hired, but "with their families—wives, sons, and daughters—work for themselves, on their farms, in their houses, and in their shops, taking the whole product to themselves."

Hired men in the system of "free labor" are not "fatally fixed" in their dependence, but are enabled *by* that system to achieve self-sufficiency *through* their labor. Lincoln went on finally to reveal the importance of affording men the ability (through education), and ensuring them the opportunity, to carve out their independence: "No community whose every member possesses this art, can ever be the victim of oppression in any of its forms. Such community will alike be independent of crowned-kings, money-kings, and land-kings." In Lincoln's account, risk-taking has precedence over security, and the purpose of material progress through the system of free labor (rather than material well-being through the conservation of already created capital) is to sustain the health of free democratic government: the economic arrangement exists for and serves the political order.

Seen in this light, the young Turks might appear to be young Lincolnians. In fact at least one of them described the platform wranglings as a struggle between the party of Coolidge—a man of Lincolnian sensibilities—and the party of Hoover, who held more in common with the early New Dealers than is commonly recognized and who was not at all liked by his Republican predecessor in the White House.

That the traditional faction of the party in Dallas did not hark back to the Lincolnian understanding can perhaps best be seen in the platform plank dealing with agriculture. (The Subcommittee on Strengthening American Agriculture at the hearings was chaired by members of that faction, notably Senator Dole.) One sees therein the traditional commendation of the free market: "The primary responsibility of government in respect to agriculture is to create the opportunity for a free and competitive economic environment supportive of the American farmers' and ranchers' industrious and independent spirit and innovative talent." Accordingly the platform rejects "the Democrats' public utility vision of agriculture which views it as a problem to be minimized by further political and bureaucratic management." But the sentence following the first one quoted above proposes that for some unprofitable farms and ranches "it is in the public interest to provide reasonable and targeted assistance." And after the criticism of Democratic management one reads the following: "Our new programs will bring flexibility to adjust to rapidly changing export market conditions and opportunities, and, in a timely and effective manner, respond to the inherent, uncontrollable risks of farming and ranching." But the idea of government as an administrative body charged with reducing or eliminating economic risks, or of securing against the effects of bad choice or luck, is to a large extent *the* New Deal idea that was behind policies from Social Security to the convoluted farm price support programs of the 1970s. Much different from *this* idea was the notion imparted by Lincoln's speech to the Wisconsin farmers:

> Some of you will be successful, and such will need but little philosophy to take them home in cheerful spirits; others will be disappointed, and will be in a less happy mood. To such, let it be said, 'Lay it not too much to heart.' Let them adopt the maxim, 'Better luck next time'; and then, by renewed exertion, make that better luck for themselves.

Democracy or Tyranny

The character of the struggle between these factions in Dallas was only obscured by the media's labeling them "pragmatists" and "ideologues." "Pragmatism" implies a grasp of the practical or of the matters at hand, while "ideology" suggests a willingness to disregard such matters in the uncompromising service of some theory or idea. But there is no reason to suppose either that practice should not be guided by ideas; or that ideas need exist in a realm other than the real; or that there are some practical questions on which compromise is not appropriate. Describing the struggle as one between "pragmatism" and "ideology" was a disservice to both groups. Indeed theirs was a *political* struggle, and in politics thought and action are inextricably interwoven. The *difference* between the debate in Dallas and debates in most other election years was that in Dallas the debate confronted certain fundamental questions about what American democracy is in essence; these used to be called "regime" questions. *Whenever* regime questions are raised in a nation founded on principles derived from nature, those first principles are brought to the forefront of discussion. And once *that* happens, it indicates that a fundamental disagreement exists about the meaning of the things that unite us as a people, or in other words, that we are *not* united as a people. Thus it is not surprising that charges of fanaticism and extremism (which is what "ideology" connotes) arise. The paradigmatic recurrence to principle in our history was Lincoln's antebellum appeal to the principle of equality in a "house divided" on the issue of slavery; and so he was branded as, among other things, an anti-Christ by many proslavery politicians. Likewise in 1984 political disputants tended increasingly to use analogies, secular as well as religious, which were designed to place their opponents' position outside the pale of legitimate American political debate. What that indicated was nothing less than that, again, the meaning of democracy among the American people, had become controversial.

Such a controversy, of course, is too weighty to rest on one comma in a party platform plank regarding taxes; and indeed that comma alone does not bear the whole weight of our suggestion, however much publicity the issue generated. Other positions were taken in the platform with the support of the young Turk faction which were said at the time to be revolutionary. We will next turn to some of these in order to show the common thread among them—a thread which, we have already suggested, was spun from rejection of the terms of political debate as assigned by adherents of New Deal thought. We have also suggested that this reform movement might be illuminated by comparison with Lincoln's.

Lincoln's free labor argument was intimately related to his rejection of slavery and thus with his understanding of democracy. Lincoln shrank from an economic understanding of man which, whether inspired by capitalist or socialist sympathies, tends to impute a low motivation to every human action.

(One reason indifference to slavery angered Lincoln, as he proclaimed in Peoria in 1854, was that "it forces so many really good men amongst ourselves into an open war with the very fundamental principles of civil liberty ... insisting that there is no right principle of action but *self-interest.* ... ") The 1984 Republican platform no longer spoke merely of a world divided between capitalism and socialism, but rather of a world split between democracy and tyranny, and the elevation of thought responsible for that shift had an enormous impact on the level of policy throughout the document.

The foreign policy section of the Dallas platform was written in a subcommittee co-chaired by Jack Kemp. The plank proceeded from a statement at its head which invoked and defined the idea of American democracy in words echoing those of 1776, and which insisted on a genuine difference—characterized as a *moral* difference—between democracy and the Marxist-Leninist state: we (but not the Soviet Union) recognize a human right by nature, and only we therefore regard human beings as equal regardless of their class or their race. Grounded in *self*-understanding, the highest end in the hierarchy of American foreign policy goals was said to be the defense (or indeed the expansion) of democracy, which translates first of all as the survival of the American people and their free institutions. This lent a new character to a debate about what to do that had come to speak of peace itself as the chief goal of foreign policy: the use of force now became an option that did not necessarily contradict the policy's ultimate goal. Thus, for instance, the platform strongly advocated aid to anti-communist forces in various countries, distinguishing a "moral difference between the use of force for liberation and the use of force for conquest."

But the clearest policy innovation following on the change in terms of the foreign policy debate showed up in the platform's unreserved advocacy of the Strategic Defense Initiative (SDI)—the development of space based means of fending off attacking nuclear missiles. This signalled a Republican repudiation of the strategic doctrine of Mutual Assured Destruction (MAD) to which leaders of both parties had subscribed for almost two decades. The traditional Republican faction's position on this was that SDI would be useful for purposes of Soviet-American arms reduction talks and thus could be negotiated away in trade for Soviet concessions on offensive weapons. Consistent with the "new" elevated understanding which permeated the young Turk-dominated platform, the survival of the American citizen became more than a card on the negotiating table once defense, rather than peace simply, became foreign policy's ultimate goal.

In this context it should be mentioned that one ballyhooed concession made in the platform to the traditional Republican faction (represented in this case by Senator John Warner, co-chairman of the Subcommittee on National Security) was the deletion of the word "superiority" in regard to the military relationship America sought *vis-a-vis* the Soviet Union. Deterrence of war, they argued, did not require the superiority explicitly called for just four years before in the 1980 platform, but only military equivalence—an argument which seemed to constitute only another form of the MAD strategy. But this victory of the old guard vaporized in the light of other pledges which survived the platform debate. For example, "this we pledge to our people and to future generations: We shall keep the peace by keeping the country stronger than any potential adversary." And again, "We plan to do everything necessary so that, in case of conflict, the United States would clearly prevail." The young Turks were not in the end to be denied. If American democracy was held to be good and *essentially* different from what President Reagan once called the "evil empire," then it was not to be thought dangerous, but rather entirely moral, to strive to be mightier than the tyrannical adversary of freedom.

The topic of morality naturally leads to the so-called "social agenda" of the Dallas platform, which was to a large extent a challenge to the judicial activism of the last quarter century. That activism was to become a matter of open institutional controversy during the second Reagan term, when Attorney General Edwin Meese and various Supreme Court Justices would take their respective cases to the public, Meese echoing the platform's advocacy of a renewed attention to "enduring principles of conduct and firm standards of judgment." On one level the complaint was procedural, but it hinged ultimately on the very meaning of constitutionalism.

The public school prayer issue had arisen with the implementation of policies which evolved from a judicial interpretation of the First Amendment that prescribed an absolute "wall of separation" between political or public concerns and the "private" concerns of religion. Likewise the abortion controversy arose only after the Supreme Court discovered a "right to privacy." In one stroke the Court voided all state and local legislation regarding the matter, nationalized what had been a local police power issue, and withdrew from political authority what had been considered *moral* concerns just as the religious ones had been withdrawn earlier. Attempts in Dallas to soften platform language supporting political measures in response to these judicial actions met with no success.

There seemed to be two major lines of argument presented in defense of the platform's assertiveness—one concerning the role of morality, the other concerning the position of federalism in American life. By calling for judicial "deference towards state and local officials" while insisting that judicial authority "must not expand at the expense of our representative institutions" (and in this it was true to the Jeffersonian teaching which it cited), the platform suggested that some degree of federalism whereby *real* political authority is exercised by states and localities must be retained in the national democratic order. Where, for example, it discussed the authority over education or over the selection of books and ideas to be taught in public schools (arguing that this is necessarily a *political* authority), the platform held to the view of education as a "local function, a state responsibility, and a federal concern." If parents are to keep the "primary right and responsibility for education" which is properly theirs, they can only effectively exercise those rights and duties on a local level. The *diversity* that results from decentralized administration, as Tocqueville called it, is to be expected in a large *democracy*, of which it is one of the most telling characteristics. The impulse to eliminate diversity on a national scale is, on this showing, undemocratic and perhaps tyrannical.

The impulse in the 1960s and 70s to subvert local authority took its most controversial forms in the above mentioned Supreme Court rulings, which explains why the structural issue of federalism in recent times became intermingled to so great an extent with the question of morality in politics. But there is indeed an organic or natural connection between the two.

"A society is only as strong as its families," according to the Dallas platform, "for they nurture those qualities necessary to maintain and advance civilization." The family's nurturing role was a recurring theme in this Republican document. The attack of welfarism, for instance, could not be fully understood apart from the contention that it has served to destroy family unity by providing "incentives to set up maternal households," the primary locus of long-term poverty since the 1970s. So also with other analyses of policies: their effects on the family in any particular instance were never far from sight. The vitality of the family, like that of religion which directs attention beyond material existence, was presented as a precondition of a politically healthy and just democracy because both serve as the cradles of citizen character or civic morality. Cultivation of that morality is a *public* or *political* concern, by this argument, for it is what renders possible an understanding of the principles on which freedom of conscience, speech, and dissent is grounded.

What was at stake in the Republican "social agenda," then, beyond the question of procedures, was the issue of whether American principles are rightly understood to be supported and undergirded by morality. Are American citizens free individuals, equal in that abstract sense alone, or are they equally moral creatures? The question had been raised before, notably by Lincoln in regard to slavery, when he argued that human equality is manifested in rights only so far as those rights are defined and limited by an understanding of the common nature of human creatures. His opponents denied the moral component of equality, in the course *then* of defending *states'* rights, and by that denial they ended up, as logical consistency dictated, by rejecting the principle of human equality altogether as a governing principle of public policy. And just so, the Dallas Republicans suggested, did the new effort to de-moralize American politics go hand in hand with a rejection of the principle of individual equality as the basis for policy in our time.

"The Republican Party is the party of equal rights. From its founding in 1854, we have promoted equality of opportunity." So stated the 1984 platform—perhaps forgetting some lapses in the party's 130 year history—but on firmer ground in proclaiming its own stance to be that of the "party of Lincoln." It vowed what, to be Lincolnian, it had to vow—namely, to oppose in an unqualified manner "attempts to dictate results" in society. Equality of *result* or of *condition* was the goal of a policy that had become known by the euphemism of "affirmative action." Policy dictating it had in some instances been mandated by the courts, while the highest court had upheld the constitutionality of its practice. The principled understanding of unalienable rights as adhering equally to individuals (not to groups) had given way to an understanding of rights as unequal and alienable. They were unequally distributed on the basis of one's membership in so-called "discrete and insular" minority groups (an Orwellian classification that included about three fourths of the nation's population), and alienable since they were dependent on the shifting political status and fortunes of each group. The traditional Republican wing was successful in including in the platform a number of proposals or flattering statements, aimed at appealing to such groups, which cut across the grain of the document. (A paragraph on the rights of the handicapped stands out in particular.) But what generally characterized the "grain" itself was a stance resting on principle, holding that "affirmative action" of any sort was incompatible with rule by non-arbitrary, equal, constitutional law.

The importance of moral character in democracy, or of a citizenry which sees beyond the realm of material self-interest (or, as Coolidge once put it, of a yeomanry with religion), is clear in a regime founded on the principle of equal opportunity. For such equality *necessarily* implies an inequality of condition, just as the quest for equality of condition *necessarily* requires discriminating treatment in affording opportunity. The 1984 Republican platform was at its best unequivocal in choosing between these, as candor would demand. The platform framers had to be, to some extent, concerned that inequality of result or condition "not be taken too much to heart." But they were not, properly speaking, Darwinians in their counsel, as the Governor of New York had charged a month previously at the San Francisco Democratic convention. Darwinism demands the subordination of the weak in order to serve the strong, a charge Coolidge had rebutted nearly seventy years ago in saying that his view "does not mean the survival of the fittest, it means the sacrifice of the fittest." Like Coolidge, the Republican young Turks held out hope for an improvement in the condition of all.

Their promise was of an opportunity for escape from the "poverty trap," understood in the platform's terms as a condition of dependence produced by redistributionist policies. Hope for escape was held out in the form of policies intended to cultivate an improved condition of life to be derived from *new* wealth, which is itself derived from free labor. And with that promise we come full circle in these brief considerations of this platform. The principle of equality as that platform defined it in Dallas, which justified its posture on foreign policy and which underlay its "social agenda," was also the core idea animating the platform's advocacy of the "opportunity society." In that too its position echoed Lincoln's, who wove similar threats of thought together when he wrote that "The hired laborer of yesterday labors on his own account today and will hire others to labor for him tomorrow. Advancement—improvement of condition—is the order of things in a society of equals."

Conservative Populists

The Dallas platform's criticism of the Democrats was toned down in its final draft; still theirs was branded as the party of redistribution, contraction, isolation, despair, and fear. The vision offered as an alternative, as we have traced it through the platform, proceeded to a post-New Deal understanding by restoring the primacy of the idea of democracy itself to the policy-making process: what is good for democratic government, and all that it entails, is good policy; and what is bad for it is bad policy. Characteristic of the new Republican rhetoric was Kemp's speech on the convention floor, charging the Democrats with being "soft," not on communism (as had been charged at times in the past) but rather on democracy itself.

The conservatives who succeeded in Dallas, and who hoped to direct the Republican Party thereafter, were so "bully" on democracy that they had been labelled "populists" by supporters and detractors alike. Yet their "populism" is very different from what is traditionally connoted by the term.

"Populism" is historically connected with the attitude of the early progressives, and later also of the New Dealers, according to which the *institutions* of government were impediments to the progressive spirit of the people; that attitude called in practice as well as in theory for a critique of the constitutional separation of powers which were thought to be preventing the *national* majority from effecting quick and continuous change through a leader—the president. The executive branch of government, the sole branch with a true national constituency, was strengthened considerably during FDR's tenure. In the 1950s and 60s it was still a commonplace among political scientists that there was a "deadlock of democracy" caused by the resistance in Congress to presidential agendas. Again, the separation of powers was at fault; the Constitution was flawed. But, strangely, with the advent of the "silent majority" which elected Richard Nixon in 1968 and 1972, progressive academics, undergoing a radical change of heart, suddenly lost faith in the "imperial presidency," as it was now called, and targeted it as *the* threat to national well-being. An attack on that office ensued in practice, culminating in such post-Watergate legislation as the Federal Budget and Impoundment Control Act and the War Powers Act, leaving the president stripped of his constitutional power and authority. As the Congress had by then ceded to the bureaucracy much of its own legislative authority, the attack on the presidency did not signal a return of the attackers to the fold of conventional piety of the separation of powers or of structured democracy. Rather, in a sense, it *did* seem to represent a loss of trust in democracy itself, or in the ability of the people to wield political authority in the regime *even* if through the political institutions.

In professing faith in American democracy the new Republicans were not recurring to that populism which opposed institutional structures as hindrances to the rule of the people. There is no hint in the platform of opposition to the separation of powers which the Founders devised as the surest way of preserving stable and energetic *representative* and *political* government; a provision for legislative challenge to the judiciary, such as the platform called for, was made by the architects of the Constitution. Rather than populism, what the new Republican advocacy seemed to imply was an older form of democracy that in no uncertain terms preferred structured *political* authority to *bureaucratic* authority.

The Dallas platform advocated not only a challenge to judicial supremacy by the political branches of government, but also a redistribution of power between the political branches which would restore some of its former power to the executive. For example, it proposed a presidential line-item veto power in the federal budget process. But more important to restoring representative government than any single policy proposed *in* the platform is the character *of* the platform's partisanship as a whole. We will conclude by explaining briefly what we mean by this, in the course of which certain reservations that we have as to the possibility for effective realignment along the lines we have outlined will be brought to light.

The Platform and Realignment

We have suggested what the victory of the young Turks in Dallas meant in the context of the convention itself. But whether it *will* mean anything of great import to the nation is a different question. We suggested what the significance of platforms *could* be, but that significance was said to be predicated on the disciplined and principled character of the party that it symbolizes. Whether the Republicans can become such a principled party in the future is the great question. That they did not emerge from Dallas as such a party is clear.

The platform noted that many attempts by President Reagan during his first four years to realize his mandate had been stymied by the legislative branch of government. What it did not, for obvious reasons, make clear is that in this regard the Republican Senate had been nearly as unhelpful as the Democratic House of Representatives. Indeed, during Reagan's second administration, the Senate would stonewall nominees of the president to various positions *on the basis of* their adherence to the principles set forth in the 1984 platform. Several questions arise from this anomaly. For example, why is the Republican Party split institutionally to this extent in its attempt to govern? And did the 1984 platform and election represent a significant step in the direction of Republican health?

Given the character of Ronald Reagan's campaigns in 1976 and 1980, many had reason to expect a fundamental shift in public policy following his first victory. That shift never took place. Basic policy change requires a healthy political party as its vehicle, because the party is the connecting link across the institutional separation of president and Congress. Lincoln's House of Representatives in 1860 was composed of a better than two-to-one Republican majority; Roosevelt's in 1936 had more than three Democrats for every Republican. The state of *poor* health in which the Republican Party under Reagan found itself is evident on two counts. The first, already alluded to, is that in many instances the President's Senate "partisans" voted and acted as if they were in opposition, suggesting a conspicuous lack of partisan spiritedness. The second is more obvious: even after the gains of 1984, Reagan was faced with a 253 to 182 Democratic majority in the House of Representatives. Seventeen million more people voted for him than for Republican Congressmen in 1984, representing the distance between the realignment that could have been and the indecisive outcome that was. Like the interruption of the separation of powers that has weakened the executive branch, so also might the weakening of the American party system be blamed in part on the rise of the bureaucracy. We argue that bureaucratic strength will remain intact so long as the parties remain weak.

In a short and insightful study entitled *Congress—Keystone of the Washington Establishment* (Yale University Press, 1977), Morris Fiorina suggests that bureaucracy has stripped the increasingly powerful legislative branch of government of its partisan character, to the point that the House of Representatives now ignores even the most violent shifts in public opinion. (Whereas almost half of all congressional seats, on the average, turned over in nineteenth century elections, since the Second World War almost nine out of ten incumbents who seek reelection have done so successfully.) To describe briefly the situation as Fiorina paints it: the bureaucrat is now the individual administratively empowered to provide services to the congressman's constituents, relieving the latter of the difficulties that they encounter because of distance and lack of accountability; thus the congressman has become dependent on the agencies and bureaus for the votes which reelect him. For their part the agencies are dependent on congressmen for their budgets, and a three-legged system of dependency has arisen in which the congressman becomes a go-between upon whom the people depend in dealing with the powerful but impersonal bureaucracy.

The effect of this arrangement on the powers of the president is obvious, considering that he is neither included in nor necessary to the constituent service process. The effect on the citizen is to encourage him to think of himself as a member of an interest group which is dependent upon Congress and the bureaucracy to preserve its status. The effect on the congressman is that he tends to eschew controversial or partisan campaign issues and depreciates his role as lawgiver, preferring instead to sell his ability to deliver services to constituents, acting as liaison to the bureaucracy. Thus, he campaigns less on his position regarding taxes or the proper response to Communist aggression in Central America—issues concerning which his constituents might disagree—

and more on his capacity for bringing benefits to farmers, drillers, blacks, Hispanics, small business, Social Security recipients, women, labor, the handicapped, college students and any other interest groups in his district. The effect of this system on the party is to weaken the link between it and the congressman. As a result of his non-issue oriented posture, he is elected on a different basis from the president, who is chosen more because of his adherence to the party's principles embodied in the platform, such as that discussed in this essay. And the effect on the bureaucracy is that it thrives and prospers despite serious popular opposition.

As long as this situation—less a "deadlock" of than an "armlock" on democracy—persists, realignment will be a chimera. On one level it appears inescapable: bureaucracy is already the villain of the national majority yet simultaneously remains as the kingpin of national policy. The hopeful outlook of the movers of the 1984 platform hearings—that as the bureaucracy was created in a partisan or political manner by adherents of the New Deal understanding, so it can be controlled or dismantled politically—did not in itself offer new hope to the majority: presidential candidates had for years displayed like confidence in their abilities. What *was* new in Dallas, and what might prove most significant in the long run, is, first, that those spearheading this perennial attack were almost all members of Congress, indeed of the House of Representatives, and were therefore proof that the circle of dependence could be broken; and second, that they would be aware of the bureaucratic system facing them if they ever advanced one of their own to the White House.

What effect did the Reagan landslide have on realignment? Consider that the platform battle at Dallas, a microcosm of the struggle on a national scale which realignment would require, was fought in relative secrecy because the White House directorate had decided to scrap a plan to hold public hearings around the country. Instead, public debate, limited to a single day at the convention site, proved to be a mere formality. The fight, of course, was joined at the first week's platform hearings, as we have shown. Secretary Lewis failed to prevent that fight, but the nonpartisan spirit of his attempt haunted the autumn campaign.

Reagan campaign officials were candid in admitting that their strategy involved widening the base of their candidate's mandate by avoiding partisan controversy. One obvious problem with this strategy is that a nonpartisan mandate is an ineffectual weapon to brandish in the face of determined partisan opponents. (As should have been expected, within three months of election day all talk of a Reagan mandate disappeared in the heat of the legislative battles in the next Congress.) The 49 state sweep by Reagan was less *politically* desirable than a narrow electoral college victory would have been if it brought with it a voting majority in Congress. But to constitute the party victory requisite to realignment would have required a very partisan appeal to— and a very partisan election by—the American people.

We believe the Reagan landslide, then, was not decisive for realignment. If there was substantial movement toward political reconquest and realignment in 1984, it took place at the platform hearings because they gave the young Turks a head start in the impending struggle over Ronald Reagan's successor in 1988. The little publicized battle within the Republican ranks in August 1984 was nationally significant in raising the possibility that the victors there might find themselves in a position to carry it into the national arena in later presidential contests. But to be successful in displacing the entrenched bureaucracy the leaders of the party that wishes to join the contest will need more, finally, than a principled platform; they will need the stomach for a struggle which will be neither pleasant nor pretty. Yet those who do revive such a party can take heart from the example of Lincoln, whose spirited effort was directed and supported by the principles informing his party's platform. They should remember that partisan politics in America serves high nonpartisan ends. Unlike the promises held out for self-interest by the advocates of administrative science, the political principles of democracy can serve as objects of genuine nonpartisan love. He who can command that nonpartisan love earns *and deserves* the greatest partisan devotion.

The General Election Campaign: Going For The Gold

Dennis J. Mahoney

Americans, unlike the people of many democratic countries, go to the polls at regularly specified intervals. We can, with a high degree of confidence, predict the date of the national presidential election twenty or one hundred years from now: it will be on the Tuesday following the first Monday in November of a year evenly divisible by four. Unlike Britons, or Canadians, or Australians, who may be called upon to vote in snap elections following short campaign periods, Americans are virtually certain of when they will be called upon to cast their ballots.

The candidates, the parties, the committees, the consultants, and, of course, the media, begin their planning years in advance. The campaign finance reform laws of the 1970s cause the formation of "exploratory committees" long before the first primaries; although the federal communications regulations keep aspirants from announcing their candidacy quite so early, we are treated to announcements that the candidates plan to announce. And the delegate selection itself gets pushed ever further back.

And yet, despite all the warning, despite the years of planning and the months of coyness and maneuvering, and even despite the grueling process of garnering delegates in caucuses and primaries, Americans make their choice for president after a campaign that seldom lasts longer than ninety days. Primaries and conventions are but the warmup and the preliminary heats; the race is all. In three months, more or less, the candidates put themselves and their programs before the people, and then, in one day, the selection is made.

The Olympic Summer

There are two great quadrennial rituals, two great contests conducted at four year intervals. One is the American presidential election campaign, the other is the Olympic Games. In most cases, the two have very little to do with one another. The athletes gather in Munich, or Montreal, or Moscow, and they divert attention for two or three weeks from the campaign. But 1984 was different. This time the Olympics were held on American soil, in the president's own home town.

It started innocently enough. In mock reminder of an ancient ritual, a flame was kindled on Mt. Olympus in Greece and carried by a runner with a torch to the place where the games would be held, there to light a sacred flame that would burn during the competition. But how we watched the progress of that torch! When it reached our shores, that foreign, pagan flame was suddenly Americanized. The organizers of the games laid out a route that took the torch through every region of the Republic; in one-kilometer intervals, citizen after citizen took his turn holding it aloft. And, almost unaccountably, the people came to line the route and cheer the runners on—and they brought their flags.

And then, at last, the Games themselves capped the celebration. Held between the Democratic convention in July and the Republican convention in August, they became what must surely have been one of the decisive events of the election year. President Reagan flew to his home state, California, to declare the games open. And what games they were! Boycotted by the Soviet Union and its allies and clients, the games were dominated by the American team, which earned an unprecedented number of medals before appreciative American audiences. There was an orgy of patriotism and national self-confidence; Americans felt good about themselves and their country, and therefore about the incumbent administration.

Moreover, unlike the previous several Olympic games, conducted at great cost to the taxpayers of the host countries, the 1984 games were conducted by private enterprise and by volunteers, and actually made a profit. Americans did what no one had been able to accomplish since the games were revived in the nineteenth century. And this, too, worked to the benefit of the incumbent, who, unlike his opponent, advocated free enterprise and volunteerism; and who projected unfailing confidence in American know-how.

The spirit generated by the Los Angeles Olympics pervaded American public life during the summer and fall of 1984. In a way, the presidential campaign itself was almost like an Olympic event. Of course, American electoral campaigns are customarily referred to as "races," and, unlike most of the final heats at Los Angeles, the presidential race was never really close. But it is not too farfetched to treat an Olympic race as a type of the presidential race, perhaps the 800-meter run or the steeplechase. And the defending champion ran the race to the cheers of "USA! USA!" Like the American Olympians in Los Angeles, he was going for the gold.

Mondale at the Starting Line

In most election years, the beginning of the general election campaign can be dated at the close of the second major party convention or, perhaps, at Labor Day. The beginning of the 1984 general election campaign must be dated at 12 July, four days before the Democratic national convention opened. That was the day when Walter F. Mondale announced that he had selected Representative Geraldine Ferraro of New York to be his running mate.

In many ways, the selection of Ferraro was the most characteristic act of the Mondale campaign. Ferraro had been preselected for him by the National Organization for Women (NOW), a group that had decided that it was entitled to have its candidate become the candidate of the Democratic Party. And the

Mondale-Ferraro campaign was a campaign of entitlements, characterized by nothing so much as its appeal to organized groups of one sort or another. Ferraro became the running mate because the group whose candidate she was established a claim of greater entitlement than those with which it competed. Nevertheless, before the final selection was announced, Mondale arranged to have the candidates of the various entitlement groups parade to rural Minnesota. At first blush, it may have looked like a parade of supplicants to beg favors from the anointed one; but it soon became clear that Mondale was the supplicant, begging each ethnic group or special interest for support.

Off they trooped to Minnesota: a black man, a Hispanic, a southerner. But there was never any doubt that Ferraro—the NOW candidate—had the superior claim. The only real question was whether Mondale would accept NOW's first choice, a liberal, Italian, Roman Catholic, urban female from the Northeast, or NOW's second choice, a liberal, Jewish, urban female from the West. Mondale chose Ferraro; and his party's commitment to entitlement politics was confirmed when Gary Hart, on the verge of losing the nomination to Mondale, and therefore in the position where most presidential candidates would be looking for a running mate with a block of delegates at his command, announced that he, too, would pick Ferraro.

Mondale went further. Restrained by the exigencies of entitlement politics from balancing his ticket, Mondale decided to balance the campaign. After choosing a liberal, Northeastern member of Congress as his running mate, Mondale announced that a Southerner would become chairman of the Democratic National Committee (DNC). His choice was Bert Lance, the hapless Carter aide who seven years before had failed to obtain Senate confirmation as the head of the Office of Management and the Budget. Of course, Mondale failed to reckon with the incumbent chairman of the DNC, Charles Manatt, who proved unwilling to step aside. Mondale then created a new post for Lance, general chairman of the campaign. The post had no apparent duties and no formal place in the campaign hierarchy. But it was a symbol that the South, too, had entitlements. Unfortunately, even conferring a wholly honorific title upon Lance drew criticism from the rest of the party, and, only three weeks later, Lance resigned.

When the delegates to the convention had duly nominated Mondale and ratified his choice of Ferraro, Mondale took to the rostrum to announce the theme of his campaign. "I will raise your taxes." That is what Mondale said, and the delegates cheered him for it. "I will raise your taxes." It was not really a surprise; entitlement politics is an expensive business, and somebody has to pay for it. "I will raise your taxes." He must have said many other things besides; and, of course, he predicted that whoever was elected would have to propose a tax increase. But there it was, the first promise of the general election campaign: "I will raise your taxes."

The finale was something to behold. All of the delegates and alternates had flags to wave: little plastic American flags, much like the ones Americans all over the country were waving as the Olympic torch passed by. And all the flags were alike, because the Mondale people had bought them all and had placed them on the delegates' chairs during the dinner break.

Reagan Ready to Run

After the Democratic national convention and the Los Angeles Olympic Games, the Republican national convention was an anticlimax. Although some members of the press had floated a "rumor" that the incumbent would bow out after one term, no one who went to the convention had any doubt that he was going there to renominate Ronald Reagan. There was some manufactured suspense about the platform—just how emphatically would the party come out against tax increases? But even that turned out to hinge on the placement of a comma. Even the handful of Republican liberals who had tried to embarrass the party in previous years by pressing federal lawsuits to challenge delegate allocation rules were quiet: having lost in the courts they publicly retreated into silence.

In Ronald Reagan, the Republican Party had a special kind of candidate, an incumbent who wore the mantle of incumbency well. And it just might be, as some suggested, that the mantle was teflon-coated—no criticism seemed to stick to it. Reagan had, after all, campaigned in 1980 on the promise of a balanced budget, and yet, four years later, the government under his administration was running the largest peacetime deficits in history. He had campaigned on the promise of determination to resist and to retaliate against terrorism, and yet there had been no decisive action following any of numerous terrorist incidents, and a terror bombing had forced the withdrawal of American peacekeeping troops from Beirut, Lebanon. He had campaigned on the promise of prosperity without inflation. And yet the country was only just recovering from its longest postwar recession.

And yet Ronald Reagan looked like a sure winner. The last American president to serve two full terms had been Dwight D. Eisenhower. John Kennedy had been felled by an assassin's bullet; Lyndon Johnson withdrew from the race for reelection after losing the support of his own party; Richard Nixon had won a second term by the greatest landslide ever, only to resign when the extent of his own meanness and squalor of mind was revealed by Watergate; Gerald Ford was tripped up by Nixon's shadow; and Jimmy Carter had proved unable to meet the demands of the office. Reagan captured the American imagination as no one had done since Kennedy; and when he promised four more years just like the first four, Americans were ready to climb on the bandwagon.

Running for a second term can be a politically dangerous business. Jimmy Carter, campaigning against President Ford, had invented a "misery index"— the sum of the inflation and unemployment rates. Again and again Carter had alluded to the worsening of the "misery index." But when Carter himself ran for a second term, the "misery index" was higher than it had ever been under Ford. When Reagan, campaigning against Carter, told voters that they should base their vote on the answer to the question, "Are you better off now than you were four years ago?" he risked having the same question posed against him in 1984. But Reagan was able to go before the convention—and later before crowds everywhere—and ask, "Are you better off now than you were four years ago?" confident that his listeners would roar back "Yes!"

The Hurdle of Financial Disclosure

There is a certain self-indulgence permitted the American voter in a presidential election. The campaign becomes a window on the lifestyles of the rich and famous. Voyeurism was elevated to the status of a virtue after the Johnson and Nixon presidencies. The press extorts from the candidates the promise of full financial disclosure, and the sordid details are spread before an eager public.

Geraldine Ferraro got caught. At first, Ferraro tried to escape the full-disclosure trap by announcing on August 12 that her husband, John Zaccaro, objected to the release of his tax returns and financial records as an invasion of his privacy. The plea for a double standard, however, ill became a feminist spokesman like Ferraro. Finally, on August 20 (the opening day of the Republican national convention) she released a mass of data to the press. It soon became evident why full disclosure had not come earlier. Among the disclosures were Zaccaro's involvement in questionable real estate deals, possible violations of the financial disclosure requirements of the House of Representatives, and possibly illegal arrangements for the financing of her congressional campaigns. It also turned out that the Zaccaros, whether as a result of bad advice or otherwise, owed some fifty thousand dollars in back taxes.

On August 21, Ferraro held a nearly 2-hour long press conference to explain and defend her financial records. The affair was Ferraro's equivalent of Richard Nixon's famous "Checkers" speech of 1952. There was some sloppy record keeping, she admitted, and an accountant had given her bad advice that she had followed. But she denied all wrongdoing; she had explained everything to Mondale, and Mondale was still behind her.

But the Ferraro-Zaccaro financial situation would not go away. Perhaps more politically damaging than the disclosures about mishandling money was the revelation of how much money Ferraro had to mishandle. Suddenly the Italian-American housewife from Queens, New York, appeared to be a millionairess real estate tycoon. Her appeal to the working people of the middle and lower middle class was thoroughly undermined. Although it had never been clear how Ferraro was expected to draw to the Democratic ticket the support of any voters outside the NOW radical feminist clique (who had nowhere else to turn in any case), from the time of the financial disclosure she had to be counted by the Mondale camp as a pure liability.

As the campaign wore on, Ferraro became increasingly strident. She published a letter in which she claimed that the position of the Roman Catholic Church against abortion was not univocal, and had to back down when confronted by her bishop; what she had meant, she said, was that some individual Catholics disagreed with the Church's position. In discomfiting sequence to Mondale's attack on Reagan for allegedly making religion an issue in the campaign, Ferraro engaged in a public spat with the Roman Catholic Archbishop of New York, and then delivered herself of the opinion that the President was not a "good Christian."

Although selected in part to effect a traditional aspect of Democratic ticket balancing—a Roman Catholic vice presidential candidate to balance a Methodist presidential candidate; an Italian-American vice presidential candidate to balance a Nordic presidential candidate—Ferraro seemed increasingly bent on alienating both Catholics and Italians. No wonder, then, that Mondale increasingly distanced himself from his hand-picked running mate.

Jogging Down the Backstretch

The six weeks between the end of the Republican convention and the first of the televised candidates' debates found Ronald Reagan taking it easy. If it resembled anything in recent American political history, the Reagan approach most resembled Jimmy Carter's "Rose Garden strategy" of 1980. The incumbent rarely left the White House grounds, his managers having decided to protect their lead in the polls by minimizing the opportunity for their man to blunder in public. Meanwhile, the media experts began to flood the airwaves with commercials depicting scenes from American life in a warm, sunlit glow. The theme: America's back (from where?), standing tall.

Mondale, on the other hand, was running furiously; and so was Ferraro, although Mondale was careful to keep his distance from her. In order to stir public interest and to attract media coverage, the Mondale camp embarked on a one-issue-per-week strategy. Mondale's speeches and statements, as well as the thirty- and sixty-second television commercials that consume the bulk of campaign funds in modern times, were keyed to a selected list of topics and changed each week so that it appeared that the candidate was saying something new all the time.

One of the themes Mondale sounded most insistently was that Reagan had been unnecessarily truculent in dealing—or refusing to deal—with the Soviet Union. The charge was often repeated that Reagan was the first American president since World War II who had failed to meet with the leader of the Soviet Communist Party. Mondale made the charge, and the media commentaries picked it up, without mentioning the fact that the Soviet Union had gone through three leaders (Brezhnev, Andropov, and Chernenko) during Reagan's first term of office, and that, in consequence, the Soviet hierarchy was in turmoil and disarray and in no hurry to meet with any Western leader. The charge sounded too good to pass up just because it made no sense when analyzed coolly.

Nevertheless, on September 1 Chernenko made a speech urging a new round of disarmament talks; Reagan responded on September 25, during his address to the United Nations General Assembly, welcoming such talks and advocating a better working relationship with the Soviet Union in order to reduce world tensions. A few days later, when Soviet foreign minister Andrei Gromyko came to the United States to address the United Nations General Assembly, he went on to Washington for a three-hour "forceful and direct" conference with President Reagan at the White House. That Gromyko should visit and talk with Reagan even as Mondale was attacking Reagan for not talking with the Soviet hierarchy was a signal that even on September 28 the probable outcome of the election was apparent in Moscow.

During September, also, Mondale attempted to make the federal budget deficit a major campaign issue. On September 10, Mondale announced his economic plan. It called for $85 billion in new taxes—most to be levied on the very rich and on corporations—and $105 billion in reduced expenditures—mostly from national defense programs. At the same time he pressed the claim that the Republicans had a "secret plan" to raise taxes after the election. Unfortunately for the Republicans, Vice President Bush seemed to lend some credibility to the Mondale charge when, unlike the President, he refused publicly to rule out the possibility that the administration would ask for a tax increase.

Still later in September, Mondale tried out the environmental issue. A Mondale administration, he said, would "take polluters to court, not to lunch." Not too surprisingly, he won the endorsement of the Sierra Club. But none of the weekly issues seemed to strike a responsive chord in the American people; the opinion polls consistently showed Reagan leading Mondale by margins ranging between 15 and 20 percent.

Through it all, except for such "nonpolitical" events as his United Nations speech and his meeting with Gromyko, President Reagan acted as if he were above the fray. The Republicans, Reagan said, were "America's party"; what the Democrats were he left for his hearers to guess. The campaign's media people produced and broadcast a series of promotional announcements for television featuring warm, earthy colors; happy, busy people; and star-spangled, high-flying flags.

Stumbling Through the Debates

The candidates' debate has in a short time become an institution in American political campaigns. The first face-to-face public confrontation of candidates for the presidency was that between Vice President Nixon and Senator Kennedy in 1960. The reportage attending that media event should have been enough to deter any future candidate from entertaining the notion of repeating it, but repeat it they have. Carter and Ford, Carter and Reagan, they have taken their turns before the cameras in a somewhat stylized display.

There were two such manufactured confrontations between Reagan and Mondale during the 1984 general election campaign, and, for only the second time, there was a debate between the two major party vice presidential candidates. Mondale had originally asked for six debates, which would have been the most ever held. Reagan had originally been willing, and that only reluctantly, to agree to one. Of course, as the challenger, Mondale had more to gain from a large number of debates: even if he did not do especially well, he would still be sharing a national forum with the President, facing him on an equal footing. In the end the candidates agreed to two debates. They were conducted under the auspices of the nominally nonpartisan League of Women Voters. The first, covering domestic policies, was held at Louisville, Kentucky, on Sunday, October 7, and the second, covering defense and foreign policy, was held at Kansas City, Missouri, on Sunday, October 21.

One is forced to wonder just how the voters are expected to judge the debates. Is formal debating skill a prerequisite for the presidency? Are glibness and a facility for juggling numbers in one's head virtues we seek in a national leader? What, then, are the debates about? The format for the debates in 1984 suggested that the purpose was to put before the viewers and voters the contrasting policy positions of the candidates by putting on the record their answers to identical questions. That, at least, seems a laudable purpose.

The media, however, demand winners and losers, even when the format does not easily conduce to their identification. Debate coaches and forensics instructors were conscripted to tote up the points earned by the candidates as if the candidate debates were part of some high school tournament. The instant analysis teams were brought in to repeat and summarize what the candidates had said, as if the national audience was too dull to know what it had heard. And, of course, the pollsters were mobilized. "Did you hear the debate? Who won?"

To what extent was the public taken in by the media hype? Not very much, and not for very long. The planners of the debates did better than they knew. The format they designed was meant to allow the voters to compare the candidates' stands on the issues. And if a candidate took a stand with which the voter did not agree, what did it really matter that he did it elegantly, or wittily, or in accordance with the debate coaches' handbooks? The real question was not, "Who won the debate?" The real question was, "Now that you have heard both men speak on the same issues, with whom do you more nearly agree?" Because the media pollsters would not ask that question, the voters had to wait for their chance to answer it.

Actually, to refer to the two events as "debates" is to bow to convention rather than to reality. Unlike the head-on confrontations between John Kennedy and Richard Nixon in 1960, the arrangements of 1984 would be more accurately described as joint press conferences or joint interviews. At each appearance, the candidates were questioned by a panel of four journalists, rotating among themselves and alternating the opportunity of first response between the candidates. Like a presidential press conference, the debates seemed designed to allow the journalists to display their own superior opinions before the public in the guise of questions.

Like a press conference, also, the debates focused on details, on individual programs, and on statistics. The American people were called upon to choose between candidates for the highest national office who professed to have diametrically opposed understandings of how the country ought to work and how the government ought to be run, and yet, when the candidates were on the same stage those differences were minimized as a direct result of the formula chosen for allocating air time.

The first debate was all but universally regarded as a great victory for Mondale, or, at least, as a serious defeat for Reagan. The President tried to deal with the journalists on their own terms rather than rising above them. He quoted statistics, he cited numbers; he tried to convey in the debate an approach to the presidency directly contrary to that he had been trying for three and a half years in the White House to dispel. Jimmy Carter had been a master of detail and of statistical data, but his presidency had been a failure at least partly because Carter immersed himself in the details and lost sight of the big picture. The Reagan presidency had been just the opposite of that: Reagan had set the tone, defined the outlines of policy, and presided over the board of directors of the Reagan Revolution. The details he had left to others.

But, apparently stung by the charges that he was not completely in control of his administration, or that he was merely a figurehead for a collective presidency actually run from behind the scenes by staff members and other appointees, the President tried to demonstrate that he was at home with statistics. His tactics were faulty; his counterattack was a failure. Even in his conclusion, which should have been a set piece, a carefully rehearsed five-minute speech to catch the minds and imaginations of the audience, Reagan resorted to quoting numbers. The real damage, however, resulted from his distracted air, his sometimes rambling answers to the journalists' questions, and his obvious fatigue by the end of the ninety-minute ordeal.

Mondale's performance in the first debate was a winning one only by contrast with Reagan's losing performance. He tried to needle Reagan, and he rather too obviously contrived to lure Reagan into offering him straight lines for preplanned "zingers." Mondale was dull and colorless in his own presentations. The difference was that no one had ever called Mondale a "great communicator," and so no one was surprised at his failure to communicate greatness. Mondale had only to appear competent and self-assured, as, indeed, he did; Reagan was expected to be a master rhetorician, as, indeed, he was not.

Democratic campaign strategists looking for an issue and journalists looking for a story latched on to one perception of the participants in the first debate: Reagan had appeared old. The "age issue" was always a bit remote from the reality of the campaign—it is scarcely a justification for voting for someone with whom one disagrees that he is younger and more active than the candidate with whom one agrees. But for the two weeks between the debates the media trumpeted the "age issue" and worried openly whether Reagan was up to four more years of holding the world's most demanding job.

The "age issue" was what Reagan arrived in Kansas City prepared to dispel. His now-famous one-line gag about not exploiting Mondale's youth and inexperience would not have been sufficient for the purpose had Reagan's performance not borne out the contention that the President was alert and healthy enough to be trusted with his office for four more years.

Mondale, who recognized that something dramatic was needed if he was to have any hope of even coming close in the November election, had chosen a new issue. Again and again in the October 21 debate he asserted that Reagan was not in charge of his administration, perhaps did not even know what was going on. Whenever it was his turn to speak, Mondale returned to that theme; and when it was Reagan's turn, Reagan disproved the assertion. It was as if Mondale had prepared no fallback position. Even when the chosen line of attack was failing, Mondale did not attempt to stress any positive points about himself, but continued to try to score negative points at his opponent's expense.

Still, those who were responsible for Reagan's debate preparations must have winced as the President made his concluding statement. There probably are thousands, or even millions, of Americans who watched the second debate and who, to this day, wonder where Reagan's oratorical excursion down the California coast might ultimately have wound up and what, if anything, it might have had to do with the defense and foreign policy issues that were supposed to be the subjects of the second encounter between the candidates.

The Home Stretch

President Reagan's poor showing in the first debate forced him to campaign more actively and more combatively. Even during the two weeks between the debates he took to the road, and to the air, and even to the rails, to assume the offensive against Mondale. But after the second debate it was less a campaign swing than a victory tour. In the closing days of the campaign, with a Reagan victory as a sure thing, the Republican strategists seemed to begin to think about the possibility of a fifty-state sweep. During the last two weeks, occasions were found for Reagan to venture into Minnesota, the one state that looked as if it might give its electoral votes to Mondale, the favorite son.

For his part, Mondale still had some weekly issues to raise. One was the "sleaze factor" alleged to attend Republican administrations. Reagan had not been helped a great deal when Jacob Stein, who had been appointed to look into charges some Democrats had raised regarding the conduct of Attorney General-designate Edwin Meese, reported on September 20 that there was no basis for prosecuting Meese. Stein refused to comment on the ethics of Meese's activities, because that was beyond the scope of his inquiry, and therefore left an opening for the media to insinuate that Meese was operating in the shadowy interstices of the criminal law.

Then, on October 1 a state grand jury in New York, convened by Democratic prosecutor Mario Merola of the Bronx, indicted Raymond Donovan for allegedly defrauding the New York City Transit Authority. Although Donovan pled "not guilty," he had to take a leave of absence to defend himself. The timing of the affair could not have been better if the Democrats had planned it.

Mondale's final issue-of-the-week, launched to coincide with the second presidential debate, was an all-out attack on the President's strategic defense initiative (SDI) with the slogan, "Draw the line at the heavens." The attack's success depended on the Mondale side's ability, mostly through short television announcements, to depict SDI as a new escalation of the arms race and as the militarization of space. That this coincided with the attack on SDI made by America's international adversaries did not seem to bother Mondale's campaign organization. By this time it was clear that any chance Mondale was to have of winning the election hung on the potential for identifying and exploiting a major "negative" issue. SDI, or "Star Wars," as the media liked to call it, just might have been such an issue.

Of course, the American people did not necessarily perceive SDI in the light in which Mondale tried to portray it. They recognized that since the Soviet government had achieved rough strategic parity with the United States in the 1960s, our national security has depended on the deterrent effect of the potential for massive nuclear retaliation. So long as an effective strategic defense system was technologically infeasible, Americans had accepted deterrence (even in its later form, Mutually Assured Destruction) as inevitable. When President Reagan told them that a real defense might be possible, they were willing to give it a try. Of course, Reagan's fatuous pledge to share SDI technology with the enemy was somewhat dismaying, but not so dismaying as Mondale's pledge to cancel the program before it was begun.

Republican supporters who had seen Reagan campaign for the governorship of California in 1966 and 1970 must have been surprised and distressed by what happened in the final two weeks of the 1984 campaign. Twice, in the California campaigns, when a Reagan victory had become a sure thing and the margin of victory looked like being very impressive, the final days of the campaign were spent on an effort to elect the "Reagan team." The objective was to bring as many Republicans as possible into office in order to transform the electoral majority into a workable governing majority. Reagan campaign spots on the radio and television were used to encourage voters to elect Republicans to statewide constitutional offices and to the legislature.

But in 1984 the final two weeks of the campaign were spent building up an enormous presidential landslide. Funds were spent, and the candidate's time was spent, chasing the elusive prospect of Electoral College unanimity. The much-discussed prospect of a partisan realignment was brushed aside in favor of accumulating superfluous votes for the top of the ticket. Such behavior was to be expected in 1972, when the candidate was Richard Nixon, who needed the personal reassurance of a landslide victory. But it ill became the reelection campaign of Ronald Reagan.

In the event, of course, the landslide was huge, but there was no fifty-state sweep, let alone an Electoral College shutout. Both Minnesota and the District of Columbia gave their electoral votes to Walter Mondale. Republican candidates for other offices did not fare so well. And for that result, Reagan and his campaign operatives were greatly to blame. Not only were the media mavens who interpret our political life for us given the opportunity to call the election a personal, rather than a political, vote of confidence, but during the second Reagan term he would be dealing with a Congress only slightly less hostile than during his first term. The second opportunity for realignment may have been thrown away.

Appendix: The Candidates

Walter F. Mondale

The Democratic Party's nominee for President of the United States in 1984 was Walter Frederick Mondale of Minnesota. Mondale was born in Ceylon, Minnesota, in 1928; he is married, with three children. He attended the University of Minnesota and the University of Minnesota Law School, being graduated from the latter in 1956. He entered Minnesota politics, while still a student, as a member of the Democratic Farm-Labor Party, hitching his wagon to the then rising Hubert H. Humphrey. After a brief period of private practice of law, Mondale joined the state attorney general's staff, and, in 1960, himself became the state attorney general. When Humphrey was elected vice president, in 1964, Mondale was appointed to fill his vacancy in the United States Senate. After twelve years in the Senate, Mondale ran for president in the Democratic primaries in 1976. When he, along with other establishment Democrats, was defeated by Jimmy Carter, Mondale accepted Carter's offer of the vice presidential nomination. For the four years of the Carter administration, Mondale was a loyal follower and supporter of the president, although, in the 1984 campaign, he would try to portray himself as a sharp critic within the administration of some policy decisions and programs.

Mondale has always belonged to the liberal wing of the Democratic Party. He was the protege of the late Senator Humphrey who, except during his own vice presidential years, was probably the leading spokesman of his day for expansion of the welfare state, federal enforcement of civil rights, and conversion of the national government into an instrument for the redistribution of wealth and income and the dominant force in American life. Mondale became a Sen-

ate spokesman for Johnson Administration civil rights policies and an enthusiastic supporter of the "Great Society." In the late 1960s, he opposed expenditures for space exploration—including the nascent space shuttle program—
because the money would be better spent relieving urban poverty. As measured by the ultraliberal Americans for Democratic Action, Mondale's ideological voting score as a Senator was always 90% or higher.

Never the flamboyant orator that Humphrey was, Mondale was an organization man, a team player. During his four-year term as Carter's vice president, Mondale was the one Washington insider in an administration that was
self-consciously outside the establishment of Washington politics. Mondale
was apparently distrusted by the "Georgia mafia" and by other key members
of the Carter team, including Hamilton Jordan, Carter's chief of staff. For his
own part, Mondale often appeared ill at ease as the mediator between the
Carter people and a national political apparatus that they never understood
or cared much to understand. But Mondale was a dutiful team player and, by
his own account, was privy to all options considered by Carter on policy questions. Both Carter and Mondale have described the latter's role in the administration as one of helping to shape policy. Like all modern vice presidents he
was the nation's First Mourner at international funerals, but he also travelled
widely as the personal emissary of Jimmy Carter to foreign political leaders.

During the four years between campaigns, Mondale was nominally a member of a major Democratic law firm in Washington, but, in fact, he was virtually a full-time candidate from the end of the 1980 campaign until the end
of the 1984 campaign. Thus, the years following the 1984 election will be the
first in which Walter Mondale will be a genuinely private citizen.

Geraldine Ferraro

Geraldine Anne Ferraro Zaccaro gave up a seat in the House of Representatives to accept the Democratic Party's vice presidential nomination in 1984.
Born in New York City of Italian immigrant parents in 1935, she is married
and has three children. Her husband is a wealthy attorney and businessman
with extensive real estate holdings. Ferraro herself attended Marymount College and Fordham University Law School, being graduated in 1960. From
1974 to 1978 she was a prosecutrix in the office of the local district attorney
(her cousin), specializing, for three years in the investigation of sex crimes and
spouse abuse. Unlike most law enforcement professionals, she became convinced that crime was caused by poverty and social injustice. In 1979 she was
elected to Congress and, when chosen as a vice presidential candidate, she had
served for about five and a half years.

Ferraro's position on those issues of national politics on which she had an
established position was about as far left as it is possible to be in either of the
major national parties. Apparently from the time of her election she conceived
of herself not as a Congressman representing a district in the borough of

Queens in New York City but as a member of Congress representing women in general. She set out to be a spokesman for "women's issues," in the cant used to described the agenda of the radical feminist movement. She became active in the National Women's Political Caucus and in other feminist organizations. But she also hewed the line of organized labor (supporting the AFL-CIO 91% of the time), and she became a special protegee of Speaker of the House Thomas O'Neill.

Ferraro was a member of the "Hunt Commission," the body that had the task of rewriting the national convention delegate selection rules of the Democratic Party after the 1980 election. She was one of the key backers of the proposal, implemented in 1984, that appointed "superdelegates" should make up a significant proportion (14% in 1984) of the total number of convention delegates. She was also chosen to be the chairman of the platform committee at the 1984 convention.

From the time that it became clear that the National Organization for Women would dictate the choice of Walter Mondale's running mate, Representative Ferraro was the front runner. Only San Francisco Mayor Dianne Feinstein was a serious contender, but Ferraro's "demographics" were better than Feinstein's, especially as the nomination of the latter would not improve Mondale's chances of carrying her home state.

Ronald Reagan

Ronald Wilson Reagan, the fortieth President of the United States, was born in Tampico, Illinois in 1911. He attended Eureka College, majoring in economics and being graduated in 1932; he is divorced and remarried, and has four children. In his first career he was a radio sports announcer and a motion picture actor. His acting career was interrupted by World War II, during which he served as an Air Force officer, although his assignment was making training films. After the war, he was for six years the head of the Screen Actors' Guild, a labor union.

Although a one-time liberal Democrat, Reagan had become more conservative during the 1950s, and in 1962 he joined the Republican Party. In 1964 he toured the country speaking on behalf of Republican presidential candidate Barry M. Goldwater. So effective was his advocacy that, even though Goldwater lost the election, Reagan was sought after as a candidate in his own right. In 1966 he was elected Governor of California, an office that he held for two four-year terms. He ran for the Republican presidential nomination in 1968 and 1976 before his successful attempt in 1980.

As governor and as president, Reagan has publicly advocated a conservative position, calling for a reduction in the size and cost of government, a balanced budget, a strong national defense, and a stress on the importance of families, communities, and basic morality. Nevertheless, both as governor and as president, Reagan has gained a reputation as a "pragmatist," one not so committed to a principled position as to allow it to interfere with the day-to-day political business of compromise and accommodation.

At age 73 on election date in 1984, Reagan was the oldest man ever elected to the office of president.

George Bush

George Herbert Walker Bush, the Vice President of the United States, is a man marking time until he is free to resume his own bid for the presidency. Born in Milton, Massachusetts, in 1924, he attended the prestigious Phillips-Andover Academy, a private high school in Massachusetts. During World War II Bush served as a naval aviator, and he was, for a while, the youngest pilot in the Navy. He later attended Yale University, being graduated in 1948; he is married, with five children. His early career was spent in the petroleum industry; in 1953 he cofounded Zapata Petroleum Company, and five years later he spun off his own company, Zapata Offshore Company, in Houston, Texas.

Bush has been active in Republican politics at least since 1964, when he ran for the United States Senate against liberal Democrat Ralph Yarborough, winning a larger share of the vote (43.5%) than any other previous Republican in Texas history. Two years later he was elected to the House of Representatives. Four years after that he gave up his seat to run again for the Senate, losing this time to Lloyd Bentsen. From 1970 to 1973, Bush was the United States Ambassador to the United Nations. In 1973 he was elected chairman of the Republican National Committee, steering the party through the final months of the traumatic Watergate affair.

In 1974, President Ford sent Bush to Beijing as the de facto American ambassador to Communist China. Fifteen months later, Ford named Bush the Director of Central Intelligence, giving him the task of reorganizing and reinvigorating the Central Intelligence Agency. Although the intelligence post is nominally nonpartisan, Bush resigned when Jimmy Carter was elected president. All told, Bush has one of the fullest and most diverse resumés of anyone in government today.

Although he began his political career as a supporter of Barry Goldwater, Bush is reputed to be a representative of the moderate, or liberal, wing of the Republican Party. During the 1980 Republican primary campaign, when he was running against Ronald Reagan for the presidential nomination, Bush was wont to refer to Reagan's proposed tax reductions as "Voodoo economics." After he became Reagan's running mate, several of his key advisors transferred to the Reagan team, including James Baker, Bush's campaign manager, who became the White House chief of staff during Reagan's first term.

Like Walter Mondale before him, Bush has become a firm backer of the man he previously opposed for the nomination. Reagan has made Bush a member of the White House policy making apparatus, and has assigned him such functions as chairmanship of the National Security Council crisis management task force. He has also been given diplomatic assignments, such as explaining American defense and arms control policies to the leaders of several European nations. Bush clearly has his eye on the 1988 campaign, when he is expected to seek the Republican presidential nomination.

Demography of 1984's National Majorities

John Adams Wettergreen

Interpretations of the Election

President Reagan's victory was so overwhelming that patterns are not obvious. Nevertheless, pundits and partisans offer their interpretations.

The business of interpreting the 1984 election began well before November 6, 1984. By January, Republican and Democratic experts alike had concluded that nothing much would be decided at the polls. John Sears, once a professional Republican campaigner, predicted, "This isn't likely to be a big election in the broad context of things." Democrats concurred. Fred Dutton, from the extreme left of that party, saw the up-coming election as part of "a period of continual drift." The more moderate Horace Busby put it this way: "We [Americans] don't have anything to turn to politics to decide for us." Nor could Kevin Phillips "muster much excitement" about this election, although he had made a living since 1968 by predicting that precedent-setting Republican victories ought to be just around the corner. These men's views were typical of the opinion of the sophisticates of the national media. Accordingly, political reporting of both the primary and general campaigns tended to focus upon electoral tactics, often to the exclusion of reports on the important differences of political principle between the candidates or on the deep divisions in the country, if any, produced by those differences.

The opinion of the national press was quite different from the opinion of the major political organizations, which declared that 1984 was crucial and acted accordingly. In early October of 1983, the AFL-CIO broke one of its founding principles by openly and officially endorsing Walter Mondale for the Democratic nomination. Following the example set by the union, the National Organization for Women examined all the candidates for the Democratic nomination before its national convention and, in effect, extracted from them the promise of a female vice presidential nominee. This promise was kept by Walter Mondale when he chose Representative Geraldine Ferraro, NOW's candidate, as his running mate. In the past, both the AFL-CIO and NOW carefully avoided intraparty squabbles, and worked for any Democratic nominee. However, George McGovern's stunning defeat in 1972, followed by Jimmy Carter's freakish nomination and narrow victory in 1976 and his unequivocal defeat in 1980, made suspect the party's natural capacity to nominate a winner. So, when the Democrats proclaimed, "A fundamental choice awaits America," in the opening words of their platform, this was somewhat more than the ordinary hyperbole of election year: the prestige and political judgment of the oldest and most powerful Democratic factions were at stake in Mondale's candidacy.

The Republican National Convention's loudest cheer came when President Reagan asserted that this year's election offered "the clearest political choice of half a century." These words were not surprising. At least since his speech on behalf of Barry Goldwater's presidential candidacy, Ronald Reagan has been urging the nation to "come to a time for choosing." The choice is clear, Reagan said on October 27, 1964:

> Either we accept the responsibility for our own destiny, or we abandon the American Revolution and confess an intellectual belief that a far distant capital can plan our lives better than we can plan them ourselves.

He thought the choice was the same in 1984; when a student at Bowling Green University asked him what would be the principal objective of his second term, the President replied, "Returning government to the people." Toward the end of the campaign, President Reagan seemed to suppose that the choice had been made at last. On the eve of the election, he speculated that a "historic realignment" of the political parties, which would result in Republican hegemony over the whole central government, might be about to happen. Republican hopes for 1984 were as great as for any time in this century.

The election was scarcely over before the business of interpreting the results began. Democrats claimed that Reagan's victory was merely personal or accidental, but not fundamentally political. House Speaker O'Neill, as partisan as ever, claimed to believe that the election was merely an endorsement of Reagan's "cute [Irish] smile." The historian Arthur Schlesinger, Jr., admitted that "rekindled nationalism" and "the state of the economy" helped Reagan's victory, but insisted that the victory had no permanent significance. That voice of liberal Democratic hopes declared, "[T]he popular coalition that elected him is unstable. . . . Only Reagan could have assembled Wall Street sophisticates and backwoods zealots into the same coalition." This line of analysis had been present under the surface of Mondale's campaign, as when the contender had professed, "I like Reagan," while explaining that the American people really disagreed with the President on "the issues." Remarks like these might make one suppose that, despite the fact that the presidency is awarded to the winner, presidential elections are beauty contests.

Such arguments are aimed immediately against the political authority of the President, but ultimately they deny the principle of majority rule. Indeed, one prominent Democrat did state, quite frankly, the antidemocratic interpretation of the election. Lucius Barker, a political scientist at the Joint Center for Political Studies and a delegate pledged to Jesse Jackson at the Democratic National Convention, reflected upon Reagan's triumph:

Are you a decent nation? If you are, you did not give Ronald Reagan the mandate the Republicans are claiming. If you are not decent, then your mandate carries no authority.

However, Jesse Jackson himself, more graciously and more realistically than most other Democrats, merely remarked,

> The combination of God, prosperity, hope, and national security was [Reagan's] package. That is not fundamentally an anti-black thrust.... Our themes of tax hike and "doom is around the corner" and "deficit is the first priority"—though they are true—were themes that did not capture the imagination of the American people.

Jackson, like most Democrats, has not abandoned hope that the Democratic party can become once again, unambiguously, the national majority party. Accordingly, in the aftermath of the election Democrats claimed that Ronald Reagan's majority was not the national majority. This interpretation is obviously partisan: perhaps for that reason the national press could never take this interpretation seriously. Nevertheless, it could be correct.

Ronald Reagan's partisans claimed almost total victory for him—for his character, his record, his policies, and his principles—but they did not and could not claim a victory for his party. Republicans were more honest than Democrats in acknowledging the limits of their political authority, because they had achieved so much less than they needed and desired; they had failed to achieve a majority in the House of Representatives and only barely maintained their majority in the Senate, while winning the national election overwhelmingly. This was no historic watershed election, like those of Jefferson's Democratic Republicans in 1800, Lincoln's Republicans in 1860, or Franklin Roosevelt's Democrats in 1932. For in those elections the winning parties not only captured the control of the legislative and executive branches, but did so in such a way as to ruin the political prospects of the other party for two generations. The best the Republicans could say of 1984 was said by a *Wall Street Journal* editorial, "this election has definitely accelerated the process of realignment." Accordingly, Republicans pointed proudly to the increasing number of Americans, especially younger ones, who identified themselves as conservatives and who registered as Republicans. They seemed to believe, as do some social scientists, that early political experience ("partisan self-identity") would bring partisan realignment, as though "the process of realignment" goes on independent of political choice.

Democrats can reasonably hope to regain their political hegemony: Republicans seem incapable of building a national partisan majority. Thus, some commentators claim that the country is in a period, not of partisan realignment, but of general political "dealignment," a period during which the traditional political parties just disappear. There is some evidence of a lack of partisan spirit, especially among Republicans. For example, when Senator Howard Baker quit his majority leadership for private life, saying that his colleagues were "elected bureaucrats" and that his position was that of "janitor," he betrayed in himself and in the Senate's Republicans a lack of the stomach for the exercise of national legislative power. Similarly, when the President's campaign cut short his tour on behalf of Republican congressional candidates because the opinion surveys showed "slippage" after the first televised debate, the possibility that a Republican national majority would be represented in the House was sacrificed to the certainty of a great victory for the President. And it ought not be forgotten that, in this country, to rule is to legislate. Republicans might have done better by heeding the advice of Representative Tony Coelho, chairman of the Democratic Congressional Campaign Committee, "We're the incumbents. They have to beat us." For, whatever else may be proven by it, the 1984 election shows that no "realigning process" is going to beat the Democratic party. However, if the 1984 election was not a watershed like those of 1800, 1860, and 1932, if it did not create a new national balance of political power, was it then, as the Democrats claim, just a political accident caused by the personal charm of Ronald Reagan?

Different and contradictory opinions, even of so unambiguous a victory as President Reagan's, are possible because we have the secret ballot: Americans are not required to give any public or official reason for their votes. Of course, everyone knows that American government is founded upon public opinion, or that all civil officials ought to represent "Us, the People." However, because of our secret ballot, popular opinion is never officially articulated, except insofar as it is articulated by the governmental officials elected by the people. In other words, as *Federalist* 51 explains, our government is designed to have no interest or will independent of society's; precisely because government is controlled by public opinion, the only publicly articulated opinions which really count politically are those of governmental officials. When the opinions of officials fundamentally disagree, then only an election can properly settle the disagreement. In 1984, there was fundamental disagreement among our political leaders and they did appeal to the people for a resolution of that disagreement, but the disagreement was not resolved. Therefore, the results even of the presidential election seem ambiguous.

Who was correct about the 1984 election, the political intellectuals and their followers in the national media or the partisans at the national parties' conventions? Did Americans make any fundamental choices in 1984, or did they just choose to continue an inoffensive, incumbent administration? We shall examine the divisions in the country, insofar as they were revealed at the polls and by surveys of public opinion, in order to answer these questions.

Our inquiries will be organized by the three most common opinions about the 1984 election. First, the President's victory was merely personal, and was not an endorsement of his political principles, policies, or party. Connected with this opinion is the view, common among Democrats and Republicans, that Walter Mondale is personally unattractive: at worst, a colorless, wimpy whiner; at best, a man devoid of "a vision," "new ideas," or a sense of direction for the nation. From this point of view, the election was more a rejection of Walter Mondale's personality than an endorsement of Ronald Reagan's character, but in either case it could not be of much political significance, because merely personal judgments were involved. Incidentally, this belief in the political irrelevance of moral character is very common among social scientists, although since the Watergate scandals and the resignation of President Nixon they have been reluctant to express it publicly.

Second, the election as a whole, i.e., both Reagan's victory and Mondale's defeat, involved no issue of political or partisan principle, but was simply a question of self-interests. Again, this view is expressed by both Republicans and Democrats. For, on the one hand, Republicans like to claim that Walter Mondale's candidacy was that of special interest groups, like labor unions and the various beneficiaries of federal social programs. Mondale gave credence to this opinion by his constant appeals for "compassion for the elderly, the black, the poor, the sad, women, the handicapped, and the blind," and by his lack of compassion for those whose taxes would pay for his compassion. On the other hand, Democrats insist that Ronald Reagan's appeal was mean-spirited and selfish, and that he had deliberately refused to discuss "the issues." The President gave credence to this opinion by his repetition of the same question all across the country, "Are you better off now than you were four years ago [with Carter-Mondale]?"

Third, the election divided the nation by ethnic and economic class, and in particular it divided black from white, but it did not produce any principled basis for national unity. Here again is a bipartisan view, and one hard to deny. Blacks and poorer Americans voted in overwhelming majorities for Walter Mondale and other Democrats; many other ethnic groups did the same. Furthermore, the national government that resulted is solidly Democratic in the House, narrowly Republican in the Senate, and solidly Republican in the Presidency, as though there were three national majorities.

Before turning to the polls and surveys of opinions to test these interpretations of the election, a brief caution about surveys is in order. To some, the condition of public opinion in the United States seems paradoxical: How can popular opinion govern in the United States, when the only authoritative opinions are those expressed by governmental officials? That is, how do we know that government does represent the public, if the public as such never expresses its opinion? Accordingly, especially in this century, attempts have been made to articulate political opinions in a manner absolutely independent of the government while at the same time being true to the interests of the people. These attempts have resulted in the professionalization of journalism and in the development of the profession of the pollster. Today's journalists and pollsters claim to be able to articulate the opinions of the citizenry better than politicians: pollsters, because they are scientific; journalists, because they are professionally and politically disinterested or objective. Yet journalists and pollsters have political opinions which color their work at least as much as they do the work of politicians; after all, politicians have a private interest in being "objective" about politics, which the national press lacks. More importantly, pollsters and journalists seldom have political opinions different from, much less deeper or more interesting than, politicians—although they invariably believe they do. For example, even the most disinterested pollsters, like the University of Michigan's Survey Research group, never inquire very deeply into the structure of public opinion, but simply provide a quantification of the degree of public agreement with the most common political opinions of the day. For example, the Michigan researchers ask respondents whether they have a "warm" or "cool feeling" toward this or that candidate. Other pollsters—above all, Louis Harris (who was financed by National Public Radio during this campaign)—are so partisan that one must conclude that they are only looking for the degree of public support for their own political views. To make matters worse, pollsters do not always understand political reality very well, and so their samples— those whose opinions they survey—are not representative. This was obviously the case in 1980, when every major national pollster predicted a "toss-up" between Carter and Reagan, because the pollsters failed to understand Ronald Reagan's appeal to traditional Democrats. What follows has been gleaned from the results of all the major national surveys—Roper, Gallup, Harris/National Public Radio, *U.S.A. Today*, ABC News/*Washington Post*, CBS News/*New York Times*. However, to compensate for the biases of their questionnaires and their samples, I shall supplement their results with the election returns from selected states, congressional districts, and counties.

A Merely Personal Victory?

To claim that President Reagan's reelection was a personal victory, is scarcely to distinguish it from any other election in American history. Typically, our electoral system pits one person against another—not one party, ideology, race, section, or interest against another. Conventionally, the voters are said to choose "the best man." Therefore, it would be surprising if citizens did not rely upon their judgments of a candidate's character when casting their votes.

It is impossible to say precisely how important judgments of character are relative to other factors, e.g., judgments of economic interest, partisan attachments, envy, judgments of the public interest, racial or ethnic attachments, etc., in the mind of the typical voter. However, all the available evidence from opinion surveys shows that, in general, judgments of character are decisive. Often, journalists, social scientists, and even politicians have deplored the citizens' reliance upon their judgments of moral character, because they believe that such judgments cannot be objective and that personal qualities have little to do with politics; the intellectually preferred position is usually that a candidate should be chosen with reference to his stand on "the issues." This understanding of how political choices ought to be made is fundamentally misguided. The political issue in American elections is almost always, "Which person deserves to hold office?" Not to decide that question on its merits would be wrong, because partisan and political issues change almost daily while the person remains in office. Furthermore, a candidate might have what the voter regards as the correct political principles and the correct position on the issues, but lack the character necessary to act successfully. Therefore, it is quite prudent on the part of the American voters to put judgments of character before every other factor in their deliberations.

In 1984, some surveys revealed how sophisticated the American citizens' judgments of character are. Again and again, the major national pollsters found that the President was preferred to Walter Mondale for his "leadership qualities." Journalists persisted in identifying this very vague term with the President's ability to "communicate," especially by means of television, even though all the major pollsters found that Walter Mondale did as well or better than the President in his performance in the televised debates. Journalists also enjoyed reporting that Ronald Reagan possessed a generally sympathetic character; in the words of Walter Mondale, "I like the President. I think he's a nice guy." However, in a national survey, the *Los Angeles Times* exit pollsters found that Mondale was preferred to Reagan (by those who had a preference in these regards) for his sympathy for the average citizen, for his performance in the television debates, and for his clearer vision of the future. Indeed, in all the merely personal qualities except three, the Democrat was preferred. The President was preferred for his "strong qualities" (86 percent to 14 percent), for his political capacity (71 percent to 29 percent), and above all for his willingness "to stand up to the Russians" (93 percent to 7 percent). These results were supported even by Louis Harris' surveys, which consistently showed two-to-one leads for the President in "inspiring confidence" and "restoring respect for America." In sum, not so much Reagan's softer qualities—his compassion, persuasiveness, and humor—as his toughness—stubbornness, spiritedness, and patriotism—impressed the voters.

Incidentally, this interpretation of the political relevance of character might be borne out by the widely-reported phenomenon of "the gender gap," i.e., the fact that Ronald Reagan did better with male voters (63 percent) than female (56 percent) in 1984, as well as in 1980 (49 percent vs. 44 percent).

None of this is to say that President Reagan is not a nice guy; one might even speculate that the voters were pleased to discover that a tough guy could also be nice. Yet, the President's oft-reported affability and geniality simply did not show up in surveys as politically important. Most voters, it seems, distinguish between merely personal qualities and personal qualities which are politically relevant. Accordingly, the Gallup surveys which attempt to separate the Presidents' personal from their political popularity show Ronald Reagan on average to be only slightly more popular personally (42 percent favorable vs. 40 percent) than Richard Nixon, and that in the depths of the economic recession Reagan's unpopularity rivaled that of Richard Nixon in the depths of the Watergate scandals. Walter Mondale, one might say, was regarded as the more attractive private personality, but Reagan was regarded as the more attractive political personality. Or, as Democratic campaign strategist Pat Caddell put it, a politician "may be viewed as likable and genial and nice, but that does not translate into political popularity." It does not, because voters consider who would be a good president, not who would be a good pal, when they go to the polls.

The *Times* exit poll confirms the view that character was more important to political issues only to this extent: among those who thought that no important political issues were at stake in the election, a large majority (79 percent) preferred the President. Although only a relatively small percentage of the voters (7 percent) were of this description, their numbers would account for about one-third of President Reagan's margin of victory.

Most voters did suppose that important political issues were at stake. One-quarter of all voters thought matters of public finance were crucial; this seems to have been the opinion of the candidates. Public finance is complex, involving as it does policies for limiting aggregate governmental spending, balancing the budget, raising taxes, and lowering the deficit. Here, again, the sophistication of the voters is fairly clear. Among all voters, the preferred solution to the federal budgetary troubles was reduction of domestic spending (about 50 percent), ahead of reduction of military spending (about 40 percent) and tax increases (about 10 percent); strangely, pollsters did not ask about support for "supply-side" tax-cuts, although Roper surveys show that about 70 percent of Americans believe they pay too much income tax. Those who favored reduction of domestic programs favored the President overwhelmingly (about 4 to 1), while those who favored increasing taxes and cutting defense programs clearly favored Mondale (about 60 percent to 40 percent); Reagan, be it remembered, had opposed increasing taxes and reducing military spending, while leaving the door open for both, but he had unequivocally favored reduction of domestic programs. Therefore, on the central political issue of 1984, one must conclude that the American electorate understood what the choices were and, on that basis, chose Reagan.

With what reason, then, did pollsters—notably, Harris—claim that Americans chose Reagan despite their greater agreement with Mondale on "the issues?" To understand this claim, two aspects of opinion questionnaires must be considered in more detail.

In the first place, pollsters typically do not ask respondents to say with whose position on a political issue they agree; perhaps they think the voters do not know those positions very well. Instead, they usually ask questions in this format: "Which candidate would do better at... [e.g., limiting the arms race, standing up to the Soviets, reducing the deficit, protecting the environment, keeping politics out of religion, etc.]?" The problem with such a format is that a respondent might suppose that a candidate would "do better" at something, and for that very reason be opposed to him. Or, the respondent might think that that something just is not very important politically. In either case, what pollsters and journalists call "agreement on the issues" is an extremely ambiguous condition.

Consider the controversies over the legality of abortion and prayer in schools. When Harris asked, with reference to these controversies, "Who would do better at keeping religion out of politics?," a substantial majority (60 percent to 25 percent, at the peak of the controversy) answered, "Mondale." However, Protestant fundamentalist and Roman Catholic Christians, for whom these controversies are vital, preferred Reagan at the polls: fundamentalists by 80 percent to 20 percent, up 19 percent from 1980, and Roman Catholics by 59 percent to 41 percent, up 12 percent from 1980. On the other hand, Mondale's stand on questions of religious morality helped him with Jews, for whom keeping religion out of politics is fundamental; Jews clearly preferred Mondale (68 percent versus 32 percent, 23 percent ahead of fundamentalist Jimmy Carter's Jewish vote in 1980), but they are only about three percent of the electorate. To mainline Protestants, Mondale's superiority on the religious issues was not politically decisive; he received 39 percent of their vote, the same as Carter. Therefore, although the Harris survey's results might be perfectly accurate, the conclusion that most Americans agreed with Mondale in these controversies is far too simple.

Second, with the possible exceptions of the controversies over abortion and prayer in schools, questions of public finance dominated the campaign. Thus, pollsters simply did not ask about a number of important issues; in particular, they avoided questions on the issues of Reagan's 1980 campaign ("supply-side" tax cutting, bureaucratization, and deregulation). Moreover, on political questions other than the central ones, pollsters used the broadest, blandest categories: they asked about "protecting civil rights," not about affirmative action, comparable worth, the Civil Rights Commission, the Voting Rights Act of 1980, or the Equal Employment Opportunity Commission; they asked about "protecting the environment," not about acid rain, the administration of the Environmental Protection Agency, or emissions control standards; and so on. In addition, surveyors of public opinion seldom discriminate between broad matters of principle or policy and narrow political questions. For example, the *Los Angeles Times* exit poll found that those who thought that "Foreign Relations" were politically crucial clearly preferred Reagan (67 percent to 33 percent), but that those who thought that "Nuclear Arms Control" was crucial preferred Mondale by the same clear margin—as though the one had nothing to do with the other.

Given the rather haphazard way in which the pollsters inquire about political controversies, there really can be no solid evidence for the claim that, in general, the voters agreed with Mondale on the issues but nevertheless voted for Reagan on the basis of his personality or for some other reason. There is, however, clear evidence for the claim that the majority preferred the President's character and that it also agreed with him on all the major political questions of the campaign. The more profound question of the relation between moral character and political position is absolutely untouched by the pollsters, although in the minds of the voters they must be related.

Economic Interest and Political Principle

We have seen that both candidates believed they offered a clear political choice, and that the voters agreed with both in this regard. Ultimately, was this choice one of political principle or was it one of economic interest? It would be a strange election indeed—an absolutely unprecedented one!—in which economic interests were not important. So the key questions are: was the electorate moved by political principles? Or did voters abandon their political principles for the sake of their material interests? Or was there a harmony of interest and principle?

All the national surveys demonstrate that President Reagan's famous rhetorical question—"Are you better off now than you were four years ago?"— was politically acute. For among those who thought they were better off, the President enjoyed a four-to-one advantage. However, Mondale enjoyed a similar edge among those who thought they were worse-off. Therefore, the crucial fact was that more than twice as many thought they were better-off as thought they were worse-off; about 40 percent thought they were in about the same condition as in 1980, and Mondale and Reagan split these voters. In these circumstances, Walter Mondale really had little choice but to argue that the good times were illusory or would not last; after all, he could not tell those who thought they were better off they really were not. We cannot inquire here whether Americans really were better off economically or otherwise, much less whether they will remain so. However, it is very instructive to consider why so many did think they were better off, despite the fact that the first years of Reagan's administration were not very good economically.

Ronald Reagan is commonly thought to be the man of the Sunbelt, of the growing, prosperous states of the South and West, as distinguished from (and even opposed to) the Frostbelt, the old industrial states north of the Ohio River and east of the Mississippi. There is considerable truth in this generalization, as the returns indicate:

	1984 (Electors/two-party vote)	1980 (Electors/two-party vote)
Sunbelt	228/62%	213/57%
Frostbelt	211/56%	226/49%

Although Reagan improved his support in the Frostbelt more than in the

Sunbelt, he did better in the Sunbelt in both elections. Interestingly, in the Frostbelt, Reagan actually won fewer electoral votes while winning more states in 1984 than in 1980, because of the shift of population and so of electoral votes to the South and West.

Ronald Reagan's popularity in the Sunbelt is not a geographic or sectional phenomenon so much as it is an economic one. It reflects his growing support among those with a particular kind of economic interest: growing wealth and/ or income, as distinguished from established wealth and/or income. To be sure, Mondale was the candidate of the poor; those with incomes under $10,000 per year[1] preferred him (55 percent to 45 percent). And the better off a voter was, the more likely he was to prefer Reagan. However, at all income levels above the very lowest, Reagan enjoyed solid majorities. Moreover, Reagan was more popular in the poorer states than in the richer states. It is useful to remember that the Sunbelt is both faster growing and poorer than the Frostbelt:

	Frostbelt	Sunbelt
Income per capita 1983	$12,138.33	$10,682.68
Income per capita Increase (1980-1983)	23.4%	23%
Income per capita Increase (1975-1983)	99.4%	100.5%
New Construction (Billions, 1983)	$56.16	$114.0
New Construction (increase, 1983)	28.1%	32.6%

Indeed, as these statistics indicate, the Sunbelt is not only poorer than the Frostbelt, but also the rate of growth is only slightly better. In addition, unemployment there has been only slightly lower during Reagan's tenure (7.3 percent versus 8.1 percent in 1981 and 9.6 percent versus 10 percent in 1983), despite the markedly lower weekly unemployment benefits ($110 versus $124 in 1983). However, the Sunbelt's prospects for the future, as indicated by new construction contracts, are brighter. Those who suppose that America is "de-industrializing," and is therefore in need of an "industrial policy," must have in mind the Frostbelt and especially the Great Lakes states: manufacturing output (as a percentage of gross national product) has been stable since the 1950s, and productivity has increased, despite the decline of the automobile, steel, rubber, textile, shoe, and apparel industries which predominate in the Frostbelt.

The important economic characteristic of Reagan's support was not so much whether a region is well off as whether its prospects were improving. Accordingly, Reagan did fairly well in established industrial centers, if they

---

1. The official poverty-level for a family of four was $10,178 in 1983.

were prospering and growing in population. Returns from three centers of "smokestack" manufacturing are typical:

	1984	1980
Pittsburgh	43%	45%
Detroit-area	54%	44%
Wayne Co.	42%	36%
Suburbs	67%	55%
Birmingham, Al	60%	53%

Detroit has been relatively prosperous, but it is losing population; Birmingham, the population of which is about 56 percent black, has prospered, and the Birmingham area (Jefferson County) is growing. Pittsburgh is declining in production of wealth and in population.

Burgeoning cities, with young populations, low unemployment, and rapid economic growth supported President Reagan even more strongly in 1984 than 1980:

	1984	1980
Lexington/Fayette, Ky.	64%	50%
Dallas	67%	60%

However, in Sunbelt cities which were growing less quickly than Dallas and Lexington and which, more importantly, have been centers of new industrial development for a decade or more, the President did only a little better than in the prosperous industrial centers of the Northeast:

	1984	1980[2]
Santa Clara County, Ca.	56%	58%
Tucson area	57%	59%

Indeed, some of the quite old industrial centers of the Northeast supported the President nearly as strongly as did the Sunbelt; Connecticut, Delaware, Massachusetts, and perhaps even Maryland are remarkable in this regard. The common view of the Frostbelt derives mainly from the Great Lakes states, including Pennsylvania. Relative to the South and West, these states have older industrial plants. Their populations are shrinking, and their unemployment rates (and unemployment benefits) are well above the national average. More significantly, the new construction rates are well below the national average in the Great Lakes, and per capita incomes, although at or above the national average, are growing at one-third the rate in Sunbelt states. Among these states, Indiana stands out as the state with good prospects (outside the Gary-area). Much like the Sunbelt, Indiana is relatively

---

2. Percentage of two-party vote. Anderson was very strong in Santa Clara County ("Silicon Valley") in 1980.

poor, has lower unemployment benefits (and rates), and it is building. It is the Great Lakes state which supported Reagan most heartily (62 percent).

Considering such economic conditions and patterns of political support, one can appreciate the political acuity of Reagan's question, "Are you better off . . . ?," all the more. Apparently, insofar as voters gave it an economic meaning at all, they did not understand the question literally: "Compare your present assets and incomes with your assets and incomes in 1980." They assessed their hopes. For, if economic interest in the 1984 election were simply a matter of income and assets, then President Reagan should have won the one state that he lost. Minnesota is among the more prosperous and wealthier states in the Frostbelt and indeed in the Union.

The economic interests favoring Mondale are not altogether obvious. Labor unions had backed him very heavily, and from the beginning to the end of his campaign, but the union's members did not support him enough to make a difference; about 52 percent voted for him. His really heavy support came in northern urban cores. For example, Mondale's whole margin of victory in Minnesota was provided by Minneapolis. He also won central New York City, Boston, Philadelphia, San Francisco, Baltimore, Cleveland, and Washington, D.C., with majorities of 65 percent or better. However, in the suburbs, including the blue-collar suburbs, one finds equally heavy support for Reagan. To some extent, Mondale's urban support is a characteristic of his support by blacks and urban ethnic groups. The decisive economic interest, however, seems to be governmental.

Surveyors and demographers have not paid much attention to the selfish interest in governmental programs and employment, even though this is clearly an important economic interest in our society. Mondale's campaign emphasized the beneficence and munificence of the central government very heavily, and this did not go unheard. Consider, for example, that, while working class suburban areas generally preferred Reagan with majorities over 60 percent, Prince Georges County, Maryland, preferred Mondale (59 percent); Prince Georges is home of many members of public employee unions. The communities of more affluent bureaucrats around Washington, D.C.—Alexandria and Arlington, Virginia and Montgomery County, Maryland—preferred Mondale much more narrowly (about 51 percent). These results show how powerfully opposed to the President the bulk of public employees are, especially if one considers that affluent suburban areas did not usually favor the President quite as heavily as working class ones. The opposition is not only by the federal government's employers. There are similar results from other centers of governmental activity: Albany, New York; Salem, Oregon; Harrisburg, Pennsylvania; etc.

The only places that supported Mondale more heavily than urban cores and bureaucrats were the centers of elite higher education. The communities of Harvard, Yale, the University of Wisconsin, and even the University of Virginia supported Walter Mondale more heavily than the nation supported

Ronald Reagan (60.4 percent); the vote at Harvard was nearly four-to-one against the President. Of course, these are centers of American liberalism, but they are also places which are heavily dependent upon government programs, grants, and contracts.

Mondale was stronger where there is more dependency upon federal programs and employment. For example, the rate of federal Aid to Families with Dependent Children (AFDC) is more than triple the national average, and quadruple the Sunbelt average, in Washington, D.C. More generally: the AFDC rate is 65 percent higher, AFDC's payments are almost 45 percent higher, and unemployment benefits are 12 percent higher in the Frostbelt than the Sunbelt. The differences are even greater between the Great Lakes states and the Sunbelt. Of course, federal aid to agriculture is 250 percent higher in the Sunbelt than the Frostbelt, but that aid is a very small proportion of total federal assistance to the various states (one percent in the Frostbelt and four percent in the Sunbelt). Besides, federal aid to agriculture typically takes the form of loan guarantees, rather than outright grants, so the dependency it cultivates is less complete. Accordingly, in the agricultural states, Mondale's popularity was proportionate to the degree of federal assistance; the two best farm states for Mondale, Iowa and North Dakota, are by far the most heavily dependent on federal agricultural aid.

No one should conclude that Mondale's support was any more selfish than Reagan's, but it would be accurate to conclude, as is common, that the pro-Reagan interests were more "anti-government" than the pro-Mondale interests. This difference is often attributed to the "populism" of Reaganites. Although Reagan, like William Jennings Bryan, did enjoy the support of what Arthur M. Schlesinger, Jr., was pleased to call "backwoods zealots," the Populist movement is long since dead, killed off by Progressives and New Dealers. What is more striking is the relation between support for Ronald Reagan and centralization of administration. That is, where the presence of the federal government is strong, so is support for Ronald Reagan. It is often forgotten that the federal presence is, and has always been, greater in the West and the South than in the North and the East. About half the land west of the Mississippi is owned by the central government, as compared with about one-twentieth east of the Mississippi. Similarly, while the amount of federal aid per capita is lower in the West and South, the number of federal bureaucrats per capita is far higher: in the West there are 12 per 1000; in the South, nine; in the old industrial Northeast, four. So-called "anti-government" sentiment runs strongest, not where Bryan was once strong, but where the federal government's influence is most obvious—especially if that area's private sector is thriving.

Because Big Government is still relatively new, we do not yet have a very clear picture of the economic and political interests it fosters. Even so, the clearest pattern of economic division produced by the election seems to be between those who were (or thought they were) economically dependent upon government and those who were not (or did not think they were). These economic interests are quite naturally related to different political principles: those whose interests would be advanced by a welfare/redistributionist state favored Mondale: those regions in which the President was especially strong, were prosperous not because of, but despite governmental programs.

Partisan Divisions

Politically, the most impressive result of the 1984 elections was the difference between the presidential returns and the returns at lower levels. In particular, the Republicans won 97% of the Electoral College's votes, but only 42% of the seats in the House of Representatives. What explains the differences between the presidential and congressional returns? To answer this question adequately, we shall have to return to some of the fundamental principles of American constitutional government. However, before doing that, we must consider some common opinions about the character of the national support for the political parties.

Republicans have tried to downplay the Democratic victory, claiming that Democrats were able to maintain their majority in the House by gerrymandering after the 1980 Census. As evidence of this, they point to the fact that Republicans received 49.9 percent of the popular votes cast for the House of Representatives. As further evidence, Republicans note that the Democrats had 49 uncontested seats; Republicans enjoyed only 14 unopposed seats. Since thirty of the unopposed seats were in the South and so were presumably conservative, some Republicans liked to claim immediately after the election that Democratic dominance of the House is not nearly as great as their numbers indicate. Finally, Republicans claim that they lost many races very narrowly, so that not only did gerrymandering prevent them from getting safe seats it also made them squander resources on narrow victories and defeats.

These Republicans claim far too much. In the first place, because votes in uncontested races are not counted, national popular vote totals for the congressional races do not measure popular support very accurately. After all, precisely if the claim about gerrymandering were true, Democrats would have to enjoy some substantial popularity at the local level. On the whole, the same kind of support is necessary for the enjoyment of unopposed seats. The fact that many unopposed seats are also conservative does not make them any the less Democratic; in the Congress, Republicans have never before been able to count on Democrats, however conservative, for any partisan vote, as the votes of conservative Democrats in the 98th Congress demonstrate. Finally, that Republicans lost many seats narrowly was certainly true, but so did the Democrats. In fact, the Republicans won 16 close races and the Democrats won 14.[3] Consider also the senatorial races, i.e., in races in which redistricting could not have been important. Republicans won 17 of 33 seats, while polling 50.6% of the two-party vote. Nor could redistricting have much to do with the facts that Reagan ran ahead of 22 of the Republican candidates for the Senate, and that he polled more votes than the Republican candidates for the House in 45 states. So there really was a rather clear difference between the popular support for the President and that for all other Republicans nationally. Democrats claim that the difference was due to the citizens' intentions to check the President with Congress. Strangely, no pollster had enquired about this, and so we must rely upon the election returns, which provide no support for the Democrats' contention.

Most strikingly, there was far more popular interest in the presidential than the congressional election: 15.7 million more people voted for president than for congressmen; because Mondale ran 448,000 votes behind the Democratic congressional candidates, one might conclude that that 15.7 million voted for Reagan. If anything, this suggests that voters were more concerned to check the Congress with the President than the other way around. Furthermore, if voters did intend to check the president with the Congress, then they should have returned a Democratic majority to the Senate as well as the House. In sum, if the voters intended any checking to result, then it would be checking of the House of Representatives; after all, the Senate, at least as much as the president, is designed to limit the power of the House. In addition, Republicans were able to gain 13 seats by defeating Democratic incumbents, and to win in 18 of the 25 districts for which there were no incumbents. On the other hand, Democrats were able to defeat only three Republican incumbents; all three were very close races, despite the fact that in one the Republican was a convicted felon and in another he was a notorious adulterer. Given the political advantage of incumbency, these results show that, at the margin, citizens were inclined toward Republicans for the House. However, above all, the Democrats' claim is vitiated by the fact that they conducted neither national, nor, so far as I know, local "Check the President" campaigns, whereas Republicans did attempt a sporadic, national "Support the President" congressional campaign.

A more striking pattern of support for the Democrats occurs along ethnic or racial lines. We have already noticed that Walter Mondale enjoyed the support of a massive majority of black Americans. He also had the support of a majority (53 percent) of "Hispanics" (an extremely ambiguous category, which includes Mexican-, Cuban-, and Puerto Rican-Americans, and increasing numbers of South and Central Americans). These patterns are continued in the House returns. The Democratic candidates won all of the ten congressional districts which have the highest proportion of Black Ameri-

---

3. I counted a close race as one in which the difference between the candidates was less than 10,000 votes.

cans (86 percent of the popular vote, four unopposed seats); some of these districts were designed by federal courts, on the principle of affirmative action, to return black Representatives. The Democrats also won all of the top ten Irish (61.9 percent, three unopposed seats), "Hispanic" (64.8 percent, three unopposed seats), and Polish (64.2 percent, none unopposed) districts. Republicans were very strong among Germans (66.3 percent), English (60.6 percent), and French (65.4 percent, but three unopposed Democratic seats), but these ethnic groups are not (or have not been) concentrated in congressional districts as are the traditionally Democratic groups. In sum, of the ninety districts with the heaviest concentrations of various ethnic or racial groups, the Democrats won 62 (53 percent of the popular vote, plus 15 unopposed seats). In other words, Democrats have been significantly more successful, as well as more practiced, in ethnic and racial appeals.

By their very nature, racial and ethnic appeals are more effective at the local level than at the national level. At the national level, such appeals likely to lose more voters than they gain, because every racial or ethnic group is a national minority. Moreover, at the national level, racial and ethnic appeals are not likely even to gain the groups to whom the appeals are directed, because most voters understand that ethnic and racial ties as such cannot be nationally respectable, although they may be very real locally. For example, the rather blatant attempt of the Democratic party to appeal to Italian-Americans seems to have backfired not only for Walter Mondale, who did worse (37 percent, down three percent) than Carter among Italian-Americans despite Mrs. Ferraro's presence on the ticket, but perhaps even at the Congressional level, where Democrats received 51 percent in the heavily Italian districts, the same percentage as identify themselves as Democrats. This kind of reaction might have been expected by the Democrats, for surveys show that substantial majorities (from 72 percent among "Hispanics" to 90 percent among Germans) of every ethnic and racial group—except blacks (55 percent)—believe that the national government has no special obligation to any ethnic or racial group.

The character of the support of racial and ethnic groups for the Democrats is much the same as that of the other demographic classes which are commonly thought to compose the New Deal coalition. Organized labor, certain ethnic and racial groups, the South, and the heavily urbanized/industrialized Northeast strongly support Democrats for the House of Representatives. However, for the last five or six Presidential elections, the Democrats have been unable to coalesce these groups nationally; more recently, the same trend seems to have appeared in senatorial races. One might put it this way: the New Deal coalition still exists; however, it is not a national coalition, because it must be put together every day in the House of Representatives.

The only genuinely national support for the Democrats comes from the economic interests (including blacks) which are heavily dependent upon Big Government. Numerically, the Big Government faction could become a majority only if Social Security recipients were included in it. So far, Republicans have attempted, more or less successfully, to neutralize the extremely touchy issues swirling about the Social Security programs. As a matter of political principle, as distinguished from merely selfish interest, Big Government has less popular appeal today than a decade ago. Indeed, it is an old Republican canard that the Democratic party is the party of Big Government, for the New Deal did not favor bigger government for its own sake, but as means to the solution of particular problems. Thus, the current Democratic leadership including Mondale and Speaker Thomas P. O'Neill have attempted to supply a moral-political principle for Big Government, by claiming that Big Government stands for "compassion."

Most leading Democrats simply do not understand that their party has been incapable of a genuinely national political appeal for almost two decades. Typically, Paul Simon, who defeated Charles Percy for an Illinois Senate seat, put "assistance to the least fortunate," as the most important way for the Democratic party to serve the country; not even the welfare state, but income-redistribution without objective standard of need, would appear to be the aim of Senator Simon's Democratic Party. Only Democratic Governor Bruce Babbit of Arizona sees the disjunction between the national and the local support for Democrats. Writing in the *Wall Street Journal*, Babbit remarked:

> This two-tiered party is the creation of ticket splitters who reject the national party as offering little more than a compendium of constituent-group wish-lists. At the state level, however, voters still perceive Democrats as independent advocates for the public interest, even though that can mean parting company with traditional supporters.

Governor Babbit's rather gentle way of saying that, as a national party, the Democracy has lost its principles, reminds of the prudence of the Framers of the Constitution, who understood that the public interest is something different at the local level than at the national level, and who framed our political institutions accordingly.

Consider the political purposes for which the House, Senate, and Presidency were designed. As we read in *The Federalist*, all three were intended to be democratically representative, but each of something different: the House was to be representative of the people's narrower or more parochial interests, in order to treat effectively the more urgent or short-term ("bread-and-butter") issues; the Senate was to represent the States as states, i.e., as the important independent political subdivisions of the nation, and so to be concerned with "the national character," i.e., with the broadest matters of policy, including the consistency of all policies with one another; the President's mode of election was designed to produce an executive with broad national support, in order that the administration of government be swift, efficient, and uniform throughout the nation. The Framers supposed that the public good would be served by the cooperation of these three, and toward that end provided constitutionally for the involvement of the President in some of the deliberations of the House and Senate. Public evils were to be avoided—certainly not eliminated—by the House and Senate checking one another, as well as by the House and Senate together checking the President. As a result of this three-tiered system of representation, the Framers hoped, government would govern in accord with the will of a genuinely national majority, which would, in the words of *Federalist* 51, "seldom [be formed] on any other principles than those of justice and the general good." Of course, the Framers did not contemplate national political parties as formers of the national majority; perhaps they did not suppose that national majorities would be especially difficult to form. However this may be, the existence of parties did not change the constitutional functions of the House, Senate, and presidency so much as augment them.

The arrival of Big Government in the past two decades changed the operation of American constitutional government. Administration of many local interests is undertaken from the center by the federal bureaucracy, or by the bureaucracy in conjunction with Congress, and especially with members of the House, who have closer local connections; about one-half of the federal bureaucracy has been independent of the executive branch since the mid-1970s. This means that, within the national government, there exists not only the "two-tiered" concern with the public interest noted by Governor Babbit, but also an institutionalization of both tiers, which frustrates the creation of a single, genuinely national majority. In this circumstance, Democrats have become incapable of a genuinely national appeal to the public interest, because their political power is so much the effect of their bureaucratic programs servicing local or parochial interests. But Republicans are almost equally incapable of a national appeal which is harmonious with the various local [non-national] interests represented [serviced] by members of the House. The classic instance of this is the widespread popular support for reduction of domestic spending and the equally widespread popular resistance to cutting any particular domestic program. Therefore, it should not be surprising that President Reagan was most popular in those regions where localized economic development proceeded in the face of a large federal presence.

Conclusion

Have we reached that "Deadlock of Democracy" which political scientists feared so much in the late 1950s and early 1960s? Is American society incapable of the formation of a national political majority? The election of 1984 shows that the Democratic party, as it is presently constituted and as it is likely to be constituted in the foreseeable future, is incapable of forming a national political majority. What of the Republicans?

In two states, Texas and North Carolina, the Republican party ran genuinely integrated campaigns, and won seats in the House and Senate while returning large majorities for President Reagan. It is sufficient for present purposes to note that House and Senate candidates ran with one another, as well as with President Reagan: Republicans presented a united front. Yet it should also be noted that these states are parts of what used to be the solidly Democratic South. Texas Democrats, who still have nine unopposed seats, lost four close races, permitting a Republican increase to ten of twenty-seven seats. In North Carolina, Republicans won four of six close races, gaining five of eleven seats. Demographically, both states are rather typical of the Sunbelt.

These races show how very difficult it would be for the Republican party to gain a genuine national majority. That is, they indicate what a massive effort would be required for the Republican party to achieve a partisan realignment. For North Carolina and Texas Republicans ran under the most favorable conditions and still did not gain majorities of the House delegations.

Although the election of 1984 was not the revolutionary event for which Republicans and Democrats seemed to hope at their national conventions, it also was not the politically unimportant affair which the political intellectuals and journalists promised. Voters clearly accepted Ronald Reagan's politics and rejected Walter Mondale's. Moreover, unlike in the election of 1976, the voters clearly preferred a man with the courage of his convictions, not just a nice guy with a "democratic personality." In presidential politics, two important changes were effected. First, the open interest-group liberalism of labor unions, the National Organization for Women, and the Rainbow Coalition, and the dealing that goes with it, appears to be dead in the Democratic party; the newly elected Democratic Chairman, Paul Kirk, declared that he intended to "shed the interest-group image" of the party. Second, the political era stretching from Theodore Roosevelt's "New Nationalism" and Woodrow Wilson's "New Freedom," when every self-respecting party and candidate was outfitted with a collection of new social and economic programs—"a vision"—seems to be over for the foreseeable future, as public attention shifts to the problems of paying for these programs and administering them justly.

Yet the pundits of the media were correct in one respect: the decisive political issue of our time was not decided. At all levels of politics, selfish and parochial interests were very much drawn up along lines of political principle: expansion of the private sector versus expansion of the public sector, or economic growth versus redistribution—not to say, government of the people versus bureaucracy. Despite the fact that neither national party chose to present this issue as the central matter of public choice, the election of 1984 reveals that this principled difference—not the differences between blacks and whites, men and women, rich and poor, Sunbelt and Frostbelt—is the most intransigent in the nation today.

The Campaign Strategy of the 1984 Election: Partisan Realignment or Minority Party Victory?

Thomas F. Payne

The purpose of this essay is to discuss the strategies used by the two major parties as they contested the 1984 presidential election. Such a discussion may seem beside the point. So overwhelming was Ronald Reagan's victory over Walter Mondale that it hardly seems that the Republicans needed any campaign plan at all beyond raising the standard of the President's reelection and calling the voters to rally to it. On the other side of the coin, it seems that the Democratic candidates likewise had little need for any campaign strategy. In retrospect—and perhaps even in prospect—it does not appear that any maneuver of theirs, no matter how adroit, could have fended off inevitable defeat. It is important to understand, however, that this situation did not arise spontaneously but was the product of underlying factors in American political life and of the actions of political leaders who acted with reference to these factors. It is important to come to an understanding of these factors, therefore, for a number of reasons. The second term of the Reagan presidency will in large measure be shaped with reference to the forces which brought it to power, and politicians both within and without the administration will act with reference to them as they position themselves for future national elections.

Coalition-Building: An Overview of the Strategies of Presidential Campaigns

The strategy of any campaign, whether electoral, military, or of some other kind, is determined by a number of factors. Among them are the resources available to the contestants, the ground over which the campaign is to be waged, the leadership and organization available to the two sides, and the object of the campaign. Of these factors, the object is by far the most important, since all other factors assume their importance with respect to it. The objective of the two parties in a campaign for the American presidency can be very simply stated. It is to win a majority of votes in the Electoral College, the body that officially elects the president. According to the Constitution, each state is entitled to a number of electors equal to the number of senators and representatives that the state sends to the Congress. Again according to the Constitution, each state is free to determine how it selects its electors, but in practice, every state has adopted the same winner-take-all, popular-election method of choosing its electors. In each state, the party runs a slate of electors pledged to vote for the party's nominee, and the slate receiving the largest number of popular votes in a given state becomes the official electors for that state and casts its votes in the electoral college for its party's nominees.

Because a candidate wins all of a state's electoral college votes by winning a plurality of its popular votes, a candidate may be elected legally by capturing less than a majority of popular votes, either in any single state or nationally. Thus it is possible for a candidate to be elected by a minority of the voters, if that candidate captures a plurality of popular votes in enough states to form a majority in the Electoral College. This is the minimal object of any presidential campaign. However, because the United States is a democracy, albeit a constitutional one, a president so elected would lack an element of legitimacy and would govern under a cloud. Therefore, few presidential campaigns have consciously pursued the minimal goal of securing the bare requirements of legal election. In fact, only occasionally has a president been elected by a minority of popular voters. Most presidential campaigns seek to satisfy both the legal and the democratic requirements of election by winning a popular majority of voters so distributed as to be a popular majority in states with a majority of electoral votes.

Because the major parties are not thoroughly united entities, but coalitions of regional and ideological interest groups, the first step in amassing this twofold majority is to secure the unity of the party's leaders and of its rank and file behind the nominees of the party's convention. Once the party base is secured, the party and its candidate will attempt to broaden their base of support by appealing to other economic and political interest groups so as to form the properly distributed national majority. In this work, the starting positions of the two parties are not equal. One party will have a decided advantage over the other. Although analogies drawn from chess are frequently used to illuminate the complexities of politics and political strategies, politics is not chess. There is no gamemaster to clear the board after the last game and start the two candidates and parties off equally in terms of resources and position on the board. Presidential campaigns take place within the dynamic panorama of American politics, and the conditions under which every campaign is conducted are shaped by currents of influence flowing from previous elections, the incumbent's conduct of his presidency, population shifts, long-term economic developments, and other factors.

Moreover, not even the inequality of political advantage is itself evenly distributed, with one party being advantaged in one election, but disadvantaged in the next. Both of the two major parties have gone through long periods in the past when the advantage in presidential electoral politics could be expected to be theirs. From 1832, generally considered the beginning of the modern two-party system, until 1860, the Jacksonian Democrats dominated American politics, with the Whigs in the minority. From 1860 until 1932, the Republicans were the dominant party, their domination being renewed and modified in 1896. Since Franklin D. Roosevelt's election in 1932, the conventional wisdom has been that the Democrats are the dominant party. However, there are reasons to believe that since 1968, this has no longer been true, or, if true, true only with qualifications.

During the period of its dominance, thirty-five years on average, the majority political party can confidently expect to be supported by a relatively stable coalition of voters. This coalition is put together during the periodic crises in American electoral politics called "party realignments." Because party realignments are something like political volcanoes which decisively reshape the political terrain over which electoral campaigns are fought, it would be wise to say something about their dynamics here. The focus of this discussion will be on the realigning elections of 1860 and 1932. The first of these brought Lincoln and the Republicans to power and led to the Civil War. The second of these occasioned the New Deal Democratic coalition of Franklin Roosevelt to power and led to nearly a generation of liberal domination of American public life. The election of 1984 must be seen as taking place in the shadow of this generation of dominant liberalism.

Party Realignments and Electoral Strategies

Party realignments are generally the product of two factors: a crisis in national policy; and changes in the composition and distribution of the electorate. In the period before the party realignment of 1860, American politics were agitated by the issue of the opening of Western land. The most spectacular and divisive component of this issue was, of course, the question of the introduction of slavery into the new territories, but there were other important matters of policy to be resolved as well. Were the lands to be sold to westward immigrants, or were they to be given away free? If there were to be no charge, would the lost revenue be made up in import tariffs which would favor the interests of Eastern manufacturers over the agricultural interests of the South and Midwest? Finally, of course, there was the question of states' rights and secession.

The Republican party became dominant in 1860 because it provided the nation with an agenda for settling these questions definitively. In the years following 1860, the Republicans crushed the secessionist movement of the South and proclaimed the supremacy of the Union over the states. They opened the West up to free labor and excluded slavery. They passed the Homestead Act, which gave most of the West away free to small holders, and they subsidized the building of a transcontinental railroad by giving what was left of the West away to the railroads. They also passed tariff measures moderately favorable to industrial interests. Once these innovations had been introduced, their perpetuation came to be in the interest of a large segment of the population which benefitted from them, either directly or indirectly. At least for the next generation, therefore, the Republicans could be sure of their votes.

Prior to the realignment of 1932, the most pressing issues facing the nation stemmed from the industrialization of the economy during the preceding generation and the urbanization of the work force. The most obvious manifestation of the problems connected with these developments was massive unemployment and retirement insecurity once a large segment of the population had become dependent upon wages for its livelihood. A concomitant set of problems was composed by the necessity of integrating the urban work force, largely composed of European immigrants or their descendants, into the fabric of American cultural and political life, theretofore dominated by Republicans, who were White, Anglo-Saxon, and Protestant and who dwelt in small towns. Therefore, the coalition which elected Roosevelt so decisively in 1932 and reelected him and other Democrats in 1936, 1940, 1944, 1948, 1960, and 1964 had as one of its major components the ethnic working folk of the cities of the northeastern and mid-Atlantic states. This coalition also included all the states of the old Confederacy, which likewise resented the Republican-WASP domination of the nation. Roosevelt's New Deal with its Social Security system, regulation of industry, relief for unemployment, and programs of agricultural subsidies which benefitted the largely rural South, served the interests of this voter coalition and kept the nation Democratic for the next 36 years, despite interludes of Republicans in the White House.

The formation of such coalitions of economic and political interest groups in party realignments is usually presaged by a shift in population patterns which express themselves as sectional realignments in the Electoral College. Prior to the realignment of 1860, the Jacksonian Democrats' domination of American politics manifested itself in the lock the Jacksonians had on the electoral votes of the "New West," chiefly the states of the eastern Mississippi River Valley, both north and south of the Ohio. The states of old New England were generally controlled by the opposition Whigs, as were Pennsylvania and the old planting states of the Eastern seaboard. In New York the Democrats of Tammany Hall could generally swing the state's electoral votes into the Democratic column and win the election for the Democrats, although both New York and Virginia were swing states which could go either way and on which a great deal of electoral strategy focused therefore. The key election of 1860 took place against a background of further population shifts caused by the westward migration and the admission of new states, with new electoral votes, to the Union. The slavery question sundered the unity of the former "New West" and forced the states of the Midwest into the Republican alliance with their formerly Whiggish rivals in New England and Pennsylvania. The South, both old and new, became unalterably and solidly Democratic (except during the period of Reconstruction), while the border states and New York with its Democratically inclined Irish Catholics were the swing states.

The party realignment of 1932 was also preceded by changes in the population which were the precursors of a political realignment of the sections. During the period preceding the First World War, there was a huge migration of European Roman Catholics and Jews into the cities of the Northeast. By 1932, the children of these immigrants were able to vote, and they did so in numbers large enough to carry the New England and mid-Atlantic states out of the Republican alignment and into the camp of Roosevelt and the Democrats.

The discussion of the dynamics of partisan alignment and realignment leads to the following conclusions about the strategies of parties in presidential campaigns. The electoral strategy of the dominant party must be to maintain unity within its own ranks, thus preserving the coalition which brought it to power. The minority party, on the other hand, must maintain unity in its own ranks and try to drive a wedge between the various components of the majority coalition by appealing to disaffected factions within the majority party, offering them candidates and policies more to their liking and likely to attract their temporary support. The minority party will also try to nominate men who are in a sense "above party politics" (i.e., men whose accomplishments are so outstanding that they may be said to deserve to be elected president despite the status of the party nominating them). For this reason, when minority parties have won the presidency, they have frequently done so by nominating successful generals. During the long period of Republican party dominance (1860-1932), the unity of the party was often threatened by rifts between the party's Eastern base, which preferred an uninflated currency and protectionism in tariff policy, and its base in the Midwest and West, where debtor agricultural interests favored inflation. No less troublesome to party unity was the division between more conservative elements of the party with vested interests in the spoils system and the progressive elements favoring reform. Nonetheless, during this period the Democrats were able to take advantage of the Republican fissures in only four of 28 presidential elections.

During the period of uncontested Democratic party dominance in this century (1932-1968), party unity was always in danger because of tensions between the party's Northern and Southern wings over questions involving the civil rights of Southern blacks. Roosevelt was able to maintain the unity of the party by suppressing attempts to raise the issue at party conventions, but after Roosevelt, Democratic party leaders were not so successful in avoiding this issue. This failure had no real effect on Democratic electoral fortunes until 1968, when Southern disaffection with the civil rights policy of the national Democratic administration was one element among many contributing to the defeat of Hubert Humphrey and the election of Richard Nixon. Thus, between 1932 and 1968, the Republicans were able to capture the White House only twice (in 1952 and 1956), and then only by nominating Dwight D. Eisenhower, whose personal prestige as one of the victorious generals of World War II was probably more responsible for his election than the fact of his nomination by the Republicans.

In the election just completed, the Democrats appeared to be following the classical strategic plan of the majority party, as Walter Mondale seemed to be trying to rally the Roosevelt coalition to its old allegiance by raising the issues of economic security and the equitable distribution of wealth. These issues had been responsible for the realignment of 1932 and had undergirt the campaign rhetoric and party platforms of every Democratic campaign since that time. In the primaries, Mondale had been the candidate for nomination of the established Democratic leadership. As the officially nominated candidate of the party he ran a most orthodox campaign, trying to unify the party by offering a bit of something to all the interest groups within the party, attacking the Republicans for unfairness by supposedly favoring the rich in tax policies, and promising to reserve and extend the benefits of the welfare state, albeit in the most cost-effective way possible. Reagan, for his part, appeared to be having recourse to the expected strategy of a minority party candidate. He took full advantage of his incumbency by taking every opportunity to "look presidential" (e.g., by travelling to Europe for the commemoration of the Normandy invasion and to Los Angeles to open the Olympics). In his campaign rhetoric he emphasized the successes of his administration and the unpopularity of the Carter-Mondale administration as he asked the voters, "Are you better off now than you were four years ago?"

In the end, Mondale did not succeed in rallying the New Deal coalition, and there is substantial reason to believe that more than the personal popularity and political success of an incumbent president prevented this. The New Deal coalition was not there to be rallied. Since 1968, a number of the elements of the old alliance, e.g., the South and the Roman Catholics, have abjured their unswerving loyalty to Democratic presidential candidates, and those elements of the coalition remaining true to the party do not seem to be strong enough to dominate national elections. Moreover, since 1968, new groupings of voters have been entered on the political balance sheet. Their partisan allegiance is not clear, but it is certain that at least at the level of presidential politics, these new elements are not unqualified New Dealers. These changes may not amount to a thorough realignment of the parties at all level of politics, but they do add up to a change in the strategic political environment at the national level and to substantial advantages for Republican presidential candidates. The adroit use of these advantages were as responsible for Reagan's election in 1980 and his reelection in 1984 as were the failures of the Carter-Mondale administration and the popularity won by Reagan during his first term.

The Unravelling of the New Deal Coalition

The changes brought about in American politics since 1968, much like the clearly identifiable realignments of earlier years, have their roots in a crisis in policy and in changes in the demographic profile of the voting-age population. The policy crisis might be termed the crisis of the liberal welfare state, while the population changes have been caused by the coming of age of the postwar baby boom and by large-scale migrations from the states of the Northeast and Midwest to the South and West.

The policies characteristic of the liberal welfare state as it reached its fully developed form in the mid-sixties were: the redistribution of income from the more-well-off to the less-well-off; the containment of Communism; the protection of the civil rights of blacks; and the substitution of forms of social organization and norms of behavior based on the findings of modern social science for more traditional values. The pursuit of these policies created tensions within the Democratic party and a sequence of policy crises for the nation at large as taxation, inflation, and the federal deficit necessitated by policies of redistribution came to be regarded as burdensome by an increasing number of voters; the war in Vietnam discredited the policy of containing Communism; the attention given to blacks provoked resentments among whites, especially Southern whites; and the changes in the national mores provoked protest movements over such issues as abortion, school prayer, drugs, and law and order generally.

As a result of this crisis in policy, a number of changes in the characteristic voting patterns of significant groupings of the citizenry has taken place. First, the Democratic Party has lost its hold on the formerly solid South. The loss became evident in 1968, when George Wallace, the segregationist former governor of Alabama, ran on a third party ticket and carried a majority of Southern states and a majority of Southern electoral votes. Thereafter, the South has not given its electoral votes to any Democratic presidential candidate with the exception of Jimmy Carter, the candidate of 1976, who, as former governor of Georgia, could be considered the South's favorite son. To be sure, the Democratic party remains powerful in the South, largely because of the large number of incumbent Democratic officeholders and the died-in-the-wool Democratic tradition of many Southerners. Nonetheless, at the national level the South seems to be Republican-prone for the foreseeable future and this inclination is being continually reinforced by the migration of Northerners from the Midwest and Northeast into the South. The middle-class immigrants tend to be Republican-oriented, and even the working-class immigrants tend to be more open to Republican influence than were working class Americans of a generation ago. Unions are weak in the South, and therefore Southern workers are less subject to the pro-Democratic influence of organized labor's political action apparatus.

A second change has been the weakening of the Democratic hold on the ethnic population of the cities of the North. A generation ago, this population was overwhelmingly working class and open to the influence of the labor movement. By the late 1960s and the 1970s many of these voters had made it into the middle class. The increasing burden of welfare state taxation has made the Republican Party increasingly attractive to them, and the attenuation to the old ethnic ties has undermined their loyalty to the Democratic Party, the party of the European immigrants. In addition, those elements of the ethnic population which remain working class tend to be turned away from the Democrats by the increasing McGovernization of the party.

Of course, there has always been some possibility that increases in the number of black voters could compensate the Democrats for the erosion of their position among white Southerners and ethnic Northerners. However, this remains just a possibility. Blacks are a potentially powerful voting bloc, but they tend not to register and vote as frequently as whites. In order to increase black influence in presidential elections, as well as to increase his own influence within the Democratic Party, Jesse Jackson spearheaded a large black voter registration drive as part of the 1984 campaign. The ultimate impact of these efforts remains to be seen, however.

The third major change in partisan politics to take place in American politics since 1968 has been the McGovernization of the Democratic Party, the sustained leftward drift of the party's preferred policies and of the personal persuasion of its activists. The roots of McGovernism lie in the civil rights movement of the mid-1960s and the antiwar protest movement of the late 1960s and early 1970s. Large numbers of college students were involved in these political activities, which in their initial states were organized outside the boundaries of traditional party politics. In 1968, however, in order to further its goals, the student left decided to enter the Democratic Party and gain influence on national policy thereby. As this generation of student activists has become older, they have risen in position and influence within the Democratic Party.

The two attitudes characteristic of the student left, both in its bygone youth and in its approaching middle age, are a doubt about the legitimacy of the American political and economic system and a concern with the victims of the system's inequities. Three broad policy lines can be associated with this attitude. The first is dovishness in foreign policy and the abandonment of the containment of Communism. The second is the promotion of racial justice understood as the imposition of affirmative action and other forms of racial entitlements in hiring and other forms of economic activities so that those who had been discriminated against in the past, blacks and women, might be free of the effects of past injustice. The third policy line of the McGovernites is the advocacy of "reform" both within the Democratic Party and the nation at large. Again reform meant the imposition of quotas for the selection of delegates to party conventions and other officeholders so that those previously excluded from power, again blacks, women, and other minorities, might at last be included (presumably in order to defend what they had gained in racial justice).

The presidential campaign of 1972 was the occasion of the massive entrance of the student left (both undergraduate and postgraduate) into Democratic party politics. It was inevitable that the nominating convention they controlled would nominate George McGovern, the candidate of peace (in Vietnam) and of reform, who had rewritten the rules of Democratic delegate selection in the wake of the 1968 convention to provide for racial, sexual, and age group quotas. McGovern's nomination was opposed by Democratic Party regulars, including the Democratic officeholders of the Northeast, men most obviously epitomized by bread-and-butter politicians such as Tip O'Neill, who owe their positions to the organizational strength of the pre-McGovernite Democratic Party; Southern Democrats, whose typical representative might be found in men such as Senator Huey Long of Louisiana; and organized labor, symbolized by the person of George Meany, president of the AFL-CIO and staunchest of anti-McGovernites. McGovern's resounding defeat by Richard Nixon in 1972 provoked the party regulars into a determined counterattack on the McGovernites during the 1974 miniconvention. Their efforts achieved some temporary success, but by the election of 1976, Democratic officeholders found it no longer profitable to continue to oppose the McGovernization of the party. During the 1976 campaign, the Carter–Mondale ticket made substantial concessions to the McGovernites in their campaign rhetoric. In office, the Carter–Mondale administration appointed a substantial number of McGovernites to second and third-echelon posts in the government. So pleased was George McGovern with the Carter–Mondale appointments that he extolled them as exactly the same as he would have made, had he been elected.

The McGovernization of the Democratic party has probably been the major reason for the decline of the Democratic Party as a force in presidential politics. This leftward movement has accelerated the flight, referred to above, of white Southerners and ethnic Northerners, out of the Democratic coalition. Moreover, the presence of the McGovernites in large numbers within the ranks of the party activists imparts a leftward skewing to the Democratic nominating process. Candidates for the nomination must therefore campaign in the primaries further to the left than is prudent, given the moderately conservative mood which has pervaded the American electorate since 1968. In itself such a state of affairs need not be disastrous since a successful primary candidate, once he has won the nomination, can move toward the political center. Candidates for the Republican nomination normally campaign to the right in the primaries in order to win the support of activists and then campaign toward the center in the general election. However, such is the ideological commitment of the Democratic McGovernites that they do not permit their nominees a similar freedom. This element of inflexibility contributes to the unravelling of the Democratic coalition, as local candidates find it to their advantage to dissociate themselves from the national ticket. These facts influence Democratic campaign strategies, and created acute problems for Walter Mondale in the 1984 campaign.

The fourth major change in the American political landscape to have taken place since 1968 as the result of the crisis in liberal policy is the rise of the New Right and its entrance into the Republican Party. This development was presaged by the Goldwater presidential campaign of 1964 and by the third party candidacy of George Wallace. Throughout the course of the sixties, the Gold-waterites and the Wallaceites had each registered their separate protests against the regnant liberalism, but it was not until the 1970s that they joined forces against their common liberal foe. The Republicans who nominated Goldwater in 1964 were in that wing of the party that rejected the New Deal root and branch, and that, had its candidate been successful in 1964, would have tried to undo the policies connected with it. Goldwaterite grievances against the New Deal Democrats were primarily economic in nature. The Goldwaterites considered the redistributionist and regulatory policies of the New Deal as economically unsound per se and as subversive of the economic basis of constitutional liberty. In foreign policy, the Goldwaterites tended to be isolationist. For instance, at the 1964 Republican convention, antiunion re-marks were more heartily applauded than anticommunist ones. Although the Goldwaterites claimed that the majority of Americans agreed with their doc-trine of self-reliance and individualism, the public tended to see them as rather typically Republican country club elitists and their movement as a rebirth of the "economic royalism" Roosevelt had campaigned against in 1936.

The Wallaceite movement, on the other hand, was not based primarily on objections to the economic policies of the liberal welfare state, but to its social policies. In the South, the home base of the Wallace movement, Wallace's ap-peal was grounded on resentment against the Civil Rights Act of 1964 and the Voting Rights Act of 1965. In the North, where civil rights for blacks were less controversial, the Wallace vote was a protest against black urban rioting, the rising crime rate, and the widespread feeling that the welfare state was too solicitous of the undeserving. In time, this movement of the disaffected lost its identification with the person of George Wallace and became less interested in issues involving the black citizenry. The lasting effect of the Wallace movement was to create a precedent for voting against liberal Democratic candidates among social classes prone to Democratic loyalties in the past. As the liberal social agenda came more and more to be the policy of the federal government, these unorganized, largely grass roots conservative elements became ever more open to the organizational efforts of conservative activists. Opposition to gun control, opposition to the Supreme Court's ban on prayer in the public schools, opposition to abortion, a widespread anxiety over the decay in mor-als and the rising crime rate, a concern over the flaccidity of liberal defense and foreign policies—all these issues became the standards to which conservative leaders rallied a constituency, thus giving the conservative movement the vital element it lacked in the mid-sixties, popular appeal.

By the 1976 campaign, the New Right was sufficiently organized to be a factor within national politics. A grass-roots movement, it challenged the nomination of Gerald Ford, the candidate of the established Republican lead-ership. By 1980, Ronald Reagan, the candidate supported by the New Right rank and file, won enough popular support in the primaries to assure him an unopposed nomination at the party's national convention. However, it would be a mistake to assume that with this victory, the New Right became the Republican establishment. Within the Republican party, the New Right exists in alliance with liberal Republicans, neoconservatives, and moderate Republicans. The first group is quite clearly on the wane within the Republican party, while the second cannot be said to be truly a factor within the party like the other three. Rather neoconservatism represents a set of political convictions and policy preferences among certain Republican officeholders, intellectuals, and "policy professionals." In other words, there are no neoconservative Republican masses, but only neoconservative Republican intellectuals and officeholders whose appeal is both to the Republican New Right and to the party moderates.

The party's moderate wing may be said to be its true establishment. The titular leader of the moderate wing is former President Gerald Ford, while its active head may be said to be former White House Chief of Staff and present Secretary of the Treasury James Baker. According to the press, the difference between the moderate Republicans and the New Right is that the former are more "pragmatic," whereas the latter are more "ideological." These distinctions are facile and fail to give a complete account of the differences between the two groups. By and large, the formative political experiences of the moderate Republicans have been in the fifties and sixties, when the Democrats dominated electoral politics and liberals dominated the national policy agenda. A significant proportion of the moderate wing of the Republican party has held appointive office in the executive branch of government during the Eisenhower, Nixon, and Ford administrations. They constitute the reserve of administrative talent available to Republican presidents, and it is their almost inevitable prominence and power in Republican administrations that entitles them to be called the Republican establishment. The marriage within the Republican party between the rambunctious and electorally conscious New Right and the self–styled pragmatic managers of the establishment has been a stormy one. It could not be otherwise, in view of the differences in collective personality between the two wings of the party. For the foreseeable future, therefore, one of the principle tasks of the Republican national leadership and of the Republican national candidates will be to prevent either of the partners from divorcing the other or seeking a separation at election time.

The four political changes enumerated and discussed above are taking place against a background of demographic changes occasioned by the coming of age of the postwar baby boom, the economic development of the South and West, and the southward and westward migration of the population induced by this economic development. These demographic shifts work together to give the Republicans a considerable potential advantage in presidential elections. Together the states west of the Mississippi River and the states of the old Confederacy command 270 electoral votes, slightly more than the majority needed to elect a president. Since the election of Nixon in 1968, the majority of states of the West have been carried by the Republican ticket in presidential elections. The once solidly Democratic South has voted for the Democratic ticket only once since 1968, when in 1976, it was carried by the South's favorite son, Jimmy Carter. By and large, the states of the South and West are inclined towards the Republicans because their populations are conservative, i.e., skeptical of the wisdom of governmental activism in society and in the economy. Since they rightly see the Democratic Party as the party of governmental activism, they vote for Republican candidates. However, there are at least two factors at work in the South and West which prevent the prudent observer from concluding that for the foreseeable future, the Republican party will have a lock on these electoral votes, and therewith on the presidency.

The first destabilizing factor is the fact that many of the most populous states in the Southern-Western bloc (Texas, California, Oregon, and Washington) are inclined toward a Republican allegiance only by very narrow margins. The states of the Pacific West (California, Oregon, and Washington) are simply less conservative, hence less Republican-inclined, than the less populous mountain states and the southern states east of the Mississippi. Texas would seem to be the most conservative of states, but within that state, the organizational strength of the local Democratic party is such that Texas Democrats can give Republican national candidates a run for their money almost any time they please. The prospective loss of any of these states in a national election would badly disorganize Republican strategic plans and force them to look to the states of the East and Midwest to make up the lost votes. Of course, one way open to Republicans to nail down the votes of these states would be to nominate local politicians with intense personal popularity in the critical states of Texas and California. That Ronald Reagan was such a figure no doubt contributed to his nomination by the Republican party in 1980 and was a powerful asset in his 1980 and 1984 campaigns.

The second factor to be considered in gauging long-term Republican prospects in the South and West is the relative youth of the populations in these states. In the majority of the states of the West, Texas and California included, 40 percent or more of the population is between 25 and 44 years of age. In other words, the political effects of the coming of age of the baby boom will register most powerfully in the states which are at the center of Republican hopes for continuing success in national elections in the future. There are a number of reasons for the Republicans to look upon this situation with confidence, but not with complete confidence. The baby boom generation is less emotionally attached to the New Deal than its parents, and tends to regard the income redistribution policies of the liberals as hostile to its own prospects for economic wellbeing. In the language of the current debate over economic policy, it is more inclined to want its slice of an expanding economic pie than to haggle over its share of an unchanging or shrinking pie divided up by the government. In this sense, the baby boomers are conservative, but this does not mean that they will embrace wholeheartedly the programs and policies of the conservative activists now so prominent in the Republican party. The Republican New Right is not only committed to economic growth over wealth sharing, but it is also committed to a free-market economy. Moreover, the Republican Right is conservative on social, as well as economic, issues. The baby boom generation, however, is not necessarily in favor of a free market as the only means of promoting economic growth. It seems to be quite willing to entertain the possibility that new forms of governmental intervention might lead to greater prosperity. In addition, very many of the baby boomers have been to college and are quite liberal in social matters. Therefore, it may be possible for future Democratic candidates to exploit these possible tensions between Republican conservatives and the baby boom voters. The candidacy of Gary Hart in the Democratic primaries will be viewed as a precursor of the Democratic exploitation of this possibility, should it ever become actual. Hart, a student political activist in the sixties and early seventies, ran as a liberal in social matters and as a neoliberal in economics (i.e., as committed to economic growth through governmental direction of the economy). He did quite well in the states of the West and among the baby boom voters.

Key Strategic Decisions of the 1984 Election

Presidential campaigns begin at the party's summer nominating convention. Important decisions are taken there by the candidates and the party leadership which shape the fall campaign. Indeed, it is something of an exaggeration, but not much of one, to say that convention decisions constitute a sort of script which is enacted during the campaign. Among the most important decisions are: the content of the party platform; the choice of a vice–presidential candidate; the election of the party's national chairman.

The platforms of the two major parties are frequently disparaged as insignificant documents. Although the candidates seldom disavow the platform or any of its planks formally, they are not obliged to run on it, let alone to govern in terms of its provisions. Nonetheless, it is a mistake to dismiss entirely the work of the party platform committees—or of their sisters, the rules and credentials committees. Within these committees, whose deliberations precede the nomination of the candidates, the parties "get their acts together." A national presidential campaign fundamentally has two complementary objectives, the creation of a coalition of interests around a constellation of policies, and the presentation of this coalition to the nation as the desirable ruling coalition. Generally speaking, the platform deliberations of the party facilitate these objectives by providing the various factions with an opportunity to test their strength against one another and work out an informal *modus vivendi* for the campaign and for the subsequent administration, should the campaign be successful. This platform also serves to sketch out in broad outline the political profile the party and its candidates will present to the electorate in order to win its votes.

The choice of a vice-presidential candidate also serves a unifying function. In the provenance of electoral politics, the vice-presidential candidate "balances the ticket" by adding to it strengths in which the presidential candidate is deficient and giving it access to sources of support which the presidential candidate cannot command in his own right. For instance, during the period 1932-1968, the Democratic presidential nominee was usually from the Northeast and with a more or less liberal background. His running mate was, as a rule, from the South or from the border states, and more conservative in reputation. (Roosevelt's choice of Harry Truman for the second spot on the ticket in 1944 conforms to this model.)

The choice of a national party chairman is nominally in the province of the party's national committee, the deliberative and executive body that runs the party's affairs when the national convention is not in session, but in practice, the party's presidential nominee will name the chairman. The task of the national chairman during presidential campaign is to coordinate the party's presidential campaign with the efforts of the state and local parties on behalf of senatorial, congressional, and other local candidates. It is not always an easy job. Aside from certain money at his disposal for supplementing the war chests of local candidates, he has no means to discipline local candidates and parties for failure to support the national ticket. For the most part, the national chairman can only persuade by showing state and local parties and candidates that it is in their interest to support the national ticket. When the national ticket is perceived as strong, this is relatively easy to do. But if the national party or its candidates are perceived as weak, then the job becomes immeasurably more difficult.

Walter Mondale intended to use the platform committee to unite the party squarely behind his own candidacy. In January of 1984, Mondale had begun the primary campaign season as the anointed candidate of the established leadership of the Democratic party. He also had the support of the McGovernite wing and of organized labor. He still had their support by the time of the summer convention, and had the nomination all but sewn up despite the fact that he had been forced to face very powerful challenges in the primaries from Gary Hart and Jesse Jackson, who had arrived at the convention with a large number of delegates committed to them. To Mondale, this situation resembled much too closely the situations obtaining at the Democratic conventions in 1968, 1972, and 1980. In each of those presidential years, the candidate who ultimately won the Democratic nomination had faced strong competition in the primaries, and the nominating conventions themselves had been the occasions for huge and unseemly political brawls between supporters of the leading candidate and delegates committed to his rivals. According to Mondale, these quarrels had been the main reason for Democratic losses in those years. Mondale was determined to prevent similar, destructive brawling at the 1984 convention and decided to use the platform committee deliberations as the chief means to that end. The result was that an extraordinarily large number of interest groups came forward at the platform committee hearings to press their cases for new programs or the expansion of old ones. For the sake of a unified and tranquil convention, none was turned away.

In the past, such a proceeding was the very essence of the Democratic Party. As the party of the New Deal, the Democrats were committed to the creation of prosperity and the equitable distribution of income through governmental action. They habitually sought to institute new spending programs or to expand old ones in order to funnel tax money to groups targeted for subvention. Throughout the seventies and on into the eighties programs of this sort had become increasingly controversial as their costs grew. The symbol of the expanding cost of government programs and wealth redistribution became the federal deficit, the amount of money the government has to borrow each year in order to pay its bills. By the election of 1980, a growing national consensus began to see the deficit as a major impediment to prosperity as the government borrowed much of the money required to finance economic growth. Until 1980, the deficit had been a Republican issue, as politicians of that party had advocated either tax increases or spending cuts in order to balance the budget. In 1980, however, under the leadership of Ronald Reagan, the Republicans took up a new position on the deficit. While still opposed in principle to a large number of government spending programs or to their expansions, the Republican national convention had committed itself to tax cuts as a means of stimulating the economy and generating the revenues necessary to pay the government's bills. The tax cuts which the Reagan administration pushed through the Congress during the President's first term had been popular with the electorate, but the deficit had not been reduced. Throughout the president's first term, the Democrats had attempted to make an issue out of the tax cuts and deficits by blaming the latter on the former, and both on the Reagan administration. These facts together with the Democratic platform presented Walter Mondale with a difficult political problem. He could not do as Democratic candidates had done in the past; he could not promise increased spending under the tacit assumption that deficit financing would pay the bills. This option was not available to Mondale because the Democrats had already made the public sensitive to the issue of the deficit. Nor could he promise that increasing tax revenues from an expanding economy would pay the deficit off. That would be to concede the election to Ronald Reagan. The only thing left to Mondale was to promise a tax increase and to attempt to justify it as the only responsible course of action. He did precisely this in his acceptance speech by telling the Democratic convention and the nation that tax increases were inevitable no matter who was elected. By so doing, he was attempting to seize the moral high ground in matters of economic policy. He implied that the Reagan administration had plans for a tax increase—after all, tax increases were inevitable—but was concealing them until after the election. Thereby, he hoped that the public would be persuaded that his course of action in office with respect to the economy would be more responsible, even if less palatable, than Reagan's.

Mondale's decision to promise a tax increase and charge the Reagan administration with planning one secretly was the master stroke of the Mondale campaign. The tax cuts had been the centerpiece of Reagan's first four years in office, but moderate Republicans in Congress and the White House had been able to force the President to raise taxes in the summer of 1982. In fact, despite the President's bias against taxation, the administration had never spoken with one voice on the tax and deficit issue. Mondale's plan was to exploit this vulnerability and undermine the President's credibility on economic issues. That it failed to do serious damage to the Reagan campaign has been attributed by some political observers to Ronald Reagan's teflon-like qualities as a politician: because of his personal geniality, so the story goes, nothing damaging sticks to him. This is too easy an explanation. It is much more likely that the voters saw in Reagan a political figure whose strongest biases were against increased taxes, but who would increase them if necessity, political or economic, forced him to. Conversely, in Mondale they saw a political leader inclined to expand government spending and who would restrain that tendency only in the face of necessity. Given the choice between a bias in favor of taxes and spending and a bias against, they chose the latter.

Mondale's second strategic decision of importance was the selection of Geraldine Ferraro to be his running mate. Throughout June and July, the primaries having concluded with Mondale's nomination by the convention all but certain, he had been under heavy pressure to pick either a black or a woman as his running mate. Such a choice was recommended as quite in keeping with the New Deal Democratic tradition. Blacks and women were the most recent interest group to be acknowledged to be "outside the system" and in need of being brought in through appropriate policies favoring them, much as the Democratic Party of the thirties and forties had brought ethnic Roman Catholics and the labor movement inside the system. Supposedly, the nomination of a woman or a black on the national Democratic ticket would not only be a step forward in providing justice to these groups, but it would also insure their loyalty to the Democratic Party for the next generation. In selecting Geraldine Ferraro as his running mate, Mondale was responding not only to these prescriptions, but also to imperatives running much deeper than the now fashionable concern with women and blacks. Geraldine Ferraro was from New York, a state which Mondale had to carry and which had been one of the key components of the New Deal coalition of Northeastern and Southern states. Ferraro was also ethnic and Roman Catholic. On the ticket, she was to represent the sober middle class virtues of hard work, patriotism, and solid family life which had characterized the personal and civic morality of the ethnic Catholic neighborhoods that voted so heavily for Franklin Roosevelt and John Kennedy. In summary her candidacy was designed to bring these erring brethren back to the fold that had been leaving ever since the sixties.

Geraldine Ferraro failed notoriously in her role as rallying point for the ethnic Catholics. As a lawyer, a prosecuting attorney, a member of Congress, a rich woman in her own right, she could not convincingly project the image of a wife and mother struggling to provide opportunities for her children. The press revelations about her husband's personal finances did little to enhance her reputation on that score. However, it would be a mistake to conclude that Ferraro's failure as a symbol was exclusively due to personal failings. In the House of Representatives, Ferraro had been a centrist Democrat. Mondale planned to run her as a centrist Democrat, but as a centrist Democrat, Ferraro had to campaign to the left of her natural ethnic constituency. This voting bloc is conservative on social issues and is anti–abortion, but Ferraro had a pro–abortion voting record in the House and was perceived as a pro–abortion candidate. In addition, Ferraro had been given the unpleasant task, usually assigned to vice-presidential nominees, of attacking a sitting president personally. She did so by reviving the image of Ronald Reagan as a trigger-happy cowboy not to be trusted with nuclear weapons. Such tactics no doubt ingratiated her to feminist activists, most of whom are left-leaning, but it again did little for her among ethnic Catholics, most of whom are hard liners on defense issues.

The third major decision made by Walter Mondale was his attempt to dismiss Charles Manatt, a Californian, as chairman of the Democratic National Committee and to replace him with Bert Lance, a figure from Georgia whom Jimmy Carter had unsuccessfully attempted to appoint as Director of the Office of Management and the Budget. Mondale's move was made quite precipitously in the week before the convention, and when opposition to it developed, he was forced to back off. Mondale's reason for wanting Lance as national chairman seem fairly obvious. As a Southern politician, Lance, like Ferraro, would serve to rally a once solidly Democratic constituency around Mondale. What is more, Lance had a reputation for being able to handle Jesse Jackson, who had challenged Mondale in the primaries and who was behaving as if estranged from the party, its leadership, and its presidential candidate. If Lance and Jackson could work together, Mondale's chances in the South would improve. Lance's fellow Southern Democratic party leaders still commanded powerful organizations in their states, and Jesse Jackson was undertaking to register and organize black voters. If Lance could prevail upon his Southern colleagues to support the national ticket out of party loyalty and the prospective spoils of a successful presidential campaign, and if he could persuade Jackson to go all out for Mondale in the fall election, then perhaps Mondale would have a chance of winning some of the Southern states which, all other things being equal, would probably go to Reagan.

Mondale's desire to shore himself up with local Democratic parties was entirely warranted, even if his attempt to fire Manatt on the eve of the convention

Manatt had organized in Manatt's own state was maladroit in the extreme. The national Democratic Party had won only one election since 1968, and its string of losses had left the party with a considerable debt following the 1980 election. State and local Democratic parties tended to regard the national organization as something of a burden, as it came to them repeatedly for funds and workers. This is almost exactly the opposite of the situation obtaining in the Republican Party, where the national committee is extremely well organized, very efficient in fund raising, and able to use the money it raises to develop state and local party organizations. Manatt, a business executive who had reorganized the California Democratic Party after the two-term governorship of Jerry Brown, was brought to the Democratic national chair in order to reorganize the national party and enable it to pull its own weight financially. He had been reasonably successful in this, but not so successful that he was able to insure close cooperation between the national Democratic campaign and state and local parties. In the South, during the fall campaign, state and local politicians tended to regard the national Democratic ticket as a liability and sought the means to dissociate themselves from it, at times having recourse to obvious pretexts to avoid having to share the same platform with either Mondale or Ferraro.

The situation obtaining in California was also symptomatic of the deteriorated relations between state and local parties and the presidential campaign. In that state, the Mondale-Ferraro campaign decided that it either could not or should not rely on local Democratic party workers and volunteers to do campaign work. Instead, it relied almost exclusively on workers provided by political action committees of the national labor movement. As a result, campaign events in California were scheduled without timely notice of them being extended to the state and local party apparatus. The state party in California was also not especially cooperative when the national ticket attempted to use the state for fundraising purposes. California Democrats had done a lot of fundraising for the Carter-Mondale ticket in 1980, but they felt that they had given much more than they had received. They seemed, therefore, to have decided to husband their resources for the 1986 gubernatorial campaign and the concurrent senatorial race, in which Alan Cranston's seat would be at hazard. Mondale's attempt to fire Manatt did not necessarily cause the trouble between the Mondale-Ferraro campaign and the California state party. There is no evidence that Manatt or anyone connected with him tried to sabotage the Mondale-Ferraro campaign out of spite. The point to be observed is that the Mondale-Ferraro ticket had trouble putting together the sort of local campaign effort needed to win a properly distributed national majority. The causes of this difficulty should be sought not in the attempt to replace Manatt but in the gradual leftward drift (McGovernization) of the national Democratic party over the last dozen years, while the nation as a whole has moved to the right. As the national party has become less and less popular with the electorate, it has become less and less popular with local Democrats, who have their own local interests and campaigns to think about.

In 1980, Ronald Reagan had campaigned to unseat an incumbent president. There are three rules which a challenger must observe if he is to be successful in this task. First, he must give the voters a reason for voting against the incumbent. Second, he must give them a reason for voting for him. And third, he must not make any mistakes which would give the voters a reason to vote against him. In 1980, the electorate believed that it had been given more than enough reasons to vote against Jimmy Carter. In order to prove this, one has only to remember how well Edward Kennedy did against Carter in the primaries. In early June, shortly after the end of the primary season, Reagan gave the voters a reason to vote for him by promising to cut taxes (as well as to restore the national defense and curb government spending, policies which he had been associated with before June 1980). Therefore, in the fall campaign, it only remained for Reagan to avoid making mistakes, such as saying things which would offend blocs of voters or making himself look like either a crank or a warmonger. This he achieved, despite some memorable gaffes early in the campaign. In 1984, campaigning as the incumbent, Reagan had had to observe only two rules: take as much advantage of the incumbency as possible and make no mistakes that would give offense or make himself look ridiculous or belligerent. The question to be explored here is what mistakes the Reagan campaign feared making in 1980 and 1984, aside from the gaffes to which the President is at times prone.

The chief mistake which the two successful Reagan campaigns seemed to be bent on avoiding was that of alienating either the moderate or conservative wing of the party by making too many concessions to either one of them. In 1980, Reagan was the first avowedly conservative candidate to win the Republican nomination since Barry M. Goldwater in 1964. Reagan and most of those around him were active on behalf of Goldwater, and the memory of that campaign was still with them in 1980. After Goldwater's nomination, it will be recalled, the moderate Republican governors of Michigan, New York, and Pennsylvania refused to support the national Republican ticket, holding the Goldwater nomination to be a political embarrassment. At the 1980 convention in Detroit, Reagan was determined to forestall a similar secession of party moderates, which could have been occasioned either by the conservatism of Reagan and his supporters on social issues or by Reagan's plans to cut taxes if elected.

As it happened, there was no fight in the platform committee over the Reagan tax cut plan. The proposal was so new and attractive that no one was willing to oppose it, not even George Bush, who had attacked the plan during the primaries as "voodoo economics." Moreover, party moderates probably did not have the strength to attack the plan, even if they had wanted to. Reagan had won so many delegates in the primaries that the convention was unquestionably loyal to him. Nonetheless, a defection by moderate state and local party chieftains after the convention had adjourned was still considered a possibility and the desire to prevent it was no doubt one of the reasons for selecting George Bush as the vice-presidential nominee. Bush had been Reagan's only substantial opposition during the primaries, largely because he was the standard around which party moderates had rallied. He had also been the most outspoken critic of Reagan's economic plans. By accepting the nomination, Bush signaled that the moderate Republicans could live with conservative innovations in policy. By offering it, Reagan signaled that he could work with party moderates. There would be no purge of the Republican Party, once Reagan took power. This reassurance of the party moderates insured their support of the presidential campaign in the fall.

However, there was a fight at the 1980 convention over social issues. Conservative Republican women were there in great numbers in press the platform committee to express opposition to the Equal Rights Amendment (ERA) and to abortion. There these determined women were met by equally determined liberal Republican women out to foil conservative efforts. The conservative women were more numerous than their liberal foes by at least an order of magnitude, and defeated them handily, with little help from the Reagan campaign. Several liberal Republican women were alienated in the process, but their revolt did not spread to party moderates. The reason for this probably lies in the very considerable grass roots strength of the anti-abortion, anti-ERA movement. Although nominally nonpartisan, these movements are conservative in nature, and thus more inclined to favor the electoral fortunes of Republican candidates over Democratic ones. The moderate Republicans were therefore unwilling to tangle with Phyllis Schlafly and her followers.

The convention of 1984 was as conservative as the convention of 1980, and its platform committee produced a very conservative document. Its most controversial provision was the plank expressing four-square opposition to tax increases as Republican policy. Moderates in the White House were uncomfortable with this plank since it seemed to them an unwise restriction on their ability to manage the economy as the exigencies of the times might require. The conservatives in the platform committee won out, but again, no moderate secession followed. Again, for the moderates to secede would have been extremely unwise politically. The centerpiece of the Reagan domestic policy had been the tax cuts, and it made little sense to fight both the President and the party conservatives on this issue. After all, the economy was improving. However, the confusion within Republican circles over the possible necessity of tax increases created a situation which Mondale attempted to exploit.

The Democratic convention held in July gave the Mondale-Ferraro ticket a temporary increase in popularity, while the August Republican convention had failed to give similar stimulation to support for the Reagan-Bush ticket. Nonetheless, by Labor Day and the onset of the official campaign, it was quite clear that Reagan's advantage over Mondale was so considerable as to be overwhelming. The economy was recovering and the nation was at peace. Mondale's attacks on Reaganomics as unfair and as the midwife of misery for the poor failed to ring true. Nor did he achieve much by trying to compare Reagan's policies in Central America to those that had given the nation over a decade of war in Vietnam. In sum, Reagan had the issues on his side. Moreover, his own personal popularity and his strength in the West and South virtually assured him of reelection. The only thing left for Mondale to do was to try to discredit the President personally and show him as unfit to hold his office. Normally campaigning of this sort, known as mudslinging, does little good: he who slings mud loses ground, as the saying goes. Nonetheless, in the debates, Reagan played into Mondale's hands by giving Mondale a chance to show him up without attacking him directly. As everyone who watched the televised debates knows, Reagan fumbled during the first debate and was unable to answer with authority some of the questions put to him. This failure enabled Mondale to renew the charges previously circulated in the press that Reagan was not in command of his own government. As a result, Reagan experienced a temporary drop in the polls. However, by the second debate, Reagan was able once again to take command of the situation and to debate Mondale to a draw. Since Reagan was the incumbent, a draw was sufficient. In the first debate, Mondale had temporarily succeeded in giving the voters a reason to vote against an incumbent, but throughout the whole campaign, the second debate included, he was never successful in giving the voters a reason to vote for himself.

Conclusion

Did the election of 1984 represent a party realignment or a minority party victory? On the basis of the advantages enjoyed by the Republican candidates in their campaign and the burdens born by the Democrats, it would seem that the presidential election of 1984 was a realigning election. The Republicans entered the election with a decided advantage in terms of sectional allegiance. The South and West with a majority of the electoral votes between them were theirs, and had been theirs for virtually every election since 1968. In all likelihood, they will continue to be inclined to favor Republican presidential candidates, and the Democrats will only be able to challenge the Republicans for the electoral votes of these sections by nominating candidates who are popular in those sections. The Republicans' possession of such a stable sectional base is a sign that they have become the dominant political party.

The Republicans also show signs of being the dominant party in that they have capitalized on the prevailing disillusionment with the welfare state among younger voters. It is the Republicans who set the terms of national policy debates. Walter Mondale tried to turn Ronald Reagan's tax cuts against him by making an issue of the deficit and by promising to raise taxes. He failed to do so. However, it is less important to note that he failed than to observe that he was being forced to campaign in terms of popular Republican policy initiatives. The ability to set the agenda of the policy debate is a property peculiar to the dominant party.

For their part, the Democrats show every sign of being the minority party. Their strength of their former sectional base in the South and Northeast has been undermined by the defection of the South and by the shift of population out of the Northeast. Their national organization is weak, with its treasury almost continuously depleted or nearly so. State and local candidates find it in their interest to distance themselves from the national Democratic candidates. Finally, they are divided between those who want to out-Republican the Republicans in devising new ways to promote economic growth and those who prefer the redistributionist policies of the welfare state. All of these conditions are characteristic of a minority party.

Nonetheless, the election of 1984 does not represent a complete partisan realignment. Both in 1980 and in 1984, the Republicans failed to capture the House of Representatives, despite winning control of the Senate and the White House. According to the patterns of previous realigning elections, they should have done so and it is not clear what this failure means. Some might argue that the electorate's loss of confidence in the welfare state is a tentative thing and that this tentativeness resulted in the Democrats retaining control of the House of Representatives. Others might argue that continuing Democratic control of the House is a result of the power of incumbency. It is by now a well documented conclusion of political science that incumbency is a far more important factor than party identification in determining the outcome of congressional elections. Therefore it might be possible to argue that it was not the Democrats who retained control of the House, but the incumbents, who happened to be Democrats. Finally there are those who would argue that the Republicans would control the House, if it had not been for artful redistricting by Democratic state legislatures. Those who hold this opinion point out that all the Republican congressional candidates received more votes than all the Democratic congressional candidates in districts where both parties contested the election. Had this vote been more equitably distributed, so the argument goes, the Republicans would control the House now, and given time, they will sometime in the future.

All these arguments have a limited validity, but probably the most important single reason for the failure of the Republicans to take control of the House of Representatives lies in the nature of the welfare state itself. While the public at large may regard the welfare state as intrusive in its activism and burdensome in its demand for taxes, the individual citizen, as a beneficiary of the largess of the welfare state, is bound to the welfare state by multiple bonds of self-interest. Thus dissatisfaction with the welfare state as a whole makes itself felt at the level of presidential politics, where the interests of the nation as a whole are considered, while at the Congressional level, private and parochial interests are more influential in moving the electorate to vote as it does.

For these reasons, it may be said that the election of 1984 represented a partial partisan realignment. On the level of presidential politics it is complete, but on the level of congressional politics, it is still incomplete. Whether or not it will remain only partial is a question which cannot be answered with authority. It is quite possible that it will remain incomplete, with the Republicans dominating the White House, the Democrats dominating the House, and the Senate seesawing between them. If this situation comes to pass, then it will be a sign that the public's attitude toward the welfare state remains ambiguous. Alternatively, it is possible that the partial realignment could be completed, with the Republicans sweeping all three of the elected portions of the federal government in some future election. Finally, it is possible that the partial realignment could be reversed, with the Democrats coming to power with a mandate to revise and expand the welfare state they have created. The situation is unprecedented, and the patterns of the past provide us with no certain guide.

Party Rules

Josiah Lee Auspitz

Seen from the standpoint of national party structure, the 1984 election appears as an episode in a continuing postwar morality play. Since 1946, when Republicans briefly recaptured both houses of Congress, there have been regular predictions of a postwar "realignment" based on what have seemed compelling demographic and attitudinal surveys. Yet 1984 was the third postwar election in which an incumbent and generally successful Republican President won a landslide victory without any corresponding landslide to his party at other levels. This pattern contrasts sharply with the single such instance of a postwar Democratic presidential landslide, in 1964, which brought massive gains to the Democrats in gubernatorial, senatorial, congressional, and even statehouse elections. Given the very different character and factional support of the three Republican presidents involved—Dwight D. Eisenhower, Richard M. Nixon, and Ronald W. Reagan—one must attribute the shallowness of the idea of realignment not to personality or ideology or campaign tactics, but to more abiding features of the two-party system.

The rules of the two national parties provide a touchstone to the deeper factors involved. This essay will argue that the characters of the national parties bear a remarkable congruence to their rules, that the conduct of nomination campaigns is inexplicable without understanding the rules of the game, and that the recurring pattern of broad support for the Democrats coupled with second-term GOP presidential landslides is itself reflected in the logic of the rules.

More pointedly, it will argue that the Democratic rules have since 1936 painfully evolved from an underlying view of party as a coalition of interests towards a vision of a national programmatic party capable of overcoming the fragmenting effects of the separation of powers. It will suggest that this latter, "responsible," view of party, has dominated national debate and resulted in a thoroughgoing restructuring of the presidential selection process. At the same time, the Democratic view of party has generated such deep problems in both intra-party affairs and in the conduct of government as to have made a Democratic presidency difficult to sustain.

The Republican rules, by contrast, do not embody an alternative vision. This essay will argue that the GOP has since 1916 overlaid a once coherent view of party with a series of factionally motivated rules changes that now leave its national structure in disharmony with the party's own stated ideals and with Abraham Lincoln's reading of the Declaration of Independence. The result is a preoccupation with short term success and marketing technique at the expense of principles that might command long term loyalty. Quasi-Republicans desiring a more principled politics have found solace in a variety of tax exempt nonpartisan and ideological movements that ape but never fulfill the constitutional role of a national party.

In all, the essay will suggest that if party rules be taken as an indicator of moral seriousness about our presidential selection system, the Democrats are, for all their weaknesses on other fronts, by default the leading national party, but because the constitutional role for a national political party itself requires rethinking, this is scant comfort either for the Democrats or for those, of whatever persuasion, who are concerned about the future of the American experiment. But to make this argument will first require a brief discussion of rules in general, of rules within the context of political parties, and of the relevant history of the most important rules among the Republicans and the Democrats.

Are There Neutral Rules?

In a rule-of-law society we are accustomed to draw a sharp distinction between substance and procedure. We like to think of procedures as neutral, as providing an unbiased framework in which substantive matters can be worked out. Yet our political debates suggest otherwise. Even the most technical rules—rules of apportionment in representative bodies, rules of evidence in court proceedings, rules of administrative procedure—are also matters of controversy and compromise precisely because they are known to tilt outcomes, build in biases, or vindicate symbolic assumptions.

In American history, the prime example of deep controversy over a technical rule was the mid-nineteenth century interpretation of the three–fifths rule in Article I, Section 2, of the Constitution, by virtue of which a slave was counted as three–fifths of a person in apportioning direct taxes and seats in the House of Representatives. From one point of view, given rigorous expression by John C. Calhoun, this rule proved that the Constitution itself was preeminently a document of compromise, a pact among the states bearing no organic or logical relation to the Declaration of Independence. For how could it be "self-evident that all men are created equal" if slaves were counted as only three–fifths men? Moreover, the failure to give statistical equality to all persons was for Calhoun evidence of the legitimacy of different weightings of constituted interests in the branches of government themselves. For him the separation of powers built in a doctrine of concurrent majorities that both entrenched and legitimated compromise as the reigning principle of the American regime. The House of Representatives, the Senate, and the presidency were each based on a different representative principle. Thus, by Calhoun's account the majoritarianism of American government was pluralist and consensual. It required concurrence of the peculiar majorities based on population, statehood, and a combination of the two in the Electoral College.

The opposing point of view, best enunciated by Lincoln, turned the same question on its head. Because for Lincoln it was self-evident that all men are created equal in rights, it was also self-evident that the three–fifths rule was a temporary expedient that would have to be superseded. Just as the Constitution itself provided for the cessation of the slave trade by a date certain, the country would in time have to abolish slavery and to supplant the three–fifths rule with one consonant with the principle of natural right enunciated in the Declaration. The principle of natural right, given concrete embodiment in the doctrine of popular sovereignty, was constitutive of the American regime and therefore, in the rare cases of conflict, overrode the doctrines of compromise and concurrent majorities. It provided, moreover, the only plausible link among polyglot Americans. Even in his day Lincoln observed that the British ancestry of the Signers was not shared by "perhaps half our people who are ... German, Irish, French, and Scandinavian," but who, recognizing in the Declaration "the father of all moral principle in them ... have a right to claim it as if they were blood of the blood and flesh of the flesh of the men who wrote that Declaration."

For both Lincoln and Calhoun, then, a technical rule of apportionment raised fundamental questions. For both, it was important to ground the final authority of the rules in some criterion above short term interest. With the principle of natural right this is, on its own terms, self-evidently the case. But even Calhoun's doctrine of compromise and concurrent majorities has more than an opportunistic rationale. It distinguishes the longer term commitments of a founding compact from mere short term compromise. And the doctrine of compromise itself, though rooted in the balancing of interests, is blindfolded in not inquiring into the substance of the interests it implicitly protects. Thus, in both Lincoln's and Calhoun's positions there remains an abiding sense that procedure must be defended with a general and enduring rationale consistent with the entire body of the laws.

What is noteworthy here is that even in a dispute so dramatic as to have been resolved by a civil war and subsequent constitutional amendment, the distinction between substance and procedure still holds. In a rule-of-law society procedures need not be perceived as inherently neutral, indeed they cannot be so long as they stem from one or another view of citizenship, but they must, like the statue of Justice herself, be blindfolded to short term outcomes.

Opportunism Versus Principle in Party Rules

Within political parties, however, an argument for the purely opportunistic character of the rules is more common than elsewhere. For parties may be seen as chartered conspiracies to seize the offices of government and to exercise them in accordance with a well-defined partisan will. On this view, their internal rules should be instrumental to partisan interest. And since on this view the overriding rationale of the party is rooted in success, so (it may be argued) should debate over rules within the parties directly reflect relationships of power. Those with greater power should, on this view, feel no reticence about setting rules unambiguously favoring themselves, constrained only by the dictates of prudence to broaden their alliances and appeal.

The extreme expression of the opportunistic view is to be found in the Marxist-Leninist tradition, where it is argued that law itself must be subservient to the dictates of partisan will. Procedure is not then independent of substance but a tactical means of enforcing certain substantive outcomes as the "party interest", where party is defined as a progressive vanguard.

But in the United States this view of party as the unconstrained movement of unmoderated interest is what the framers of the Constitution called the "mischief of faction." As they saw it, the perennial attempt to subordinate procedure to substantive interest is ultimately subversive of the whole basis of a rule-of-law regime. If, then, there were to be parties in America—as there were from the outset—they had to be constrained by principles derived from the nature of the regime itself. There thus grew up a robust but principled view of party, foreshadowed in the refusal of *Federalist* 10 to apply the term "faction" to those united by "opinion" rather than "interest" and fully developed in the writings of Martin Van Buren, who distinguished "party" in the positive sense from "faction" in the pejorative usage of the framers.

For Van Buren, the defining mark of party was the reflection within its inner constitution of the spirit of the Constitution whose offices it seeks to win. Since the system of national nominating conventions took root during Van Buren's political ascendancy, he may be viewed as a framer of this system and his thoughts on it, interspersed with lively partisan polemic, have a constitutional ring. Van Buren himself thought a national party should be structured to bridge rather than exacerbate sectional division, to represent citizen as opposed to corporate interests, and to encourage national integration with adequate respect for states' rights. Only within these broad principles, was he willing to tolerate opportunistic maneuver, and indeed, to revel in it. For his procedural machinations he earned his sobriquets; "the Fox of Kinderhook," the "Little Magician," the "wire puller."

Van Buren's doctrine and practice have stamped debate over party rules with a dual character to our own day. On the one hand, it is generally conceded, following Van Buren's writings, that there must be principled standards derived from some overarching view of the American regime itself, else we have not a party in the American sense but some compounding of the logic of "faction" in the pejorative sense of the Framers. On the other hand, in practice it takes take a disciplined political intelligence to discern the extent to which any given politician, Van Buren included, is animated by such standards, even when he invokes them. For in party politics both the highest American ideals and the meanest stratagems are regularly cast in procedural terms. Since factions within the parties are wont to elevate their short term interests into absolute claims, it takes a certain sifting to distinguish stratagems from principles.

The 1984 nominating conventions pose problems of this kind for both parties. Among the Democrats there were well publicized criticisms by Jesse Jackson and Gary Hart of Hunt Commission changes in the Democratic rules on proportional representation. On the Republican side, where discord was muted, there were nevertheless proposals of a fundamental kind in the Rules Committees of the Convention and the Republican National Committee (RNC) involving the "victory bonuses" central to the allocation formula of the convention itself. In both parties, the discussion was continued by resolution into the following four years—a "fairness commission" for the Democrats, a special subcommittee of the RNC Rules Committee on the how the rules as a whole affect minority representation. Taking both parties together, the 1984 rules debates, which were of only minor interest to the press for their ephemeral factional implications, raise, at a deeper level, issues about federalism, majority rule, proportional representation, incentives to party success, and voting rights.

Rules Change As a Delayed Response to Trauma

Party rules governing the national nominating conventions may be divided into three parts. First and most revealing, there are formulas of allocation or apportionment. These stipulate how the total number of delegates is to be divided among the states and congressional districts. Because they affect the voting rights of party members in all parts of the country, allocation formulas provide a party's philosophy of representation writ large. Second, there are rules of delegate selection. These stipulate how members of the national convention are to be selected within the states and congressional districts. These embody the party's philosophy of representation writ small. They may vary from state to state and they specify how individual delegates represent their constituencies. Third, there are housekeeping rules: rules stipulating the order of business, the composition of committees, the manner of voting, the powers and composition of the national committees, the certifying of credentials, and so on. These internal procedures reflect the party's standards of civility.

The two parties differ significantly in all three areas, as well as in their posture towards the state laws governing the conduct of presidential nominating campaigns. For each party the structure of the rules reflects a distinctive history, which though influenced tangentially by events in the rival party, is more directly the product of internal rivalries and self–induced traumas. The response to trauma typically takes a long time to work itself out. Like the Gilbert and Sullivan hero who was born on February 29 of a leap year, the national parties age quadrennially. The process of trial and error that might take a decade in a legislative program can thus be stretched out over a generation or two in matters of basic party structure. Until 1974, when the Democrats introduced the midterm miniconvention, party rules could be changed only by a vote of the national convention itself, and (notwithstanding Herbert Hoover's attempt to introduce a midterm convention into the GOP in 1934) this is still the glacial Republican way of doing it. Thus, it is not atypical to find a party still responding in 1928 to a situation that arose in 1912, or settling in 1940 an old score from 1924, or still recovering in 1988 from the shocks of 1968.

Moreover, there has always been remarkable stability among the specialists who write and interpret the rules. Behind the shifting fortunes of presidential candidates and their issues, there is a stable group of experts, an identifiable rules establishment whose members form a sort of specialized bar in the law and lore of party rules. It is not unusual for the same faces to appear for 25 years on the rules committees and commissions of national party organs. These men and women are conscious of themselves as shaping the very basis of presidential competition and have a professional's benevolent disdain for those in the press and public whose interest is limited to the merely substantive and charismatic dimensions of politics. Since the coalition that passes a major structural change is likely to be self-entrenching, only determined presidential leadership or some major trauma produces fundamental alteration.

Thus, in this century, there are for each party very few periods of fundamental change. The Democratic Party set a new structural definition for itself in 1936 and when this proved untenable at the 1968 Chicago convention, it responded with a succession of commissions bearing the names of their chairmen—McGovern-Fraser after 1968, Mikulski after 1972, Winograd after 1976, and Hunt after 1980. In the course of its reexaminations it has gradually developed a new structure, and since this is a subject on which there is already a considerable literature, the account here will concentrate on the Democrats' underlying philosophy of representation and on the influence of the Hunt Commission rules changes on the 1984 campaign. The Republican story, on the other hand, though known in its broad outlines to the rules establishment of the party and a handful of serious political journalists, has yet to receive the attention of the political science profession. The sketch provided in the appendix to this essay, being the first such account, will be more detailed and historical, and will serve as a case study in the factional bargaining that has characterized rules changes in both parties.

The Democrats: From Coalition to Party

From election to election the Democrats have had regular occasion to recall Will Rogers's famous remark, "I am a member of no organized political party. I am a Democrat." Their squabbles, ultimata, defections, and excesses are legendary, and yet appealing to the adventurous and untidy American mind. Not. without reason is the past half century of Democratic dominance commonly referred to as the New Deal "coalition." A coalition, as such, is not a party in Van Buren's principled sense. Rather, it is a compounding of factions, each of which allies itself with the others to achieve some narrow interest. The one-party South with its congressional seniority and military bases, the northern urban machines and labor unions, the populist farmers of the West, the children and grandchildren of immigrants looking for white collar jobs, the victims of discrimination and poverty, wealthy patricians, college professors, government contractors—these were the motley members of the New Deal coalition. Yet under the circumstances of depression, war, and postwar aspirations for a middle class America, they could all be united around an expanding role for government.

Big but benign government thus became the Democrats' trademark. Their achievement as a party was to elevate it to more than a mere patronage relationship. They defined it in terms of the implementation of new "freedoms" or rights—the right to a secure old age, to an education, to a job, even to the ownership of a home. The thrust of these rights was to make accessible to all the "equality of opportunity" to be middle class, and with this status to achieve the material prerequisites of citizenship in a moderate regime.

In associating itself with this vision, the Democratic Party became an emblem of America itself, in which age-old rivalries of region, class, religion, race, and national origin were acted out, moderated, reconciled, and, to a remarkable degree, homogenized. Just as the Republicans—with their faith in free labor, high tariffs, gold, homesteading, and infrastructure investments— were identified with the formation of a national industrial economy in the half century from 1876 to 1928, so the Democrats in the succeeding half century identified themselves with the extension of the benefits of this economy to every sector of society. The building of the middle class was their project. In pursuing it, they turned a coalition into a party, predicated upon an expanding role for the federal government.

One convention rule reflected and accelerated the change. In 1936, by voice vote, the Democratic National Convention adopted majority rule. Until that time the party had, with the exception of the 1840 convention, used a two-thirds rule for the nomination of a presidential candidate. The two-thirds rule had imposed consensus politics upon the disparate members of the coalition, and gave the states rights' South a sectional veto on the selection of the presidential candidate—a power that reinforced the leverage of southern seniority in the national legislature. Majority rule, by contrast, enabled the formation of a presidential party capable of independent action. To be sure, the elements within the coalition still retained control over their local bases of power. But majority rule changed the pattern by which the political intuitions of Democratic presidents were formed. By using shifting majorities within the party, presidential initiatives became irresistible so long as the role of government continued to expand. For how could a prudent coalition member reject today a philosophy of government that would predictably benefit his constituents tomorrow?

But what if circumstances decreed that government was overextended? What if a Democratic president had to accept limitations on his programs and to make hard choices among priorities? This was the question that faced Lyndon Johnson, who embodied in his person and his policies the tension between the principled and patronage basis of the Democratic party. Johnson, author of ambitious civil rights legislation, even more ambitious Great Society programs, and the still more ambitious "nation-building" effort in South Vietnam, asserted that the country could have "guns *and* butter," that is, could sustain an expanding role for government on all fronts. The realization that government could not expand on all fronts split the Democratic party in 1968.

The peculiar character of the split posed a problem for the rules. The mass base of the war protest movement were younger members of what James Q. Wilson had earlier described as "amateur Democrats"—those for whom a politics of principle and program was more important than direct patronage. They were geographically mobile, and though sometimes preponderant in suburban areas or university towns, they were not distributed to take advantage of nomination politics, which has always revolved around control of state delegations. The Democratic convention was especially known for a style that favored the older, coalition style of bargaining, in which brokers maintain power by keeping bloc strength intact.

Even in the absence of favorite son candidacies, a variety of procedural devices was available to achieve monolithic state delegations. The South preferred the unit rule, by which an entire state delegation was pledged to vote in convention as a bloc. In the northern industrial states the same effect was often achieved by other means. Nonbinding primaries were used to give an illusion of popular participation, while unpledged slates of delegates controlled by party bosses went to the convention. Where state conventions selected delegations, winner-take-all devices on the district or county level assured that localized "reform" minorities would be filtered out before reaching the statewide level. And of course, at the grass roots, in caucus states, the use of inadequate publicity, shifting venues, and inconvenient times favored those who controlled the party machinery.

These devices, which enhanced the bargaining power of organizational leaders, inhibited the representation within the party of the unorganized but potent middle class constituency whose creation was the pride of the New Deal. The war protest movement brought this contradiction to a particularly bitter crisis, but did not create it. The reform issue of rescuing the party from the "bosses" was a perennial one, and it would obviously be pressed with greater insistence as the party came to fulfill its dream of a middle class constituency made secure by the Four Freedoms of the New Deal.

The standard reform device that served the aspirations of an educated middle class had been pioneered by the Progressives: the direct primary, of which Wisconsin had since 1903 provided the prime example. Prior to 1968 the effect of primaries in the Democratic Party was more symbolic than numerical. Striking results in primaries might help to winnow out a large field of organization-backed candidates, but, as Estes Kefauver learned, a genuine insurgent could never win a Democratic nomination on the mere strength of primary victories. If, as many speculate, Robert F. Kennedy might have won the 1968 nomination after his California primary victory, it would not have been because of the numbers of delegates it gave him but because of its persuasive effect on the minds of organizational Democrats.

The problem for the Democratic rules, then, was twofold: first, how to develop more supple mechanisms to represent nonorganization Democrats; second, how to balance these with the coalition politics that were still the bedrock of the party's power. This dual problem, exacerbated by the 1968 experience, was really the working out of a dynamic that had been set in motion in 1936. The solution to it has taken up the efforts of four separate post-1968 commissions. Since those proposing various reforms were also counting delegates for this or that candidate in the next convention, the road to a balanced system of representation has not been smooth. Overreactions in the direction of "reform" have been followed by counterreactions, also overdone, in the direction of coalition style bargaining.

Yet so much attention has been lavished on the bumps in the road—the tawdry factional tactics, the brief but lamentable experimentation with quotas, the landmark lawsuits, the unanticipated consequences of well-meaning reforms—that the extraordinary achievement of the Democrats as a party during the post-1968 period is rarely remarked upon. While the Republicans looked on passively, the Democrats thoroughly revamped the entire presidential selection system by which both parties compete. The result was to provide an outlet for constituencies, however they might define themselves, who were not a majority in their geographical area, but who wished to make their voice felt through a presidential candidacy.

The 15-year program of change in part merely implemented a long-standing reform agenda: the elimination of the unit rule, the opening of the closed caucus, the end of the artificially harmonious state convention, the widespread use of direct primaries, the frank declaration on the ballot of delegate preferences. In part, it laid the juridical grounds for a national party apparatus with a capacity for independent action barely dreamed of in 1936: the Democratic National Committee was changed from a confederal to a federal body and given rulemaking power between conventions; it was supplied with legal machinery to assure the compliance of state parties with its directives; and (since the Democratic Party is wedded to an expanding federal role) both parties now draw on federal funds to make them independent of business and labor for their conventions and presidential campaigns. But the really fundamental rules change was a modified form of proportional representation (PR).

Because PR has often been seen as unamerican, it is remarkable that this device achieved immediate acceptance in every state Republican and Democratic party in the country, save the California GOP, where a winner-take-all primary was preserved as a favorite son device for Ronald Reagan. Yet not until the 1984 campaigns, when Hart and Jackson found it in their interests to question the thresholds of proportionality set by the Hunt Commission, has the use of PR received any sustained public notice. It is important to understand the role that proportionality has come to play in transforming our nomination politics from a sectional to a national affair, and why the Hunt Commission moved the Democrats (and with them the country) from a pure to a mixed proportional system.

How the Democrats Introduced and Modified PR

Proportionality was introduced to break the monolithic state delegation. The national party's right to impose it upon the state parties was upheld by the Supreme Court as the result of a case brought in 1972, when McGovern's own victory in the winner-take-all California primary was invalidated and he was reduced (ironically, under the guidelines of the McGovern-Fraser Commission) to a share of the delegates proportional to his popular vote. At the same time a delegation led by Mayor Daley was unseated in Illinois for not following the guidelines on racial and sexual quotas. But whereas the use of quotas (also upheld by the courts) was dropped after it served its tactical purpose (Rule 6A2 now specifically prohibits the "imposition of mandatory quotas at any level of the delegate selection process or in any other Party affairs"), the rule that delegates should be parceled out in proportion to popular vote has rapidly become an accepted fixture of American nomination politics. In 1974 the Democrats, fearing the power of George Wallace in winner-take-all primaries, turned proportionality "guidelines" into an explicit rule that would be legally binding on state parties. They wrote a 15 percent threshold into their rules, so that any candidate who exceeded this percentage in a binding primary, caucus or state convention would be entitled to a like percentage of the delegates.

The proportionality rule accommodated the need for diversity within delegations. It moved the Democrats from coalition building among sectional blocs to a process centered on national candidate-led constituencies distributed in differing proportions throughout the 50 states. But in doing so it raised the possibility of fragmentation. From the start there was strong criticism that setting the proportionality level too low (originally a 5 percent minimum was proposed) would encourage single-issue and narrowly based candidacies, of a kind common in the short-lived coalition governments of continental Europe. The Democrats seemed headed toward some version of the French Fourth Republic or the Israeli Knesset in which majority rule became difficult. The Carter blitz in 1976 and the simple one-to-one encounter in 1980 had avoided this result, but the logic of the rules encouraged it. Even a 15 percent minimum made a deadlock a strong probability once federal funding became available to enable a candidate to stay the course of a losing campaign. With delegates mechanically pledged to candidates who could not deliver them to another candidate, and with polling and media professionals displacing the old bosses, who would broker a deadlocked convention? Barbara Walters? Lou Harris? Pat Caddell?

It was this underreported problem of fragmentation and deadlock—not the well-publicized factional maneuvers or even the steps to shorten the primary season—that was the serious business of the Hunt Commission. The 70-member group resolved the problem in two ways: first, by reducing arithmetically the probability of a deadlock; second, by assuring that if a deadlock should occur the convention would have the flexibility to break it. To reduce the probability of a deadlock, it raised the threshold from 15 to 20 percent in caucus states and to a range of from 17 to 25 percent in primary states, depending on the number of delegates per congressional district. This step alone limited the number of viable candidates to three or at most four. To further encourage a quick winnowing of the field to a two-way contest, states had a further option of awarding an extra bonus delegate to the front-runner in each congressional district.

The Hunt Commission also permitted states to opt out of proportional representation altogether. Under this option a state could choose to elect delegates directly on a winner-take-all basis at the congressional district level. These delegates, though they declared a preference for a presidential candidate, were like all other delegates, bound only to "in all good conscience reflect the sentiments of those who elected them." It was expected that winner-take-all delegates, having run on their own names, as independently elected representatives of their districts, would be especially likely to move to a more viable candidate should the need arise. In the phrase of Terry Sanford who provided a learned rationale for this option (*A Danger of Democracy*, 1982), they would be "thinking delegates." Their presence would help to a "deliberative convention" in the event of a deadlock. In 1984 seven states with a total of 28 percent of the convention delegates chose the winner-take-all, congressional district option in conjunction with nonbinding primaries.

Finally, the better to assure a flexible convention, an exceptionally large number of slots was reserved for officeholders and party officials: 568 slots (14 percent) for those who were specifically unpledged, and another 305 (8 percent) for other elected and party officials who, though pledged, were presumably men and women long practiced in putting their noses to the wind. In all, roughly one-half of the delegates to the 1984 Democratic Convention were chosen under conditions that made them unlikely to be mere automatons. As a simple matter of bargaining logic, the presence of a large contingent of officials would discourage narrowly based candidates from persevering to produce a multiballot convention. For even if a single-issue candidate were to hold together a bloc of delegates on the convention floor, the first bargains struck by winning candidates would almost certainly be with the more individualized swing group of "superdelegates," as the unpledged officials were called.

The designation of so large a number of elected and party officials marked an important philosophical shift towards the national programmatic party first glimpsed in 1936. Congressmen, governors, mayors, senators, state legislators, and party chairmen have always attended Democratic conventions. But 1984 is the first time they were there by specific provision of the rules. This constituted a formal movement away from the separation of powers as a rationale for the convention nomination process. It is a step toward the system which prevailed prior to 1832, when the congressional caucus served as a presidential nominating body. Admirers of the British system favor this kind of process, which assures that a president will also be an effective leader of his party in the legislature. The American convention system, by contrast, mandates a uniquely presidential competition with a premium on public and electioneering abilities rather than the quieter legislative skills. But a convention with nearly a quarter of the seats reserved for party officialdom reintroduces an element of prenegotiation by the nominee with the legislative, gubernatorial and mayoral officials with whom he will have to deal. The inclusion of so large a group of officials is a significant step in the direction of what many political scientists have admiringly called "responsible party government," a concept not easy to reconcile with the separation of powers.

The Hunt Commission thus made two important departures. First, it Americanized the system of proportional representation by introducing conditions conducive to deliberation and majority rule at the convention. Second, it gave formal recognition to the nonpresidential wings of the party in choosing the nominee, incorporating thereby a strong dose of the doctrine of "responsible party government." It thus was a milestone in the unfolding of the New Deal vision of a disciplined but diverse national party capable of sustaining vigorous, majoritarian, but not necessarily consensual presidential initiatives. Yet the irony of 1984 is that notwithstanding the clear thrust of the formal provisions of their rules, the Democrats conducted a nomination campaign that was perceived by the public not as the crucible for programmatic leadership but as a throwback to the worst aspects of the coalition-building of an earlier age. How did this come about?

The 1984 Nomination Campaign: From Party to Coalition

In large part, the "old politics" air of the 1984 Democrats stemmed from rules decisions made at the state rather than the national level. The most significant of these was the movement away from binding primary elections. In 1968 the Democrats had conducted 17 binding primaries to select delegates in the 50 states and the District of Columbia. This did not include "beauty contest" primaries that had no effect on delegate selection. By 1972 the number had risen to 24. In 1976 and 1980 the number of binding primaries was 30. In 1984 this was reduced to 17. In addition, there were the seven winner-take-all congressional district states, six of which held "beauty contest" primaries on the same day as the election of delegates. These seven were erroneously counted in widely reprinted statistics prepared by the Democratic National

Committee as binding primaries. Even the usually authoritative *Congressional Quarterly* reported a net change of only six states from direct to indirect representation, whereas the actual change was from 30 to 17 direct primaries, a reversion to 1968 levels. Moreover, since indirect representation was introduced in several of the largest states, the effective role of direct primaries in delegate selection in 1984 actually receded to below its 1968 level.

Since the direct primary is the traditional bellwether of middle class reform, movement from it signaled accurately that organizational forces, particularly those of organized labor, were making a major investment in nomination politics. As if to epitomize the shift, the national party won in 1981 a long-standing battle to refuse to seat delegates directly elected in the Wisconsin open primary. For most of this century Wisconsin's open primary was *par excellence* the symbol of progressive reform. It was set up in 1903 in the belief that party registration compromised the independence of the voter and the secrecy of the ballot. It required all voters to choose ballots in primaries without declaring or publicly recording a party affiliation. It was thus open in the sense that any voter could choose either party's ballot on election day. The Wisconsin primary was extended to presidential nominations in 1911 and was made binding on delegates to both major party conventions in 1949. It had great prestige not only because of its longevity but also because it tested the enthusiasms of weak party identifiers in a swing state.

In 1973, when George Wallace seemed a special threat in the open primaries of Wisconsin and Michigan, the Mikulski Commission recommended that participation in Democratic primaries be limited to registered Democrats only. A rule was written to this effect in 1974 but it made an exception for states like Wisconsin where legislatures refused to allow public registration of party preference. The Winograd Commission eliminated this exception for the 1980 convention. In doing so it was influenced in part by a study of crossover voting that showed the Wallace vote in 1972 and the McCarthy vote in 1968 coming from weak Democrats and non-Democrats. In part, it was emboldened by the Supreme Court opinion in the 1972 Illinois delegate case (*Cousins v. Wigoda*, 1975) which gave party rules priority over state law in seating delegations. The new rule provoked a showdown with Wisconsin which went to court to protect its pioneering ballot.

Unanimously, the Wisconsin Supreme Court ruled that the Wisconsin primary constituted no infringement on the rights to free assembly of the national Democratic Party. Three U. S. Supreme Court Justices, Lewis F. Powell, William H. Rehnquist and Harry A. Blackmun agreed. But the U. S. Supreme Court majority in 1981, in a 6-3 opinion by Justice Potter J. Stewart, saw the Wisconsin case as sufficiently similar to *Cousins v. Wigoda* to decide it on the same principle: the party's First Amendment right to free assembly permitted it the final say in delegate selection. Wisconsin Democrats could choose to hold their primary as they wished, but they could not force the national convention to seat their delegation. For old time's sake, Wisconsin still held its open primary, which was won overwhelmingly by Hart. But it was a "beauty contest" only. The actual delegates to the Democratic convention were elected later in sparsely attended caucuses which sent a Mondale slate to San Francisco.

The Wisconsin case captures the trend of the rules changes for 1984. In general, the Democratic rules establishments, with strong prodding from organized labor and supporters of Mondale and Kennedy candidacies, wanted to avoid a repetition of the surprise nominations of 1972 and 1976. Closed primaries meant a more predictable electorate. Caucuses, attended by party faithful, were still more routinized. And shortening and "front–loading" the primary season gave further hope that no upstart candidate would arise. Each of these measures, of course, had sincere advocates on other grounds than as a counterreaction to the democratic pressures of the 1970s. But unlike the proportionality rules, establishment-oriented provisions lacked any organic relation with the longer term attempt of the Democratic Party to adapt to the growing, independent-minded middle class constituencies that its programs had helped to create. In fact, the movement toward caucuses, by drawing on the more committed voter, had the potential of repeating at the state level the bitter confrontations that had occurred at the 1968 convention between the older regulars and the younger issues-oriented activists.

By contrast, the proportionality changes, though they also had an anti–insurgent effect, arose from the inner dynamic of the transition from a broadly based interest group coalition to an equally broadly based programmatic party. Still, the net effect of all the rules changes seemed to the casual observer simply a piling on of devices to assure a surprise–free outcome—a self-defeating effect if it were to give the impression that the grass roots voter was being taken for granted, or that the state parties were being coerced by a centralized party bureaucracy in Washington.

To bring this message to the primary voters was the opportunity spotted by Senator Hart (but not by the more highly publicized Senator Glenn) just two months before the New Hampshire primary. Because of the heavy role of "thinking delegates" and of organized labor in caucus states, Hart had only a remote chance of piling up an arithmetic majority. Walter Mondale had collected endorsements from unions, issues groups and office holders that assured him a preponderance of delegates in the nonprimary states. But if Hart could humiliate and delegitimate Mondale in direct electoral combat, without overly antagonizing the party regulars, he could hope to change the minds of flexible delegates.

The shortened primary season gave him no time to make a reasoned case with the many detailed issues papers he had prepared during the previous year. He could only refer to himself as the candidate of "new ideas" (that is, of the post-New Deal middle class). This had special appeal to the young and to weak party identifiers and gave the Hart campaign surprise victories in states where large number of independents could vote in the Democratic primaries.

But it also provoked a counterattack by Mondale, who first charged that there were no such new ideas ("Where's the beef?"), and then that anyone who targeted a campaign at weakly partisan primary voters was not a "real Democrat." Hart shot back that Mondale was the candidate of the "special interests"—that is, of all the groups and office holders whose endorsements he had collected, to which the press responded by popularizing a special interest term for Hart's most enthusiastic supporters, "yuppies."

The effect of the exchange was to emphasize the very tension that the restructuring of the party had tried to resolve—between the coalition bedrock and the emerging middle class basis of the Democratic party. The rules changes helped to prolong the agony. Mondale, with his strength among office holders and in caucus states, could persevere in the face of serious primary reverses. At one point, chancy victories in Alabama and Georgia kept him in the race after defeats all over the country. Hart, for his part, could not be deterred by delegate totals that showed him far behind: so long as the polling results proved him the stronger candidate against Reagan, there were enough "thinking delegates" to abandon Mondale. To convince them, he needed a striking victory in which his margin was not furnished by independents, dismissed by the regulars as interloping mischief makers. There was only one early primary that could play this role: Pennsylvania, where state law excluded independents from party affairs. Pennsylvania was a strong organized labor state where Jimmy Carter, who had only the backing of a few dissident unions, had wrapped up the nomination in 1976 by beating the preferred candidate of the AFL-CIO Executive Board, Henry Jackson.

But in 1984 a unified labor movement was well prepared in the Keystone State. Pennsylvania was now a congressional district, winner-take-all state where delegates ran on their own, without any proportional tie to the "beauty contest" primary. Hence it was appropriate and legal for labor to set up "delegate committees," independent of the Mondale campaign, to support candidates in each congressional district pledged to Mondale. The combined expenditures of the official Mondale campaign and the independent labor committees vastly exceeded the expenditure limits which Mondale had accepted as a condition for receiving federal funds. When it turned out that these delegate committees were only nominally independent—that in violation of the law they had been the product of prior planning with the Mondale staff— Hart quite correctly complained: "Give the money back!" And after Mondale in fact did make a financial adjustment, Hart raised the ante: "Give the delegates back!" But the one thing Hart could never take back was the fact that he had lost the Pennsylvania "beauty contest," which alone could have provided the electoral evidence he needed. And because he had been unfairly outspent, he could hardly be expected to make a quick and harmonious settlement with Mondale.

Thus, the ordeal of the Democrats went on until Hart's finally decisive loss in New Jersey on June 5. The Garden State had a large independent crossover vote housed in sprawling middle class bedroom suburbs—Hart's natural constituents until he disparagingly compared New Jersey's toxic wastes to California's scenic beauties. His overwhelming victory in California—and indeed in every noncaucus state west of the Mississippi—was not persuasive to party regulars once he lost New Jersey fair and square. By then he and Mondale had had six months to drill home that the Democrats were a party of "special interests" which now might be taken to include the fickle young, urban, and professional voters who made up the "yuppies" and a party which could choose between stale old ideas and vapid new ones. In case the picture of the Democrats as a coalition of "special interests" had not been sufficiently conveyed, Walter Mondale spent his triumphal weeks before the convention reviewing a parade of potential running mates, all of whom were described by his staff and the press in terms of their region, religion, sex, and ethnicity rather than on the terms on which Carter had chosen Mondale: competence and compatibility.

All this was certainly not inherent in the logic of the Hunt Commission changes, which were aimed at bridging the very divisions that the campaign reopened. But the national rules, in tandem with the changes at the state level, did significantly shape the pattern of the self-destructive competition that ensued. The fact that the field of serious candidates was rapidly reduced to two was exactly what the logic of the rules encouraged. The fact that the bipolar split occurred along the very fault lines the Democrats had been trying to bridge was a sign that the transition from coalition to programmatic party was far from complete.

The one success of the rules was to discourage future campaigns conceived like that of Jesse Jackson. Jackson discovered the bipolar bias of the Hunt Commission changes late in the game. He had hoped, among other aims, to wield a significant bloc of delegates as a bargaining counter at a possibly deadlocked convention. When he discovered, belatedly, that the rules changes militated against a powerbroker's role, he was dismayed. He first attacked the winner-take-all congressional district option. He pointed out, accurately, that of the seven states that had adopted the winner-take-all option—California, Florida, Illinois, Maryland, New Jersey, Pennsylvania, and West Virginia—all but the last had large urbanized black communities concentrated in a few congressional districts. At first he claimed, inaccurately, that the rules diluted their influence. But he dropped this complaint as it became apparent that his real rivals in these states were black mayors and congressmen who would have preponderant influence over even those delegates pledged to him. He reached a sort of gentleman's agreement in which organizational black Democrats would not call attention to his weak control over his delegates while he used his considerable media appeal to help them increase registration for the party.

His role in increasing turnout made party professionals treat him kindly even when he charged that the proportionality thresholds had deprived him of his rightful voice in the convention. He argued that he had received 19 percent of the vote in those states that had primaries, but had garnered only nine percent of the delegates at the convention. If the truth had been told, the answer to his complaints would have been that his was exactly the kind of candidacy that the Hunt Commission had aimed at discouraging—not because it was grounded in a racial constituency but to the extent that it was unable to reach out beyond that constituency. The Hunt Commission changes did indeed reduce the role of "third force" candidates who wished merely to bargain at a deadlocked convention by reducing the arithmetic probability that such a convention could arise. The fact that Jackson persevered with his campaign, persuading many black voters that the rules were somehow unfair, and gratuitously, persuading many Jewish voters that blacks were allied against them, added to the impression that Hart and Mondale had done so much to foster: that the Democratic Party was a coalition of voracious and irreconcilable interest groups.

If in the movement of the Democrats towards a programmatic party, the Hunt Commission was a step forward, the 1984 nomination campaign was a step backward. Even so, and even with the establishmentarian attempt to "shorten" the campaign season, the rules changes both permitted the full emergence of an underfunded insurgent with majoritarian potential and prevented a candidate without majoritarian potential from deadlocking a convention. And, the changes in PR thresholds worked as planned to winnow down a large field to a meaningful, if divisive, two-way race. The presence, moreover, of office holders at the San Francisco convention gave it recognizable personalities who could, if the need arose, contribute towards a deliberative convention.

The Interaction with the GOP in 1988

Enter the Republicans. To portray the election defeat of the Democratic ticket as just deserts for the nomination campaign would be stretching the point. Rules and nomination fights are all the more delectable to party professionals because there is no inevitable electoral consequence. The professionals understand that elections more often turn on peace, prosperity, personality, and potluck than on lingering memories of the nomination campaigns. Though Republicans had reason to be grateful to Gary Hart and Walter Mondale himself for pioneering the picture of Mondale as a soft-minded panderer to "special interests," they had more reason to be grateful for an upbeat economy. But rules disputes in one campaign do set the stage for the next. Whatever changes the Democrats make for 1988 will proceed from the agendas that various factions took away from San Francisco in 1984. This time, however, Republicans are also scheduled to have a contested nomination.

The interaction between the two parties will introduce elements not present in 1984. The suspicion by party regulars of independent and crossover voters, for example, is harder to justify when both parties have contests. Then the movement of independents into a primary is a fair test of a candidate's appeal to swing voters who may determine the general election. The further arguments of political science professors against the open primary on the grounds of "responsible party government" also become less persuasive in a more free-wheeling election year.

Similarly, in a dually contested year the arguments in favor of party caucuses have less powerful backing. When there is an incumbent president seeking a second term, he favors caucuses because they minimize risks in his own party. The opposing party establishment can argue persuasively for caucuses to mobilize and unify its own activists against a known opponent. When both parties have crises of leadership simultaneously, however, it seems less dangerous to air "dirty linen" in direct primaries. The balance between party caucuses, which mobilize activists, and direct primaries, which test electoral appeal, is more likely to shift to the primary.

One thing is certain about 1988: the peculiarities of the two parties' national rules decree that it is the Democrats who will set the national fashion on delegate selection. The Republican National Committee does not have any rulemaking power between conventions. The GOP rules explicitly defer to state law on matters of delegate selection and timing of primaries—or as the lawyers say, the GOP rules incorporate state law by reference. Thus, any changes which the national Democrats impose are likely, without contrary action in the few state legislatures controlled by Republicans, to be legislated at the state level for both parties. For example, in 1988 as in previous years since 1976, the Democratic threshold on PR will, in the absence of state-by-state GOP alternatives, become the Republican threshold as well.

The rules agendas of the several Democratic factions, then, have more than parochial interest. On four counts—the balance between caucus and primary states, the modification of pure proportionality, the congressional district winner-take-all primary, and the timing and structure of key primaries—the measures adopted by the Democrats may have greater impact on the Republicans than among themselves.

Within the Democratic party the caucus is becoming more neutral among factions. The old wisdom that it favored organized labor does not hold in states where the issue-oriented activists of the 1960s have become the hard-boiled professionals of the 1980s. In primaries, organizational Democrats have often suffered from defections to media-oriented candidates, but this, too, could change if they support a charismatic candidate. The strongest eristic argument for a caucus system among the Democrats, then, is not intraparty but interparty—namely, that widespread use of caucus systems tends to inhibit rapid Republican growth.

For without the experience of participating in a GOP primary, Democratic and independent voters are slow to redefine themselves as Republicans. Instead, they see votes for this or that Republican as judgments of personality.

Ambitious GOP leaders have often pressed for open primaries, at least as a transitional phase, to accelerate the movement of fluid voters into their party.

Caucuses, by contrast, usually draw those who have had some prior organizational activity. In areas with strong GOP traditions, caucuses reinforce mainstream Republicanism, with participants drawn from existing ward, precinct, and local candidate organizations. In the South, however, and wherever grassroots GOP organization is sparse, caucuses are likely to attract issues-oriented activists. As with the Democrats, such activists generally need a few elections to develop a political style that is more than a liability in a national campaign. And this is particularly true of those elements of the evangelical and right-to-life movements likely to invest efforts in Republican caucuses.

No generalization can hold for all states, but nationwide a fashion for direct primaries and particularly for open primaries benefits the GOP, while a fashion for caucuses helps it to retain its existing strength where it is already strong but gives it predictable national liabilities where it is weak. Thus, the plan of southern Democrats to group their states into a regional primary (objectionable on Van Buren's principles for reintroducing the sectionalism that the national parties were set up to counteract) would, as a tactical matter, benefit the GOP by enabling many closet Republicans in the South to make their first party-identifying act. But Democratic legislatures could thwart the GOP potential of this device by scheduling caucuses rather than primary elections.

The Democratic proportionality thresholds have even more profound spillover effects among Republicans. The Hunt Commission countered the thrust of PR towards fragmentation and deadlock by making the Democratic convention more "republican"—that is by introducing indirect forms of representation and raising the proportionality thresholds. The most prominent device was reserving about a fourth of the slots at the 1984 convention for officialdom. The Democrats virtually promised at the 1984 convention to lower the proportionality threshold to 15 percent, the pre-Hunt Commission level. But at the same time their Fairness Commission plans to increase the overall fraction of officials. In tandem these two devices will give freer play to diversity in the primaries and yet retain the ability to assure a smooth convention.

Republicans, who hew closely to the separation of powers as a rationale for their presidential convention, have no such provisions for party officialdom. As a result, the lowering of national proportionality thresholds will have greater fragmenting effects among them. If no single candidate stampedes public opinion, how will they winnow down a multicandidate field? In the past they have been able to rely on their majoritarian instincts to avoid an impasse. But the movement of issues—oriented activists into the party opens the GOP convention to the iron logic of pure proportionality. Any media-oriented candidate whose supporters are more concerned about issues than about winning can, by persevering through to the convention, hope to have more leverage in the GOP system than Jesse Jackson had in San Francisco.

The flexibility of a GOP convention may thus depend on those states which avail themselves of the new winner-take-all, congressional district option permitted under the Democratic rules. In 1984 this pro-organization option was used by Republicans in six states that usually elect "moderate" Republican governors. In four of these—New Jersey, West Virginia, Illinois, and Pennsylvania—the GOP would appear to be strong enough to retain or initiate its own system without Democratic cooperation. Elsewhere, the future of this device requires some cooperation from Democratic legislative majorities.

The striking thing about such issues is that, short of preempting the ground with federal legislation, Republicans have no way to affect them on the national level. At the state level they can make changes only where they either control the state legislatures (as in Michigan in 1984, New Jersey after 1986, Indiana always) or where a tradition of deference permits the parties to choose significantly different systems for presidential competition. Michigan Republicans acted promptly in 1985 to make their district caucuses the opening event of the nomination campaign. The California GOP's winner-take-all direct primary will be of special interest since it commands the largest bloc vote of delegates in the history of U.S. nominating conventions. In 1976 and 1980 the California result came after the nomination outcome was clear. But if the California date were moved or if the GOP nomination is closely contested, the California GOP will doubtless be asked to eliminate what many Republicans in smaller western states see as a circumvention of the party's prohibition against unit rule voting. Even here, however, a legislated change would require the cooperation of California Democrats. The most aggressive initiative by a state Republican Party has been taken in Connecticut where the GOP has sued, with initial success, to hold an open primary in defiance of a closed primary law imposed by the Democratic legislative majority.

On the whole, the Democrats have used constructively their power to set the national conditions of delegate selection. They have provided a proportional voice to national constituencies whose members may be in a minority in a given state. And they have allowed candidates based in such constituencies to test their majoritarian appeal. Insofar as the Democrats have ground factional axes, it has been against each other, and we have seen that the piling on of devices to overcontrol the 1984 nomination campaign backfired upon them. But not since they gave their national committee the power to make midterm rules changes has there been the prospect of a campaign year without an incumbent running for nomination in either party. In planning for 1988, the Democrats may for the first time consider the effect of their rules on the Republicans.

Allocation Formulas

Thus far, our discussion has addressed delegate *selection* and representation *within* state delegations. In this area, both parties have adopted the main

Democratic innovation: the splitting of the monolithic state delegation. They differ nationally on the inclusion of ex officio delegates and at the state level on the California primary.

In the area of delegate *allocation*, or apportionment *among* the states, however, the differences between the two parties are pronounced. The Democrats use a standard based half on the Electoral College and half on the national vote for president. The Republicans use a standard based on the Electoral College and a complicated set of "victory bonuses" and grandfather clauses. That the differences are significant may be seen by comparing the convention representation of neighboring large and small states in 1984, with their electoral vote (EV) in parentheses:

	Pennsylvania (25)	Delaware (3)
Dem dels	195	18
per EV	7.8	6.0
per capita	1/61,000	1/30,000
GOP dels	98	19
per EV	3.9	6.3
per capita	1/121,000	1/31,000

As the table shows, Delaware had roughly the same number of delegates at both conventions in 1984. In both parties its delegation was about six times its Electoral College vote, with each delegate representing a population of roughly 30,000. Pennsylvania, by contrast, had a GOP delegation about one-half as numerous as that among the Democrats, with 3.9 times its Electoral College vote in the Republican convention versus a factor of 7.8 among the Democrats. Each delegate at the GOP convention in Dallas represented 121,000 Pennsylvanians, about double the number as at the San Francisco convention.

Greater differences between the two parties prevail on standing convention committees dealing with rules, platform and credentials, and on the national committees which manage party affairs between conventions. GOP party committees are purely confederal, with all states represented equally, as in the U S Senate or the United Nations General Assembly. Democratic convention committees are roughly federal, with each state having about a third of its Electoral College vote. The Democratic National Committee is also roughly federal, except that the party chair and vice chair from each state are added to each delegation, while a countervailing group of 25 voting at-large delegates is added to counterbalance this confederal element with urban-oriented representation. The following table compares the same neighboring large and small states:

	Pennsylvania (25)	Delaware (3)
Convention Committees		
Dems	8	1
GOP	2	2
National Committee Members		
DNC	11*	4
RNC	3	3

(*Plus two of the 25 at-large delegates)

Among the Democrats a well-articulated philosophy of representation accounts for the basis of the convention and its committees. The formula used to determine delegation size is based on two standards, Electoral College vote and vote for president in the previous three presidential elections. The use of the Electoral College has a prima facie legitimacy, since this embodies the federal logic under which the president is elected. The use of popular vote for president is the party's way of recognizing a national popular membership that cuts across state lines. Unlike European parties, the major American parties have never kept national membership rolls. State party registration requirements vary too much to be useful as a guide to membership. As the best substitute, the Democrats take national party vote over a three election period as the base of its national constituency. This rewards high turnout and party loyalty and shifts the Electoral College standard in a popular and participatory direction. It fits also with the post-1976 use of federal funds by the major parties. Because it is taxpayers, as individuals, without regard to the Electoral College system, who are now financing the conventions and presidential campaigns, the Democrats' deviation from the Electoral College has a further justification in terms of the new basis of campaign finance introduced by the Federal Election Campaign Act of 1975.

Within the states, the allocation of Democratic delegates among congressional districts may be determined by state parties from one of four possible options, combining standards of population, Democratic registration, and Democratic statewide vote for governor and for president. These options give some play to state variation and to factional wrangling, yet all derive from a simple intrastate standard: "one Democrat, one vote." This same standard is the basis for the measured deviation from the Electoral College at the national level, and it coheres with the Democrats' belief in a national programmatic party capable of transcending state lines and the separation of powers.

The Republican allocation formula, by contrast, deviates from the Electoral College by virtue of a system of "victory bonuses" linked to presidential, gubernatorial, and senatorial elections, and House delegation majorities. Each state begins with a base of delegates equal to three times its Electoral College vote. To this it can then add a number of delegates equal to 60 percent of its Electoral College vote if it has voted for the GOP presidential ticket in the previous election. All further victory bonuses are then awarded uniformly to states without regard to population, GOP vote, or Electoral College weight.

For example, every state that votes for the presidential ticket in the previous election gets 4.5 bonus delegates regardless of its size. In addition it receives one bonus delegate for the election of a Republican governor, one for each Republican senator, and one for winning a majority of its House delegation. In all, a state can win up to 8.5 uniform bonus delegates to add to its base.

For Delaware with a base of nine delegates, adding the maximum of 8.5 (rounded to nine) uniform bonus delegates produces a doubling of its delegation size. For Pennsylvania with a base of 75, the addition of nine bonus delegates represents an increase of only 12 percent. Such a system produces a mathematically certain dilution of the franchise of Republicans in the more populous states. Dilution will occur regardless of Republican turnout, registration, or electoral victory. The comparison between Pennsylvania and Delaware in the table above is typical. These two states were chosen because in 1984 they earned the same allotments of bonus delegates; each had one less than the maximum possible. Yet Pennsylvania's victory bonuses earned it a delegation 3.9 times its Electoral College vote, while Delaware earned 6.3 times its share on the same standard. The relation between these two factors is about three-fifths, a figure that raises more than an eyebrow in an American constitutional idiom.

Moreover, a special grandfather clause adopted in 1972 assures the small states a few extra delegates even if they fail to win any elections. Under this provision, it is a mathematical certainty that a populous state like Pennsylvania can never reach Electoral College parity with Delaware, even if Pennsylvania receives the maximal number of bonus delegates and Delaware receives none at all. The following table illustrates the possible ranges of delegations (parentheses give delegation size as a multiple of Electoral College vote):

GOP Delegation Size

	Pennsylvania (25)	Delaware (3)	Pa/Del Ratio
Maximum	99 (3.96)	20 (6.67)	.59
Minimum	75 (3.0)	12 (4.0)	.75
Actual 1984	98 (3.92)	19 (6.33)	.62

The third line gives the ratio of representation of Pennsylvania to Delaware on an Electoral College standard. It is derived by taking Pennsylvania's delegation as a multiple of its Electoral College vote and dividing it by Delaware's. Thus, when both states achieve their maximal delegation size, Pennsylvania's representation is diluted to slightly under three-fifths (.59) that of Delaware. Note that even if every Pennsylvanian voted Republican for every office, Pennsylvania would have a delegation of 3.96 its Electoral College vote. If not a single Republican vote were ever cast in Delaware, that state would have a delegation equal to 4.0 times its Electoral College vote. The reader must bear in mind that these comparisons are based not on a one person, one vote standard, but on the Electoral College, in which small state voters already have a greater weight than those in the more populous states. The GOP formula makes Electoral College parity between a large state like Pennsylvania and a small one like Delaware a mathematical impossibility.

The GOP has since its founding made the Electoral College the basis of its convention. It has never accepted a states' rights rationale for its national convention. It also claims to believe in "incentives," and the preamble to its rules specifically inveighs against any form of "favoritism." What, then, is the rationale for the disparities between large and small states?

The short answer is that the party has no adequate rationale consistent its stated ideals. The curious GOP allocation formula is better understood in terms of a tainted and traumatic factional history than in terms of any coherent philosophy of representation. A historical account of the bonus system is provided in the appendix. The initial introduction of three uniform bonus delegates for presidential victory resulted from factional bargains struck at the 1920 Republican Convention. Underlying the bargaining was a shared sense that the party could afford to accord some American citizens less punctilious consideration than others. One bonus device, first adopted in 1916 at the insistence of the Progressive faction, tacitly accepted the denial of the franchise to blacks. The second device, the uniform victory bonus, worked as an ethnic gerrymander against newer stock Americans, who were overwhelmingly concentrated in the more populous states. Official and semiofficial Republican documents circa 1920-1924, in rhetoric that contrasted sharply with Lincoln's view of the Declaration as providing the basis of unity among polyglot Americans, held that the newer immigrants from Southern, Central, and Eastern Europe were poor material for citizenship. The uniform victory bonus tilted the Republican convention toward the smaller states of the West and northern New England, which were thought to contain a more genuinely American population.

Once legitimated in the rules, the uniform bonus had a career quite independent of the factional rivalries and nativist prejudices that attended its birth. The word "bonus" had instant appeal to convention rank-and-file, and the one-state one-vote structure of GOP rules committees assured that uniform bonuses could be reported favorably to the convention. By 1960 the uniform bonus had doubled its weight in a convention of the same size, and the party had even extended the bonus principle to the RNC. A series of adverse court rulings led to a redrafting of the formula in 1972 and to the introduction of the party's first presidential victory bonus geared to the Electoral College. At the same time, factional pressures led to the retention of the old uniform bonus for presidential victory.

Like the Democratic quotas of 1972, the GOP formula of that year withstood a landmark court test that was resolved in 1975. But unlike the Democrats, the Republicans did not in subsequent years distinguish between what the courts would allow and what it behooves a major party to retain. As we shall now see, the party's 1984 rules deliberations suggest that the GOP allocation formula as a whole has yet to achieve a level of coherence or principle comparable to that of the Democrats.

1984: The Petrified Formula

At the 1984 convention, three new bonuses were proposed: the state legislative bonus, the so-called Puerto Rico–District of Columbia bonus, and the Indiana Plan for a turnout bonus geared to GOP vote in three previous elections. All three proposals were defeated in the convention rules committee. And in the recorded debates on each, an important consideration was the opinion of counsel that any change in the 1972 formula might permit dissidents to reopen litigation under conditions of federal funding that invited closer scrutiny by the courts. Nevertheless, the three proposals shed light on the infirmities of the current allocation system as they are perceived by members of the Republican rules establishment. Each of the proposed bonuses derived from some logical extension of the existing formula. All of them drew upon the idiom of "incentives" and "federalism" that became canonical after the courts used it to approve the 1972 formula.

The state legislative bonus is a perennial favorite. It would enable a state to win one bonus delegate for each house of the state legislature with a Republican majority. (In Nebraska's unicameral, nonpartisan legislature, the election of a Republican speaker would be worth two bonus delegates.) This bonus seemed to its proponents a perfectly reasonable extension of the existing uniform bonuses for Republican governor, senator, and majority in a state's delegation to the House of Representatives. As a delegate from North Dakota put it, the convention, though based on the separation of powers, should provide an incentive for any statewide Republican victory with a tangential bearing on winning the presidency. State legislatures drafted reapportionment plans for the House of Representatives, which in turn voted for the president in case of an Electoral College deadlock. Hence the existing bonus for control of a House delegation majority logically required a state legislative bonus to complete the system. Opposition to the proposal came from the South, whose representatives argued that their region would qualify for none of the 39 bonus delegates to be so added and that the bonus would thereby shift the regional and ideological balance of the convention to the less "conservative" states that elected GOP legislatures.

The proposed Puerto Rico–District of Columbia bonus specified that no state would receive fewer delegates than the 14 assigned arbitrarily to Puerto Rico and Washington, D.C. (When the bonus system was redrafted in 1972 its obvious effects against urban concentrations of black and Hispanic voters in the populous states made it prudent to offer attractive inducements to the two delegations led by black and Hispanic Republicans.) Under the 1972 grandfather clause a state could fall only as low as its 1972 total, which for many small states was 12 delegates. Moreover, if, as a technical amendments

158 / Josiah Lee Auspitz

subcommittee recommended, the 1972 safety net were removed, small states that received no bonus delegates could fall as low as their base of nine delegates. To a delegate from Rhode Island, among others, it seemed a violation of federalism that states should have fewer delegates than nonstates. Both of these proposals, which would further intensify the disparities between large and small states, came to the convention with a positive endorsement by vote of the RNC.

A countervailing proposal for a turnout bonus was presented to the convention rules committee, where it died after exhausting the requested time for debate. Its author, James Neal of Indiana, had been a supporter of the 1972 formula as Indiana State Chairman. He continued to support it but saw a need to "refederalize" the convention by adding population-based elements. Without some countervailing popular element, he could find no federal rationale for the 4.5 uniform bonus delegates for presidential victory, especially since the party already had a presidential bonus geared to 60 percent of a state's Electoral College vote. He proposed adding to the existing formula 1076 delegates (twice the Electoral College number) geared to GOP turnout in the three previous presidential elections. He argued that this would recognize the individual Republican voter, encourage party loyalty over more than one election, give institutional force to the Reagan-Bush majority, satisfy the desire in all states for more delegates, and provide a realistic incentive to state parties to increase turnout, a contribution more within their power than the victory of the presidential ticket. Any objections to the increased size of the convention could be countered by reducing the number of alternates. Figures compiled by the RNC staff suggested, moreover, that his plan was factionally neutral. Had it been in effect in 1976, the last contested convention, the shift in votes between Reagan and Ford would have been a negligible 0.4%, or eight delegates out of more than 2000.

The Indiana Plan was successfully opposed with the accurate argument that many more states would lose in relative share of the convention than would gain—a telling point in a committee where all states have two votes. However, middle-sized states with nothing to gain in relative share—Connecticut, Iowa, and Kansas—supported the Indiana proposal, while self-described "conservative movement" delegates from more populous and more weakly Republican states—Maryland, New York, and Massachusetts—spoke against the Indiana proposal even though it would have increased the representation of their constituents. Opponents of the proposal used materials distributed by Morton Blackwell's Committee for Fair Republican Rules, which asserted (erroneously) that the dilution of voting power of Republicans in populous states in the 1972 formula did not go beyond the "Madisonian" standard inherent in the Electoral College. These materials are of historical note because Blackwell subsequently claimed to be the author of the 1972 formula.

Ironically, if all three bonuses had been passed, the GOP would have had a more plausible formula in terms of "federalism" and "incentives." Using the

Electoral College comparisons of the previous tables, the Indiana turnout bonus would have greatly decreased the disparity between large and small state delegations in 1984 (again, ratios of delegation size to Electoral College vote are in parentheses):

	Pennsylvania (25)	Delaware (3)	Pa/Del Ratio
Indiana Plan	22 (7.33)	157 (6.28)	.86
1984 actual	19 (6.33)	98 (3.92)	.62
Indiana + RNC bonuses	24 (8.0)	159 (6.36)	.79

Note the last column: even if one were to add to the Indiana bonus the RNC–approved bonuses for state legislative victories and the Puerto Rico–District of Columbia factor, the GOP formula would fall into a range much closer to the Electoral College. The advantage of bonuses would still be with the small states, but only if they earned victories. In the event they did not earn uniform bonuses, they would fall slightly below Electoral College parity with the large states, so that the bonus system would pose incentives and attendant risks to them as well. Here, for example, (again using the presidential voting figures for 1972-1980 in calculating the Indiana turnout bonus) are the delegation sizes for Pennsylvania and Delaware if both states earn no uniform victory bonuses:

Minimum Delegation Size

	Pennsylvania (25)	Delaware (3)	Pa/Del Ratio
'72 (Blackwell) Formula	75 (3.0)	12 (4.0)	.75
Indiana + RNC bonuses	134 (5.36)	14 (4.75)	1.13

Though not ideal, the unplanned combination of the Indiana and RNC bonus proposals, demonstrates that within the rationale of incentives and federalism, it is still possible for there to emerge a package of incremental improvements that would reduce the deviation from the Electoral College, refederalize the convention, recognize the individual Republican voter, reestablish the distinction between states and Puerto Rico, and even accommodate demands for more uniform bonus delegates.

But the political dynamics of GOP structure make piecemeal reform difficult. On the one hand, bonuses that add uniform delegates are perennially popular in committees dominated by the small states, but they risk renewed litigation so long as the GOP accepts federal funding. On the other hand, bonuses oriented to GOP vote or population or (as in the Steiger proposal rejected in 1972) victory in congressional districts have little chance of passage in a confederally based committee if members vote their narrow state interest.

As it stands, therefore, the GOP structure would appear to be petrified. Between conventions, the RNC Rules Committee dutifully develops new bonuses only to have party lawyers tell the assembled convention rules committee that the changes cannot be enacted for fear of suit. In part as a precaution against legal action, the convention rules committee in 1984 passed a study resolution to examine the effect of the GOP structure as a whole on minority participation in party affairs. Since the newer minorities of concern to the party—Hispanics and urban blacks—are every bit as concentrated in the populous states as were the immigrants from Southern, Central, and Eastern Europe of the 1920s, exhaustive research is scarcely needed to establish the chilling effect of the GOP structure upon their participation.

Housekeeping Rules

The rules by which a matter may reach the floor of a convention are superficially the same in both parties, but very different in their effect. In each party matters must be reported onto the floor from the appropriate committee, be it platform, credentials, or rules. In each party a dissenting resolution may reach the floor by a petition of 25 percent of the members of a committee. But because the composition of convention committees is so different, the potential among the Republicans for justifiable cries of foul play is much greater than among the Democrats. Democratic convention committees on rules, credentials, and platform are proportioned to a state's convention strength. GOP committees, as we have seen, allot two votes to each state regardless of the size of its convention delegation. Thus, an issue of interest to the small western states—say, the 55 mile per hour speed limit—will be routinely included in GOP platforms in order to avoid a 25 percent petition and a convention floor vote, while a similar issue that concerns populous states—mass transit, industrial pollution—can be safely ignored. The ten most populous states, with 55 percent of the population, cannot muster the votes to bring a minority plank to the floor.

Until 1976, the committee structure did not prevent minority planks from reaching the floor: the "six-delegation rule" permitted any six GOP state delegations to petition on the floor for a vote. In 1980 it remained ambiguous whether the six delegation rule applied to minority resolutions or suspension of the rules. In 1984 the work of a technical amendments subcommittee explicitly restricted the six-delegation rule to a motion for suspension of the rules. It also specified that the Rules of the House of Representatives not Roberts Rules of Order would be used on the convention floor. Under the Rules of the House, a suspension of the rules requires a two-thirds rather than a majority vote.

A GOP convention is thus more controlled than a Democratic one. Traditionally, the Republicans have relied on a sense of civility outside the rules to preserve a smoothly run convention. When their good manners break down, as happens every generation or two, the problems of reconciliation are compounded by the unfair advantage that one side or the other has taken of rules that did not bear close scrutiny to begin with. The Democratic rules assume a level of conflict that requires more serious attention to formal procedure.

It should be repeated that, notwithstanding the structure of its committees, the GOP does not accept a states' rights rationale for its national convention. Though the committees are unrepresentative of the convention, they can never act in the place of the convention. The rare matter in which a committee might have a final say is decided by weighted voting in which each state's representation reflects the strength of its delegation to the convention. For example, if the party should have to replace the presidential or vice-presidential nominee in the middle of a campaign, the RNC does it by weighted voting, in a process that was made explicit in the rules for the first time in 1984, but has been included in a continuing resolution by every convention since 1928.

A final difference is worth noting on the role of minority and sectional groupings in the two national committees. After the enlargement of the DNC in 1974 members formed caucuses (the black caucus, Hispanic caucus, labor caucus, and so on), but official recognition of them was dropped in the aftermath of the 1984 election, a further step in the movement from a coalitional to a programmatic definition of the national party. The RNC, on the other hand, explicitly recognizes the existence of hyphenated Republicans. Prior to 1984 it reserved nonvoting seats on its executive committee for "auxiliaries" representing black, Hispanic, and "heritage group" (mainly ethnic Roman Catholic and Asian) Republicans. After 1984 the RNC still preserved its nonvoting tokens but shifted them from the executive committee to the main body and added to their number Jewish and labor auxiliaries. The RNC executive committee, meanwhile, was restructured along explicitly sectional lines, with representatives drawn from four regional caucuses accorded formal recognition in the national rules.

The Parties Compared

We can now compare the two parties with respect to three criteria. First, there is Van Buren's criterion that a major party reflect in its inner constitution some defensible interpretation of the spirit of the regime whose offices it seeks to win. Second, there is the organization of party for actually winning elections. Third, since what one wins in an election is the authority to govern in a system marked by the separation of powers, there is the problem of the place of party within the American constitutional order. There is no single right way to meet these criteria. Yet one can discern better from worse.

Representative Structure

As we have seen, the Democratic Party structure reflects the doctrine of responsible party government. To adapt it to the pluralist, postcoalitional character of American presidential politics, the Democrats have pioneered a limited role for proportionality within a majoritarian system. They may continue to tinker with elements of this system to meet the demands of one or another candidate or faction—notably the thresholds of proportionality, the numbers of officeholding delegates, the scheduling of the primary season, and the balance among three devices for selecting delegates: direct primaries, congressional district primaries, and caucuses. But though the role of the individual elements may change, the overall structure of their system remains coherent; it springs from an integrated vision of a national programmatic party with room for diversity and play for factional conflict.

The implicit rationale for the Democratic structure may be stated as follows: the Democratic party conceives of itself as a national party, with three centers of participation: the state parties; the elected governors, mayors, and members of Congress; and the diverse mass of voters who loyally vote Democratic. Its allocation formula for the national convention recognizes all three centers of participation, and any successful nominee will be disciplined in the course of his campaign to deal concurrently with all three constituencies.

The national character of the party is reinforced juridically by the active use of the party's court-approved right to override state law in matters of delegate selection. It has asserted this power over issues of scheduling, affirmative action plans, and the prohibition of the open primary. To legitimate the centralization of such decisions, as well as the use of federal funds for its convention and presidential campaign, the party has restructured its national committee and convention committees on a federal basis, roughly reflecting the Electoral College strength of the states. It has, after some experimentation, explicitly repudiated quotas. (As among the Republicans, provisions for equal representation of the sexes are somehow not considered quotas.)

In all, one must concede to the Democrats a dignity of purpose. Beneath their petty factional strife, they have been engaged in a profoundly serious enterprise: to bridge the deep fault lines in the New Deal coalition. If they are in the end able to transform that coalition into a majoritarian programmatic party, their work on party rules will have been a crucial precondition to this historic achievement.

The Republican rules can claim no such dignity. The best that can be said is that they retain elements of nineteenth century statecraft that still provide the skeleton of a coherent alternative to the New Deal notion of a centralized programmatic party. Since 1916, however, the GOP rules have suffered additions that put it out of alignment with an Electoral College standard and with the preamble to the rules themselves. The extent of the disparities, a three-fifths dilution of large relative to small states, requires a rationale. On the face of it, there is none for the single device that produces most of the disparity: the uniform victory bonus of 4.5 delegates for delivering a state's Electoral College vote to the presidential ticket. Though one might plausibly argue, in defense of other uniform bonuses, that a GOP governor or senator has a political significance regardless of the size of his state, the electoral vote of that state has no significance outside the Electoral College itself.

In the 1920s one might have argued that national campaigns were so largely conducted through the state parties as to justify a special uniform bonus to them. (However, because two-thirds of the money for the 1920 campaign was raised nationally, there is no record of such an argument having been made.) But whatever the case in 1920, state parties do not remotely deliver victory to the presidential ticket today. Nowadays presidential campaigns are centrally run. The strategic interplay of the two major candidate organizations far overshadows state party effort in determining victory. The large incentives for presidential victory—both the 60 percent Electoral College bonus and the 4.5 uniform bonus—thus have an arbitrary and capricious effect. For example, Carter's sweep of the South in 1976 deprived that region of delegates to the GOP convention in 1980. A Humphrey candidacy would have had just the opposite effect. What influence did southern state Republican parties have on the Democratic nomination process? Here is another instance where decisions made by the Democrats shape the structure of the GOP convention.

More objectionable in representative theory is the self-entrenching factionalism that results when the number of seats in a representative body is greatly expanded to reward one or another region on the basis of a single election victory. That body would then be prone to nominate candidates who would again campaign in the favored regions and produce the frozen sectional politics that for Van Buren it was the first duty of a national party to counteract. Happily for the country, the pattern of elections since 1972 has avoided such an outcome by a combination of the first Carter nomination and three GOP landslides, in which all regions win bonuses. But if there are several closely contested elections in a row, any flexibility in the Republican convention will proceed from campaign choices made by the Democrats.

Of course, the courts have ruled that a political party has a First Amendment right to assemble under its self-chosen rules. But here, too, a comparison with the Democrats is instructive. The courts, as we have seen, permitted the Democrats to enforce racial quotas and to eliminate Wisconsin's open primary. Yet that party dropped the quota system and for 1988 even gave up its hard-won ban on Wisconsin's open primary. The GOP, by contrast, has had more difficulty distinguishing enduring principles from expedients.

Party Success

But isn't the GOP formula "successful?" Doesn't the emphasis on "victory bonuses" indicate a winner's mentality? Does not the relative harmony in the GOP over rules provide a welcome contrast to the wrangling of the Democrats? And are not one-time election victories, of the kind rewarded in the GOP rules, the whole function of a party in any case?

A framework of intraparty representation does not cause success at the polls. (If one wished to make a simpleminded scorecard, the statistics would, of course, favor the GOP's nineteenth century, pure Electoral College formula, under which it won all but three presidential elections from 1860 to 1912, rather than the subsequent bonuses, under which it has won eight and lost eight elections.) And in point of fact, the real success story of the post-war era has been the ability of the Democrats to sustain themselves as the ongoing majority in the face of obsolescence of their philosophy of government. Their attention to the professional points of politics is no small part of this achievement. In the postwar period, the United States remains the only country in the industrialized West in which the more business-oriented party has yet to win full control over the government. In sixteen of the forty years from 1946 to 1986, the Democrats have held the presidency and both houses of Congress; the GOP has never had this honor. Of the ten presidential elections, the GOP has won six, a figure due not to party victories but to the success of its three incumbent presidents in winning second terms by establishing an identity independent from the party.

Right now, to the limited extent that rules affect "winning," the post-1984 Democrats are structured for long term health, while the Republicans are structured for long term trouble. As in 1946, when a realignment of attitudes toward the GOP was so marked as to give Republicans majorities in both houses of Congress, the national GOP structure presents the party with competitive liabilities that, regardless of the outcome of this or that election, limit its potential.

First, Republicans continue to allow the Democrats to set the terms of national presidential selection to suit their needs, with no guarantee that this process will benefit the GOP or the country. Second, the Democratic system, without the correctives introduced by the Hunt Commission, is conducive to deadlocked and ideologically polarized convention politics. Specifically, the proportionality thresholds, which will be lowered for 1988, enable issues-oriented activists to achieve a larger role than they could earn in a majoritarian electoral competition. A campaign conceived on the model of Jesse Jackson's has far greater potential in a Republican convention, where no places are reserved for officeholders. Third, the narrow and aging base of GOP party loyalists creates an especial problem in caucus states, where any issue that motivates insurgents can produce caucus takeovers by activists who have not yet mastered the idiom of national electoral politics. Whereas a caucus system stabilizes the Democrats it has the opposite effect on the Republicans; it is noteworthy that organized labor opened 1985 with a plan to extend caucus selection. Fourth, the representative system of the GOP remains a potential liability in itself in a political culture which takes issues of representation issues seriously. A GOP convention in which the result were not preordained would open to closer public scrutiny the party's committee and convention structure, which have no ready parallels in any state Republican Party. Finally, the flouting of its own ideals in its rules reinforces the fashionable view of Republican activity as ignoble. For most of this century those seeking a principled politics have done so in some nonpartisan way. Both the progressive and conservative movements have been populated by quasi-Republicans loath to invest themselves in party affairs. Yet there is no evidence that such movements, even with the benefits of tax exemption, can fulfill the constitutional role of party.

Parties and the Separation of Powers

The rules thus raise a deeper question about the place of party within the American constitutional system. For fifty years the heirs of the New Deal have advanced the notion of a national programmatic party. The mission of party, on this view, is to overcome the separation of powers—to unite with a common purpose the branches of federal government and to provide further bridges between Washington and the state and local governments. Though party has always worked informally in this role, there has been no formal link between a president and his congressional party since 1832, when the national convention replaced the congressional caucus as the instrument of presidential nomination. Franklin Roosevelt's attempt after 1936 to pack the Supreme Court and to purge his congressional majority failed as a means of enforcing a unity of purpose led by the executive branch. In reintroducing a formal link in 1984 between the president and other party officials the Democrats have built into the nomination process a more moderate version of the doctrine of responsible party government.

The doctrine so dominates public opinion that most Republicans act with only a dim and vestigial awareness of an alternative. The nineteenth century elements of the GOP structure, however, are grounded in a different conception. By nominating a presidential candidate independently of the other branches and levels, the GOP in effect recognizes a distinctive competence and independence in the presidency, which ought not to be artificially precompromised in the nomination process. The mission of the presidency on this view is not to impose a unified managerial will upon the other branches, still less upon the country as a whole. A Republican president, having been elevated by a convention that respects the separation of powers, would stress the complementary rather than the bargaining relationships among the several branches and levels. He would follow a policy of restraint in his own office and concentrate his policies in those spheres where the protection of American citizenship itself is at stake. Party unity, on this view, would then consist not in insinuating dogmatic and detailed policy objectives into the other branches but in fostering a shared resolve on the enduring bases of the American regime.

For the party of Lincoln, one of these enduring bases was the sacredness of the franchise, rooted in the still more basic principle—the "father of all moral principle," as Lincoln called it: equality in natural rights. Natural right is not, as is sometimes thought, exclusively compatible with a one person, one vote standard. But it does require that distinctions among citizens be neither arbitrary nor invidious. If devices that dilute the franchise of some Republicans serve no purpose save factional convenience, they subvert the integrity of the franchise, and thus undermine any Republican effort to define an alternative to the centralized programmatic party that is the lasting heritage of the New Deal.

While the Democratic rulemakers have been struggling to develop a workable conception of party as an institution bridging the separation of powers, the Republicans have allowed their more traditional conception to deteriorate. In this, they have taken a cue from their three elected postwar presidents. Eisenhower considered himself from the start to be a national leader above party. Nixon, though a creature of the GOP, in 1972 campaigned independently of it with an advertising-oriented New Majority Party. Reagan, though a party leader in California, owed his national prominence more to his role in the conservative movement, a consciously transpartisan faction. True to this base of support, he campaigned in 1984 as the inheritor of the conservative strands in the New Deal coalition. In all, the postwar leadership of the GOP has tended to view the party as a merchandising device, robbed of moral import. On this score the Republicans seem closer to the mugwump prejudices of a public openly contemptuous of partisan politics.

Prognosis: Politics Versus Marketing

Though the structure of a national party is a rarified topic for most students of politics, it is the bread and butter of presidential aspirants. Candidates and their staffs are uniquely motivated to master and manipulate party structure. Thus, the rules shape not only the future of the national party but also the intuitions of America's political leadership.

Van Buren's original idea for the political party followed from a Jeffersonian ideal of citizenship. For him the national party was the only institution to have as its basis the interests of individuals as citizens rather than as members of corporate or sectional groups. A weakening of party was thus a weakening of the institutional voice of the citizen against the voice of special interests. The national party provided the long term discipline without which political leaders would cater to corporate over citizen power.

True to this vision, the Democrats in the years 1980-1984 took formal steps to promote their transition from a coalition of interests to one possible conception of a citizens' party. Because no immediate electoral profit accrued, the impatient among them began after the election to denigrate the achievement of the Hunt Commission and to seek some purely managerial nirvana. The Republican example, however, shows that a pure managerialism is insufficient. The GOP played out a third act in its postwar "success story": it won its third second-term presidential landslide with a marketing strategy based upon the weakening of party allegiance. It then rejoiced in postelection polls purporting to show realignment. But these ephemeral figures mask a deeper, qualitative reality: the increasing shallowness of the tie between the voter and the party.

Instead of a quasireligious commitment, party affiliation under the marketing approach has increasingly become an individualized consumption item. The association of the GOP brand name, through the Reagan-Bush ticket, with favorable consumer conditions is very different from the building of loyalty that will sustain leaders through crises and reverses. As the perennial minority party, the GOP has thus far benefitted relative to the Democrats from the increasing fluidity of the electorate. But that same fluidity blocks it from consolidating any gains. Meanwhile, the party system as a whole, and with it the ability of the American polity to sustain commitments, suffers. If Americans are discouraged from forging enduring relationships with their own political parties, why should one expect from them the more abstract discipline of sustaining long term policies?

There is no inevitability about whether a marketing approach or a less evanescent, more morally coherent conception of presidential politics will prevail. In a commercial republic the two must always coexist. True, a persistent strain in the American national character demands moral coherence in politics. Foreign observers at many times—Alexis de Tocqueville, Gunnar Myrdal, and Jean-Francois Revel come to mind—have attributed American moralism to the principle of natural equality in the Declaration of Independence. But that abstract principle can be evoked in advertising even when it is violated in practice. Nothing guarantees that the national political party must be ennobled by intelligent participation in it. Nor is the political party the only means by which a wide variety of citizens can experience sustained commitment to democratic ideals.

Still, in times of peace, the national political party is an especially serviceable institution for national integration. In recognition of its role, the Federal Election Campaign Act in 1975 gave the two major parties a financial subsidy to serve as a regulated duopoly over our presidential politics. Leaders of both parties, understanding that public financing would open their activities to closer public scrutiny, voluntarily accepted millions of tax dollars for their conventions and their campaigns. Their inner rules, like those of other government contractors, reveal at a superficial level how they are spending tax monies. At a deeper level, however, the Republican Party and Democratic Party should not be confused with ordinary government contractors. Their duopoly is exercised over the franchise, upon which the authority of representative government is predicated. If the service they provide is faulty, citizenship itself is cheapened. Parties are not simply rival marketing organizations like Hertz and Avis, or Coke and Pepsi. At stake in their competition is the ability of the polity to sustain civic engagement.

The Democrats still have an uphill struggle to make theirs a post-New Deal party of citizen concerns, but their work on rules has laid the ground. For the Republicans, the vision of a principled citizens' party, rooted in Lincoln's reading of the Declaration of Independence, is a glorious memory. Is it a living memory?

Appendix: A Short History of Republican Bonuses

The Factional Background

"Bonus" delegates first entered the GOP in the factional bargaining that followed the traumatic events of 1912. The GOP convention of that year dissolved without even adopting a rules report; and the breakaway Progressive Party (or Bull Moose) ticket led by Theodore Roosevelt polled more popular and electoral votes than the incumbent president, William Howard Taft. The Bull Moose bolt, which enabled Woodrow Wilson to become the second Democratic president since the Civil War, called forth a protracted series of rules changes that led ultimately to the introduction of three bonuses in the GOP allocation formula: the Congressional District bonus (adopted 1916, revised 1921, 1923, 1940, 1952, abolished 1972), the uniform victory bonus (adopted 1923, revised 1940, 1948, and 1972), and the 60% Electoral College bonus (adopted 1972).

The first of these three, the Congressional District bonus was adopted in 1916 at the insistence of the Progressive faction. It was the first major change in the allocation formula since the party's founding. From 1860 until 1912 each state's delegation consisted of four at-large delegates and two delegates per Congressional district. This pure formula, twice each state's Electoral College vote, had unanticipated results after 1876, when Republican fortunes waned in the South and the typical southern delegate came to represent only a handful of Republican voters. Reformers claimed that these "rotten borough" delegates were unduly influenced with offers of patronage jobs. A special complaint concerned Negro delegates whose votes were allegedly bought and sold for cold cash, postmasterships not being available for them so long as Southern Democrats exercised Senatorial privilege to block "black and tan" appointments.

At the turn of the century Ohio-led regulars controlled the southern delegations and Progressives sought to curb the advantages this gave party regulars. As early as 1900 the Roosevelt forces had proposed that each congressional district receive one delegate for every 10,000 GOP votes cast. Many northern congressional districts might have exceeded their Electoral College allotment of two delegates; but since the franchise was widely denied in the South, and specifically denied to Negroes who habitually voted Republican, the measure would have reduced southern representation dramatically and Negro representation almost entirely. In 1908 a less drastic proposal was put forth: a minimum vote threshold by which congressional districts would earn their two delegates. This came to the floor for a roll-call vote, the first on a major shift in the allocation formula in the history of the GOP. The Taft regulars defeated the measure narrowly, and thus set the stage for their even narrower victory over Theodore Roosevelt in 1912.

At the Chicago GOP Convention of 1912 when Theodore Roosevelt challenged the party's incumbent president for the nomination, there were six contested roll-call votes on procedural, credentials and platform issues. A majority was 540; and the "Taft Steamroller" won all six test votes by narrow margins, ranging from 542 to 597. In every vote the Taft regulars relied heavily on an overwhelming share of the 242 delegates from the states of the Old Confederacy. Only North Carolina among the states of the Solid South lined up on the Progressive side.

The Bull Moosers accordingly made a reduction of southern voting strength a firm condition for rejoining the party after 1912. To reunite the party the National Committee took the extraordinary step of promulgating a new allocation formula in the Call for the 1916 Convention. No longer would every congressional district be awarded two delegates by right; henceforth, it would have to earn its second delegate by casting a minimum of 7500 votes for the GOP nominee for Congress or the President in the previous election. As an added gesture to the Roosevelt forces, the "previous presidential election" for 1916 was set at 1908, not 1912. The new formula retained the Electoral College structure of the convention but by forcing a congressional district to earn its second delegate reduced southern representation at the 1916 convention by a third and cut the proportion of Negro delegates in half.

Once they were back in the party the Bull Moosers pushed successfully for further steps favorable to a renewed Roosevelt campaign for the 1920 nomination. After American entry into the Great War they used "pro-German" statements made by an old Taft regular, John C. Adams of Iowa, to his Dubuque constituents in 1914 to block him from the chairmanship of the RNC. In his stead they installed Will H. Hays who, as party chairman of Indiana, had reconciled progressives and regulars. Hays promptly set up national party headquarters in New York and appointed a prestigious 180-member Advisory Committee on Platform and Policy that has remained unsurpassed as a model in consensus-building for an out-of-power party. His efforts helped to assure that a fully united GOP would emerge on the offensive in 1920.

But Teddy Roosevelt was not to lead the charge. His premature death, in 1919 at the age of 60, left no other progressive candidate able to unite business interests with both eastern and western reformers. Disarray among progressives laid the ground for the "smoke-filled room" that arranged the nomination of Warren G. Harding on the tenth ballot in 1920. Hiram Johnson of California, thenceforth the leading progressive standard-bearer, records in his memoirs that Harding came to him after the third ballot to report that the Senatorial group which was in control of the convention had ordained that he, Harding, would emerge victorious after the eighth ballot. He asked Johnson to be his running mate. Johnson declined, but subsequent events suggest that he did extract a pledge for the further reduction of southern representation at the 1924 convention.

Since the Rules Report reaffirming the 1916 formula had already been accepted on the second day of the convention, a change in the allocation formula for 1924 could only be engineered in an irregular manner. Following the nomination of Calvin Coolidge as Harding's running mate, Senator Henry Cabot Lodge, the Permanent Chairman of the Convention, used a new agenda item entitled "unfinished business" to allow the Chairman of the Rules Committee to introduce an unusual resolution stipulating that:

> ... the National Committee, notwithstanding any rule heretofore adopted, is hereby authorized and directed within twelve months from the date of the adjournment of this Convention to adopt a just and equitable basis of representation in future National Conventions, which basis shall be set forth in the call for the next convention and be binding upon the same and all other future conventions until otherwise ordered.

A motion to table was made by a white Texan, who thought the resolution out of order; he was seconded by a prominent Negro leader from Louisiana on the grounds that the "resolution has for its object the cutting down of our representation in the South in National Conventions." The motion to table was defeated by voice vote and the National Committee was charged with adopting a new formula by June 12, 1921, and promulgating it in the call for the 1924 convention.

As it turned out, the RNC did its job twice, once in fulfillment of the convention resolution and a second time in violation of its timetable. First, it produced a new formula on schedule in June of 1921: it raised the threshold from 7500 to 10,000 votes for the second congressional district delegate and added a lower 1000 vote threshold for the first delegate; and it added a provision by which a state received two additional at-large delegates if it had voted for the GOP ticket in the previous election. Then, in a surprise coup in December of 1923, the RNC rescinded the 1921 product and issued in the Call a revised formula that better favored Calvin Coolidge in the early phases of his struggle with Hiram Johnson for the 1924 nomination: it retained the 10,000 vote threshold but awarded the second delegate by right, a proposal that added about twenty delegates to Coolidge's base. And it raised the uniform victory bonus from two to three delegates.

Though the 1921 and 1923 versions were substantially different in their factional impact, they were similar in concept. Both had two bonus elements. They both retained, in more stringent form, the 1916 device of a threshold for congressional district delegates based on a minimum GOP vote. They added to it a second and entirely novel element: a "uniform victory bonus" for presidential victory in a state. These devices were well understood to have more than technical import.

In the 1921 and 1923 RNC deliberations, the 1916 minimum threshold device met principled as well as self-interested opposition. Prior to the June 1921

RNC meeting Charles D. Hilles, the national committeeman from New York and former secretary to President Taft, circulated a statement charging that for the GOP to reduce southern representation on the basis of low vote totals was to legitimate the denial of voting rights in the South. Representative Tinkham of Massachusetts appeared before the RNC to urge that it take no step on southern delegates without first endorsing his bill for a commission of inquiry to enforce Section 2 of the 15th Amendment, which provided that states denying the franchise to their citizens have their representation in Congress reduced accordingly.

When the Tinkham resolution was defeated, a black RNC member, Henry Lincoln Johnson of Georgia, protested vociferously against the party's hypocrisy: the RNC would diminish convention representation of the victims of disenfranchisement without even making a gesture towards reducing the congressional representation of the perpetrators. He charged that the GOP did not "have the guts" to enforce the Constitution. "Sit down, Henry! Sit down!" was the abrupt response of the Party Chairman, according to a contemporary press account. Negro Republicans repeated the same arguments with better success in special hearings in December of 1923, when a formula more favorable to the "rotten borough" South suited the Coolidge renomination calculus. Moreover, it was known, at a time when the GOP had begun to court white voters in the South, that the disenfranchisement was not limited to blacks. The entire South had in 1920 cast fewer presidential votes for both parties than had the state of Illinois.

Though these arguments did not succeed in eliminating the congressional district bonus they militated for finding some other device to reduce the relative representation of the south. The device, which came to be called the "uniform victory bonus," was the first formal break with an Electoral College rationale. It awarded states a uniform number of bonus delegates, irrespective of population, Republican vote or Electoral College strength, for having carried for the ticket in the previous presidential election. The uniformity of the bonus—three delegates per state—added a confederal tilt to the Electoral College basis of the convention. A California proposal to add a countervailing bonus based on GOP vote was rejected, so that the balance in the Electoral College between statehood and population was violated in favor of statehood.

Since the Harding-Coolidge ticket had carried all but the southern states in 1920, the uniform victory bonus measure was widely touted as a further means of reducing southern representation and thus of fulfilling the 1920 bargain with the Progressives. Moreover, since the RNC was composed of one member from each state, the purely confederal rationale of the uniform victory bonus reflected the structure of the body that had to approve it. But the measure had another well-recognized effect in the context of contemporary debate over immigration restriction. A confederally grounded bonus system skewed the balance of the convention away from the populous states that contained the bulk of the newer stock immigrants, much as similar county unit systems were used within state parties to shift the balance of power to the rural, sparsely populated counties. Party professionals are always acutely aware of the political demography of apportionment schemes—indeed, they think of little else; but in the period 1920-24, something new was added to the calculus, a concern for the ethnic and religious balance in America itself.

The Nativist Background to the Uniform Bonus

The years 1920-24 were a period of intense nativist agitation on many fronts. This was the period when labor unrest was linked to 'alien' influences, when constitutional amendments outlawing parochial schools were proposed in several states, when the Ku Klux Klan claimed a third of the delegates to the 1920 Democratic convention, when Henry Ford's *Dearborn Independent* circulated the *Protocols of the Elders of Zion*, when intellectuals embraced purportedly progressive and scientific theories about racial differences and eugenics and believed that a new "objective" measure, the IQ test, proved newer Americans intellectually inferior to the older stock. The term "race" in the common parlance of those days referred not only to distinctions among white, black and yellow peoples, but among varieties of Europeans, who were, in turn, most often subdivided into Mediterranean, Alpine, and Nordic "races," according to whether they came from southern, eastern, or northwestern Europe.

Though recurrent spasms of nativism had been a part of GOP history, one might suppose it unlikely that the RNC, the party organ charged with redrafting the GOP allocation formula, would allow itself to be associated with nativist views. It was in those days a small, nuts-and-bolts committee, with one member from each state, infrequent meetings, no corporate or permanent staff, and a determination to express only consensus views. Moreover, as a loose confederal body charged with representing party interests throughout the country, the RNC would seem, even if it were so inclined, the least likely group to express views that might offend any potential Republican constituent, not the least of whom were the ethnic voters in such Republican cities as Cleveland, Philadelphia, Chicago, Baltimore, and Newark.

It is, therefore, a remarkable sign of the depth of nativist and racialist opinion during this period that unmistakable evidence of it appears in the two major publication efforts representing the 1920-24 RNC.

The first of these, *Reports of Subcommittees of the Advisory Committee on Policies and Platform*, was, as we have seen, an exemplary effort at consensus-building by an out-of-power party. By its own account, the 180-member Advisory Committee distributed 100,000 questionnaires to party activists in preparing its reports, which were released, along with a booklet of the original questionnaires, in May of 1920. The Report of the Subcommittee on The Immigration Situation chaired by Frederick H. Gillett, Speaker of the House of Representatives, contains rhetoric and analysis remarkable for its contrast with Lincoln's views on the incorporation of immigrants into the American mainstream:

> ... Only men of a certain type could have built this great nation ... the newer immigration is profoundly altering the racial constitution of our people.... There has been a marked shift in the sources of immigration from northwestern to southern and eastern Europe.... This change has introduced races and nationalities differing radically from those which constituted the bulk of the population of the United States at the time of the Revolution, and of the immigration stream from 1776 to 1882 ...
>
> The goal of our entire immigration policy is a unified nation. This implies a minimum number of members of the population who are subject to civic limitations on account of their birth.... It must be realized, however, that it is not the mere formal citizenship which is of importance, but genuine adoption into the American life.... The law furnishes practically no assurance, beyond a candidate's own assertion, that the alien has become an American at heart."
>
> The question of the treatment of Asiatic immigrants is peculiarly delicate and difficult. The general principle of the practical exclusion of these races is sound. No democracy can afford to admit large groups of people whose racial or national characteristics are so different from those established in the country as inevitably to set the newcomers off into socially isolated groups. This is emphatically true of Asiatic races.

The second major publication, *The National Republican*, an explicitly partisan weekly, served in the period 1920-24 as the quasi-official organ of the RNC. Popularly priced at $1.50 a year, it reached a peak press run of 500,000 during the 1920 election and had an average paid circulation of 200,000 thereafter. Its editor, George B. Lockwood of Indiana, was RNC Secretary from 1921-24. John T. Adams, who finally succeeded Hays as RNC Chairman from 1921-24, was a founding investor and editorial contributor. Its status as the premier party organ was generally recognized, and there was talk in 1924 of the DNC setting up an organ to counter it. It published biographies of RNC members, regular reports on the activities of the National Republican League, Republican women's and college groups. Its historical articles were used for Republican women's study groups.

Most of its authors were prominently identified with the GOP. It printed a page of editorials of its own, signed by Lockwood, as well as reprinted editorials from general circulation newspapers whose opinions it endorsed. During the Adams chairmanship a weekly column with his picture and title appeared opposite the editorial page. After the 1924 election the *National Republican* moved to monthly publication and became more independent of the official party, but during the 1921-24 period it spoke with the authority of a party organ.

Compared with the rabid nativism and racism of other publications, including the high-brow ones, the *National Republican* is notable during this period for its rhetorical restraint. There was nothing in it to suggest religious prejudice against Roman Catholics and Jews; indeed, there was an occasional piece to counter such prejudice. The immigration and Asian exclusion issues were muted. In general, the pens of Lockwood and Adams were kept pointed against the Democrats rather than against any elements of the population. Nevertheless, even here there was an acute awareness of the dangers posed by the undigested immigrant masses in the northeastern states. The following editorial comments by Lockwood on "Americanization" suggest that the role of the states with heavy immigrant populations was a matter of real concern:

> There never was a time when there was a greater need of real Americanization than now. A study of the census statistics relative to our foreign population will startle anyone who has not made himself familiar with the facts. In a half-a-dozen of our eastern and New England states approximately one-half of the total voting population is foreign-born. In some states this proportion exceeds one half. In others it lacks a little of being one-half. In half-a-dozen other states the foreign-born population constitutes a very large per cent of the total voting population— so large a percentage that they easily control the balance-of-power between the old political parties . . .
>
> One would naturally suppose that these immigrants would readily support the policies and institutions which made this country an attractive place as compared with their homeland. In a great many cases this is true, but in a majority of cases the contrary is true. They immediately begin to take sides in American politics not from the standpoint of how proposed policies will affect this country but how they may affect foreign countries.
>
> They view the question of a tariff not from the standpoint of American industry and American wages, but from the standpoint of how a tariff will affect their 'home country.' They view the immigration law, the prohibition laws, the courts, local and federal authorities, and all policies affecting our foreign relations, such as the handling of the foreign debt, not from the angle of Americans and how such policies work to the injury or the benefit of the United States, but from the angle of their native country . . .
>
> Our foreign population can never be said to be 'Americanized' until they have lost this foreign viewpoint in considering American policies. Moreover, until they are 'Americanized' in the real sense of the word there exists a very grave danger of America's losing its national integrity, its national individuality, if such a term may be used, and becoming, as tersely expressed by Theodore Roosevelt, a 'polyglot boarding house.'

And in December of 1923, in support of President Coolidge's recent message to Congress that "America must be kept American," the *National Republican* reprinted a long editorial from the Newark *News* reviewing the "Five Waves of Immigration" and making use of the then current vogue for IQ tests. It noted that immigration from southern and eastern Europe began to appear in 1890 during the wave of Scandinavian immigration and then dominated the fourth wave, from 1903-1914:

> As a result of the changed character of the later waves, we have acquired since 1890 a foreign-born population of 14 million, of whom only 7,500,000 can show

as much as the low average intelligence of class five in the army tests.... We have taken in each year fewer than 230,000 aliens of the higher grade of intelli gence ...

Another result is that, the country over our cities have become foreign ... there are now 24,556,729 native-born whites of native parents in our cities to 26,063,355 whites of foreign birth or foreign stock, of whom 10,356,983 are foreign born. In the cities along the Atlantic seaboard the foreign preponderance is much greater, running perhaps as high as 65 per cent."

Another reprinted editorial defended immigration restriction by the need of America to prevent an increase of its "unassimilable elements" and noted that the new national origins legislation was superior to the previous 1921 bill because it "favors the countries of northwestern Europe, which have furnished America with its best type of immigrant in the past." (The 1921 bill set up quotas limiting immigration to 3% of the foreign born from each country in the 1910 census; the 1924 bill used 2% of each country's foreign in the 1890 census to determine national origin quotas.)

There seems, in sum, reasonable evidence that RNC rule-makers, among them the Party Secretary and Chairman, were vividly conscious that measures reducing the relative representation of the populous states in GOP conventions would shift the balance of the party away from areas dominated by those more recent immigrants, widely thought deficient in intelligence and susceptible to unAmerican bloc appeals at every level of government and on every kind of issue. And it adds some piquancy to this conclusion to observe that during the very weeks in 1921 and 1923 in which the uniform victory bonus was developed, immigration quotas were the main item in the news. In May of 1921, when the uniform victory bonus first surfaced after a meeting of an RNC subcommittee with President Harding, the first immigration bill was signed. In December of 1923, when the bonus was increased, Calvin Coolidge sent his "America must be kept American" message to Congress urging a shift in quotas to assure a preeminent place for immigrants from northwestern Europe.

Of course, the balance struck between the congressional district and uniform victory bonus elements of the new formula reflected the balance of factions within the party. Foremost in the minds of the rule-makers was the need for a formula that would meet two short-term exigencies, producing a relatively united GOP in 1924 and avoiding credentials fights in southern delegations like those that had marred the 1920 convention. The 1921 version reflected the balance of forces in that year, while the 1923 formula, which added a safety margin of southern delegates for Coolidge early in the prenomination maneuvering, was the product of a president not personally bound by any pledges made at the 1920 convention.

A key figure in both versions was the adroit and thoroughly professional C. Bascom Slemp, the Virginia Republican congressman who became Coolidge's secretary and handled liaison with the Congress and the RNC. In the end, when the ruthless decision was made to renege on the 1921 formula, the Johnson forces found themselves isolated. Two RNC members from the eastern wing backed the change. Senator George Wharton Pepper, an ally of Pennsylvania Governor Gifford Pinchot, proposed the new version. National Committeeman Hamilton F. Kean of New Jersey also backed it and won unanimous support for his measure to add to the RNC a National Committeewoman from each state. An editorial in the *National Republican* laid down the party line: the three at-large uniform victory bonus delegates should satisfy all legitimate demands of western progressives. In all, the balance between the two bonuses was the product of the politics of coalitions and compromise.

But the Calhounian principle of compromise is not the only one that can be asserted in the American regime. What is noteworthy for the notion of a principled party is that both devices adopted in 1921 and 1923 presupposed that some citizens were less worthy of representation than others within the GOP. While the rules-makers may have had their own internecine fights directly in mind, they shared the assumption that some citizens could not be considered "flesh of the flesh and blood of the blood" of others. And this is reflected in the well-known effect of the two measures they adopted.

In the case of the congressional district bonus, the factual context, known in 1916, was made clear and explicit in 1921: the major cause for low Republican turnout in the southern districts had less to do with lack of latent support than with the unconstitutional denial of the franchise. In the case of the uniform victory bonus, the political effect of the device in diluting urban representation did not need to be stated. Unitary devices were regularly used within the state parties to underrepresent the urban counties. In Maine, to take a glaring example, where the GOP went so far as to form a common front with the Ku Klux Klan in a 1920s gubernatorial race, the powerful state committee gave equal representation to all counties regardless of population, so that urban Cumberland County, with its heavy Catholic population was equally represented with Androscoggin, with its heavy potato crop. Thus, a departure from the Electoral College in the direction of a uniform bonus was recognizable to all party apportionment experts, *prima facie*, as a dilution of the voting power of the heavily populated areas of immigrant settlement. Since these voters held the balance of power in the more populous states, it was feared that Republican officials beholden to them might succumb to bloc influences.

It has been observed by an historian of the Republican Party, George H. Mayer, in a monograph on the GOP in the New Deal era, that the hold of the New Deal upon black and newer stock voters was far from inevitable. Notwithstanding the example of Tammany, most urban machines were Republican in the 1920s, and the Negro vote was overwhelmingly Republican even in 1932. The seeds of the GOP demise he attributes to party complacency in the 1920s: "Besides neglecting its traditional constituents, the Republicans showed a tendency to take for granted the support of blacks and of new immigrant groups from southeastern Europe. . . . Republicans spearheaded the drive to restrict immigration, and made no secret of their dislike for Catholic newcomers from central Europe. They treated the Negro differently but no better, partly because his voting power was as yet negligible and partly because he was not likely to defect to the Democrats, who took an open stand for white supremacy."

The 1921 and 1923 rules changes gave evidence of such attitudes. But more: they embalmed them in the permanent structure of the party. And worse: bonuses became legalistic "precedents" upon which to build.

From Bonuses to 'Incentives'

In 1940 the party intensified both bonuses. Though voting rights in general elections had not been enforced in the South, the 1940 convention set a threshold of 1000 votes for the second congressional district delegate, so that it was possible for a district to lose both delegates. This measure belatedly restored the provisions agreed upon in 1921. The same convention doubled the maximal uniform victory bonus to six delegates by giving three more for victories in gubernatorial or senatorial elections—a means of preserving the over-representation of the smaller states even in the event of a landslide loss like that of 1936.

In 1948, a year when the percentage of Roman Catholic delegates to the GOP convention was still only 6%, the uniform bonus was redesigned to be awarded *en bloc* by granting six at-large delegates for any one of three statewide victories—presidential, gubernatorial or Senatorial. This meant that almost every state outside the South would predictably "earn" the full bonus of six delegates. Since the bonus was not proportioned to population, Electoral College or Republican vote, it further diluted the representation of the populous states. Here is the way bonuses affected delegation size for two states with 16 and 3 Electoral Votes which qualified for the same bonus delegates at the 1940, 1944, 1948, and 1952 conventions:

	New Jersey (16)	Wyoming (3)	NJ/Wyo Ratio
1940	32 (2.0)	6 (2.0)	1.0
1944-48	35 (2.2)	9 (3.0)	0.7
1952-60	38 (2.4)	12 (4.0)	0.6

The figures in parentheses give the size of each delegation as a multiple of Electoral College vote. Note that in 1940 both New Jersey and Wyoming, having voted Democratic in 1936, got no bonus votes and thus had delegations equal to twice their electoral college vote. In 1944-48, both states earned three bonus delegates. By 1952, under the 1948 revision, both states earned the full six uniform bonus delegates, and predictably continued to do so for the duration of the six-delegate *en bloc* bonus rule through the 1972 convention. For Wyoming this was equivalent to four times its Electoral College vote, while New Jersey had a delegation equal to 2.4 times its Electoral College strength. To put it another way, relative to Electoral College strength, Republicans in New Jersey had exactly 2.4/4 or three-fifths the representation of those in Wyoming after 1948, a fraction that is a red flag in American constitutional parlance. Note that the three-fifths dilution is relative not to a one man, one vote standard but to the Electoral College, which already favored the citizens of Wyoming over those of New Jersey by 4:1.

The "precedent" of the bonus device was even extended to the Republican National Committee. As we have seen, thanks to the Kean initiative, the RNC had since 1924 been composed of two representatives from each state—one National Committeeman and one National Committeewoman. In 1952 a victory bonus rule awarded a state an additional voting seat for its state chairman if that state gave its electoral vote to the presidential ticket, elected a GOP governor, or had a Republican majority in its combined House and Senate delegation. This measure passed the convention on a roll-call vote with the South in unanimous dissent. (At the same time, without a roll-call, the threshold for the second congressional district delegate was raised from 1000 to 2000 votes.) This extraordinary application of bonusthink was short-lived: the party dropped the RNC bonus in 1968 by adding all state party chairmen to the body by right.

In the 1960s the legal climate became less favorable both to unitary bonus devices and to thresholds that legitimated the denial of voting rights. In 1962 in the landmark case, *Baker v. Carr*, the Supreme Court introduced the "one person, one vote" standard for state legislative apportionment. Since that time unitary devices which dilute the vote of urban areas have been under legal attack at the precinct, county, and state legislative district level. Within state parties, the creation of precincts and state senatorial districts or equal population led to the demise of inequitable county unit systems of representation in state party committees. The Maine Republican State Committee, for example, continued to use the old counties but accepted population as the major basis for apportionment among them in 1972. And a survey by this writer and Thomas Levergood of all the state party rules in 1982 revealed that population or Republican vote had become the major basis for apportionment of seats in every state party convention and committee. Only one state convention had a uniform victory bonus among counties of unequal population: sparsely Republican Arkansas, and even here it was an innocuous device giving extra delegates to the rare counties which elected GOP justices of the peace.

At the national level, however, the one person, one vote standard has no legal force for the simple reason that the Electoral College system itself insures a disparity in representation of more than 4:1 between voters in the most and least populous states. Uniform devices as such can, if there is some non-discriminatory rationale for them, pass muster with the courts. For the GOP bonuses, therefore, a new rationale was devised to improve their chances of legal survival. The stimulus came from a series of reverses in the federal courts in a lawsuit brought by the Ripon Society and individual Republicans in the large industrial states. The 1972 convention, in fact, was briefly under a federal court order to revise its allocation formula. Though the order was stayed by Mr. Justice Rehnquist on eve of convention at the petition of the Arizona Republican State Committee, it was clear that the party would need a coherent rationale to take back into court after the election. There were also pressures from the state parties to increase the size of the convention. And of course, as in the past, factional rivalries determined the balance among the devices used for revision.

The "conservative" faction, at that time a coalition of southern and western states, plus Indiana and parts of other delegations, perceived its interest as retaining the maximal role for the bonus device. It was the calculation of the aides to Ronald Reagan, who led winning side in a floor fight, that the uniform bonus alone, because of its favoritism to small states, was worth more than 100 delegates to the California governor in 1976. The "moderate" faction, led by Congressman William Steiger of Wisconsin, sought to introduce population-based elements to countervail the anti-federal effect of the bonus. The "conservative" side won handily and the following changes were made:

The base of the convention was raised from two to three times a state's Electoral College strength. The maximum uniform victory bonus was raised proportionately from six to 8.5 (rounded to nine), but since it was no longer awarded *en bloc* its distorting effects were less automatic. A state would now win 4.5 delegates for a presidential victory, and one each for each GOP senator, governor, or majority of the House delegation. The congressional district threshold provision was dropped entirely. And there was introduced a new and much larger victory bonus by which a state could win a bonus of delegates equivalent to 60% of its Electoral College vote by carrying for the ticket in the previous election. All fractions were rounded to the higher integer. A grandfather clause was added assuring that no state could fall below the size of its 1972 delegation, and special provisions were made giving Puerto Rico and the District of Columbia a flat 14 delegates. A new Preamble declared that the "intent and purpose of these rules" was to assure that the GOP remained an "open party" dedicated to "equality of opportunity" and opposing "favoritism" of any kind. In the event the formula failed to survive a court test a rule was drafted empowering the RNC to approve a new formula by weighted voting.

The key innovation, both legally and factionally, was the 60% victory bonus proportioned to Electoral College vote. This had the potential of adding more than 300 delegates to the convention, along with a maximum of 250 for the presidential part of the revised uniform bonus.

On legal grounds, the complexity of the new formula enabled the GOP to argue that the entire bonus system was actually a complicated "incentive" device to encourage and reward state parties for success. With courts both skittishly and properly reluctant to intervene in intraparty affairs, this was a winning argument. During the 1970s the courts generally stressed a political party's first amendment rights to wide latitude in setting its own rules, and the Washington D.C. Court of Appeals, declined to substitute its judgment for that of the party on the efficacy of an incentive device: "Whether or not it is an effective incentive, it may be the only one that a national party has to offer." Moreover, the court argued that so long as each element of the new formula could be defended as bearing some "rational relation to party success" the courts had no business intervening, even if they disagreed with the rationale. And since, as it argued, quoting an outdated political science text, national parties were for presidential campaigns "confederacies of state parties" even uniform devices bore a plausible relation to the (confederal) realities of a national campaign.

The court's view of the facts and circumstances, antique when it was asserted, would have to be revised substantially today, when not only presidential campaigns but the RNC itself are highly centralized, truly national operations, using the state parties mainly to circumvent funding limits. Nevertheless, the 60% bonus was successful as a forensic device. The pre-1972 suit was mooted and the new formula, after initial reverses at the district and appeals level, was sustained by the full U.S. Court of Appeals of the District of Columbia meeting *en banc*, and the case was denied further review by the Supreme Court.

On a factional calculus, the 60% bonus built in the possibility of a self-entrenching, permanent, sectional majority in the convention. At the time of its drafting, it was expected that the GOP would easily win the South and West but might lose portions of the Frost Belt to the Democrats. By giving a very large premium to winning states, it would put them in a position to dominate the next convention, nominate a candidate who would campaign to win these states, giving them, in turn, enlarged delegations for the next convention, and so on in perpetuity. The landslide elections of 1972, 1980, and 1984 have foiled this sectional logic, while the Carter sweep of the Solid South in 1976 reversed it, but the overall policy of enlarging the membership of a representative body to give bonus seats for "victory" always holds the potential for self-entrenching factionalism.

Since 1972 additional uniform victory bonuses for state legislative majorities have regularly been voted by the RNC, but they have not been favorably reported out of the Convention Committee on Rules and Order of Business, where party lawyers have warned of possible relitigation if the 1972 formula is changed in any way. The 1975 court decision on that formula came before federal funding was available to the major parties. Anticipating that the GOP might choose to accept federal funds, the court warned that this might subject it to closer scrutiny. It also noted that the case had been brought on a strict one person, one vote basis and had not alleged invidious discrimination in the origins or operation of the bonus system. Such allegations, too, would invite closer scrutiny by the courts. Finally, it included a third caveat: the formula was sustained because it seemed to the court, on the basis of its inspection of the election system, to bear a rational relation to party success given the (confederal) realities of presidential elections. This, too, it said, could change.

Ironically, the most forceful juridical arguments casting doubt on the future of the 1972 formula have come from the GOP itself. After the 1984 election the Republican National Committee made a major investment of resources in a legal action and attendent public relations campaign to oppose the pro-Democratic gerrymandering of Congressional districts. In doing so, it articulated an exceptionally activist interpretation of the Fourteenth Amendment and of judicial intervention to protect the sanctity of the franchise. It further proposed a broad definition of "gerrymandering" to include computerized programs that follow a one person, one vote standard. To convince skeptics that its positions were not merely opportunistic, the RNC chose to file its arguments against Republicans, in a friend-of-the-court brief urging the U.S. Supreme Court to invalidate the redistricting plan of the GOP-dominated legislature of Indiana. Of course, if the pro-Republican Indiana redistricting were overturned, the overturning of pro-Democratic redistricting in other states might give the GOP a chance of winning a House majority in 1991. But the RNC's activist view on the justiciability of gerrymandered formulas, its strong opposition to "discriminatory" gerrymandering on Fourteenth Amendment grounds, and its especially broad definition of gerrymandering itself would, amusingly, also appear to undercut any public defense of the the the gerrymandering effect against the populous states of the national GOP's uniform victory bonuses. Regardless of the formula's technical legal status, then, it is a skeleton in the Republican closet, limiting a fully competitive position with the Democrats on the rule-based dimension of two-party politics.

FURTHER READING: Previously uncatalogued transcripts of the 1921 and 1923 RNC meetings that approved the new bonus formula were deposited by the RNC Convention Office in a mixed box of materials in the National Archives in April 1985 and made available for the first time for scholarly purposes as this book went to press. The proceedings address the constitutional, racial, and party-building implications of the device used for reducing southern representation. The proceedings are dominated by black republicans, who are given a full hearing, and are important primary documents in black as well as republican history.

Money In Politics:
Campaign Finance Reform and the 1984 Election

John Marini

Money and Politics

The 1984 election was the third presidential election to be conducted under the guidelines laid down by the Federal Election Campaign Act of 1971, which, as amended in the wake of Watergate, produced the most sweeping piece of campaign finance legislation in American history—the FECA of 1974. This act, amended in 1976, by necessity of a Supreme Court ruling in *Buckley v. Valeo*, and further amended in 1979, has had profound implications for electoral politics in the United States. Through campaign finance law, Congress has established separate procedures and different revenue sources for financing the election campaigns of members of Congress as opposed to those of presidential candidates. It has also attempted detailed regulation of the process of partisan politics through federal finance legislation. Congress has created a regulatory bureaucracy—the Federal Election Commission—whose purpose is the on-going enforcement of campaign finance legislation. This legislation, furthermore, has tended to inhibit local party activity in presidential elections because of the complexity of complying with campaign finance laws. Rigid enforcement of federal campaign guidelines have necessitated more centralized organization and detailed control over spending.

The political effects of the finance reform legislation of the 1970s were profound. There was no doubt that laws governing a candidate's funding would also, as Michael Malbin has said, "affect their campaign's structures . . . guide their strategy, and . . . influence the role and structure of the parties and interest groups that want to support or oppose them."[1] Practically speaking, Congress mandated publicly financed presidential campaigns and privately funded congressional elections. By limiting the amount of money a citizen could contribute to a candidate for public office or to a political party, it changed the role that private wealth once played in campaign finance. Centrally organized methods of raising large sums of money in small increments, such as direct mail solicitation—often independently of parties—had become increasingly

---

1. Malbin's views are found in his introductions to two volumes he edited, *Money and Politics in the United States* (Princeton, NJ: Chatham House, 1984) and *Parties, Interest Groups, and Campaign Finance Laws* (Washington, DC: American Enterprise Institute, 1980).

important. Given limitations on the amount of money individuals could give to political campaigns, it was almost inevitable that political action committees (PACs) would become more important than ever in electoral politics. There is no limit to the total amount a PAC may contribute to all candidates. But, individuals may give no more than $1,000 per candidate per campaign, and no more than $25,000 to candidates or committees in a single year. It is ironic that a law designed to reduce the influence of special interests, especially by limiting individual contributions, has accelerated the growth of PACs. PACs increasingly focus on congressional campaigns, where, because there is no public funding, there are no limits on campaign expenditures.

Before political campaigns were so regulated and public funding of presidential campaigns became a political necessity, individual private wealth, largely unregulated, was the principal source of money in all American elections. Since 1976, the United States Treasury has become the largest contributor to the election campaigns of candidates for public office, providing over one third of the costs of elections in each presidential campaign since then. Moreover, public financing of presidential elections has transformed the funding sources of congressional campaigns. Although congressional elections are privately funded, the revenue sources have become increasingly nationalized. And congressional incumbents have become ever more dependent on PAC financing. As Michael Malbin has observed, "the importance of business PAC growth is not that it increases business power but that it nationalizes the process, replacing the local wealthy entrepreneur with national organizations." The private funding of congressional campaigns could not but cement the ties between incumbents and the interests that supported them. Nonetheless, the importance of PACs and their proliferation could not have taken place without the growth of the bureaucracy that occurred in Washington in the period before campaign finance reform. Campaign finance reform becomes intelligible in light of the fact that the Democratic Party, which succeeded in nationalizing politics in the New Deal coalition, also succeeded in centralizing administration in Washington during the 1960s and early 1970s. The centralization of administration that occurred during this period resulted in a wedding of the interests of the legislature and the bureaucracy. The growth of the neutral bureaucracy—largely the creation of a partisan majority—is the key to the apparent decline of partisanship in the United States. The great success of the Democratic Party membership in retaining its seats at the congressional and state level—partly as a result of the benefits derived from centralization—enabled it to produce the kind of legislation which inhibited the creation of a new consensus or a new majority.

It was not merely coincidental that such reforms were undertaken in a period of institutional turmoil and intense partisan struggle, which pitted a Democratic controlled Congress against a Republican president (Nixon) intent upon decentralization. Furthermore, the national majority which elected that president was animated by far different principles in the partisan presidential election of 1972 than was evident in the typical congressional contest. Increasingly, congressional campaigns have sought to avoid partisanship, appealing more and more to the organized interests of electorally decisive minorities, while at the same time stressing constituent services for individual voters. That kind of appeal presupposes a centralized bureaucracy, or regulatory apparatus, through which economic, political, and social problems can be articulated, and private interests reconciled. As a result, incumbent members of Congress have become almost unbeatable, and the Democratic Party continues to form a majority in the House. The acceptance by the national elites of the legitimacy of the goals of the Great Society led them to abandon the national majority and its political embodiment—the presidency—in favor of the diversified interests of the legislature and the bureaucratic state. Consequently, the disjunction between presidential electoral politics and politics at other levels inhibited a realigning election. Furthermore, parties declined in proportion to the rise of a national, centralized bureaucracy as the chief instrument of government and the chief governmental source of private or local benefits. Thus, as John Wettergreen has stated, this "disjunction between particular private or local interests, which are administered to individually and not legislated for nationally, and the national or public interest, which is articulated by presidents or aspiring presidents is likely to continue."

The rise of the bureaucracy furthered the demise of parties, and the capacity of the majority rule is endangered by denying the element of consent. The consequence of bureaucratization has been an increased tension between the executive and the legislature regardless of party, and increasing apathy among voters. This is so because nearly all important administrative decisions, not to mention political and economic decisions, are made in Washington by a centralized bureaucracy, which is not accountable to the elected chief executive. Furthermore, the interests of the legislature become closely allied with—and committed to the perpetuation of—an executive bureaucracy. The bureaucracy, ostensibly nonpartisan, will retain effective control when backed by Congress.

In practice, a genuine separation of powers is undermined to the extent that the president is unable to control the administration or force it to conform to the demands of a contemporary majority. Rather, the president, with the party, remains impotent, the symbol of an impotent majority. In the absence of crisis, and without the necessity of a majority consensus, administrative rule replaces political rule. Campaign finance reform is reflective of the fact that the characteristic activity of Congress is no longer legislation in the general interest, but regulation and administration of the smallest details of the economic, social and political life of the nation. The shift of the government's activities from governance to regulation implies a shift of the political standard from public to private interests. Perhaps the most durable legacy of Watergate will be seen in the effects of the campaign finance legislation of this period, which was made possible largely because of the change in public opinion occasioned by Watergate. That change subsequently undercut presidential authority and undermined the principle of majority rule in the general or public interest of the nation. It is difficult if not impossible to understand the importance and the impact of money in politics, as regards the 1984 election, without some understanding of the political conditions and the partisan environment which produced the necessity of campaign finance reform.

The Politics of Campaign Finance Reform

Too little attention has been paid to the fact that campaign finance reform grew out of the institutional struggle between the President and Congress and the interests and constituencies which supported them. The kind of reform that was undertaken in the post-Watergate period, including campaign finance reform, is most useful, and most beneficial to the legislature, in a society in which the political or governing function gives way to the administrative or regulatory function. Such a shift demands that the center of political and economic life is tilted toward an alliance of Congress and the executive bureaucracy, which has the effect of undermining the political rule of the elected chief executive. Whereas Congress once concerned itself with issues of general importance, and legislated on the basis of broadly-based principles, it now intervenes routinely on behalf of its constituencies in the affairs of the executive branch. It conceives its task to be one of overseeing the bureaucracy. It insists upon ensuring that important economic and regulatory decisions be made at the behest of the relevant committee or subcommittee member of Congress. Furthermore, it presupposes the necessity of preventing unified presidential control of departments and agencies in the executive branch, as well as unified control over the mechanism of fiscal policy, to say nothing of personnel control.

For practical reasons, it became clear to the leadership of Congress that a president could not have primary responsibility for unified control of the federal budget. Such control had given the President the ability to determine national priorities in economic and fiscal policy, as well as foreign policy. The reforms of the budget process, the electoral process, as well as the internal reforms of Congressional procedures, allowed party leaders in Congress the ability to direct the administrative state regardless of the national majority's selection of the President. Animated by the Democratic leadership in the House, whose security from electoral defeat derived largely from the advantages of incumbency (which are associated with federal largess, and administrative control), the reforms in campaign legislation were only part of a much broader agenda of reform that occurred in the mid-1970s.

Those reforms went a long way toward consolidation of a centralized administration, which best serves the interests of the legislature and organized groups, at the expense of the president and the national majority. In the process, they have protected and reinforced the prerogatives of incumbent congressmen, while at the same time inhibiting the possibility of a presidential realigning election. This was accomplished by severing the connection between the party and candidate in presidential elections. Candidates, not parties, are funded by the national treasury. The effect of this legislation was that campaign finance reform laws have weakened the link between presidential candidates and the political parties and have made it more difficult for parties to mediate between policy makers and organized groups. It is not surprising that the most radical reforms of the 1970s were put in place after the emasculation of the presidency.

It is somewhat ironic, that at the height of the rhetoric concerning the "imperial presidency," few raised any objection to the attempt by Congress to regulate directly the process of presidential elections on the ground that such regulation violated the principle of the separation of powers. The Constitution does not clearly assign Congress the power to exercise direct control over the process of presidential elections. As James Ceasar has noted, "Congressional elections under the Constitution are treated very differently than presidential elections. . . . The sole provision relating to presidential elections refers to selection of electors: Congress has the power to determine the time of their choice and the date on which they vote." But, he notes, in the case of Congressional elections, Congress is "given broad powers . . . to pass laws regulating the times, place and manner of holding elections for senators and representatives." Yet is was automatically assumed to be the case in the early 1970s that Congress has an absolute right to regulate and subsidize presidential elections by means of ordinary legislation. Justice Hugo L. Black, in the Supreme Court's opinion in *Oregon v. Mitchell*, had given legal expression to this view. He stated, "it cannot be seriously contended that Congress has less power over the conduct of presidential elections than it has over congressional elections."

The acceptance of this view, Ceasar suggests, "makes it easy to ignore the small inconvenience of the Constitution's different wording in the two cases." He believes that the convention debates and *The Federalist Papers* "clearly show that many of the Founding Fathers were concerned with protecting executive independence from legislative interference. Making the president's method of selection substantially independent of congressional control was a means to this end. The very limited discretionary control that the Constitution gives Congress over presidential elections probably reflects a concern over the basic question of separation of powers." It is surprising therefore, Ceaser contends, that attempts to nationalize the nominating process and campaign finance legislation, by bringing it under direct control of the federal government, were not opposed on the ground that such fundamental changes should require a constitutional amendment. The states, also, were apparently unlikely to object, for they had become little more than administrative units. When one recalls the popular rhetoric of the day, it is not surprising that these

188 / John Marini

reforms were unchallenged on Constitutional grounds. The grave threat to the Constitutional order, it was widely believed, was posed by the "imperial presidency."[2]

The political crisis which occurred in the second Nixon term which precipitated the institutional quarrel culminating in Watergate, resulted from Nixon's unwillingness to recognize the supposed neutrality of the bureaucracy. This constituted an implicit repudiation of the Progressive era view legitimized by the New Deal and made operative in the Great Society, that government could be an "engine of compassion." Nixon apparently believed that the presence of a nonpartisan bureaucracy had resulted in a distortion of the principle of representation. It had prevented the majority from ruling. The purpose of his policy of decentralization and executive reorganization—the heart of his proposed New American Revolution—was to decentralize power and bring the bureaucracy under political control, thereby restoring a representative government.

Those opposed to Nixon sought to retain a centralized administration, and to continue the tradition of liberal consensus politics that every recent President regardless of party had adhered to since the New Deal. The Democratic Party in Congress, though firmly in control of the legislature, appeared unable to make a principled appeal of sufficient moral authority to animate a national majority. However, it was increasingly able—largely as a result of nonpartisan appeals—to insure that incumbent congressmen would not be defeated. With continued control of the central political branch of government, the Democratic leadership had the institutional means to dominate the bureaucracy in their interest. But, with regard to public opinion, they remained merely a powerful faction, for unable to become a national majority, they lacked the moral authority to govern. More simply, the people had not, and apparently would not, consent to their rule. It became clear to the congressional leadership, however, that it could not allow a president to govern, regardless of the electoral mandate, who sought to destroy the structure which maintained its power. Republicans, too, in Congress, were alarmed by what they perceived to be a growing institutional imbalance between the branches, which threatened not only the prerogative of Congress as a body, but those benefits which make incumbency so advantageous to individual members.

The institutional or political quarrel was settled decisively in the wake of Watergate; Congress prevented presidential use of power in a direction it opposed. But the battle to shape public opinion did not end, nor could a new consensus be forged concerning the use of power without the animating force of a national majority. After Watergate, Congress attempted to restore a new political balance between the branches. Or, more accurately, it sought to

2. Caesar's analysis is contained in his *Reforming the Reforms: A Critical Analysis of the Presidential Selection Process* (Cambridge, Mass.: Ballinger, 1982), see especially pages 119-120.

achieve a new equilibrium—wherein both branches could have access to the bureaucracy—but neither could rule.

Campaign finance legislation was but one attempt to prevent the kind of realignment that can only be brought about through presidential leadership and broadly based party revitalization, which would of necessity require partisan campaigns at every electoral level. A Democratic consensus had created the federal apparatus which allowed congressmen the luxury of standing for election without the necessity of being partisan. Democratic incumbents could almost always be reelected, but they appeared to be unable to capture a national majority. And, candidates who could win the Presidency, opposed the extension of the bureaucratic state. Furthermore, Republicans, in Congress, also perceived the threat posed by the majority and the president. Many Republican congressmen viewed the conflicts within government as an institutional rather than a partisan quarrel. William Brock was typical of those Republicans who supported campaign finance reform, not on the grounds that it strengthened the party, but because it strengthened Congress's hand against the President. Consequently, he was not alarmed at the prospect of a weakened party system. He noted that, "while those who support public financing are generally those who want to see a strong Congress vis-a-vis the Presidency, as I do, public financing will probably see the rise, or could lead to the rise of a multi-party system, or at least a weakened party system."

Nearly all incumbent congressmen supported campaign finance reform because limits on contributions, but not on expenditures, have seemed to help to entrench incumbents, especially those in the House of Representatives. Moreover, public funding of presidential campaigns has led private groups, particularly the new legitimized PACs, to channel their resources into congressional contests. Nearly every study has shown that professional contributors donate money to incumbents, who hold powerful positions in Congress.

It is commonly believed that PACs were brought into being by the FECA and the 1976 amendments. But that legislation only accelerated their growth. As Bernadette Budde has commented, "those of us who have been active in the PAC movement for a decade or more are amused by the assumption, for we watched the development of PACs over a long period." She suggests it was not the Federal Election Campaign Act and the Federal Election Commission that promoted the PAC movement; rather "it was every other law and every regulatory body that began intruding into the business of business. A clear pattern emerges when reviewing who does and who does not have a PAC—the more regulated an industry and the more obvious an industry is as a congressional target, the more likely it is to have a political action committee within the association or within companies that make up that industry, the result of that liaison is a PAC, mothered by industry but unmistakably sired by government." Moreover, the implications of the provision of the law which supported PACs were well understood at the time. Fred Wertheimer, president of Common Cause, stated, "the PAC provision was part of a much larger fight, but we as well as labor and business were paying attention to it. We could see that we were establishing a dual system, with public financing of Presidential campaigns and private financing of congressional campaigns. We knew where we were headed."[3]

Numerous political scientists have shown the extent to which bureaucratic patronage has taken the place of party patronage in the contemporary Congress. And the campaign finance system has been changed accordingly to accommodate the new circumstances. As Gary Jacobson has written, "contemporary electoral conditions are scarcely conducive to effective action by political parties. Candidates have learned to get by without much assistance from party organizations, relying instead on campaign management professionals, the mass media, and their own personal followings." The effect, he says, is that "elections at different levels have become increasingly separated from one another, reducing the shared partisan fate." Consequently, "politicians operate as individual political entrepreneurs, pursuing personal careers in a political environment where parties are a dwindling presence."

Of course such campaigns are expensive, for they rely largely on technological innovations and professional management. "Incumbent members of Congress have been able to deal with the problem by greatly augmenting their official prerequisites," which Jacobson notes are, "resources which can and-are-used to pursue reelection." Not only are incumbents in a strong position to raise money, he insists, but "challengers find themselves at a serious disadvantage in the competition for campaign funds." It is therefore difficult for a minority party to mount an effective campaign strategy against the "interacting strategies of individual members of the majority party." The reason is, Jacobson suggests, that "members pursue reelection as individuals, emphasizing personal characteristics and service to the district, carefully avoiding responsibility for the collective performance of Congress or their party." Consequently, it is difficult to "assign blame because members of the majority are so practiced at disassociating themselves from the collective effects of their individual activities."[4]

One result of the reforms has been to increase the importance of professional fundraisers, made necessary because of the limits placed on individual contributions. Consequently, a Washington based group of lawyers-lobbyists has emerged to coordinate the expenditures of the various interest groups now nationalized, in response to the growth and increased regulation of economic life—to ensure that they are directed to the proper congressional campaigns, where their dollars can be of influence. Private money which once

---

3. Quoted in Elizabeth Drew, *Politics and Money* (New York: Macmillan, 1983), p. 10.

4. Jacobson's comments are contained in his "Congressional Campaign Finance And the Revival of the Republican Party," in Dennis Hale, ed., *The United States Congress* (Boston: Barton College, 1982), pp. 313-316. See also his *Money in Congressional Elections* (New Haven, Conn.: Yale University Press, 1980).

found its way into presidential campaigns is often diverted to congressional races. Individual private wealth is increasingly less important than corporate or group wealth, and the result has been to nationalize the sources of revenue for congressional races. As David Adamany has observed, "candidates now rely more heavily on money from outside their districts or states. As Washington D.C. has become the best place to raise campaign funds, a concomitant concern is the increasing detachment of candidates from their constituencies." Moreover, the costs of getting elected to Congress have risen dramatically. Few candidates can raise such sums on their own. So they depend more and more for cash on special interest groups and lobbyists. There was a time, Brooks Jackson observed in the Wall Street Journal, "when a politician could thumb his nose at lobbyists and get his money from a few rich individuals and the party, that's not possible anymore. The election-reform act magnified the influence of lobbyists enormously."

If candidates can no longer raise significant sums from only a few donors, what are the sources of campaign money? Malbin insists that "a candidate who is not wealthy and wants to raise a lot of money has only three ways to do it: by tapping Washington issue networks; by spending huge blocks of time—much more than ever used to be spent at fundraising—at upper-middle class cocktail parties; or by delegating work to professional fund-raising specialists, many of whom rely on direct mail techniques." Nonetheless, perhaps the most important effect of campaign finance legislation, to the ongoing success of a partisan system, is the impact of that legislation on those who challenge incumbents in congressional elections. The start-up costs of an unknown challenger running for office are extremely high, and necessary campaign funds became even more difficult to raise as a result of finance reform. In the past, a newcomer could solicit the support of a few wealthy donors, and with that seed money a credible campaign could be initiated. That is no longer possible as a result of limitations on individual contributions. Consequently, many incumbent congressmen have no effective opposition.

Congress, by requiring detailed accounting procedures, along with spending limits, has forced changes in presidential campaign strategy. They have had the effect of encouraging individual, professionalized campaigns, which undermine the role of state and local parties. Richard B. Cheney, Gerald Ford's campaign manager objected to the fact that "one of the major results of the spending limitation has been to encourage the development of highly centralized campaign organizations with elaborate controls over spending." Unless a campaign develops such an organization, he noted, "there is virtually no possibility that it can account for all funds expended or adequately comply with federal regulations." The effect has been to inhibit local or grass-roots activity in presidential elections. As Cheney notes, "the experience of the Ford campaign in 1976 showed conclusively that it was easier to discourage grass-roots activity than to try to control and report it. In previous campaigns, it was possible to tell a local campaign or party official to go ahead with a project as long as he could raise the money to finance it." After the reforms, it was easier to insist that local party organizations remain neutral.

It is perhaps true that "systematic regulation of political campaigns by Congress must inevitably lead to those in power regulating in favor of themselves." Gary Jacobson has clearly demonstrated that "the most persistent trend in campaign finance legislation over the last decade has been toward restricting the financial resources available to candidates." Moreover, Jacobson suggests that "campaign spending matters, and it matters most to candidates who are not incumbents . . . what incumbents could spend makes relatively little difference. Whether or not campaigns are seriously contended depends on the resources mobilized by non-incumbents." Consequently, he has insisted that "changes in campaign finance have consistently tended to dampen electoral competition, thus favoring the very people who do the legislating." So clear is the advantage of incumbency, that the former chairman of the Democratic National Committee, Michael Kirwin remarked, the "no congressman who gets elected and minds his business should ever get beaten. Everything is there for him to use if he'll only keep his nose to the grindstone and use what is offered."

It is also apparent that members of both parties benefit from a centralized administration responsive to congressional intervention. Congress as a body has an interest in preventing effective political or presidential control of the bureaucracy. Thus Jacobson points to the fact that "party conflict has increasingly given way to activity that enhances the ability of incumbents of both parties to retain office." If the partisan divisions have become less important, David Mayhew may be right when he suggests that "in a good many ways the interesting division in congressional politics is not between Democrats and Republicans but between politicians in and out of office."

If the crucial political division is now the institutional division between Congress and the President, and the interests and constituencies, not to mention the majorities which support them, the hidden loser in the legislative-executive battles of the 1970s was the national majority. The legislation of the 1970s, of which campaign finance reform was but a part, created the conditions which allowed for the consolidation of a centralized administrative state. But contrary to the fears of many, that centralized administration would lead to an immensely strong national government, the opposite has proved to be the case. The actual result has been a weakened national government—particularly the active part of government—the executive. Bureaucratic government is big government but not strong government. Bureaucratic rule, therefore, has created the possibility of an executive apparatus without the necessity of a political executive. It has created a bureaucracy that can administer without ruling, one that is responsive to many centers of power, and lacks only a central principled purpose.

Regulating Elections: The Watergate Legacy

Campaign finance received renewed attention in recent years, purportedly, as the result of an enormous increase in the costs of running for office, particularly, those for the financing of presidential elections. Those costs had always been borne by private wealth, largely unregulated by government. They had grown dramatically, it was argued, because of a growing dependence on the use of electronic media, as well as the more specialized campaigns, which utilized the professional consultant and pollster, in the process of replacing the party boss and the volunteer worker. Given the necessity of raising vast sums of money, which was often solicited from the hands of the wealthy few, it was almost inevitable that questions concerning the relationship of wealth and decision-making in government would be raised anew.

Nor was it surprising that this issue was to be raised in the period of divided control of the institutions of the national government, at a time when the Democratic consensus had been shattered and the Party was unable to capture the presidency. The Republicans, on the other hand, were able to win the presidency, but were unable to mount a campaign of sufficient appeal to unseat incumbents in Congress. The Republican president, animated by a national majority opposed to the extension of the power of the national government, was countered by a Democratic Congress that had created the bureaucracy, and benefited from its continued existence. This state of affairs reached a crisis stage in the aftermath of the 1972 election, when the revelations of the Senate Select Committee on Campaign Practices, the so-called Watergate Committee, convinced many Americans that private wealth had succeeded in polluting the political process.

A major public goal of the campaign finance legislation of this period was the elimination of the corrupting influence of private wealth on the political process. The political rhetoric of the 1970s, which led to reform of campaign finance practices, was dominated by the theme that private wealth had muddied the waters of the democratic process of selecting and funding presidential campaigns. Ostensibly, Watergate was proof positive that this was indeed the case. Such wealth appeared to be the sole repository of the Republican Party, and the reforms of the period succeeded in drying up the traditional sources of Republican support. They also succeeded in changing the political landscape of American electoral politics.

Before the early 1970s, presidential campaign finance procedures were largely unregulated, although federal laws prohibiting corporate contributions had been on the books since 1907. In earlier attempts at reform, the major goal was the prevention of corrupt practices, particularly the buying of votes; or, the prevention of undue pressure by officials on government workers to contribute to their campaigns. The decline of machine politics, however, caused attention to shift from the buying of votes in the voting booth to the buying of votes in Congress and the buying of special consideration in the White House. Subsequently, the Federal Corrupt Practices Act of 1925 became the primary instrument of campaign finance regulation. This law required disclosure of receipts and expenditures in campaigns for the Senate and the House of Representatives, but the law did not apply to political committees set up by a candidate, and it did not apply to presidential and vice-presidential candidates. In fact, however, this act was neither enforced nor enforceable. Consequently, although the Corrupt Practices Act was universally considered a failure, no broad support for reform emerged before the 1960s. During this decade, Gary Jacobson claims, "the atmosphere changed radically, and in the early 1970s substantial and far reaching changes in campaign finance regulation were enacted. Reasons for this development are not hard to discern. The most important was the startling rise in the cost of major political campaigns."

One might reasonably be led to the conclusion that the corrupting influence of money in politics is a phenomenon of the age of the electronic media. With increased costs of campaigning, the opportunity of the wealthy to influence the political process is also greater. But it seems unlikely that the major impetus for campaign finance reform is primarily the result of the rising costs of elections. Those costs were thought to be rising because of an increasing reliance on technology. But as Jacobson has noted, "technological and political changes are not the only sources of increased campaign spending[. U]ntil 1972, campaign spending was not growing any faster than the federal budget. Both the growth in federal spending and extension of federal regulatory activity raised the political stakes enormously; decisions made by federal officials could have drastic effects on the prosperity of whole industries." More likely, the increased costs of campaigning coincided with the growth of a centralized administration, which changed the stakes of electoral victory or defeat. Moreover, Congress made it easy for those who desired access to its membership. It continued private financing of congressional elections, at the same time that it mandated public funding for presidential elections.

In reviewing the campaign finance literature of the past decades, it is clear that private financing of campaigns has long been considered a form of political corruption. Indeed throughout much of this century, campaign finance was regarded as a kind of corruption, precisely because those costs were borne by private wealth. Even Herbert Alexander, perhaps the leading authority on campaign finance, concluded that "the American system of financing elections through secret, often unlimited private donations has given undue influence in politics and government to wealthy or well-organized donors at the expense of the unorganized public." Nor is this criticism new. In 1960, Alexander Heard voiced a similar concern. In his influential study, *The Costs of Democracy*, he noted, "Concern over the private financing of political campaigns stems in significant measure from the belief that a gift is an especially important kind of vote. It is grounded in the thought that persons who give in larger sums or to more candidates than their fellow citizens are in effect voting more than once."

Louise Overacker had expressed this concern long before the use of television had turned election campaigns into very expensive affairs. In 1932, with the publication of *Money in Elections*, she pointed to the fear which animated all subsequent reformers of campaign finance. She wrote: "The financing of elections in a democracy is a problem which is arousing increasing concern. Many are beginning to wonder if present-day methods of raising and spending campaign funds do not clog the wheels of our elaborately constructed mechanism of popular control, and if democracies do not inevitably become plutocracies." Perhaps it was Theodore Roosevelt, the father of campaign finance reform, who gave quintessential expression to the problem of money in politics. In 1907, he noted, "if our political institutions were perfect, they would absolutely prevent the political domination of money in any part of our affairs."

It is not surprising therefore, that public finance legislation was first proposed by Theodore Roosevelt in his State of the Union Address in 1907. He recommended public financing of federal elections and a ban on private contributions as "a means to give the poor man a fair chance in politics." He suggested that "the need for collecting large campaign funds would vanish, if Congress provided an appropriation ample enough to meet the necessity for thorough organization and machinery, which requires a large expenditure. Then the stipulation should be made that no party receiving campaign funds from the Treasury should accept more than a fixed amount from any individual."

In the view of reformers, campaign finance legislation was an attempt to equalize conditions so as to minimize the influence of wealth and limit access to power through government regulation of the electoral process. It required utilizing such devices as public disclosure of campaign contributions, limitations on expenditures for campaigns, and restriction on amounts allowed to be contributed. The most ambitious proposals called for public funding of elections, as well as expenditure limits, contributions restrictions, and strict disclosure requirements. Congressional enactment of an elaborate set of laws regulating how candidates raise, spend and account for campaign funds, was allegedly in response to growing concern over the influence of private wealth in elections. However, one may be permitted to wonder whether the public rhetoric used to justify such reforms was indeed the principal reason for campaign finance reform.

Nonetheless, it was not until 1966 that Congress enacted the first public funding legislation, The Presidential Campaign Fund Act (Long Act). But, the Long Act never took effect. The major problem concerning legislation to underwrite and regulate presidential elections, was to decide whether political parties or candidate organizations should be the recipient of federal subsidies. The Long Act established an income tax check-off system, converting tax money into a presidential campaign fund and making that fund available to the treasurers of the political parties rather than to candidate organizations. Funds would have come from a Presidential Election Campaign Fund in the U.S. Treasury consisting of dollars voluntarily checked off by taxpayers on their federal income tax returns.

The legislation generated considerable controversy. Robert Kennedy, in arguing against the Long Act, "stressed its centralizing consequences for the party system, which traditionally has been organized as a federal system in its own right." Kennedy claimed that "any program which assured the two major national committees of $30 million or more in each presidential election would concentrate power in the hands of the national chairman . . . and diminish the role of state and local parties in the system." Congress, persuaded by such arguments, indefinitely suspended implementation of the act.

In 1971, Congress adopted remarkably similar provisions which formed the basis of the present funding system. Under the 1971 Revenue Act, the nominee, rather than the party, receives the public funds accumulated through the dollar checkoff. The Revenue Act also limits campaign spending by presidential nominees who receive public money and bans all private contributions to them. Along with the Revenue Act, Congress passed the 1971 Federal Election Campaign Act. This act repealed the Corrupt Practices Act of 1925. It had three major provisions. It significantly tightened disclosure and reporting requirements for all candidates for federal office; it limited the amount of money candidates could spend on advertising; and it limited the amount a candidate and his immediate family could contribute to his campaign.

The 1974 amendments to the FECA extended the public funding provisions of the Revenue Act to presidential primary elections and to the presidential nominating conventions of the national parties. It imposed ceilings on individual contributions to federal campaigns, which seriously limited the influence of individual private wealth on all elections. It also imposed limits on the amounts an individual could give to political parties or political committees. It imposed limits on overall expenditures from a candidate's own resources. It established detailed reporting and disclosure requirements for campaign committees, political parties, and multicandidate committees, governing both receipts of contributions and campaign expenditures. Furthermore, it created a bipartisan Federal Election Commission to administer election laws. "The FECA amendments of 1974," Michael Malbin asserts, "probably represented the most sweeping set of campaign finance law changes ever adopted in the United States, if not in the world."

Initially, it appeared that Congress intended that expenditure limits would also apply to Congressional elections, even though it was widely believed that such limits were unconstitutional. Congress, therefore, made it easy to challenge the law. As Herbert Alexander has observed, "an unusual provision of the law had authorized any eligible voter to start federal court proceedings to contest the constitutionality of any provision of law." In a decision rendered before the next presidential election, on January 30, 1976 the Supreme Court held several provisions of the FECA to be unconstitutional. The limitations on individual contributions were upheld, but the limits on overall campaign expenditures were struck down as violations of the constitutional right of free speech. The Court also held that independent expenditures could not be restricted without violating the individual's right of free speech. Only candidates for the presidency who accepted public funding were held to expenditure limits. Moreover, the First Amendment prevented Congress from restricting independent expenditures on behalf of a candidate, if the expenditures are not coordinated with the official campaign. Finally, the Court struck down the method by which members of the Federal Election Commission were appointed. Originally, Congress had a hand in the appointment of some of the members of the FEC, but the Court ruled that members of an executive branch agency must be appointed by the President.

The political reality of the reforms, given the decision of the Supreme Court, is that presidential elections are publicly financed, and congressional campaigns are privately funded, but no expenditure limits are mandatory on privately financed campaigns. In enacting FECA, a recent study reports, Congress made several policy choices: there would be strict limits on contributions, national and state expenditure limits would be tied to public funding for nomination and general election campaigns, extensive administrative regulation would be imposed, and campaign subsidies would be directed to candidates over parties. By so choosing, Congress made federal statutes and regulations major determinants of presidential campaign strategy and organization and contributed to a growing separation of presidential campaign organizations from national party organizations.

By the 1984 election, the United States had in place an election regulating system that had taken most of the previous decade to enact and to "debug." In undertaking to regulate presidential elections in this way, Congress seriously transformed electoral politics in America, and at the same time assured itself dominance of the political process by virtue of its access to and use of the federal bureaucracy. One need only witness the great difficulty the Reagan Republican Party has had in bringing about a major electoral realignment to see that its failure was in no small measure due to the Congressional Democratic Party's success in utilizing those important reforms of the 1970s. However, it was only possible to do so after it succeeded in overcoming the obstacles imposed by the presidency. In viewing the political climate which brought about the perceived need for campaign finance reform, it becomes possible to understand the nature of those reforms.

On August 8, 1974, just hours before Richard Nixon announced his resignation as President of the United States, the House of Representatives passed the FECA Amendments of 1974 by a lopsided vote of 355-48. The second Senate version of the bill, which would have required public funding of congressional election campaigns, was unacceptable to the House, and action on the bill was delayed. "As finally passed by large margins in both chambers," Herbert Alexander has written, "the bill provided public financing only for presidential elections, including matching funds for the prenomination period, flat grants to the political parties for national nominating conventions, and large grants to the major party nominees for their general election campaigns."[5] The Federal Election Commission administered the first public funding program in 1976. Those presidential candidates who were eligible received matching funds in the primary election, and full funding for the general election campaign. The major parties received public funds to pay for their nominating conventions.

This legislation would almost certainly not have become law had it not been for Watergate. The Republicans opposed it, and Nixon promised in March of 1974 to veto any bill that included public funding of presidential elections. But, by mid-August, Nixon was no longer in office. On October 15, 1974, President Ford signed the FECA of 1974. Although long an opponent of public financing, Ford declared that "the times demand this legislation." The presidency, not to mention the Republican Party, was in a state of disarray. The collapse of the Nixon presidency resulted in a fundamental alteration of the relations between the political branches of the federal government as well as the traditional sources of power within the parties.

Campaign finance legislation had been a deeply partisan issue in the last years of Nixon's first term. Congress enacted major campaign finance bills in 1970 and 1971. Nixon vetoed the 1970 bill, and Congress responded the next year with the FECA of 1971. The fundamental issue in question was the public financing of presidential elections. As Jacobson has noted: "the successful drive toward public funding of presidential campaigns began with the revival of Senator's Long's income tax checkoff idea. A section allowing individuals to designate on their returns that $1 of their taxes be placed in a special fund to finance presidential campaigns was attached to the Revenue Act of 1971, an important administration tax package." The issue provoked a strongly partisan division, and "with good reason," Jacobson suggests. "The Democrats were still $9 million in debt from the 1968 election with only a year to go until the next. Republicans, with plenty of money, not unreasonably saw it as a scheme to bail out Democrats. The immediate interest of both parties dovetailed nicely with their traditional rhetorical attitudes. Democrats could support the scheme as one that would keep wealth from corrupting politics; Republicans could attack it as an assault on individual freedom and a further intrusion of government into political life."

Nixon, of course, opposed any such plan, and threatened to veto it. Congress, to avoid the veto, delayed the law's effect until after the 1972 election and required that the money be specifically appropriated from the fund before

---

5. *Financing Politics: Money, Elections, and Political Reform* (Washington: Congressional Quarterly, Inc., 1980), p. 31.

being distributed to the candidates. It is important to note, as Herbert Alexander has remarked, that the FECA of 1971, which "passed in January 1972, a month after the Revenue Act, required fuller disclosure of political funding than ever before—a factor that was to play a key role in the Watergate affair." Watergate provided the political climate which brought about the public funding provisions of FECA of 1974; the money would be provided by a Presidential Election Campaign Fund, a tax checkoff provision of the Revenue Act.

Subsequently, the Court's decision in *Buckley v. Valeo*, forced further amendments to this legislation. The FECA Amendments of 1976 were the result. This law limited individual and PAC contributions to political parties, and increased the amount that Senate campaign committees could contribute to Senate candidates. It also limited the amount of one's own money a presidential candidate who accepted public funding could spend, to $50,000. In 1979, Congress once again amended FECA with the object of lightening the burden the law imposed on candidates and political committees by reducing paperwork. At the same time, it increased the public funding entitlement and spending limit for national nominating conventions. Major attempts to enact additional changes in campaign finance laws, including public funding of congressional campaigns, have failed. It is in the interest of incumbent members of Congress to mandate the public financing of presidential elections while at the same time becoming increasingly dependent upon organized private spending.

Public Financing of Presidential Elections: 1976-1984

The 1976 election was the first election to provide public funding for presidential prenomination and the general election campaigns. Herbert Alexander noted that this election was an unusual one in several respects. "A new law," he explains, the FECA, "limited the amount of money that could be contributed or spent. A new agency, The Federal Election Commission (FEC), administered the law and disbursed the public funds. At least partly because of public funding, a Southerner, an outsider not attuned to Washington politics and without access to traditional sources of money, won the Democratic Party's nomination and subsequently the election. He defeated an incumbent president who had not been on the ballot four years earlier." Under the law, eligible candidates seeking the presidency were to receive public funds to match small contributions from private contributors. In order to receive matching funds from the government, a candidate had to raise at least $5,000 in contributions of $250 or less from individuals in at least 20 states and had to agree to limit his campaign expenditures to $10 million plus a cost-of-living adjustment (COLA). In the general election each major party Presidential nominee became eligible for a grant of $20 million (plus COLA) to run the campaign. The candidate had to limit expenditures to that amount and was not allowed to accept private contributions for the general election. Furthermore, each major party was entitled to receive up to $3 million (plus COLA) to finance its national convention.

In the 1976 primary elections, matching funds up to $5.5 million were provided for candidates who qualified for public funding. The major parties were given $2.2 million to fund the national nominating conventions. And a flat grant of $21 million was provided for the candidates of the major parties to finance the general election. Ford and Carter both accepted public funding and were restricted to that amount, plus another $3.2 million that each national committee could raise and spend on behalf of its candidate. In 1972, the Republicans had spent more than $61 million to elect a President, the Democrats had spent $30 million in a losing effort. In 1976, the parties had an equal amount to spend, as did the candidates themselves. Furthermore, few individuals or private groups resorted to independent spending; this was probably due, in part, to a lack of familiarity with the new law. In Alexander's view, "the single greatest change effected by the new fund raising law was the elimination of the prominent role played by wealthy donors." He suggested that "only 8 or 9% of Americans contributed to campaigns in 1976, the lowest since 1952 . . . and large contributions virtually disappeared."

Campaign finance legislation also appeared to necessitate centralized organization of presidential campaigns. Because of the need to comply with numerous restrictions and rigid accounting procedures of the new law, campaigns were necessarily centralized, and local or grassroots activity was severely curtailed. The role of local and state parties, as well as the national party, was to undergo change. Jacobson noted that the National Committee of the Republican Party "moved into direct mail fund raising . . . for several reasons. One was the absence of an alternative. The Watergate revelations made all large contributions—suspect, and left major Republican contributors feeling burned and scarcely inclined to further generosity. Small individual donors were unquestionably proper, and they were easier to solicit." But this kind of fund raising is costly, and requires time in order to achieve a payoff. This strategy had unforeseen consequences, and with the adoption of the FECA amendments of 1979, the Republican Party was able to play a prominent role in the next presidential election, the election of 1980. But neither party was capable of playing a decisive role in the election of 1976.

What were the effects of campaign finance reform on the 1976 election? Alexander contends that the FECA was a "vital part of the Carter success story." Without stringent contribution limits, he noted, "better known candidates who had connections with wealthy contributors might have swamped Carter easily in the primary season. Without federal subsidies, Carter would have lacked the money to consolidate his initial lead . . . this combination had an equalizing effect because it lowered the advantage large contributors could provide while enhancing the value of small contributions." Public funding, he suggests, "allowed a Washington outsider, a regional candidate, to break into the field and establish his candidacy." Furthermore, Alexander contends, finance legislation gave Carter "one important advantage over his Republican opponent. With the nomination virtually assured some weeks before the Democratic National Convention, which preceded its Republican counterpart by one month, [Carter] had ample lead time to lay orderly plans for the fall campaign. The Carter campaign made maximum use of both the party and the federal funds made available to it." The Carter campaign also made effective use of the traditional supporters of the Democratic Party, particularly the labor unions.

A major purpose of campaign finance reform was elimination of the undue influence of special interests, and the domination of politics by private wealth. However, in Congressional decision making concerning campaign finance policy the choices made have consistently supported the interests of incumbent members. Furthermore, the Democrats have carefully avoided imposing new limits on what organized labor can do. Consequently, as a result of FECA, Malbin contends, the "biggest winner was organized labor." The reason, he suggests, is that "public financing for the general election campaign shut off private contributions to the two major presidential candidates. Contributions to the national party committees were permitted, but even this was limited. In contrast, labor was able to spend as much as it wanted to in communicating with union members and their families, registering them to vote and getting them to the polls." He estimates labor spent upwards of $8.5 million on behalf of Jimmy Carter, compared with $21.8 million that Carter could spend on his own behalf. It is no wonder that George Meany held a news conference just after the election in which he noted his expectation that the efforts of organized labor would give him access to the White House.

Nonetheless, the Republicans did not become the beneficiary of business support in 1976. As Malbin noted, "business's cautious backing of incumbents in both parties raises problems for challengers who want to mount serious campaigns without depending on labor. With large individual contributions ruled out, the three basic sources of large amounts of money are personal wealth, ideological groups and direct mail fund-raising." As a result of finance legislation, there seemed little doubt that these sources would become increasingly important in subsequent elections.

There is considerable evidence that campaign finance legislation worked pretty much as it was intended to work by Congress, at least in the election of 1976. The influence of wealth was minimized and the expenditures of the national parties were equalized. But, many were skeptical that such regulation of the electoral process had resulted in the elimination of special interests or privilege. Former Democratic Senator Eugene McCarthy insisted that "there is no question that this new law gives special preference to the Democratic party. I am surprised the Republicans did not recognize that, though they did halfway sense it, all except the liberal Republicans, whose principal function is to shoot the wounded after the battle is over." McCarthy contended that those groups who sought access to the public treasury, bought access through support of the Democratic Party. He noted, "for the first time in history, The National Education Association (NEA) endorsed a candidate. Why did they do that? Because the candidate promised money to education. I think this represents a much greater corruption of the system than large contributions do." Moreover, McCarthy suggests that any attempt by government to finance partisan politics would result in the establishment of 'state political parties' that would benefit those in power and their allies. He observed: "if somebody had come to the Constitutional Convention and said 'we want a system whereby the government will finance politics,' he would have been told this was what the revolution was against." The freedom to participate in politics, McCarthy implied, should not be dependent on the support or approval of the government itself.

In 1980, once again, both major party presidential candidates agreed to accept public financing of their campaigns, thereby foregoing private funds in the general election campaign. In the prenomination period, there was a $17.7 million spending limit for candidates who accepted public funding, although federal subsidies accounted for only about half that amount. In the general election, each candidate received $29.4 million in public funds, and the national party committees were allowed to raise and spend another $4.6 million. But, unlike the previous election, the 1980 election was significantly affected by a rise in independent expenditures—which the Supreme Court had ruled could not be limited—and, a renewed role of political parties, particularly the Republican Party, in the national campaign.

This election provided the opportunity to observe the first full appearance of the national Republican Party in its modern form. Ronald Reagan won the presidency and the Republicans gained control of the Senate for the first time in more than a quarter century. The national Republican Party, perhaps by necessity, had become skillfully and professionally organized, and had developed considerable financial strength through its directed mail fundraising efforts. Moreover, Alexander shows that the Republican National Committee (RNC) "successfully exploited fund-raising options made possible by the 1979 Amendments—options not foreseen by those who formulated the law. Under RNC auspices, some $9 million was raised from individuals and corporations and channeled into those states where such contributions to party committees were permitted and where spending for voter identification and turnout drives would have the greatest benefit." Consequently, there was, Alexander noted, "considerable grass-roots activity because state and local party committees could spend unlimited amounts of money for the presidential ticket as long as the spending was related to volunteer participation."

It was because of criticism following the 1976 election, in which it was argued that the existing law inhibited grass-roots activity, that Congress again amended the Federal Election Campaign Act in 1979. Alexander observed that the effects of the amendment were to "permit widespread dissemination of banners, pins, bumper stickers, handbills, brochures, posters, leaflets, yard signs, party tabloids, and buttons. More important, the 1979 FECA amendments allowed state and local party spending on volunteer-operated voter registration and get-out-the-vote drives, including the use of the phone banks." Although Congress appeared to condone voluntary party activity at the local level in presidential campaigns, it forbade expenditures for mass media activity under these exemptions for state and local activity, and restricted such activity it did allow to presidential campaigns alone. As for Congressional elections, Congress appeared satisfied with the result of campaign finance reform.

The Democratic Party was not nearly so successful in organizing itself to function successfully in fundraising at the grassroots. Perhaps, it did not have to. Congressional Democrats, especially, appeared to have little need of a revitalized national party. David Adamany noted that "the DNC was, following tradition, an arm of the White House; and the campaign committees on Capitol Hill worked in the shadow of Democratic incumbency." Moreover, he observed, "the evolution of political action committees, emerging as institutional rivals to parties, was well under way in the new incarnation mandated by the Federal Election Campaign Act."[6] Despite the FECA Amendments of 1979, the Carter campaign was unable to attract the kind of local support from Democratic committees that Republicans had successfully attracted. The Republican committees were able to spend some $15 million on behalf of Reagan. Democratic committees spent only about $4 million on volunteer efforts on behalf of Carter. However, Alexander contends that "the $15 million spent by Republican state and local party organizations was matched by a roughly equal amount that labor organizations spent on communications and activities intended to benefit Carter-Mondale." But, he suggests, labor's spending was not well coordinated with the Democratic ticket, and was late in the campaign, thus "it failed to have as much impact as RNC-supported state and local party spending."

There was another source of expenditures which appeared to be of some importance in the 1980 election. They were those independent expenditures, in which individuals or groups could spend unlimited amounts for or against a candidate, as long as they were made independent of—or without the collaboration of—the official campaign. In this category, Alexander has written, "the Reagan campaign attracted a substantial amount of independent spending, some $10.6 million." This was far more than $30,000 of such expenditures reported on behalf of Carter. Alexander estimates that total Reagan expenditures in this election were $64.3 million, while the Carter campaign spent $53.93 million.

In the 1984 election, as in the previous two elections, both major party candidates accepted public financing of their campaigns. Those candidates who agreed to public funding were limited to $24 million, partially subsidized by the government, in the prenomination period. Each party presidential candi-

---

6. "Political Parties in the 1980s" in Malbin, ed. *Money and Politics*, p. 71.

date was allowed $40.4 million, fully subsidized by the Treasury, for the general election campaign. Again, as in the 1980 election, independent expenditures were important, as were the efforts of parties and groups. Once again, the Republican national, congressional, and senatorial committees were successful in raising large sums of money. But, the Democratic Party's committees succeeded in reversing a steady trend favoring the Republicans. Perhaps the most important development in this campaign was that congressional Democrats matched Republican fundraising in key contests, and were able to hold down losses in the House even as Reagan won reelection by an overwhelming margin. As the Washington Post's Thomas B. Edsall reported, "in the House ... there were significant changes in the partisan patterns of fund-raising that suggests that Democrats are slowly catching Republicans in the effective distribution of money in tight contests." A Washington Post analysis of 83 House races decided by 12 percentage points or less found that "Democratic incumbents facing serious challenges out-raised their Republican opponents by a wide margin. In 52 races, Democrats raised an average of $100,000 more than Republicans, $374,000 to $247,000. In 15 races for open seats ... Democrats raised more money on average than Republicans, $353,000 to $301,000." Only in races "where Democrats challenged Republican incumbents [did] Republicans [have] a decisive financial advantage, $145,000 to $286,000. In almost all cases, however, Democrats raised at least $200,000 by the October 17 reporting date, enough for a credible race."[7]

There is little doubt that much of the Democrats' success can be attributed to Tony Coehlo, chairman of the Democratic Congressional Campaign Committee. Coehlo aggressively solicited economic interests and business PACs to raise cash for his committee, and to persuade them to support Democratic candidates. An example of Coehlo's technique was reported by Brooks Jackson in the *Wall Street Journal*. He noted that when the National Association of Home Builders decided to support a Republican challenging a Democratic incumbent, "Coehlo engineered a blunt letter from the House leadership, to the organization's chief lobbyist, suggesting 'that the Home Builder's good relationship with Democrats in the House' could be damaged if the group failed to support the Democrat's campaign." Although Democratic incumbents have always done well with PACs, it was clear that its continued success with the economic interests required ongoing control of the House, and therefore demanded a party effort. In the past, Edsall observed, "safe Democratic incumbents have received a disproportionately large share of the money for Democratic candidates, while nonincumbent Democrats have often gone begging." The Democrats' House leadership strategy was one of more effective distribution of resources so as to maintain control of the House.

The public financing of presidential elections has led to an increase of private spending in congressional elections. The primary beneficiary of private

7. "Democrats Used their Money Wisely," *The Washington Post National Weekly Edition* (Nov. 26, 1984), p. 13.

spending has been incumbent members of Congress, whose power, influence, and ability to retain office, have become legend. In the election of 1984, as in nearly every election since the adoption of FECA, special interest groups continued to favor Democrats and incumbents. In this election, incumbents received 72 percent of PAC money, up from 69 percent in 1982, 62 percent in 1980, and 58 percent in 1978. The Federal Election Commission reported that PACs gave $58 million of the $133 million received by incumbents in the 1983-84 election cycle. This was nearly 44 percent of the total collected by the 408 incumbents. In fact, 163 incumbents raised more than half their funds from PACs, including 20 of the 27 committee chairmen and the top leadership of both parties. In each of the three election cycles, incumbents have received a greater total share of their campaign money from PACs. In the 1981-82 election cycle, incumbents received 37 percent of their money from PACs; whereas in 1979-80, they received only 34 percent. It seems clear that access to the bureaucracy and the ability to intervene on behalf of interests in administrative and regulatory decisionmaking, have paid off for members of Congress. In the 1984 elections, only 19 out of 411 members of the House who sought reelection were defeated.

In viewing the three presidential elections since the FECA of 1974 has been in effect, it seems evident that campaign finance reform has heightened the tension between the president and Congress, and has made it more difficult to reconcile the demands of the interests and constituencies which elect each of the respective branches. Michael Malbin has suggested that "the rules of campaign finance seem to encourage a situation in which Presidents and members of Congress come to office with systematically different interest-group electoral bases. Legislative-executive relations might be improved...if the branches' electoral bases were made more similar." But, as Malbin knows, campaign finance legislation has done precisely the opposite, it has exacerbated those differences. Moreover, it "helped reinforce the nationalization of interest-group politics that followed the expansion of the federal government's role."[8] The ongoing regulation of these interests becomes the essence of liberal Democratic politics, and it presupposes the existence of a centralized administration. It has transformed the principal function of Congress, from one of legislation on behalf of a general or national interest to one of detailed administration and regulation of particular interests. Furthermore, members of Congress seek to avoid partisanship in the ordinary sense, ignoring parties and principles, while emphasizing service.

It is not surprising that PACs have proliferated in the wake of campaign finance laws which abruptly followed administrative centralization. The problems implicit in those reforms, pose serious questions for the viability of a free, representative democracy. As David Adamany has observed, "even when PACs do not focus mainly on obtaining direct economic benefits, they create a prob-

8. *Money and Politics*, pp. 255-256.

lem for representative government. Because money is transferable, PACs nationalize funding sources. They collect ample treasure in small individual gifts from many locales, centralize those funds in the hands of institutional offices, and make large contributions in strategically important races anywhere in the country. The real and effective contribution in these circumstances is the PAC and its leadership, not the small givers. . . . The candidate knows the programs and objectives of the PAC and it is to the PAC officer that preferred access is given."[9] Alexis de Tocqueville aptly observed the essence of this dilemma long before it had become a fundamental problem in American government. "How is it possible to reconcile extreme centralization with representative democracy?" he asked. "This is the grand problem of the times."

Politics and Money: The Ideological Basis of Reform

Are presidential nominations and elections determined by those who have the most money? Do those who contribute expect favors? Are winners expected to 'pay off' to the large contributors? Nelson Polsby and Aaron Wildavsky argued in their popular book that "this was certainly the reasoning that inspired the post-Watergate political reform of the mid-70's, which attempted to take money as an influence out of presidential elections." However, they insisted that "before those elaborate limitations were established, the evidence was slight that presidential elections were unduly influenced, never mind 'bought' by monied interests."[10] Consequently, it appears that the public rhetoric, which was crucial in swaying public opinion to favor such reform, has little basis in fact. For this reason, it is necessary to look at the political climate as well as the ideological commitment of those who were the leaders in campaign finance reform.

The polluting effect of money in politics, particularly with regard to campaign finance, has long been alleged by critics of private financing of elections. It has emerged with great regularity as an important issue of American politics. In every period of extensive reform, from those of the Progressive era to the equally dramatic reforms of the 1970s, private financing of political campaigns has been attacked as a form of corruption which threatens to undermine the legitimacy of democratic government and the principle of equal representation. The democratic animus against wealth has long proved to have powerful rhetorical appeal; once again in the 1970s, the alleged corrupting influence of wealth, graphically portrayed in the Senate Watergate Committee hearings, provided the impetus which led to the most drastic reform of campaign finance legislation in our history.

---

9. "PAC's and the Democratic Financing of Politics," *Arizona Law Review* v. 20 (No. 2, 1980), pp. 596-97.

10. *Presidential Elections: Strategies of American Politics* (New York: Charles Scribner's Sons, 1984), pp. 54-55.

Campaign finance reform legislation has always been animated by two separate goals that are not unrelated. One is to prevent corruption or the appearance of corruption in electoral politics; the other is to equalize the relative ability of individuals to influence the outcome of elections. In the popular rhetoric, measures against the corrupting influence of wealth nearly always have a special kind of appeal. However, in the opinion of the reformers, traditional campaign finance methods have always been treated as a form of political corruption, precisely because campaign finance costs have been borne by private wealth. As Alexander has written, "the American system of financing elections, through sometimes secret, often unlimited private donations, has given undue influence in politics and government to wealthy or well-organized donors at the expense of the unorganized public."

More importantly, however, finance reform has had an ideological basis—rarely brought to the surface of partisan politics—which is crucial in justifying reform, and in principle leads almost inevitably to public financing of election campaigns. At its core, this opinion is animated by a certain understanding of the meaning of equality. Reformers and critics, as well as commentators, assume the self-evidence of what has been called the "new equality." As Alexander noted, "the idea that inequality of contribution generates inequality of influence over election outcomes has often been regarded as an essential premise of the case for campaign finance reform." Thus, he suggests, "the American system of government is rooted in the egalitarian assumption of 'one-person, one-vote,' but, like all democracies, it is confronted with an unequal distribution of economic resources. The attempt to reconcile the inequalities lies at the base of the problem of money in politics." In this view, "one-person, one-vote" becomes a kind of categorical imperative, the implementation of which is the true test of democratic government: the obligation to weigh each vote equally is the essential requirement of democracy. In the process, any substantive meaning of equality as the end or purpose of the regime is replaced by a preoccupation with procedural or statistical parity. As regards public policymaking, therefore, it was easy to shift the emphasis of the meaning of equality, from one of a defense of the political principle of equal opportunity for every individual to the achievement of the social ideal of equality of results.

Equality, so understood, is not based on the political principle that all men are created equal and therefore have certain unalienable rights as individuals, which gives rise to legitimate governments whose proper task is the protection of those rights. Rather, the new equality is viewed as a social ideal which requires government intervention to achieve its ends, equality of social conditions. This view was expressed with great authority by John Rawls, in his immensely influential work, A Theory of Justice. Judge Skelly Wright, a leading jurist-scholar, noted that Rawls "recognized that dominance of wealth in the political process is inconsistent with both the philosophical meaning and the practical exercise of political equality." Wright observed that "Rawls maintained that the 'worth of liberty' was not the same for everyone, because of 'the inability to take advantage of one's rights and opportunities as a result of poverty and ignorance, and a lack of means generally." Rawls argued in his work that "the liberties protected by the principle of participation lose much of their value whenever those who have greater private means are permitted to use their advantage to control the course of public debate. For eventually these inequalities will enable those better situated to exercise a larger influence over the development of legislation." Consequently, Rawls suggested that public financing of political campaigns is necessary, "for when parties and elections are financed not by public funds but by private contributions, the political forum is so constrained by the wishes of the dominant interests that the basic measures needed to establish just constitutional rule are seldom properly presented."[11]

It is apparent that no system of private financing of politics can be equitable, given the assumptions of the new equality, which has been popularly transformed into the view that equality is but a procedural, formal or statistical requirement. Even Gary Jacobson, a political scientist who specializes in campaign finance, was led to conclude that "apart from any other defects—or any virtues—they may have, privately financed elections are open to a fundamental criticism. Political equality is the democratic ideal: one person, one vote. But the distribution of financial assets is anything but equal; money used effectively as a political resource, inevitably violated democratic equality." Rawls's theory of justice requires regulation of every aspect of political, economic, and social life to achieve social equality. In short, it requires a centralized bureaucracy. However, it is not easy to create a bureaucratic state in a free, constitutional democracy. In order to do so, it would be necessary to form a majority which would freely vote for the creation of such a state. Nonetheless, if government itself could become a faction on behalf of the goals of the bureaucratic state, the chance of its success, even without majority consent, is greatly enhanced. It is not accidental that those who support the goals of the bureaucratic state, have come to view the majority as the greatest enemy of a government committed to their attainment. Thus, political freedom is directly opposed to the demands of the new equality.

In a free society, it is difficult to regulate campaign finance directly without regulating politics. This same difficulty is posed in attempting the national regulation of political parties. It is not accidental that both occurred at the same time. As Adamany had reminded us, "American political parties are unknown to the text of the Constitution and were not mentioned by federal statutes until the enactment of political finance reforms in the early 1970's." Consequently Eugene McCarthy was not far wrong when he suggested that campaign finance regulation is inseparable from the establishment of state

---

11. *Theory of Justice* (Cambridge: Harvard University Press, 1971), pp. 225-226. See also, J. Skelly Wright, "Money and the Pollution of Politics: Is the First Amendment an Obstacle to Political Equality?" *Columbia Law Review* v.82 (May 1982), pp. 609-645.

parties. Thus, he insisted that such legislation constitutes "the broadest attack on the constitutionally protected rights of freedom of speech and assembly in ... [history]. If the men who drafted the Constitution ... had anticipated a time when one or two political parties would have been given preferred positions ... they ... would have included one or more provisions in the Bill of Rights, a provision allowing the free practice of politics and making unconstitutional any established political party or parties."

In the decade between 1964 and 1974, Congress attempted the detailed regulation of the economic, social, and political life of the nation. It was almost inevitable that it would seize the opportunity to extend government regulation to an area the founders deemed especially vulnerable, the electoral process itself. Nonetheless, many were uneasy in doing so, for they perceived this to be regulation of the political or partisan process, which opened up the possibility of government itself becoming a faction. Senator Howard Baker was one of those who was apprehensive about such regulation. He remarked, "I believe there is something almost politically incestuous about the idea of government financing, and thus inevitably regulating the procedures by which government is selected." Partisan politics is, he noted, "the most fragile and most sensitive and important part of a representative democracy.... It's terribly important to me that the government does not have control of the machinery by which the public expresses the range of its desires and demands and dissents." It was on similar grounds that the Supreme Court overturned certain aspects of FECA. In *Buckley v. Valeo*, the court majority opinion noted: "The First Amendment denies government the power to determine that spending to promote one's political views is wasteful, excessive or unwise. In the free society ordained by our Constitution, it is not the government but the people—individually as citizens and candidates and collectively as association and political committees—who must retain control over the quantity and range of debate on public issues in a political campaign."

One thing has become clear in light of a decade's experience with campaign finance reform. Campaign finance legislation has not produced the results intended by the reformers. Those reforms have not eliminated the influence of private wealth, nor have they prevented corruption or insured the allegedly simple fairness of "one-person, one-vote." As in politics generally, campaign finance legislation could not achieve a level of perfection which is incompatible with human nature. It was not possible to attain the public goals advocated by the reformers without undermining the liberty of individuals. However, there is little doubt that the reforms have had a profound impact on electoral politics, often in ways not anticipated. Perhaps this problem cannot be solved in a simple or satisfactory manner, because of the fact that the problems inherent in campaign finance present obstacles similar to the dilemma posed by democratic politics itself. The heart of the dilemma lies in the difficulty of reconciling the two central principles of democratic life: equality and liberty.

The Teflon Media

Steven Hayward

It is not astonishing that there are many journalists who have become human failures and worthless men.

—Max Weber

On June 10, 1984, the *New York Times* carried a front-page story about perhaps the most significant symbolic occurrence of the year. "More Than Olympic Flame Crosses America" was the headline of reporter Andrew H. Malcom's story, filed from Loose Creek, Missouri. Malcom had been following the Olympic torch relay across the United States since it began in New York City on May 8. The lead paragraph of the story described the scene as runners exchanged the torch at various intervals before ever present crowds.

"But something unusual and unplanned is also happening as the Olympic torch makes its way slowly across the nation these days," Malcom's story continued. "For, unseen by most of the country, as the flame moves through places like Useful, Linn and Knob Noster, Union, Sedalia and Festus, it seems to be igniting some special feelings less tied to the Olympics and more to patriotism. They show themselves in many ways, often producing tears for spectators and participants alike."

Although the astonished *New York Times* reporter never made the connection, it is plain that many people associated the torch with the Statue of Liberty, which at the time was shrouded in scaffolding, its torch removed during the restoration process. The Olympic torch would do nicely as a substitute and a catalyst, and it had the advantage of being mobile; after all, much of the population of the U.S. has never seen the Statue of Liberty. Flag-waving crowds everywhere, even in the dead of night, would spontaneously begin singing "God Bless America" and even "The Battle Hymn of the Republic." "I never expected it," one relay official told Malcom, "But there's all these feelings pent up. And a special chemistry. And when people see that torch, they relate it to patriotism. There's a hunger for that in the land. And for a hero."

Eventually all the major newspapers, news weeklies, and TV networks took notice of this stunning outpouring of sentiment over the torch. But most of the major media missed the significance of this sentiment. It is difficult to imagine, for instance, a similar outpouring of patriotic sentiment occurring ten years ago, when, in the wake of Watergate and a sagging economy, the national morale was running at ebb tide. Throughout the rest of the decade, as nearly everything seemed to go wrong, a wave of pessimism swept over the American people.

211

In the early 1980s this situation dramatically reversed. Opinion surveys now show large majorities of Americans are optimistic about the future. It is perhaps true that Americans take their future bearings from present circumstances, and so with a booming economy and several other "positive" events of the early 1980s, this reversal is not surprising. But this is to miss the point. Americans are by character patriotic, optimistic, and confident about the future, as foreign observers from Alexis de Tocqueville through James Bryce to Luigi Barzini have noted. And Americans tend to express this essential character in dramatic fashion, as the torch relay shows. Americans also project their better nature onto their leaders; "hero worship" if you prefer. Consider this panegyric of a popular president by a noted historian: "Before the nation, before the world, before coming ages, he stands forth the representative, for his generation, of the American mind. And the secret of his greatness is this: by intuitive conception, he shared and possessed all the creative ideas of his country and his time; he expressed them with dauntless intrepidity; he enforced them with an immovable will; he executed them with an electric power that attracted and swayed the American people."

George Bancroft wrote these words of Andrew Jackson in the 1850s, but these words might be applied with some felicity to Ronald Reagan, America's "warrior king" in the words of *Time*'s William Henry. Reagan is an enormously popular personal figure to an America given by character to hero worship; his heroic aura was confirmed and enhanced by surviving the assassin's bullet with aplomb.

What is not clear to the news media is whether Reagan's popularity is due merely to "imagery" or because he represents, and because he has helped to shape, the decisive political sentiments of the electorate. There is of course no denying that the President has a great "image." But is it empty image? The media in general accepts uncritically Rep. Pat Schroeder's (D-Colo.) designation of Reagan as the "teflon" president, asserting that "nothing sticks" to him, meaning, of course, that none of the Democrats' partisan criticisms stick to him. It is incomprehensible to most of the media that Reagan could be popular explicitly for his political views, and so it is not surprising that the media, which came late to the magnitude of the response to the Olympic torch (and never did grasp its meaning), would latch on to the "teflon factor" as their primary analytical lens for interpreting the election.

Much has been made in recent years of the gulf between the attitudes and opinions of the news media and the attitudes and opinions of the general population. The widely noticed 1981 survey by Stanley Rothman and Robert Lichter under the auspices of the Research Institute on International Change at Columbia University documented an overwhelmingly liberal orientation among "the media elite." Rothman and Lichter surveyed 240 journalists, editors, and broadcasters with the most influential media outlets (*New York Times, Washington Post*, news magazines, and the television networks), and discovered that this group votes Democratic by a margin of more than four-to-one and believes that government should redistribute wealth by a margin of four-to-one. Half agree with the proposition that "the very structure of our society causes people to feel alienated," and 50 percent say their fellow journalists are mostly on the left, while only eight percent say their colleagues are on the right.

The Rothman-Lichter findings have come in for some very heavy weather, especially from the media themselves, but have generally been confirmed by a more recent and more detailed survey conducted by the *Los Angeles Times*. "American newspaper reporters and editors are substantially more liberal than the general public on a wide range of issues," read the lead to the story. "But," the story hastily added, "readers seem largely convinced that the press does not permit this liberalism to unfairly influence [sic] its news coverage...." The *Los Angeles Times* poll was more extensive than Rothman-Lichter or any previous survey, with nearly 3000 journalists and editors being questioned, along with an equal number of the general public in each of the various media markets surveyed.

Despite the fact that this survey was being conducted by "one of their own" so to speak, the sensitivity about charges of liberal bias by journalists was indicated by the numbers of journalists who refused to participate in the *Los Angeles Times* survey. Complete figures were not reported in the story, but in a sidebar the writer (David Shaw) noted that "no definitive judgments can be made about the staffs of the *New York Times* and *Washington Post* because only 215 of 451 people contacted at the *New York Times* and only 60 of 286 people contacted at the *Post* agreed to participate in the poll." That this circumstance is downplayed is especially surprising since the *Los Angeles Times* wanted to focus especially on four papers, the *New York Times*, the *Washington Post*, the *Chicago Tribune*, and the *Los Angeles Times*.

The *Los Angeles Times* poll showed that reporters and editors are consistently to the left of the general public on a wide range of issues, by as much as a two-to-one margin. 74 percent of the general public favors prayer in public schools; only 25 percent of journalists do. 75 percent of the public favors the death penalty for murderers; 47 percent of journalists do. Only 24 percent of the public describe themselves as "liberal," as opposed to 55 percent of journalists.

Not surprisingly, then, 57 percent of the public expressed approval of President Reagan, while only 30 percent of journalists approve of Reagan. (60 percent of journalists disapprove of Reagan, while only 27 percent of the public expressed disapproval.) What *is* surprising is that the *Los Angeles Times* concluded that this demonstrable bias does not affect the objectivity of news reporting in so far as the perceptions of readers are concerned. This last point must be emphasized because the *Los Angeles Times* does not assert that reporters' bias does not affect their reporting, only that this potential bias is not apparent to readers.

In an astonishing exoneration of liberal media culpability, *Los Angeles Times* political analyst William Schneider said: "This poll does not prove or disprove that charge that the media is [sic] politically biased, but it does show that if there is any bias, it hasn't crept into the news coverage to the extent that the public feels aggrieved by it." Schneider bases this backhanded confidence on two general questions asked of the public, with 84 percent responding that the papers they read are "fair and impartial to all sides," but with only 54 percent responding similarly when the question asked whether the reader considered their paper "slanted" or "impartial."

That the *Los Angeles Times* should assign so much confidence to such obviously soft numbers is even more surprising in light of the survey by the American Society of Newspaper Editors which in April of 1985 reported significant distrust and hostility toward the news media by the general public. The ASNE survey, as reported in the *Los Angeles Times* in a page 14 story, found that "three out of four adults doubt their publication's credibility and that, if they do not act to improve their reputation, their privileges and the size of their readership are in danger."

On the question of bias, the ASNE survey reported: "Two-thirds of the people think there is as much opinion on the front page of the paper as in any other part, and more than half believe that the reporter's bias is evident in stories, even though they believe the reporter is trying to be objective." It is hardly likely that the public's hostility toward the media—confirmed by several other polls in addition to the ASNE survey[1]—is *not* because of real or perceived bias on the part of the media.

But to dwell merely in the realm of opinion surveys is to miss the issue: does the predominant liberal bias affect the way journalists and editors view the news they report? Certainly this is the case, even if and when journalists are not aware of it. "[R])eporters operate more from intuition and extrapolation than from sweeping factual knowledge," says *Time*'s William Henry. It takes an extraordinary flight from common sense to suppose that a reporter's political inclination and (perhaps faulty) intuition does not, at least at the margins, affect his conception of the essence of a story, no matter how "fair to both sides" he may intend to be. A reporter who believes that the two superpowers are "mirror images" of one another will report Soviet arms deployments differently than a reporter who does not so believe. And a few in the media have owned up to this. *The New Republic*'s Fred Barnes, formerly national political reporter for the *Baltimore Sun*, observes:

> In trying to scotch the idea of liberal bias in news coverage, defenders of the press rely on precisely the sort of argument they would reject if made by others. The argument, cited recently by both Al Hunt of the *Wall Street Journal* and columnist Joseph Kraft, goes like this: even if most journalists and reporters are liberal, their professionalism prevents this from influencing their stories. Now what if a judicial nominee said he was a racist but that this wouldn't affect his views on civil rights?

---

1. In a 1981 ABC Viewpoint survey, 35 percent of respondents found "television news reporters as pro-Communist in their views."

Or what if the chief of the Environmental Protection Agency declared that ownership of Union Carbide stock wouldn't influence his view of that firm's toxic waste practices? Or what if a White House official said his vacation at a company's resort wasn't a factor in pressing for tax relief aiding that company? Who'd buy such an argument? Not the press.

It is not so much that there is a double standard as much as a recognition that the journalist's craft is necessarily one of interpretation and explanation—especially in a discrete historical narrative like a presidential election. Thus it should not surprise us that, given the gulf between the media's attitudes and the general public's attitudes, the media would misunderstand the main currents and the significance of the 1984 elections. Much of the media interpreted the election in almost the exact terms of Walter Mondale: as a triumph of narrow self-interest over the public good, and as Reagan's mastery of media "imagery"—the "teflon factor."

Consider an October 26, 1984 page one story by *Los Angeles Times* reporter Robert Scheer. Scheer, former editor of the radical *Ramparts* magazine, and a professed Reagan-hater, attempted in his story "Reagan Gift: He Appeals to Opposites" to portray the President as a contradictory person, whose moral principles were not to be taken seriously, and whose appeal to voters was at root symbolic and shallow. Scheer notes that Reagan simultaneously espouses libertarian economic ideas along with traditional moral values, and suggests that there is an irresolvable tension between these two facets of Reagan's message, of which tension voters are unaware. For instance: "Nor has the specter raised by liberal critics of a Supreme Court stacked in the second term with Reagan appointees who agree with him on social issues registered much with younger voters. That is an issue for the future, and younger voters tend to be much preoccupied with the present." In this marvelous passage, as in most of the article, Scheer manages to attack both Reagan and the electorate, suggesting that if voters really thought about Reagan's ostensibly reactionary social ideas, they would automatically reject him. Scheer's judgment that "young voters are much preoccupied with the present" is typical of a liberal reporter who stretches *a priori* opinions (based on sketchy poll data) into firm generalities.

Scheer is of course right in the ordinary sense that Reagan blends libertarianism and traditionalism, the philosophical tension between these two being the subject of countless back issues of *Modern Age*. It is less certain that "libertarianism" and "traditionalism" are as opposed in practice as they are in pop theory, let alone in a more complete moral theory that takes proper account of the dialectic between ends and means. Regardless, Scheer assumes the contradictoriness of Reagan's ideas, and it was a simple matter for him to give his story the veneer of journalistic objectivity by quoting Stuart Spencer, Richard Wirthlin, and other political opportunists close to the President who cannot separate principle from expediency because, for the most part, they do not share the President's principles. "Five key Reagan staff members readily admitted, on a not-for-attribution basis, that Reagan's electoral success depends on his failure to implement most of his proclaimed social agenda." Joe Sobran has aptly named this sort of practice "ventriloquist journalism," the practice of getting a (usually unnamed) source to say what you're thinking so you can pass off opinion as "news analysis." Certainly it is true that Reagan, like most other successful politicians, appeals to diverse groups of people—that is how coalition politics works—but Scheer and much of the media miss the fact that all segments of the Reagan coalition, whether young professionals angered by high taxes, or moral majoritarians angered by permissiveness, are united in their overwhelming rejection of the liberal orthodoxy that has ruled America for the past generation. This rejection the media still cannot accept. Instead, the media presume, the voters must be idiots.

Thus, in explaining the election result on election night, the television networks adopted wholesale Mondale's presumptuous incredulity about the selfishness of the electorate. Dan Rather, Bill Moyers, Tom Brokaw, and the rest of the elite coterie saw the Reagan landslide primarily in terms of self-interest versus the public good, rich versus poor, and white versus black. Few commentators were willing even to concede the possibility that voters, through rational deliberation, had opted for Reagan because they thought he was right on the merits of the issues.

Such presumptiveness, bordering on *hubris* in the face of overwhelming repudiation by the electorate, must necessarily display itself in desperate and disingenuous ways. The "analysis" of the youth vote is a startling example. Young voters, aged 18 to 25, voted nearly two-to-one for Reagan. This not only represents a mass defection from what Democrats consider a natural constituency; it may also be a portent of lasting realignment.

The "new conservatism" of young voters is a source of acute anguish for liberals, especially since liberals oozed sophomorically about the "idealistic" youth of the sixties as being "the hope of the future." The once-championed "hope of the future" are now Republican-leaning "yuppies," and the liberals charge betrayal. Rather than allow that young voters are unpersuaded by liberalism, Ellen Goodman charges that their conservatism springs from "youthful selfishness." (They weren't at all selfish in the sixties?) Alvin Schorr wrote in the *Los Angeles Times* that young conservatives are "cowards," lacking the "venturesomeness and excitement" of their predecessors. And Arthur Schlesinger—what collection of liberal opinion would be complete without Arthur Schlesinger—attributes the new conservatism to a "cyclical retreat" from idealism to "privatism." Seldom is it conceded that the new conservatism could be the result of rational reflection.

The other tactic employed to deny the liberal's electoral rout is to attack Reagan's conservatism as surreal or as an aberration. Thus historian Henry Steele Commager wrote on the eve of the Republican convention in Dallas that "Reaganism is not true Republicanism." Commager portrayed "true Republicanism" as an opposition caricature of Democratic liberalism, which of course is what the Republican party was for so many years during its "me too" phase when the New Deal coalition was ascendant. But neither Commager nor the media (who take their intellectual bearings, such as they are, from established oracles such as Commager and Schlesinger) entertain the idea that the newly confident and unapologetic conservatism of the Republicans arises from the attenuation of New Deal liberalism. Instead we see the *Los Angeles Times* worried about "ideological reactionism" controlling the Republican Party. The *New York Times* was similarly concerned that the Republicans "risk driving away" many voters "who are offended by, for instance, the seeming callousness toward women." The *New York Times* also made the obligatory reference to ostentatious displays of Republican wealth at the Dallas convention. (There was no similar comment about the $400,000 Fisherman's Wharf party held by California Democrats at San Francisco, just as there is seldom an editorial or news analysis worrying about whether the Democrats might "offend" some voters with their stands on the issues, such as gay rights.)

Another *New York Times* editorial sought to drive a wedge between Reagan and the "extremists" running the party. The *Times* cleverly adopted the criticisms of Richard Viguerie, Howard Phillips, and other conservatives who have attacked Reagan's drift toward the center on practical policy questions and in personnel appointments. While the criticism is accurate and just, it obscures the fact that Reagan did not depart at all from the Party's conservative platform in his public rhetoric. Indeed, his hard-line acceptance speech was attacked by the media for its "stridency." The media did not persist with the "Reagan the moderate" theme and quickly returned to the "Reagan the image" theme, which seems a more effective way to controvert the potential appeal of conservatism to voters. *New York Times* associate editor Tom Wicker, for instance, wrote shortly after the GOP convention that the Republicans in Dallas were so far out of the mainstream that the Democrats would "expand their majority this fall in the House of Representatives" because "without Ronald Reagan, the Republican Party would be a weak minority."

How does the media think the Republicans should behave if they "realistically" want to become the majority party? In an editorial on the eve of the Republican convention (titled "A Course for the GOP"), the *Los Angeles Times* praised the "rump session" platform hearings held by liberal GOP senators Lowell Weicker (Conn), Robert Stafford (Vt), Charles Mathias (Md), Mark Hatfield (Or), Mark Andrews (ND), and John Chaffee (RI), "six of the most constructive [read: liberal] Republicans in the U.S. Senate," according to the *Los Angeles Times.* "It seems evident to us that the six senators are among the true party conservatives, not least for seeking to conserve the virtues that have made the Republican Party great. Among those virtues have been diversity, broad popular base, moderation, encouragement of the private sector balanced with a recognition of the importance of government, constructive problem-solving, openness to new ideas."

Nothing is more evident, the *Los Angeles Times* should be told, than that these six senators are no more representative of "mainstream Republicanism" today than were the filibustering "Dixiecrats" representative of the New Deal liberal Democratic Party twenty and thirty years ago. It seems to be inconceivable to the media that the vigorous conservatism of the GOP might be a formula for realignment and majority party status. Thus the media's worry over the Republican platform and solicitude for the few liberal Republicans who exist on the fringes of the party.

The media's myopia was no more convincingly demonstrated then by its coverage of the two parties' conventions. In both the general characterizations made of the parties, and the specific questions asked, the clear bias of the media can be seen. In a survey of CBS and NBC's coverage of the two conventions done for *Public Opinion* magazine, William C. Adams wrote: "Together, both CBS News and NBC News called the Republican party, its platform, or its dominant leaders by conservative labels 113 times. The called the Democrats by liberal labels 21 times and moderate labels 14 times. . . . Republicans were measured in ideological terms, with their distance to the right discussed and calibrated. Democrats were seldom evaluated by such criteria. The terms 'right wing' and 'right winger' appeared repeatedly in covering Republicans; the terms 'left wing' and 'left winger' were never used by CBS News or NBC News reporters covering Democrats." And Michael J. Robinson, also writing in *Public Opinion*, found "eight times as many references to the far right as to the far left in network coverage of the campaign, thus confirming his hypothesis that "the networks would be more likely to use pejorative adjectives to describe conservatives than to describe liberals." In addition, reporters tended to ask questions from the Democratic agenda when querying Republicans ("There wasn't much about arms control in your speech. . . . "), while reporters seldom asked Democrats questions from the Republican agenda, such as about abortion, tax cuts, strong defense, or prayer in schools.

The modern media by their nature tend to truncate the news, by giving brief, superficial, or "one-dimensional" analyses of the meaning of events. The media seldom report the long view, because their method limits them to focusing on immediate "events." A gradual buildup of the Soviet navy in the Pacific, for instance, is seldom reported as headline "news," whereas an incidental collision between a Soviet submarine and an American destroyer makes the big headlines.

The media approach to most political issues is similarly truncated. About poverty, for example, the typical network news broadcast will include an interview with a poverty-stricken person or fragment of a family, along with a dire report of the adverse consequences on these people of proposed changes in government welfare policy. Seldom if ever does a network report or a newspaper story on poverty consider the thesis of Charles Murray, Thomas Sowell, Edward Banfield, Walter Williams, George Gilder, and others that government welfare policy is in large measure responsible for the nature and exacerbation of poverty in America today.

The news media instead are given to purveying sentiment, and usually the lowest common denominator of sentiment. We read things like the *Los Ange-*

les Times editorial the day after the election lamenting Mondale's loss with the comment: "It was reassuring to hear the words *social justice* from the Mondale campaign. Social justice should always be a priority of the national agenda, not just one side of an election campaign or a trickle-down byproduct of economic elitism." The phrase "social justice" is without doubt the emptiest cliche in contemporary political discourse; the use of the phrase by ostensibly serious media organs belies the corruption of their manner of news analysis.

The shallowness of the news media suggests a major irony in the case of the 1984 election. It is the supposed shallowness of Reagan that informs the main critique of his political career by the media ("a dangerously simplistic vision of politics," says the *Los Angeles Times*), which is why his success is explained predominantly in terms of hollow "image" and the mean short-sightedness or self-interest of voters. But it is of course the media, especially the television networks, that emphasize style (or image) over substance in the coverage of elections. Even the television correspondents themselves admit that because of their method of reporting much of the day-to-day and hour-to-hour effort of campaign organizations is preoccupied with the "battle of the sound bite."

"Horserace journalism" is the phrase that has been used to describe the predominant manner in which the media cover presidential elections. Who's ahead? Who's catching up? Who stumbled? There is a great deal of truth to the "horserace journalism" description, but in 1984 there was no race. Reagan was so far ahead from the beginning that there was little drama to report. But the media assumed that this big gap between Reagan and Mondale was due to Reagan's superior imagery, so there were few stories which tried to explain comprehensively why Reagan was so far ahead of Mondale, few stories that considered the possibility that Reagan was ahead of Mondale because of the substantive political sentiments of the electorate.

Instead, the media lowered itself to the base level of its assumptions about image, and tried to inject the horserace element into what was otherwise a lackluster election. After the first Reagan-Mondale debate the media took up "the age issue" due to Reagan's poor performance. On Tuesday, October 9, two days after the debate, a *Wall Street Journal* page one story brought up the age issue: "New Question in Race/ Is Oldest U.S. President/ Now Showing His Age?" "Until Sunday night's debate, age hadn't been much of an issue in the election campaign," the story read. "That may now be changing." The story then cited a procession of gerontologists and psychologists speaking very generally about the progressive debilitations facing a man in his mid-70s, without any specific knowledge or information about Reagan himself. (Only 10 percent of people at age 75 suffer significant mental impairment.) *Wall Street Journal* co-author James Perry said the story had been in progress for some time, and that the timing was merely "propitious." Propitious or not, the story opened a floodgate of stories on "the age issue." All three TV networks took their cue from the *Journal* and ran stories on the age issue that same evening, and the following morning the *Washington Post, Philadelphia Inquirer*, and *USA Today* all ran front page "age issue" stories. On Thursday, the *New York Times* ran two stories; a front page story on the fact that it had become a big story, and a "news analysis" of the impact of the issue on the campaign—a perfect example of news creating itself and feeding on itself, for the "age issue" was having no appreciable impact on voters' inclinations. But suddenly the issue was everywhere, and would not go away. A *New York Times* story on the growing enthusiasm of young voters for Reagan was quick to note the irony that the "oldest" president was attracting youth. James Reston wrung the issue dry in three columns in the *New York Times*, in prose that was eminently more old and tired than Reagan was supposed to be. Arguing that the "complicated" challenges of our time could not be met "by old minds," Reston then cited Lincoln: "As our world is new, we must think anew."

The real story after the first debate, of course, should have been about why Reagan moderated his position and tried to capture some of Mondale's ground on domestic policy, just as the real story after the second debate was why Mondale felt compelled to try to sound like a hard-liner on foreign policy, moving substantially onto Reagan's ground. Rather, the story about the second debate, dictated by the media coverage of the first debate, was about how Reagan dispatched "the age issue" with a vintage one-liner. The point is that Reagan's undeniable mastery of imagery succeeds precisely because of the tendency of the media to emphasize style over substance in their campaign coverage.

The first debate did however show the media's power at its strongest. Polls taken immediately after the debate split almost evenly between those who felt Reagan had won and who felt Mondale had won, with Mondale getting only a slight edge. *USA Today*'s poll actually had Reagan the slight winner. But within a week, polls showed Mondale the overwhelming winner, mostly because in the days following the debate the media pounded away that Reagan had lost and had lost badly. It is true that Reagan did not perform up to expectations, but it was his performance relative to expectations framed in terms of image, not his performance on the issues, that formed the basis for judgment.

In addition to the media's preoccupation with image over substance, the media also display a strong streak of cynicism. For some reason, bad news seems more "newsworthy" than good news, and many reporters consciously try to emphasize negative themes even in positive news stories. The coverage of the economic recovery of 1983-84 is particularly illustrative. The economic expansion of 1983-84 (which continued at a modest clip all the way through 1985) was the longest sustained expansion since the end of World War II, with substantial growth in new jobs in addition to nominal transactional activity. Total employment grew by 3.9 million in 1983 alone, and inflation remained low.

But the news media, the television networks in particular, consistently denigrated this good news. Paul H. Weaver, writing in *Commentary*, describes the network coverage:

But as the economy itself began growing again, the nation's economic coverage became curiously schizophrenic, according to a study conducted by the Institute of Applied Economics, a small New York research group that videotaped and analyzed every economic news story on the three network nightly news programs from July 1 through December 1, 1983. The Institute's analysts identified two main types of economic news stories. One genre . . . was the news item, often short, that . . . reported freshly released economic statistics. Of these, nearly all (95 percent) conveyed a positive impression: things in the economy were getting better, the data reflected the improving trend, and the stories reflected the data.

A second genre of news story identified in the study was the longer, in-depth, interpretive news analysis, typically narrated by a reporter in the field. These stories took as their point of departure some event of the day; often the 'news peg' was the announcement of upward movement in an economic indicator. But having quickly noted the news peg, the stories would then turn to their real purpose—delving beneath the surface of the news to identify some larger, more meaningful economic reality or trend. According to the study, the networks ran 104 of these longer, more analytic, less event-oriented news pieces during the second half of 1983. Of these stories, 89, or about 85 percent, featured bad news, emphasizing not any reassuring resurgence of economic growth or welcome increase in employment, but the recession's lingering ill effects, of the persistence of structural economic problems that demanded attention now that the recession had passed.

Their length and documentary character made this second group of stories the dominant body of network economic-news coverage—and the impression they conveyed was strongly negative. . . . Presiding over the worrisome situation, these stories suggested, was an uncaring, politically manipulative administration that sought political advantage in the nation's recovery from a recession which the administration's policies had probably made worse.

Weaver goes on in his article to cite several examples, with extensive quotations from the correspondent's narrative which display clearly the cynical edge of contemporary journalism.

The root of the problem is that reporters and especially network correspondents confuse cynicism with sophistication. It is this supposed sophistication mixed with a condescension toward the public that leads journalists to slight the substance of the campaign and attribute overarching significance to "image" alone. Typical of such attitudes was a front page story by *Los Angeles Times* political reporter Robert Shogan which appeared a few days before the election. "Voters Facing the Risk of Unpleasant Surprises," with a subhead declaring: "Both Reagan and Mondale Avoiding Specifics of How They Will Cope With Critical Problems." Even though the article assailed both Reagan and Mondale for vagueness, it was *de facto* an attack on Reagan, since he was the incumbent.

But beyond that, this story and others like it expose the mandarin attitude of the press, the false sophistication by which the press see themselves elevated above both politicians and the public. Nothing could be more clear even to the half-attentive voter than the general opinions of Reagan and Mondale on the crucial issues of the day; both men have held remarkably consistent views for the duration of their long public careers. (How well Reagan has hewn to his views in office is a separate question.)

Furthermore, both parties produced lengthy platforms which, if not finely detailed, were nevertheless explicit about the fundamental principles guiding each party at the present time. If voters were somehow unaware of the differences between the parties and their candidates, it is only because the media chose to rattle on about "image" as the only campaign issue. (Mondale tried, without success, to make "issue themes" each week, which included detailed if dubious plans to deal with the budget deficit, military spending, education and labor policy, and so on. The media, though for different reasons than the voters, seemed not to be listening.)

Beyond these ordinary failings, this story also shows the way in which the media fundamentally misunderstands what democratic elections are all about. We are not electing the "Policy Analyst in Chief," but rather the single leader who sets the general direction of policy and who tries within the constraints of constitutionally separated powers to direct the vast machinery of government to implement the specifics of policy. One could imagine seeing a headline similar to Shogan's at another time: "Voters Facing the Risk of Unpleasant Surprises: Both Roosevelt and Hoover Avoiding Specifics of How They Will Cope With Great Depression." Or, "Roosevelt Vague About Details of 'New Deal.'" Such stories almost surely exist, for the media of the thirties disliked FDR with nearly the ferocity with which today's media dislike Reagan. But Roosevelt captured and transformed the sentiments of the electorate, and a new political era was born. Now, in the twilight of the New Deal era, at the dawn of a new one, the recalcitrant media fail once again to grasp the essence of the time, which leads to distorted and, one might even say, reactionary reporting. But this should not surprise us, for, as William Henry notes in his impressionistic narrative of the campaign (*Visions of America*), journalists are like the proverbial French army generals, failing to grasp the dynamic of the current battle, preferring to fight previous battles instead.

Ethnicity and Politics:
Citizens as "the mutual guardians of their mutual happiness" and the Politics of Realignment

Ken Masugi

Hearken not to the unnatural voice which tells you that the people of America, knit together as they are by so many cords of affection, can no longer live together as members of the same family; can no longer continue the mutual guardians of their mutual happiness....

Federalist 14

Introduction

What kind of regime, what kind of country have we made of the Founders' legacy? Do we resemble more the nexus of competing interest groups some see predicted in *Federalist* 10; or are we rather the "fellow-citizens of one great, respectable, and flourishing empire" vaunted in *Federalist* 14? What unique problems do ethnic differences create for Americans? How can the "cords of affection" or friendship, which Aristotle saw as perfecting justice, be established among people of different ethnic groups? Given a corresponding presence of religious diversity, how can American political ideals unite this nation?

The place of ethnicity in American politics can be best understood in light of those decisive changes in political orientation related to founding principles known as critical, watershed, or realigning elections. In fact the ethnic question, that is the question of nationality versus nationalities, has been a major issue in realigning elections throughout American history, and the past two presidential elections may be part of such a fundamental change.

But "ethnic politics" is, in the proper sense of the study of politics, a contradiction in terms, because politics deals with the whole political community, not simply with one of the parts. Of course one understands the whole in light of the parts. But contemporary political science fails to acknowledge that the whole, the regime, is of central and peculiar significance as a cause of behavior and an object for action. Hence, in its present condition it cannot enlighten us about the relationship between ethnic groups and American politics.

Although all critical elections reconsider the relationship between the parts, or citizens, and the political whole, or regime, in light of the founding principles, it would be a mistake to assume that the *ethnic* parts are at the heart of all critical elections. Nonetheless, in reflecting on whether the 1980 and 1984 elections represent any sort of political watershed or are simply an indication of the personal popularity of Ronald Reagan, one must come back to the place of ethnic groups in the relationship of America's parts to itself. To put the question in an Aristotelian way, is America more a collection of tribes or an association of citizens? Given the liberal denigration of citizenship, the tribal view predominates now in an America increasingly dominated by centralized bureaucracy, where governmental action is increasingly regarded as natural as private initiative.

This essay will reflect on ethnicity and the 1984 presidential election in light of the question of whether it was a realigning election. That is, did it raise fundamental questions about the kind of people we are? Were those questions in light of a new understanding of ourselves as a regime, that is, as both a government and a people? We are thus led back to deeper questions concerning the nature of the American regime. To see what the elections meant with regard to these issues, let us consider the two obvious phenomena, the debate over affirmative action and the candidacy of Jesse Jackson, in addition to other aspects of the election usually covered under the "ethnic politics" rubric.

We must proceed with the greatest caution when discussing the significance of ethnicity for politics. First of all, reliable data about our subject matter are hard to obtain. Certainly we have confidence that many more blacks voted for Mondale than for Reagan in 1984. But did they do so in the proportions the statisticians cite: about 90 percent for Mondale nationwide? How does this translate into black votes outside the South? One widely used means of determining how blacks (or any other group) vote is the exit poll, a measuring device shown to be highly unreliable. Another common device used to measure black voting is to sample all-black districts; yet such districts may have peculiar economic or social characteristics which would make them unrepresentative of black political behavior in other districts. And the difficulty increases for voters who cannot be surveyed in this manner. Telephone polling, and even random sampling may yield more accurate results than the exit poll. And of course stereotypes contribute to misunderstanding.

Moreover, how does one properly evaluate the "black vote?" It is a southern and urban vote. How does one factor in differing income levels? If the Republican Party were interested in appealing to black voters, how should it make its appeal? If blacks in a certain area live together, should a politician appeal to them on the basis of what makes them different from other Americans or what makes them similar? Jesse Helms was reelected with black votes, campaigning on the latter theory. As the black vote is diverse, then so are those of other ethnic groups: among Asians, Japanese Americans versus Chinese Americans (the latter tend to vote Republican more than Japanese), recent immigrants versus later ones, those in large cities such as San Francisco, Los Angeles, and Seattle versus those in smaller cities and rural areas.[1]

---

1. Consider, for example, the 1984 re-election campaign of Senator Jesse Helms, which has

Furthermore, the views of individual members who belong to ethnic groups can differ dramatically from those acknowledged to be leaders of those groups. Moreover, division exists within ethnic groups, as indicated by the Linda Lichter poll for *Public Opinion* revealing divergent attitudes on issues such as affirmative action between black leaders and blacks at large. With such divisions existing within an ethnic group perceived to be overwhelmingly Democratic and anti-Reagan, what generalizations can one make with confidence about the major parties? Despite their differences, the leadership and the generality were almost equally anti-Reagan. But the division indicates an opportunity for politicians with, say, anti-affirmative action views nonetheless to appeal to blacks. That is, politicians can campaign in black neighborhoods but not on the themes as interpreted by the black leadership. Politicians would argue as to other fellow Americans, not to their conception of what blacks want. Thus would nationality come to predominate over nationalities.

With these considerations in mind let us take up the two most evident instances of ethnic political issues in recent years, the bureaucratic issue of racial quotas (or "affirmative action") and the political issue of the Rainbow Coalition. Consider first the post-1984 election significance of the administration's inability to have William Bradford Reynolds's nomination for Associate Attorney General approved. One commentator, the late Joseph Kraft, declared that Reagan's "Second American Revolution" had been killed off by the rejection of Reynolds, who was an enemy of affirmative action-inspired quotas. The Senate committee vote broke the "populist backlash [which] shaped up as a prime feature of the second term." The rejection had followed contentious debate by an administration-dominated Commission on Civil Rights over the future of affirmative action. But the Reagan administration itself had its own divisions over affirmative action, with Reagan declining the opportunity to end it, by only slightly modifying previous affirmative action rules for government contractors. Such quarrels indicate the problem Reagan has had with his own party on an issue of fundamental principle.

The inability to act on a distinction between quotas and traditional ethnic politicking has contributed to this division within the Reagan administration. Republicans are doubtless more concerned with how an anti-affirmative action or even antiquota stance will affect their reputation among women and Mexican-Americans than among blacks. And Attorney General Edwin Meese himself has spoken in support of "increased affirmative action" and even minority set-aside programs for "socially and economically disadvantaged classes." He even claims to defend aggressive affirmative action wherever it does not produce discrimination against individuals. Yet the defense of goals and timetables may require the quotas which are widely condemned (even in

been cited as a recent example of racist political appeals. Yet, the crude means we have of discovering such things points out that Helms ran ahead of Reagan among black voters (13 percent of the vote—up from 2 percent—against 9); his campaign toward the end appealed to them on the grounds of conservatism (prayer in schools, for example).

the original draft of the 1984 Democratic Party platform). In any event, under William French Smith the Justice Department certainly did not attempt to dismantle affirmative action.

If we see such inconsistency among the Republicans, note the actions of the Democrats, now backing off from their official recognition of group identities, having seen its bad political consequences, and are now attempting to reestablish the party as one for the middle class, the party of the people, as Franklin D. Roosevelt made it, and not simply a prominority party with a flaccid foreign policy. How can a party, one-fourth of whose 1984 presidential vote came from blacks, appeal to a majority without offending one of its principal parts? How is a party, which has relied on the Electoral College votes of the South, to compensate for the massive defection of Southern white voters to Republican presidential candidates?

The Democrats, as shown by Walter Mondale's behavior toward Jesse Jackson, wish to absorb the energy of Jesse Jackson's Rainbow Coalition without the odium Jackson and some of his supporters bring with them. The rhetoric of family (heard in Mario Cuomo's convention speech) appears to be its future. What sort of family is this? Both parties had their problems with the "ethnic voter" in the campaign, and continue to bear the scars earned then, while attempting to build upon past successes. Whatever the results of the post-election disputes over quotas—and it is good to keep in mind that no single action, no single order issued or revoked appears decisive—the long term issue of the place of ethnicity in American politics appears to be as muddled as ever. Are ethnic differences to be reinforced and made part of the laws (as in affirmative action), or are they differences which are due their respect but are not a political focus or end in themselves but rather constitute another challenge for statesmanship to overcome in creating citizens who are open to friendship and, eventually, the establishment of families?

American political rhetoric frequently exhibits confusion among minority rights, civil rights, and a certain socio-economic status. Besides lumping together "minorities," who may or may not suffer from the same economic problems, the rhetoric often confuses civil rights with the achievement of a certain status. But President Reagan and the Republicans above all should know that the only guarantor of "full economic power" would be an all-powerful state. As a party the Republicans have not done what Reagan has *generally* done on the presidential level: spoken to the best in the American people.

In any event the discussion of quotas, with some significant exceptions, has not been carried on at a very elevated level. Consider the *New York Times*'s argument for not opposing such devices of affirmative action: "Many Americans share the Administration's weariness with busing and racial quotas, but they have no appetite for Mr. Reynolds's campaign to retry, in city after city, long-settled affirmative action plans." The persistence of quotas, now disguised as commitment to affirmative action "goals and timetables" is a tribute to the continued power that pressure groups have on politics. As Jeremy Rabkin wrote in *The New Republic*, "There is, after all, no great threat to the dominant groups in this country if public policy encourages demeaning stereotypical thinking about blacks or Hispanics or women." Hence in making ethnic appeals, politicians often appeal to the elite (even when they know this elite may be misinformed) rather than to the people themselves. Evidently the politicians believe that this is a more efficient way of using resources (or paying off debts) than going directly to the people. But such "efficiency" not only affects the sort of message they give and may actually undermine their educational purpose in campaigning.

Just as in other areas of domestic and foreign policy, the Reagan administration's temporizing may not only leave intact but actually affirm the tendencies of long held Democratic Party policy. In making this analysis, I do not wish to preclude statesmanlike actions or bureaucratic intrigues which may change this tendency. But the tendency itself is now more firmly established than ever.

Concerning ethnic appeals in politics, Republicans are still the moon party to the Democratic sun; the Democrats show the way. (Remember the Republicans' embarrassing choice for keynote speaker at their 1984 convention.) True, people of the same ethnic group help each other; this is the way it is done. But citizenship calls for other efforts, in which tribal origins are overcome: American citizenship means identifying oneself with a set of principles, such that men can become mature citizens, "mutual guardians of their mutual happiness." Insofar as the people still rule in this country, the bureaucratic battle over quotas can be won only by winning the political battle over ethnicity, which in turn has been fueled and guided by groups surrounding the bureaucracy (academics, as a leading example).

In this way the politics of the Rainbow Coalition reflects the problem of contemporary liberalism, its reliance on nondemocratic institutions of American politics such as the courts and the bureaucracy. The place of these latter institutions in American politics has been at issue for the last two decades (recall Richard Nixon's 1968 law and order campaign, with its criticisms of judges; Nixon's planned second-term attack on the bureaucracy; Carter's attacks on the bureaucracy; and Reagan's on specific Supreme Court decisions as well as on "big government"). Now race was certainly present in these struggles, directly in the form of issues such as school desegregation ("busing") and peripherally in issues such as street crime. But the Jesse Jackson campaign gave race a prominence unknown since the struggles of the early 1960s. The claim for justice which Jackson's Rainbow Coalition makes is rooted in older conflicts but demands a dignity higher than those of ordinary interest groups which have already received their "representation" in the bureaucracy (e.g., labor, teachers, urban groups). But do the Jackson and other "discrete and insular minorities" justly occupy a superior place to others who assert claim to the spoils of power—say, oil companies, shoe manufacturers, or social security recipients. What can justify such inequality, such, one is tempted to say, aristocracy? Clearly such a usurpation relies on a reading of American history which makes race rather than individual rights the central element in the struggle for the recognition of equality. But how are the claims of the various groups and the rights of individuals related? We must reflect, however briefly, on the founding principles as articulated by *The Federalist*, Abraham Lincoln, and some other enlightened commentators.

General Principles

Any discussion of republican government must return to *The Federalist*. *Federalist* 10 is the focus of many an analysis of American politics. The theme of republicanism should also remind us of number 14, the only other paper written solely by James Madison prior to number 37. Fourteen is important, for it speaks of themes ignored in 10: nobility (one of only two uses of "noble" by Madison in the entire *Federalist*) and empire, "manly spirit," "cords of affection," "the mingled blood which they have shed in defense of their sacred rights," "the glory of the people of America," and "public happiness"—in other words, the language of classical politics, the attempt to give "to every citizen the same opinions, the same passions, and the same interests." Madison wishes to see a nation of patriots—not a bourgeois cosmopolitanism. The "private rights" stressed so much in 10 are now paired with "public happiness" in 14. The fourteenth paper stresses the need for that uniformity of opinions, passions, and interests that the tenth paper had declared "impracticable." America has a form or soul or regime; it is not simply a bundle of colliding interests and passions, which will produce a kind of equilibrium. The American regime requires citizens who will be "the mutual guardians of their mutual happiness," not those who rely on bureaucracy and the courts.

When taking the perspective of the regime, we see that American politics, in opposing aristocracy, aims at substituting rule of law for the most common regime, tyranny. The rule of law may not be the rule of philosophers, but it does incorporate aspects of wisdom; it is a good guess at what prudent men would ordain. The rule of law means ruling and being ruled in turn: exercising both rights and duties. Those who govern themselves must in turn possess souls which rule themselves. The American democratic republic was founded to establish the rule of law and hence to create the sort of souls that can sustain it.

Tyrannical rule (of either an individual or a class) uses the ruled solely for the tyrant's purposes. Tyranny is willfulness given political expression. It quite often appears in the guise of racial or ethnic dominance; these are obvious differences on which to base action. Hence in matters related to race or ethnicity—the great example being slavery—observers see only the surface and forget the underlying problem: tyranny. Hence the slavery issue is often confounded with a racial one. Thus scholars have taught citizens to overlook the fundamental political question involved in the Civil War: Lincoln's effort to make the best practicable regime's standard, the rule of law, replace tyranny. The discipline of the rule of law must replace the pleasure of tyrannizing over others of a different race. Consider Lincoln's description of equality of inalienable rights as

> a standard maxim of free society, which should be familiar to all, and revered by all; constantly looked to, constantly labored for, and even though never perfectly attained, constantly approximated, and thereby constantly spreading and deepening its influence, and augmenting the happiness and value of life to all people of all colors everywhere.

The ability to slight race and ethnicity is in large part a reflection of America's success, even in the time of slavery. But even in the above Lincoln address the senatorial candidate made a pitch for ethnic votes:

> Why, according to [Douglas's interpretation of the Declaration], not only negroes but white people outside of Great Britain and America are not spoken of in that instrument. The English, Irish and Scotch, along with white Americans, were included to be sure, but the French, Germans and other white people of the world are all gone to pot along with the Judge's inferior races.

Earlier in his career, Lincoln had made Irish jokes, as in the Temperance Address. But Lincoln's ethnic appeals were designed to include the groups addressed as part of the Founding, despite their modest role in his attempt for electoral success. But contrast such jokes and their aim with Lincoln's 1859 reflections on the measure of civilization:

> From the first appearance of man upon the earth, down to very recent times, the words "*stranger*" and "*enemy*" were *quite* or *almost*, synonymous. Long after civilized nations had defined robbery and murder as high crimes, and had affixed severe punishments to them, when practiced among and upon their own people respectively, it was deemed no offence, but even meritorious, to rob, and murder, and enslave *strangers*, whether as nations or as individuals. Even yet, this has not totally disappeared. The man of the highest moral cultivation, in spite of all which abstract principle can do, likes him whom he *does* know, much better than him who he does *not* know. To correct the evils, great and small, which spring from want of sympathy, and from positive enmity, among *strangers*, as nations, or as individuals, is one of the highest functions of civilization.

Thus, the great themes of the Founding Fathers and of Lincoln are present, if in the background, of current ethnic politics discussions. Was the case for free government tested, and strengthened?

Two articles from an issue of *The New Republic* help us understand how such a nation of citizens can arise in recent times. Both essays point to the need to understand America as more than just a sum of its parts in terms of a regime. This first passage reflects on race relations:

> White people who argue for the segregation of the masses of black people forget the tremendous power of objective teaching. To hedge any set of people off in a

corner and sally among them now and then with a lecture or a sermon is merely to add misery to degradation. But put the black man where day by day he sees how the white man keeps his lawns, his windows; how he treats his wife and children, and you will do more real helpful teaching than a whole library of lectures and sermons. Moreover, this will help the white man. If he knows that his life is to be taken as a model, that his hours, dress, manners, are all to be patterns for someone less fortunate, he will deport himself better than he would otherwise. Practically all the real moral uplift the black people have got from the whites—and this has been great indeed—has come from this observation of the white man's conduct. . . .

Finally, . . . as white and black learn daily to adjust in a spirit of justice and fair play, those interests which are individual and racial, and to see and feel the importance to those fundamental interests which are common, so will both races grow and prosper. In the long run no individual and no race can succeed which sets itself at war against the common good; for "in the gain or loss of one race, all the rest have equal claim."

The second quotation occurs in an article just two pages later, from the same issue of *The New Republic*. It reflects on the enduring significance of American ethnic divisions for our foreign policy:

. . . [I]t has been a strange experience, unlike any that has been known in the world. This is the first period in which a conglomerate democracy has had to exist in a warring world. And the first lesson it has taught us is that it is impossible to remain a democracy and carry on diplomacy by the European model. We cannot play a part in the European world if in order to play that part we have to exhibit an undivided sovereignty. . . . Our internal tolerance is a deplorable weakness. The very fact that we have given all nationalities a chance to live at peace on territory as large as Europe, the very fact that we have solved internally the worst interracial and international conflicts, unfits us for an aggressive part in the European tangle. . . . We can be imperial only by limiting freedom within—by a policy of coercive Americanization. . . .

The United States has . . . no consistent foreign policy, and no consistent nationalism. The hyphen in American feeling depends upon the frontier which is threatened. . . . What this means is that the American people are adapted to a varied foreign policy, requiring different methods towards different Powers. They are not a homogeneous, obedient, drilled population to be wielded in any direction for any purpose. Through no intention of their own, through sheer force of circumstances, the American people are discovering the essence of practical wisdom, which is that only a fool is uniform in his conduct, but that a sensible person must be resourceful in a varied world. The raw material of an enlightened world-policy exists in the fact that our nationalism is not absolute but relative. It is at present raw material and nothing else. The fact has hardly been faced—it has never been utilized.

Now, as one may suspect from the examples the writers used, this is not a current issue of *The New Republic*; in fact the passages occur in the December 4, 1915 issue. The first quotation is from "My View of Segregation Laws," by Booker T. Washington (pp. 113-14), the second from "Hyphens and Frontiers," by Walter Lippmann (pp. 116-17). Far more blunt and discerning about these matters than anyone writing today, Washington and Lippmann approached the most significant questions concerning race and ethnicity in our politics. Washington's discussion of the races teaching each other calls to mind the classical notion of citizenship, which involves both ruling and being ruled. As in all of Washington's writings on the subject, his stress is on men's obligations to others. Lippmann notes what a miracle it is that we have any common citizenship at all. Further, the most explosive domestic ethnic issue is that of color made explicit in dealing with the descendant of slavery, segregation, but the most divisive one is that seen in the conflict of loyalties, brought to crises in times of war (before and during World War I, for ethnic Germans, and during World War II, for ethnic Japanese). What makes America *e pluribus unum*, what gives it unity in the face of foreign threats exploiting domestic ethnic differences? In other words, how is it we can speak of American citizenship, a nexus of rights and duties which apply to all, across ethnic lines?

Of the great elements of American politics—equality, liberty, and consent—we have stressed equality and that element of liberty emphasized in citizenship. But democracy cannot function without consent, and that means enlightened consent. But who can consent in an enlightened way? The history of American democracy is the history of attempts to include more and more diverse peoples in the category of those who can give enlightened consent, who can be trusted with the rights of citizenship and who undertake its duties— people, in other words, who recognize something of the fundamental meaning of human equality. Jews, Mexicans, Asians, eastern Europeans, Arabs, ... each group faces problems of "assimilation," of becoming American. The sociological or economic approach to these questions causes us to lose sight of the problem of political life. These deny or slight the peculiarly political aspect of human life. Prosperous individuals are not necessarily good citizens in Madison's sense. For becoming American means absorbing, by whatever means, rough or sophisticated, the teachings of the Declaration of Independence.[2]

Transition: The Present in Light of Past Principles

Thus we see how Americans have often overestimated the place of ethnicity in politics by ignoring what is truly fundamental: the development of citizens, free men who can be trusted with their use of freedom. Yet from George Wash-

2. For a superior example of sociological analysis see William Julius Wilson, *The Declining Significance of Race: Blacks and Changing American Institutions* (Chicago: University of Chicago, 1978 and 1980), 2nd ed. "It is also the case that class has become more important than race in determining black life-chances in the modern industrial period." p. 150. Of course the leading analyst of economic conditions and motives and their relation to race and ethnicity is Thomas Sowell. See especially *Ethnic America* (New York: Basic Books, 1981; Harper Colophon Books) and *The Economics and Politics of Race* (New York: William A. Morrow, 1983).

ington to Booker Washington we see how rights should be understood. For example, today it is often said or assumed that "civil rights" is a matter for ethnic or racial minorities. This contemporary confusion has arisen because of this "historical" error, encouraged by the bureaucracy and its allies. In opposing the past tyranny of slavery proponents of affirmative action and other recent civil rights measures advocate a new aristocracy or elite, in the form of bureaucracy and the courts. (This misunderstanding is reflected in the assumption by advocates of affirmative action that Chief Justice Roger Taney's *Dred Scott* opinion gives the correct account of the American Founders' view of slavery.) It is clearer now than at any time since 1860 that the issue of all critical elections remains the same: can self-government, a government of the rule of law, still endure? In 1980 and 1984 these concerns were manifest in national pride and defense, and the attack on bureaucratic government. It is still apparent that no one has been able to articulate clearly that self-government is the critical issue as far as the field of civil rights goes. In their haste to condemn one form of injustice, they have promoted another. The Roosevelt Revolution against "malefactors of great wealth" led to the establishment of another type of unjust regime rather than advancing toward the best regime implicit in American founding principles.

Consider, in this light, the statement attached to the U.S. Civil Rights Commission Report on *Firefighters Local Union No. 1784 v. Stotts* (104 S. Ct. 2576) by dissenting commissioners Mary Frances Berry and Blandina Cardenas Ramirez:

> Civil rights laws were not passed to give civil rights protection to *all* Americans, as the majority of this commission seems to believe. Instead they were passed out of a recognition that *some* Americans already had protection because they belong to a favored group; and others, including blacks, Hispanics, and women of all races, did not because they belonged to disfavored groups. If we are ever to achieve the real equality of opportunity that is the bright hope and promise of America, we must not deny our history and promise of America, we must not deny our history and present condition by substituting illusion for reality.

But such a notion of civil rights condemns minorities to perpetual second-class status: "minorities" become wards of the central government and ultimately its tools (consider the place of the blacks in the Democratic Party today), sycophants of centralized bureaucracy. Such "minorities" would be treated apart from the processes and procedures that other, non-minority citizens undertake to protect and advance their interests, winning some battles and losing others. Far from protecting minorities, such condescension can hinder the maturation of members of minority groups into complete citizens.

A true civil-rights policy would take its bearings by a healthy citizenship, not the smothering protection of groups by unlimited government. As it aided individuals who suffered illegal forms of racial discrimination, such a policy would measure every action by its ability to enhance the fundamental political principles of equality, liberty, and government by consent. The heart of the matter is the issue of self-government. The issue of civil rights has been distorted, virtually beyond recognition, by those who would use the slogan for their own particular purposes, which typically include an assault on the qualities the Founders and their principles required for self-government. They would advance more bureaucracy at home and more weakness abroad and thus undermine the moral qualities necessary for both self-government and self-defense, both equality of rights and consent of the governed.

In 1984 Jesse Jackson was to come forward as the great advocate of a coalition of minority groups that demanded rights as minorities, thus denying Washington's principle regarding race relations and satisfied Lippmann's fears concerning ethnic division. While attempting to argue for compassion from their alleged oppressors, they were in fact demanding the special or aristocratic privileges given recipients of affirmative action. That the issue involved in affirmative action is not race but an issue of fundamental political principle, namely that of self-government, has been noted by several observers including Jeremy Rabkin and Nicholas Capaldi, who have pointed to the tyrannical element in contemporary liberalism, as manifested in its fondness for antimajoritarian institutions.

The "unnatural voice" of Jesse Jackson: "The Great Ambulance Chaser"

When one recalls Jesse Jackson's campaign for the presidency, one immediately thinks of divisiveness—that is, Jackson's endeavor struck many as demagoguery or opportunism; Jackson appeared as the leader of a faction.[3] (To others, he appeared to promise a departure from the normal liberal politics of self-interest. To them, his Rainbow Coalition promised to improve the conditions of those previously unheeded. Despite these pleadings, we are reminded of Winston Churchill's definition of socialism as the equal distribution of misery.)

Thus the Rainbow Coalition came to sight as a threat against traditional, interest-group politics. The opinions, passions, and interest in the Rainbow Coalition revolved around race and ethnicity: how should Americans who are "the damned, the disinherited, and the disenfranchised"—mostly non—white—act politically? A common hatred of the white establishment motivated the Jacksonian coalition. Consider the remarkable logic in the following statement of its leader, reported in the *New York Times*: "Women should never again support an all-male slate. Blacks should never again support an all-white male or female slate. And part of our mission must be to destroy racism

3. The two most readily available books on Jackson tend to be critical: Barbara Reynolds, *Jesse Jackson: The Man, The Movement, The Myth* (Chicago: Nelson-Hall, 1975); and Thomas Landess and Richard Quinn, *Jesse Jackson and the Politics of Race* (Ottawa, Illinois: Jameson Books, 1985).

and sexism and unleash our brains." Early in his campaign he charged that "whites have developed over their history a lack of regard for the intelligence and hard work of black people," and that this had contributed to his failure to receive many white votes. "It is remarkable," he commented in early June, "that not one white member of the House of Representatives, not one white U.S. senator, not one governor, not one major or minor daily newspaper that is white endorsed my candidacy—not one." Jackson had a racial explanation for everything.

Moreover, the Rainbow Coalition could be directed against black politicians too; consider the heckling of Mrs. Martin Luther King and of Andrew Young at the Democratic Convention. The Rainbow Coalition is a class-oriented faction, but the racial aspect is particularly remarkable. But Jackson went beyond racial classifications to others as well, as *Los Angeles Times* writer Nancy Skelton reported:

"Something's happening," Jesse Jackson says at stop after stop now. "There *is* a 'rainbow coalition,' " he says, "reds, yellows, blacks, browns, whites, gays, lesbians, everybody is somebody, *everybody* is somebody."

Jackson has been saying that in state after state since January, often with little to show for it on Election Day. But in California it shows more signs of ringing true.

It can be heard in the exotic lilt of a Mandarin Chinese greeting: "Welcome Jesse Jackson and the rainbow coalition."

It can be seen in Sacramento when knots of white civil servants shout their approval on the state Capitol lawn.

It is evident in the sun flashing off shiny metal in the front rows at a rally: "My brothers and sisters in wheelchairs say chrome belongs in the rainbow," Jackson says. Jackson's California audiences have been large, enthusiastic and the most racially and ethnically diverse of any in the nation.

What remains to be seen, however, is just how much of the enthusiasm is just curiosity about the highly publicized first black presidential contender and how much is support that will be translated into votes June 5.

Jackson would gain about 19.6 percent of the California vote, slightly more than his 18.3 percent share of the total primary vote. Mondale's national share was 38.6 percent and Hart's was 36.2 percent. What a decline from Booker T. Washington's level of discourse! Jackson's approach to ethnicity puts us further away than ever from a proper understanding of ethnicity and politics.

Jackson's dangerous elevation of racial groupings to one of political principle transforms what is idiosyncratic and cultural into what is fundamental to the regime. Jackson's principle threatens to make the private will superior to the common good. Such "liberalism" is certainly widespread. No one supposes that a taste for Chinese food endangers political freedom, but a large proportion of shops bearing signs in the Chinese language raises questions about the quality of life and hence about political character. It is easy enough to confuse culture and politics, and certainly a relationship exists. But Jackson's emphasis on race gives such a cultural phenomenon a positively intimidating meaning. Lives appear to be threatened to be transformed politically by, say, Chinese-language signs and restaurants, seemingly a revival of the ancient city (in this case, Oriental despotism) that forbade distinctions between the private (or cultural) and the political. A Rockefeller eating a knish may gain himself political support, but he is simply using cultural traits for a political end. Jackson, however was transforming cultural traits into political ends, including the justification of the private passion culminating in tyranny and defiance of the rule of law.

Thus one must consider the radical difference between the Rainbow Coalition and traditional ethnic politics. (This difference partially explains the coolness of establishment black politicians toward Jackson.) But besides reflecting the differences among black politicians it reconsidered the place of ethnic groups in American political life at a time when scholarly opinion was divided over the persistence of ethnicity as a political factor and when "minorities" (blacks, Hispanics, and Asian refugees) were perceived as obtaining undeserved advantages such as welfare.

The political emphasis would better be placed, as ethnic appeals have typically been, on what each group can contribute to America. Even in this ordinary sort of rhetoric, used by politicians since the Founding, we see the proper relationship between ethnic appeals and politics: the diverse is refined into the one. A regime respecting both human equality and consent is established (as we saw in Lincoln's speeches).

All this emphasis on nonwhite ethnic groups has eclipsed the significance of white ethnic groups such as the Irish and the Italians. Focus on these latter groups was replaced by the greater attention paid to the various peoples labeled "Hispanic." Whereas older books on American politics (Samuel Lubell's *The Future of American Politics* [1st edition, 1951]) and even more recent ones (Richard Scammon and Ben Wattenberg's *The Real Majority* [1970]) had large sections on Germans, Irish, and Italians, recently published books on the 1984 elections (e.g., Peter Goldman and Tony Fuller, *The Quest for the Presidency 1984* [New York: Bantam Books/A Newsweek Book, 1985], and William A. Henry III, *Visions of America* [Boston: The Atlantic Monthly Press, 1985]) omit these groups, while treating Hispanics, as well as Jews and blacks. These ethnic groups were most assuredly not ignored; for example, President Reagan made a heavily publicized trip to Ireland. Of course each party has its own ethnic and political liaison organizations.

But specific appeals to this or that group may be meaningless unless it considers the development of contemporary liberalism and what that has meant for older white ethnic groups. A revealing (pre-1980 election) study of one Brooklyn neighborhood, Jonathan Rieder's *Canarsie: The Jews and Italians of Brooklyn Against Liberalism* (Cambridge: Harvard University Press, 1985), points out the problem of the appeals made by the Democratic Party and of liberalism in general. The ethnic voters of Rieder's subtitle were the main pillar of support for the New Deal, but they felt betrayed by liberalism, in the form of what appeared to be privileges for blacks (welfare, affirmative action, busing) which were simply the extension of liberal principles to them. Extension of liberalism's privileges to blacks manifested itself as a barbarism unbearable to Canarsie's Jews and Italians, who in turn reacted against liberalism. Rieder's observations confirm our own about the aristocratic dimension to current American racial and ethnic appeals: "The feeling of second-class citizenship grew among whites of all kinds . . . left-wing liberalism hardened into an orthodoxy of the privileged classes." Other, similar observations have been made for older ethnic groups such as Poles, Slavs, Italians, and Irish. The relative deemphasis on Italians is encouraged by, among other observations, the fact that despite the presence of Geraldine Ferraro on the national ticket Mondale received fewer Italian votes than Carter did.

Most indicative of the problem with the Rainbow Coalition and its need for hatred is Jackson's anti-Jewish stance and the subsequent exacerbation of black-Jewish conflict that threatened to destroy Jackson's campaign early in 1984.[4] This conflict was epitomized by two episodes, his "Hymie" comment and the Farrakhan affair. Yet, despite the mutual suspicions and hatred, both groups voted Democratic, with the Jewish vote for John Anderson in 1984 returning to the Democrats (to 32 percent, down from 39 percent, about as well as Ford did against Carter but not as well as Nixon did against McGovern). Thus the Democrats reflected the traditional grand coalition approach to securing political majorities which reflect the fundamental principle of consent of the governed. The explanation for such common behavior probably lies in a Jewish distrust of Reagan's courting of fundamentalist groups. Moreover, what major Jewish appointments had Reagan made?

But the long-standing Democratic hold on the Jewish vote had been broken by Reagan in 1980. This is another formerly solid Democratic group that now swings. And this means the Democrats will have to devote resources (policy and appeals) to attract this group. As Milton Himmelfarb put it, "Jews vote like Hispanics, only more so." (After the 1968 election he had written that "Jews had the incomes of Episcopalians but voted like Hispanics.")

It is only a mild exaggeration to make the Jewish problem the problem of all American ethnic groups.[5] How does one preserve one's cultural roots while

---

4. See William Schneider, "The Jewish Vote in 1984: Elements in a Controversy," *Public Opinion* December/January, 1985, p. 18. Schneider cites *Los Angeles Times* polling which indicates that Jerry Falwell had a far greater negative rating than did Jesse Jackson. Consider as well the *Los Angeles Times* survey of Jackson delegates (85 percent of whom are black) which found that 65 percent of them (those surveyed) view Louis Farrakhan favorably. He was viewed unfavorably by only 22 percent. Among all blacks delegates Farrakhan was regarded favorably by 47 percent and unfavorably by 38 percent. Seventy-eight percent of all Jewish delegates had an unfavorable impression of Farrakhan. Blacks and Jews accounted for 17 percent and 9 percent of the delegates, respectively. "Jackson Delegates Favor Farrakhan, Survey Finds," *Los Angeles Times*, I-1, July 16, 1984.

5. See Harry V. Jaffa, "The American Regime and the Only Greater Institution," in *Amer-*

affirming one's political identity as an American? Is Yahweh also the God of the Declaration and of those who sang "Onward, Christian Soldiers?" So has He been transformed. Moreover, the Jews' relationship to Israel raises the question of whether Jewish Americans' loyalty is one or dual. Is America one nation under one God, or a plurality of nations without a distinctive national identity, a bundle of different impressions or an abiding soul?

The Rainbow Coalition made special appeals to "Hispanics," ranging from Puerto Rican urban poor to Mexican farmers. "Hispanics" is a convenient but misleading label covering a diverse group of peoples—Mexican, Central American, South American, Puerto Rican, and Cuban. Moreover, a diversity exists just among, for example, Mexican-Americans: those in Texas and New Mexico are more likely to vote Republican than those in Los Angeles, though not much differently from those in small towns. Thus, the "Hispanic" vote must be approached in terms of federalism, and, further, the division between big-city and other environments. The increase in Mexican and other voters of Latin American ancestry makes them an important part of political strategy.[6]

This in turn raises the question of whether gains among some groups necessarily mean losses among others. Surely candidates who appeal openly to a black vote lose some white support (consider the Helms-Hunt race, or Jackson's primary race). But how does this hold with other groups—blacks versus Mexican—Americans or sometimes even poor, urban Puerto Ricans, for example. The Rainbow Coalition attempted to replace such ethnic and racial tensions with a class tension.

Ethnic voting blocs used to be Democratic party mainstays, but now the Democrats can rely only on blacks, Puerto Ricans, ideological liberals, whoever is discontented at any given time. But we should remember that this is at the presidential level: at the congressional level ethnic support of Democratic candidates remains strong. Moreover, critical elections involve not only the presidential contest but the Congress as well. And in large cities ethnic associations and other groups support Democrats (though they may lack enthusiasm, as documented by Canarsie).

The Republicans have their parallel organizations, but they lack the image of FDR, or other inspiration behind them (country club Republicans versus regular people). The problem is that many people cannot take seriously the Republican Party's 1984 convention keynote speaker, when she said,

ican Conservatism and the American Founding (Durham, North Carolina: Carolina Academic Press, 1984), pp. 251-62.

6. Incidentally, the estimates of the Hispanic vote for Republicans fluctuates considerably. Most sources cite 33 percent, the same percentage as voted for Reagan in 1980. But other sources (such as ABC News, based on exit polls) estimate 44 percent. For reflections on the various Mexican-American communities, see Peter Skerry, "The Ambiguity of Mexican American Politics" in Nathan Glazer, ed., *Clamor at the Gates: The New American Immigration* San Francisco: Institute for Contemporary Studies Press, 1985, pp. 241-257. See also Kevin B. Phillips, *The Emerging Republican Majority* (Garden City, N.Y.: Doubleday, Anchor Books, 1970), pp. 394-96.

"Nuestra casa es su casa." As Douglas Jeffrey noted in his report on the 1984 Republican convention for *The Claremont Review of Books*, with all its ethnic caucuses, "Some Republicans are playing a game they can't win, but, more importantly, one that they shouldn't be playing."

The Rainbow Coalition's Pretensions

Having surveyed the different ethnic groups, and their place in a potential realignment, we see that the Rainbow Coalition raises a deep question. What does it mean to be an American? What quality of soul does it imply? It judges people on the basis of race. The Rainbow Coalition tied one's ethnic origins to one's Americanness and put interest, as defined by the body, at the forefront of contemporary American politics. Jackson presented a pointed reply to traditional interest-group liberalism, forcing his Democratic opponents to pause in their denunciations of him, and then it was too late; he had become legitimate.

A fine example of Jackson's approach, of its violations in particular of Washington's and Lippmann's admonitions, is a completely unremarked speech of his before one of the convention's ethnic caucuses, the Asian-Pacific caucus, comprising 103 delegates and alternates. The caucus itself is something to marvel at. Common geographic origin (surely not common cultural heritage) is the formal basis for its existence, but caucus chair Thomas Hsieh was more blunt: "When we put all the bucks together across the nation... these are going to be big bucks and when anyone walks up to us for support ...I guarantee you they are going to have to tell us what they are going to do for us.... And they'd better take care of us." Color this part of the rainbow green.

How would Jackson employ the rhetoric of getting even before an audience whose average income is well above the overall national average? (Japanese-American families, for example, make over 130 percent of the average national income of all other families.) After the typical Jackson litany of reaching out to the locked out, he attempted the following means of division, campaigning as though he were in some sort of third-world country. Advocating a "no first-use policy" on nuclear weapons, Jackson said "for Asians it means no second use of nuclear weapons." Moreover, when we think "about Hiroshima and Nagasaki we should say never again, never again." (Did he consider that some of the Chinese and Filipino delegates may have taken special delight in the bomb?) Observing that "Asian people" are being used "as scapegoats for a collapsed economy," Jackson launched into the following comparison:

> It's not your fault that while the Americans were making missiles you were making cars; it's not your fault.
> While we were trying to get moon rocks and dust on the moon, you got your watches and tvs. It's not your fault. It's your values.

While our managers learned how to fire people, Japanese managers learned how to expand and make room for people. It's not your fault because you had a great idea about how to manage your work force.

Concluding with his standard comments about retiring "the repressive Reagan regime," Jackson left to cheers and applause.

Although warmly received, the Jackson speech was criticized afterwards by some Japanese-American delegates (including Congressman Norman Mineta) as an example of ignorance of their status as Americans. Prominent, of course, in these delegates' minds was the opprobrium, and much worse, many of them and their relatives knew in the days following Pearl Harbor. It was a stunning example of demagoguery and ignorance—bringing people in by reading them out—but an all-too-natural consequence of a mindset that has shunned equality of individual rights and the pursuit of excellence in favor of group rights and class claims.

This speech epitomized the erroneousness of Jackson's approach. Each regime defines itself, to a great extent, by what it holds to be human happiness and hence human perfection. Certainly individual Americans have somewhat different notions of what human happiness is according to the national origins of their ancestors. Now Jackson's rhetoric directs Americans to what divides them—the beliefs and practices of their ancestors, what they were before they were Americans. Hence Jackson's trips abroad were particularly alarming precedents for a presidential candidate. Jackson's trips and rhetoric concerning his rainbow coalition made evident the very problems Lippmann saw concerning American foreign policy toward Europe. Is this still one nation?

To see how Jackson raised fundamental regime questions, which politicians in both camps had long accepted, we should review the principal events of his campaign, including the Goodman release, the Farrakhan embrace, and the trips to Cuba and Nicaragua. We will see how Jackson's campaign raised to the extreme the question of whether America should be viewed as a collection of interest groups or as a body of citizens. To what extent should citizens support the politics of their ancestors? That is, how should ethnic groups influence American foreign policy? Jackson's trips abroad were not the obligatory candidate's trip to Europe to assert his competence in foreign affairs; Jackson himself had made such a trip in September, 1983, which was full of amateurish blunders. Rather, Jackson's campaign trips abroad went to foreign tyrannies—Syria, Nicaragua, and Cuba, when he attacked the U.S. and praised his host tyrants. He also visited Mexico, El Salvador, and Panama, in the last country meeting with a Salvadorean guerilla leader. He spoke of going to the Soviet Union, in an effort to free Andrei Sakharov, and of attempting to persuade the Soviets and the Cubans not to boycott the Olympics. Finally, and perhaps most significantly, the Jackson campaign gained considerable publicity by the tyrants' favorable actions—the Goodman release of late December 1983, and the release of 22 Americans (and 27 Cubans) by Castro in early July,

1984. Of course these activities recalled his controversial 1979 trip to the Middle East, in which he embraced Yassir Arafat. Jackson might even maintain that he has not really left his home at all, for he has said that he has "had a Third World experience right here in America."

We must keep in mind that before the Goodman trip Jesse Jackson's campaign for the presidency was foundering, and attracting little favorable coverage or support. For example, Mayor Coleman Young of Detroit said of Jackson: "Jesse, first of all, has no experience. And he has no platform. And he has no chance. . . . As a politician he's out of his league." Jackson had, after all, challenged other older, longer established black politicians, who looked disapprovingly on his self-proclaimed status as Martin Luther King's successor.

But in the midst of the Jackson campaign floundering came the Goodman coup, and suddenly Jackson—not without the blessing of the Reagan White House (perhaps itself an adroit partisan move on its part)—became a respectable figure. No longer did we have the Jackson of the dubious past criticized by fellow blacks. How odd that a foreign dictator and the White House could, in effect, have conspired to promote an irresponsible Democrat, who could only damage Democrats' chances in 1984. Both Democrats and Republicans remembered the 1973 advice of Levy and Kramer:

> A medallion of Machiavelli—the authors' highest political award—will undoubtedly go to that Republican who makes the first substantial cash contribution to an independent black Presidential candidate. For there is no better way to insure Republican victory in 1972 than to place a highly visible independent black candidate on the ballot.[7]

Of the Goodman "rescue," Senator Edward Kennedy said: "this personal initiative by Reverend Jackson will rank as one of the finest achievements by a private citizen in the history of international relations." While most observers seemed to think Mondale would be hurt most by Jackson's success, Mondale's pollster, Peter Hart, maintained that Reagan was hurt most, for Jackson had gotten results, while the President was forced to look on. Thus the Mondale camp reinforced the legitimacy of Jackson's move.

Some investigation was made of the circumstances of Jackson's visit—he was a guest of the Syrian government—but the links between the murderous regime of Assad and Jackson will probably never be completely spelled out. It is extraordinary that so much could be made of Geraldine Ferraro's finances but relatively so little of what may well have been an attempt of a hostile foreign power to manipulate the American election. This is not a wild charge, when one considers that Jackson's PUSH reportedly received $550,000 in donations from the Arab League. This is not to mention that a then relatively

---

7. Mark Levy and Michael S. Kramer, *The Ethnic Factor: How America's Minorities Decide Elections* (New York: Simon and Schuster, A Touchstone Book, 1973), pp. 191-92.

obscure black Muslim preacher, Louis Farrakhan, who accompanied Jackson to Syria, has been heavily financed by Libya.

Consider what might have been the fate of the Jackson candidacy without the Goodman boost. Even this achievement was not enough to give Jackson a majority of black support. Consider the findings of a *New York Times*-CBS poll in late June: black Democrats preferred Mondale to Jackson as their party's nominee, 5 to 3. Twenty-nine percent of all blacks surveyed said they supported Jackson; 49 percent supported Mondale. The majority of blacks did have favorable opinion of Jackson, however. Yet it should be noted that while 57 percent of all blacks surveyed had a favorable opinion of Jackson as against 18 percent of all whites who did, 69 percent of all blacks had a favorable opinion of Walter Mondale. Thus, Jackson's Democratic opponents had to indulge him and treat him as though he were a serious candidate. Moreover, the charges of anti-Semitism, which would justly flourish only six weeks after Jackson's appearance at the White House with Goodman and the President, would surely have reduced the possibility of Jackson's remaining in the race. (The "Hymie" and "Hymietown" remarks were made on January 25, but reported three weeks later.) Yet Jackson was able to withstand the criticism, or lack of it, and to persist in his campaign through the convention.

Jackson's trip also threw additional attention on the black congressional caucus, whose foreign policy votes are at the extreme left of the political spectrum of the Democratic Party. For example, the black caucus vote unanimously to condemn the American invasion of Grenada. The caucus has, however, with the conspicuous exceptions of Ronald Dellums (Berkeley, California) and John Conyers (Detroit) voted to support Israel in the same degree as other liberal Democrats. The current debate over U.S. policies in South Africa again raises the question of the relationship of domestic racial concerns with foreign policy.

Finally, Jackson's trips abroad, together with his stress on the ties between Americans of color and their ancestral lands, have raised the specter Walter Lippmann had of a balkanized America. The Rainbow Coalition raises the specter of a new, more intense civil war, based on racial and ethnic division. It was bad enough for ethnic Germans, Irish, and Jews to be subjected to such divisions, but it is even worse for more vulnerable groups such as blacks, Mexican-Americans, and Asian-Americans, the focus of Jackson's rainbow rhetoric.

Affirmative action may well continue in some form or other, even as quotas are routinely denounced. Recall the Democratic Party's original platform position: opposition to quotas while embracing affirmative action. Jackson demanded specific mention of quotas, and the party went on to approve an amendment which did not mention quotas but which embraced goals and timetables. There is surely no principled difference here. The Republican struggle over quotas reminds us that political principle concerning ethnicity is lacking in the Republican as well as in the Democratic Party.

Conclusions

How does all this affect the future of American politics? Does the reelection of Reagan represent a fundamental shift concerning the relationship of various ethnic groups to the regime, and the regime to various ethnic groups? Will the attention given Jackson simply accustom the American public to such outbursts of self-indulgence and prepare it for even more extreme displays of foul judgment? Has he permanently affirmed race-consciousness as part of the conventional wisdom?

Democrats and Republicans will continue to hunt for votes, relying on the Roosevelt coalition's instincts—using government power to benefit groups which would appear to have little in common. There is no reason to suppose that politicians cannot continue to appeal to ethnic groups just as Tammany Hall boss George Washington Plunkitt did. But today's politicians will use the largesse of the federal government to appeal to ethnic groups. Neither party seems particularly willing to emphasize the politics of the common good, appealing to people of ethnic groups on the basis of the highest aspirations of the American political tradition and thus educating citizens. Such an appeal would enhance the enlightenment of the consent all Americans give, and would serve to draw the more recent Americans closer to the political community. Thus can we avoid Walter Lippmann's thought that we must needs resort to "coercive Americanization" in order to have national unity.

In 1985, five years after the first great Reagan landslide, American public policy on the questions of race and ethnicity seems as muddled as ever. One would have thought that the traditional argument of democracy versus aristocracy ought to have been revived: privileged classes have no basis of existence and hence no rights in a regime of equality and liberty. And affirmative action creates such classes, and under its own logic cannot remove them. What was once a bureaucratic and judicial doctrine has now become legitimated as a means of conducting politics. But it appears that for now, together with the trends toward bureaucratization, government by mechanical functioning, and a foreign policy which appears to pay more attention to the concerns of ethnic groups than the geostrategic necessities of the nation, the future of American ethnic politics is characterized more by Jesse Jackson's Rainbow Coalition than it is by the spirit of the Declaration of Independence's "all men are created equal." It appears that the only alternative to the present course of events is statesmanship informed by the spirit of the Founders and of Lincoln. The spiritedness of *Federalist* 14 and of Lincoln's great Civil War speeches can be a source for directing American passions in the proper direction.

That America is a nation of many nations can never be forgotten; nor will Americans ever be merely the clashing atoms some see predicted in *Federalist* 10. Statesmanship must produce virtuous citizens who neither know nor favor this dehumanization or that of racism. Statesmanship must always seek to produce, through the variety of means at its disposal, the constant Americanization of its citizens—"mutual guardians of their mutual happiness"—through constant reference to America's origins.

The Reagan Revolution and the Legacy of the New Deal: Obstacles to Party Realignment

Charles R. Kesler

What has become of "the emerging Republic majority"? Before asking why it has not emerged, it is only prudent to review the considerable body of evidence suggesting that it has done, or gradually is doing, just that. Consider: Four out of the last five presidential elections have gone Republican, three of them by landslide proportions. After sweeping eleven new Senators into office and taking control of the Senate for the first time in a generation in 1980, the GOP has managed to retain its control (albeit by diminished margins) through two elections; in the House, Republicans remain in the minority, but are 23 seats stronger than they were before 1980. The aggregate popular vote for Congress grows increasingly Republican; indeed, in 1984 the GOP received nearly 50 percent of it, though due to Democratic gerrymandering this translated into only 42 percent of the House seats. Whereas the GOP held only 13 governorships and 17 state legislative chambers (out of 99) at its nadir in 1975, today it is ensconced in 16 governorships and 32 state legislative chambers.

The South and West of the country, which tend more and more regularly to vote Republican, continue to gain in population, representation in the Congress, and number of electoral votes. Seven of the party's 16 new Congressmen, for example, come from the once solidly Democratic states of North Carolina and Texas. Voters under the age of 30 have proved that they can be trusted to vote for a Republican presidential candidate by a margin of almost three to two. And by averaging polls taken in 1984, the Gallup organization discovered that 31 percent of those polled supported the Republican party, the highest figure since 1954. Looked at dynamically, the figures were still more encouraging: from the first to the last quarter of 1984, Republican support surged from 28 to 35 percent, while Democratic support declined from 41 to 38 percent. The *New York Times*-CBS News polls confirmed the Republican resurgence, showing the party at its highest levels of popularity since the New Deal.

This evidence is formidable but not conclusive. It may be, as some analysts infer, that a "rolling" or "creeping" realignment of the party system is going on; but the numbers could just as easily be explained as a temporary expression of gratitude for good economic times, self-confident foreign policy, and the avoidance of Walter Mondale. Loyalty and gratitude are two different, though connected, things, and in the bad economic times of 1982 the voters found relief not by reflecting that they were suffering in a good cause, but by unceremoniously voting 26 Republican Congressmen out of office. That's gratitude for you! It is not exactly party loyalty, and in most polls the GOP is far from commanding the allegiance of a majority of voters. To be sure, the Democrats are almost as unpopular, but the vast Democratic majority in the House is beyond peradventure; and so long as the electorate consistently sends such lopsided Democratic majorities to Congress, it is not credible to maintain that a realignment of parties has taken place. Democratic gerrymandering is not a sufficient excuse, because every realignment must overcome the effects of past redistrictings. Besides, as Kevin Phillips has noted, no Republican President has *ever* taken office with his party controlling so few House seats, governorships, and state legislatures.

Although the consummation of this long-anticipated change may seem to Republicans to be at hand, the truth is that a sufficient cause for realignment—a clear purpose or end that would organize and inform a new majority—has not yet been articulated. To align, after all, means both to put something in a straight line and to take sides. Putting the definitions together, one might say that in American politics a realignment means that the voters take or switch sides in order to put the country back into line with its fundamental principles, or at least with what they regard as its fundamental principles. Hence realigning elections are sometimes called critical elections because "critical" implies a "crisis," a turning point in the fortunes of the parties and the destiny of the country. Such crises marked the elections of 1800, 1860, and 1932, and to a lesser degree those of 1828 and 1896. In those years, the voters truly were presented with "a choice, not an echo"; and based on that choice—presented by a critical issue that cut across existing party lines or coalitions—an enduring majority party was formed that dominated American national politics for the next 30 to 40 years. But what was the crisis that the parties—particularly the Republican party—addressed in the 1984 election?

A Realignment of Parties

That some sort of turning point had been reached was proclaimed by both sides. "This year, the American people will choose between two diametrically opposed visions of what America should be," the Republican platform began. The Democrats concurred in the Preamble to their platform: "A fundamental choice awaits America—a choice between two futures. . . . America stands at a crossroads." In his Acceptance Speech, President Reagan agreed that "America is presented with the clearest political choice of half a century. The distinction between our two parties and the different philosophy of our political opponents are at the heart of this campaign and America's future." But what was the nature of the distinction? Let us hear the language of the Republican platform:

The Republican Party looks at our people and sees a new dawn of the American spirit.

The Democratic Party looks at our nation and sees the twilight of the American soul.

... The Republican Party's vision of America's future, the heart of our 1984 platform, begins with a basic premise:

From freedom comes opportunity; from opportunity comes growth; from growth comes progress.

... The party whose 1932 standard-bearer told the American people, as President, that all we have to fear is fear itself has itself become the party of fear.

Today we declare ourselves the Party of Hope—not for some but for all.

The Democrats, of course, saw things differently, and said so in a *patois* that was one part J.F.K.'s antitheses, one part Jesse Jackson's verbal rope-a-dope. From their platform:

It is a choice between solving our problems, and pretending they don't exist; between the spirit of community, and the corrosion of selfishness; between justice for all, and advantage for some; between social decency and social Darwinism; between expanding opportunity and contracting horizons; between diplomacy and conflict; between arms control and an arms race; between leadership and alibis.

But the words of the President undoubtedly commanded the widest audience:

The choices this year are not just between two different personalities, or between two political parties. They are between two different visions of the future, two fundamentally different ways of governing—their government of pessimism, fear, and limits, or ours of hope, confidence, and growth.

Their government sees people only as members of groups. Ours serves all the people of America as individuals. Theirs lives in the past, seeking to apply the old and failed policies to an era that has passed them by. Ours learns from the past and strives to change by boldly charting a new course for the future.

The Republicans understood the central issue of the election to be the choice between hope and fear, between optimism and pessimism, progress and decline. The Democrats, too, thought that progress was the issue, but insisted on progress with social justice, rather than progress with only the fittest surviving. Neither party questioned that the fundamental choice confronting the voters was which party would get or keep the country moving forward. Therefore, despite the ominous rhetoric on both sides, neither party admitted that the election concerned a difference over the ends or principles of our politics; what was in question was which party offered a better set or program of *means* to reach that end. Hence, the debate revolved around whether a tax increase to erase the deficit or low taxes to stimulate investment and consumption would conduce to economic prosperity and progress. The economists on each side and everywhere in between debated the question, but came to no conclusion; and the public, interested but not edified in the discussion, accepted President Reagan's formulation of the issue on the presidential level, preferring optimism to pessimism, but on the congressional level the same voters often decided to stick with the incumbent Democrat, presumably rewarding his solicitude for the district's interests in Congress—and perhaps, heeding the advice of the economist-bookmakers, hedging their bet on the President's optimism.

Indeed, they were in a sense invited to do so by Reagan himself, who preferred to run on his administration's record and his own personality rather than as the head of the Republican party—an organization that used to be the majority party, and whose long-term interests require that it be so again. In his Acceptance Speech, Reagan declared that "I began political life as a Democrat, casting my first vote in 1932 for Franklin Delano Roosevelt." He implied that it was Roosevelt's promise to cut the federal budget by 25 percent and to return authority to state governments that won his vote, and said explicitly that it was by forgetting such promises that the leadership of the Democratic party had left behind "not just me but millions of patriotic Democrats who believed in the principles and philosophy of that platform." It is perhaps awkward to ask why, if millions of Democrats were disaffected by F.D.R.'s unbalanced budgets and centralization of authority, they nonetheless—including Ronald Reagan—voted overwhelmingly for him and his party not once, not twice, but four times? In any case, Reagan never emphasized any specifically Republican tradition, seeming content to identify the party with the unfulfilled promises of the 1932 Democratic platform. Nor did he ask these long-suffering, long-memoried Democrats to become or even to consider becoming Republicans. Instead he asked them to "take a walk," in the manner of Al Smith in 1936.

In his standard stump speech during the campaign, the message was the same:

> To all those Democrats, and I hope there are many here, who have been loyal to the party of F.D.R. and Harry Truman and J.F.K., people who believe in protecting the interests of working people, who are not ashamed or afraid of America's standing for freedom in the world—we say to you: Join us. Come walk with us down that new path of hope and opportunity.
>
> I was a Democrat most of my adult life. I didn't leave my party and we're not suggesting you leave yours. I am telling you that what I felt was that the leadership of the Democratic Party had left me and millions of patriotic Democrats in this country who believed in freedom.

What about the Republicans? One might expect that the head of the Republican party would have a *positive* argument for being a Republican, hence for disgruntled Democrats and independent voters to *become* Republicans, but that is not the impression his speeches leave. It is almost as if one were called upon to vote for Republicans *faute de mieux*, there being no real Democrats left in control of their party any more. Reagan said explicitly that he was not asking Democrats to change parties; he asked merely that they take a walk with him, and presumably continue to walk with him and other Republicans, so long as the Democratic leadership continued to reject balanced budgets, greater governmental decentralization, and a resolute foreign policy. In short, just so long as the Democratic leadership turned its back on the real interests of the people: progress or opportunity for the country as a whole.

Reagan vs. Roosevelt

If we were to follow Reagan's own suggestion and look to F.D.R. and the New Deal as models of proper policy and political realignment, we would see a very different sort of rhetoric and statecraft. From the beginning of the campaign, Roosevelt made it clear that he was interested in reconstituting the Democratic party along new, progressive lines, and that the American electorate faced a fundamental choice in party allegiance: a choice between the American and un-American party, between democracy and oligarchy (the contemporary equivalent of monarchical despotism). Here are his words from his first Acceptance Speech, in the 1932 campaign that historians regard as much less radical than the 1936 race:

> There are two ways of viewing the government's duty in matters affecting economic and social life. The first sees to it that a favored few are helped and hopes that some of their prosperity will leak through, sift through, to labor, to the farmer, to the small businessman. That theory belongs to the party of Toryism, and I had hoped that most of the Tories left this country in 1776.
>
> But it is not and never will be the theory of the Democratic Party. This is no time for fear, for reaction or for timidity. And here and now I invite those nominal Republicans who find that their conscience cannot be squared with the groping and the failure of their party leaders to join hands with us; here and now, in equal measure, I warn those nominal Democrats who squint at the future with their faces turned toward the past, and who feel no responsibility to the demands of the new time, that they are out of step with their party.

In one bold stroke, F.D.R. managed to identify the Republicans with Toryism, to invite "nominal Republicans" to change names, and to warn reactionary Democrats to get in step or get out of line, i.e., out of the party. Roosevelt was intent on creating a realignment by working through and reorganizing the party—ultimately both parties—in his image. Notice, for example, that whereas Reagan appealed to Democrats as Democrats, asking them to vote for the genuine principles of their party that happen now to be in the custody of the GOP, Roosevelt entreated "nominal Republicans" to vote for *their* genuine principles, which however belonged essentially to the Democratic Party. "Nominal Republicans" had really been Democrats all along; they had belonged to the GOP in name only, not in substance. For Reagan, however, the Democrats to whom he appeals are and always have been good Democrats, members in good standing of the opposition party—whose credentials as the natural majority party, by the way, are not disputed. It is the Democratic party *leaders* who have betrayed the party's principles. For F.D.R., the leaders of the

Republican Party were genuine representatives of their oligarchical, undemocratic principles. It was their *followers*, the "nominal Republicans," who had
been in the wrong party.

But this brings us back to our first point. If the Republicans are the party of
Toryism, then the Democrats are the party of the American Revolution; and
the "nominal Republicans" are the only *genuine* republicans (small "r") in the
so-called Republican Party. The Democratic Party of F.D.R. is therefore the
sole and true legatee of the Democratic-Republican Party of Thomas Jefferson.
The opposition party is in the strictest sense an illegitimate party bent on the
overthrow of our democratic-republican Constitution. This theme was
sounded most elaborately in Roosevelt's 1936 Acceptance Speech, which is
worth quoting *in extenso*:

> ... But the rush of modern civilization itself has raised for us new difficulties, new
> problems which must be solved if we are to preserve to the United States the po-
> litical and economic freedom for which Washington and Jefferson fought.
>
> Philadelphia is a good city in which to write American history. This is fitting
> ground on which to reaffirm the faith of our fathers; to pledge ourselves to restore
> to the people a wider freedom—to give to 1936 as the founders gave to 1776—
> an American way of life.
>
> ... In 1776 we sought freedom from the tyranny of a political autocracy—
> from the eighteenth century royalists who held special privileges from the crown.
> ... Political tyranny was wiped out at Philadelphia on July 4, 1776.
>
> But, since that struggle, man's inventive genius released new forces in our land
> which re-ordered the lives of our people.... For out of this modern civilization
> economic royalists carved new dynasties. New Kingdoms were built upon con-
> centration of control over material things. Through new uses of corporations,
> banks and securities, new machinery of industry and agriculture, of labor and
> capital—all undreamed of by the fathers—the whole structure of modern life
> was impressed into this royal service....
>
> And so it was natural and perfectly human that the privileged princes of these
> new economic dynasties, thirsting for power, reached out for control over govern-
> ment itself. They created a new despotism and wrapped it in the robes of legal
> sanction. In its service new mercenaries sought to regiment the people, their labor,
> their property. And as a result the average man once more confronts the problem
> that faced the Minute Man of seventy-six....
>
> These economic royalties complain that we seek to overthrow the institutions
> of America. What they really complain of is that we seek to take away their power.
> In vain they seek to hide behind the Flag and the Constitution. In their blindness
> they forget what the Flag and the Constitution stand for. Now, as always, for over
> a century and a half, the Flag, the Constitution, stand against a dictatorship by
> mob rule and the over-privileged alike, and the Flag and the Constitution stand
> for democracy, not tyranny; for freedom, but not subjection.

Harsh words, yes. Demagogic, pretty surely. But a theme that declaimed in the
right manner and in the right circumstances could bring about a political realignment, most definitely.

The key to F.D.R.'s strategy was to read the Republican Party as previously constituted right out of American politics, to cast it beyond the pale of the Declaration of Independence, to pronounce it excommunicate and heretic and to anathematize its doctrines. Now, every critical election is in some sense a re-enactment of the crisis of 1776, a reassertion of the meaning and bounds of American republicanism. This fact goes unrecognized by many political scientists, who are insufficiently empirical to see that a critical issue is not just any issue that happens dramatically to cut across party lines, but is always *the same issue*, though in different settings. And that issue is the capability of a free people to govern themselves in accordance with the proposition "that all men are created equal." Every critical election is an authoritative pronouncement on this great question, deciding what the grounds of political consensus for the next generation or two will be; a declaration of the meaning of equality as the great American middle-of-the-road will understand, accept, and revere it; a determination of that abstract truth in particular, concrete circumstances. This is no disparagement of liberty, insofar as liberty and equality are correlative principles: we are free *because* we are equal (i.e., no one is so unequal as to have the right to rule us without our consent), but this equality is intelligible because our minds are free (i.e., we are equal human beings, rational not brute animals). Hence every party realignment involves reopening the question of justice that animated the American Revolution, that continues to animate the life of American democracy.

It would be unfair to assert that President Reagan's campaign was oblivious to this question, but it is fair to say that he never insisted on its centrality, that he did not expound it as the decisive issue of the election. The condemnation of affirmative action as an unjust and imprudent measure was present in most of his major speeches, but rather as part of a standard litany of Democratic follies, than as the vanguard of an insidious attack upon equal rights and indeed the Constitution itself. The justice of tax and economic policy—not to mention of the Administration's foreign policy—was always part of the President's arsenal of concerns, but again there was no real effort to connect particular injustices to an assault upon the Democrats' overall retreat from American principles. Republican candidates and spokesmen occasionally quoted or paraphrased the Declaration, but to no apparent purpose. One thinks of the hapless Howard Baker, addressing the Republican National Convention: "We want the world to remember that the greatest revolution for the rights of mankind was begun in this country two centuries ago—and it's not over yet," he intoned. "The right to life, the right to liberty, the right to pursue happiness are the gifts of God, not government. No government on earth should presume to interfere with these fundamental rights of men and women." New paragraph: "People can buy cars and houses and take vacations again." To such bathos the Republicans were reduced even in their attempt to prove who was worthy to inherit the American future—"the wishers, the wasters, the wanters, the whiners, and the weak," to adopt Gerald Ford's euphuistic language at the National Convention, or "the sure, the sensitive, the seasoned, and the steadfast." There was, to be sure, a serious point buried in there somewhere, but, like the party as a whole, neither Senator Baker nor former President Ford was able to articulate it.

A Realignment of Values

President Reagan, in short, was reluctant to create the serious political division that was required to shatter and humiliate the Democratic Party, and to reform the Republican Party, as F.D.R. had been so manifestly, so joyfully eager to do in 1932 and 1936 on behalf of his party. This is not to blame Reagan and the Republicans for the failure of the political earth to quake and shift in their direction. Realignments, which are, after all, comparable to wars and revolutions in their political effects, require propitious circumstances as well as felicitous rhetoric; and in 1984 there seemed to be no crisis or catastrophe on the horizon remotely comparable to the Great Depression of the 1930's. Nevertheless, not every American realignment has taken place in such a dire emergency (particularly true if one counts the lesser realignments of 1828 and 1896); and, at any rate, a statesman ought to know before hand what he wishes to accomplish in order to steer his way through the crisis, whenever and however it comes. Perhaps it is a sufficient answer to these criticisms to say that if Reagan *had* attempted to trigger a thoroughgoing realignment, he might have lost the election. As it is, however, he has lost the critical election; and even if he could not have won it due to *force majeure*, he could have done more to rehabilitate the GOP's reputation, enhancing its ability to become the majority party sometime in the future.

Yet even if these criticisms are accurate—if it will be up to Reagan's Republican successors to convert his accomplishments into a party realignment—it would be wrong to deny that the groundwork was laid, in considerable part, by Reagan himself. Moreover, we do him an injustice if we do not understand that, by his own standards, the election was a turning point. For Reagan did have a clear idea of his and the party's destination, and that goal was not so much a partisan realignment as a philosophical one. The message was most clearly conveyed in his 1980 Acceptance Speech, when he spoke of the Republicans as "a party ready to build a new consensus with all those across the land who share a community of values embodied in these words: family, work, neighborhood, peace, and freedom." Elsewhere in the speech he made plain that he was referring not to a consensus *of* these like-minded people organized within or headed by the Republican party, but a consensus *with* them that is not directed by any party. "Everywhere we have met thousands of Democrats, independents, and Republicans from all economic conditions and walks of life," he said, "bound together in that community of shared values of family, work, neighborhood, peace, and freedom." These are "values that transcend persons and parties," and in contrast to Jimmy Carter who had asked voters to "trust me," Reagan asked them to "trust your values—our values" and to hold him responsible for living up to them. It was to the majority of the American people who shared these "values" that Reagan directed his spectacularly successful appeals in 1980 and 1984, and their response to his appeals proved that the "consensus" existed. The realignment of opinion or "values" in the country at large has therefore already taken place, or at least is on-going.

One might term this the conservative rather than the Republican realignment, though Reagan himself is careful not to do so in his national addresses (he generally speaks of conservatism only in front of self-styled conservatives, though he will occasionally use "liberalism" as a pejorative). This conservative realignment does not have to be effected or interpreted by a political party precisely because the values involved are integral to the American character. But upon examination, that character is itself not transpolitical but rather the result of certain traditions—hence Reagan and other Republicans speak of "traditional American values"—that have to be handed down. Such handing down always involves choice or the possibility of choice, so Reagan asks for "a new beginning" or a "second American Revolution," the central element of which (again according to his 1980 Acceptance Speech) is the resolution "to teach our children the values and the virtues handed down to us by our families." On closer inspection, then, the "community of values" comprising "family, work, neighborhood, peace, and freedom" is not transpolitical so much as prepolitical. Its parts are either rudimentary facts of life that exist in some form in virtually every regime (family, work, neighborhood) or terms of political art that cry out for political definition (peace, freedom). In fact, it is possible for Democrats, independents, and Republicans to share these values only insofar as the *traditional* American definitions of them remain powerful. But it is precisely these traditional definitions that have been under attack in recent years by those who would, e.g., redefine "family" to mean homosexuals living together, "work" to mean that which you don't have to do to be worthy of dignified public support, and so forth.

"Values" that once could be handed down unthinkingly because there were no ready or respectable alternatives now must be chosen much more self-consciously, for there are many competing "values" or "lifestyles." Is there then any argument for "traditional values" other than their being traditional? Is there a *reason* why they should be adopted here and now? The "consensus" on these "values" is always questionable so long as there is no authoritative or political account of them. To put it differently, it is difficult to see how a "community" based on these shared values can in the long term be politically effective without a political party or some other kind of political form to defend and explain them against the myriad of non-traditional values. To be venerated, traditional values must be shown to be not merely traditional—for there are dead as well as living traditions, corrupt as well as healthy ones—but also *good*, hence worthy of being chosen for other than antiquinarian reasons. But here we reach a philosophical dead-end, because to give a rational account of "values" is, to put it bluntly, impossible. The term "values" (which did not enter our political life until before the Second World War) denotes subjective expressions or creations of the will. "Values" are, by definition, relative to the evaluating subject; unlike "facts," they cannot be known or validated by reason, but are simply preferences, the moral equivalent of preferring crunchy over creamy peanut butter.

It is another matter to prove that Reagan has this definition in mind when he uses the term. Perhaps he means by "values" what the Founders meant by "self-evident truths" or "first principles." But it is certainly true that he offers almost no account of these values other than their being "traditional," and that the formulation "traditional values" has utility as a kind of bridge between the traditionalist and the libertarian wings of modern American conservatism. These points are telling, because the political form that Reagan seems to have in mind when conceiving this "community of values" is what has come to be called the conservative movement. The "new consensus" that has gradually been forged since the New Deal is the handiwork of, or at least has been publicly defended and explained by, the conservative intellectual and political movement. Many commentators have argued that the essence of the realignment is precisely the success of the conservative movement in winning the hearts and minds of the American people away from New Deal liberalism, which has been rejected in its Minnesota-Farmer-Labor version (Humphrey, Mondale), its Southern version (Carter), and its Dust Bowl-radical version (McGovern). There is a great deal of plausibility to this view, and not just because of the Democrats' chronic inability to pick a winning presidential candidate. The leading ideas in American politics for almost twenty years have been coming from conservatives of one stripe or another—from monetarism to the new federalism, from de-regulation to enterprise zones, from the balanced budget to the Strategic Defense Initiative—and the best, and increasingly the most widely read, writers on American politics have been conservative, too. One thinks of such journalists as George Will, William F. Buckley, Jr., and James J. Kilpatrick; of such academics as Milton Friedman, Friedrich Hayek, and Edward C. Banfield; of George Gilder, Irving Kristol, and Norman Podhoretz; and of many others as well.

Yet the case for a conservative realignment flounders not only on the hard fact that voters keep electing Democratic congressional majorities that could not by any stretch of the imagination be called conservative, but also on the unpleasant truth that the meaning of conservatism is unclear even to conservatives. Modern conservatism has always been of two minds about itself, inasmuch as it has always been divided into traditionalist and libertarian camps; and its political successes have been made possible only by making the most of, but never resolving, this schizophrenia. Reagan is a virtuoso of this peculiar art. In his 1984 Acceptance Speech, for example, he rejected the polarity of Left and Right in American politics, on the ground that either one taken far enough would result in totalitarianism, whether of the Stalinist or Hitlerite species. "Isn't our choice really not one of Left or Right," he asked, "but of up or down: down through the welfare state to statism ... and ultimately totalitarianism, always advanced as for our own good. The alternative is the dream conceived by our Founding Fathers, up to the ultimate in individual freedom consistent with an orderly society." Not Left and Right but freedom and order are therefore the relevant categories. With the right mixture of freedom and order society may progress upwards, with the wrong mixture, downwards. By this formula Reagan is able to square libertarianism and traditionalism through the idea of progress, aided by their common hatred of totalitarianism and Tip O'Neill. But this attempted synthesis begs the decisive question, or rather it leaves the question to be answered by the progress of history itself, *ad hoc* because *ad infinitum*. That question is: What *kind* of freedom and order are we discussing? If "the ultimate in individual freedom consistent with an orderly society" means that order is simply the minimum conditions of individual freedom, then he has not achieved a synthesis but has accepted the libertarian argument. If, on the contrary, it means the maximum of freedom consistent with a certain kind of order that is an independent and superordinate good (time out of mind), then he has accepted the traditionalist argument. The two simply cannot be reconciled by lumping them together as "traditional values" and leaving their reconciliation to the mysterious verdict of history.

Reagan's political career was built upon his masterly ability to effect a treaty between the two conservative camps against a common enemy, but it was not, and could not have been, predicated upon a principled synthesis of these antithetical notions. Treaties against common enemies usually last only so long as the enemies are at the gate, however, and so one must wonder what will happen if liberal Democrats continue to lose presidential elections as effortlessly as they have in the last two decades. In this connection, the dispute over religion and politics that erupted in the 1984 campaign may have been a sign of things to come: it was certainly a sign of the liberals desperately but nonetheless shrewdly casting about for an issue that could split the coalition of economic and social conservatives. This attempt to recapture libertarians, Yuppies, and—admittedly not a traditional part of the conservative coalition—Jewish voters from the Republicans was partially successful, more so with the latter than with the former constituencies; but it was most important as a reminder of the contradictions within conservatism that had been papered over for the sake of Reagan's election. If the alliance between these two factions seemed more tenuous in 1984 than in 1980, perhaps it was because the alliance, forged when conservatives were out of power, had suffered strains under the pressures of actually having to govern. For most of its life, after all, conservatism had enjoyed the liberty of being in opposition; its parts had had a freedom of speech and action that they could not exercise when called upon to concert in legislative and administrative actions. Ironically, it may have been only the lack of a Republican majority in the House of Representatives that saved the unity of the Reagan coalition. If the Administration had had actually to take the responsibility of passing a constitutional amendment banning abortion on demand, for example, rather than simply fretting over the Democratic majority's intransigence in refusing to pass it, the tensions within the conservative coalition could have reached the shattering point.

The Politics of Progress

If President Reagan and the Republican Party are guilty of mistaking or underestimating the causes of political realignment, the fault lies with a persistent misunderstanding of the nature of the contemporary crisis. They have attempted to emulate the Democratic realignment of the 1930's without sufficiently reflecting on the meaning, and the legacy, of that fateful turn in our political history. By trying to co-opt F.D.R., they may have allowed F.D.R. to co-opt *them*. That is to say, they have yet to understand the extent to which the New Deal was meant seriously to mark the end of American politics: the realignment to end all realignments.

Despite differences in emphasis and tone, and divergent political tactics, the New Deal was in its purpose and self-understanding a continuation of Progressivism, especially of Woodrow Wilson's New Freedom. Progressive politics in Wilson's conception had two main parts: strong or responsible party government, and scientific administration. The former was to be the mechanism by which the ends of government were determined, allowing government's purposes and measures to change with changing popular majorities; and the latter was to supply the most efficient means to carry out the ends set by party government—to make democracy scientific. But both were means to a larger, more comprehensive end: namely, opening up American government to progress, so that it could keep pace with developments in society, which meant keeping government far enough ahead of society to allow it to offer leadership in meeting new social problems, but not so far ahead as to give the government a separate interest or to render it independent of society. Government's purpose was to help lead society into the future, to prepare society for the forward march—not to secure unalienable rights or to fulfill men's nature. Party government was justified by its utility for leadership, and scientific administration by its ability to effect the leaders' plans. Nonpartisan administration thus existed to serve partisan goals, but the party system itself existed to serve the nonpartisan end of progress.

Within this system, the parties are not essentially Democratic and Republican or even, as Jefferson, Tocqueville, and many others had thought, democratic and aristocratic, but the party of progress and the party of order. However much the latter may seem opposed to the former, the party of order in fact presupposes the existence of progress, or rather is predicated upon the assumption of progress. For the people's interest—more than that, their very identity—depends upon progress, but the people must have time to absorb and adjust to change, in order to keep progress from becoming revolution. The result is an alternation of change and rest, advance and consolidation, of periods of dominance by first the progressives, then the "conservatives," who are properly so called because their task is merely to conserve the new status quo. There is no real danger of a return to the status quo ante, because a permanent retreat from progress is impossible ("you can't turn back the clock"). History runs only forward, like a river with a swift current that cannot be fought for long. The only question left to be decided politically is the pace of the trip downstream.

This kind of party system is based not upon questions of justice or claims to rule, as in the Democratic-Republican and democratic-aristocratic models, but upon the temperaments of men. Some men are disposed to like change, others to shun it; and the balance between the parties of progress and order turns upon the number of people who are historically motion-sick at a given moment. Critical elections are exciting moments when the nation is called back to the forward march from the stabilizing but, if unrelieved, enervating effects of conservatism; for the status quo that conservatives defend always includes a legacy of untreated social problems as well as a legacy of previous reforms. Critical elections therefore represent—according to the Progressive view—the revival of reformism, every reform being understood as the wiping out of an anachronism, of a social problem that can now be solved. Thus Jefferson stamped out the last vestiges of monarchism, Jackson defeated the Second Bank of the United States, Lincoln freed the slaves and secured the West for free labor.

But all these great periods of reform had taken place within the horizon of the Constitution as originally understood, that is, as a frame of government meant to secure men's natural rights. All of these reformers had understood themselves to be perfecting American government by bringing the Constitution and laws more perfectly into alignment with the principles of the Declaration of Independence. Progressivism was however the first political movement in which reform became conscious of itself as an end in itself. "The government of the United States was constructed upon the Whig theory of political dynamics, which was a sort of unconscious copy of the Newtonian theory of the universe," Woodrow Wilson wrote in 1908. "The trouble with the theory is that government is not a machine, but a living thing. It falls, not under the theory of the universe, but under the theory of organic life. It is accountable to Darwin, not to Newton." Whereas the Framers of the Constitution had sought to limit and refine the powers of government by separating them—keeping each in its proper orbit, held in place by the force of self-interest, of ambition counteracting ambition—Wilson insisted instead on combining the executive and legislative powers by means of strong party government, allowing them to be coordinated quickly and efficiently for the purposes of social reform. For the Framers, the powers of government were limited by the ends of government, the rights to life, liberty, and the pursuit of happiness. But

these rights, drawn from the fixed nature of man as part of a permanent, ordered universe, had lost their authority when the permanence and order of the
world were disproved, or at least radically questioned, by Darwin. Natural
rights and natural law were ideas much too rigid and abstract to be guides for
political life, which like biological life must constantly adapt itself to new circumstances if the body politic is to survive. "Liberty fixed in unalterable law
would be no liberty at all," Wilson declared. "Government is a part of life,
and, with life, it must change, alike in its objects and in its practices...." Liberty is not a law or right to which politics must conform; it is itself a product
of politics, of the evolution of a community; it consists in "the best practicable
adjustment between the power of the government and the privilege of the individual," an "adjustment" guided by no principle except what the people will
accept and what the government will require—or, to put it differently, by
nothing other than the developmental requirements of the social organism.
The justification of reform for the Progressives was therefore primarily that it
was the dictate of the age, not the dictate of prudence or right. Perhaps it is
more accurate to say that reform was the dictate of prudence or right *because*
it was the dictate of the age.

The larger purpose of the New Freedom and the New Deal was to change
American politics forever by acting for the first time in full consciousness of
the obsolescence of natural law notions and natural rights constitutionalism.
Once these ideas had been shown to be anachronistic ("eighteenth-century
ideas," as we still call them today), and the American political system had
been re-established upon the new historical basis, a future realignment like the
realignments of old—meant to bring the nation back to what Lincoln called
its "ancient faith"—was rendered unthinkable. This marked the end of American politics in the old and practical meaning of the term: politics as the dispute over who should rule, or over who has the better grasp on justice and the
common good. For the debate over right and wrong as abstract principles (always implied by the tenets and arguments of democrats, aristocrats, mon-
archs, and so forth, even if the best argument never won) was made nugatory
by the fact that history would decide those questions for men. That is, history
spoke in the same way that evolution spoke: the fittest, the most progressive
or most adaptable societies, survived, and justly so. In human societies, of
course, the measures of "adjustment" or adaptation were decided by political
rather than biological processes. And in advanced constitutional governments,
this meant that history, in effect, spoke through the voters; but any governmental branch or power could conceivably be representative of the future, because the voters required leadership in order to follow their own inherent
forces of development. Wilson thought that the presidency offered the best
chance for effective leadership, but he left open the possibility that in given
circumstances the legislature, the courts, or even the bureaucracy could assume that function.

The Legacy of the New Deal

In F.D.R.'s interpretation of Progressivism, the end of politics corresponded to the moment when the scarcity of nature's resources and goods had been overcome by the liberation of human acquisitiveness: when mankind passed from an economy of scarcity to an "economy of abundance" (to use the paradoxical term that later came into fashion). As he put it in his Commonwealth Club Address of 1932, "the day of the great promoter or the financial Titan, to whom we granted anything if only he would build, or develop, is over." The present task is "not discovery or exploitation of natural resources, or necessarily producing more goods. It is the soberer, less dramatic business of administering resources and plants already in hand," of reestablishing foreign markets and otherwise "meeting the problem of underconsumption, of adjusting production to consumption, of distributing wealth and products more equitably," in sum "of adapting existing economic organizations to the service of the people." The Wilsonian emphasis on "adjustment" or adaptation is evident, though with a new economic twist. For the final social problem on the economic front has been reached. "The day of enlightened administration has come." Not production but consumption and distribution therefore form the principal task of the new day, and the virtues associated with production— moderation, frugality, industry, prudence—as well as the virtues associated with scarcity in a more political sense, the scarcity of honors, are speedily anachronized. Such virtues are not needed in a regime concerned primarily with encouraging consumption and distributing a surplus. Capitalism has produced not its own gravediggers but its own psychotherapists, ready to treat the impulses and virtues that gave rise to its present rich but deranged condition.

What kind of politics befits "the day of enlightened administration"? To quote from the same speech, "the task of Government in its relation to business is to assist the development of an economic declaration of rights, an economic constitutional order. . . . It is the minimum requirement of a more permanently safe order of things." Already in 1932 Roosevelt was advocating what in his 1944 Annual Message to Congress he would describe memorably as "a second Bill of Rights," built upon "economic truths" that in this century "have become accepted as self-evident." "Among these," he noted magnanimously, were rights to "a useful and remunerative job," "to earn enough to provide adequate food and clothing and recreation," "to a decent home," "to adequate protection from the economic fears of old age, sickness, accident and unemployment." The ground of these rights was the fact "that true individual freedom cannot exist without economic security and independence"; or, to borrow his favorite epigram, that "necessitous men are not free men." Roosevelt went so far as to declare that if "reaction" developed—if the country were to return to the "so-called 'normalcy'" of the Republican heydays of the 1920's—it would be as if we had "yielded to the spirit of fascism here at home."

If necessitous men are not free, then it is up to government to make them free by providing for their necessities. One wonders how free government in America came into being at all, given the prevalence of necessitous men in our past. Apparently, American government was unfree, or it was government of and for the few free, i.e., rich men, or it was as free as historical conditions would permit—i.e., the full meaning of freedom was as yet unknown to the Framers, who were stuck with eighteenth century notions that looked to nature rather than to man's transformation or subdual of nature as the ground of freedom. True to his Wilsonian roots, Roosevelt understood government to be a contract under which "rulers were accorded power, and the people consented to that power on consideration that they be accorded certain rights." It is not a contract into which people entered bearing inalienable or natural rights; their rights were a *product* of the contract negotiations. This idea of the social contract was sufficiently open-ended to enable Roosevelt (and Wilson before him) to explain the Constitution as the original bargain struck between the American people and their government, on the basis of so-called natural (F.D.R. preferred to call them "political") rights. Though this would explain the origins of free government in America, it also explained nicely the limitations of that original understanding. For the eighteenth century worldview would not do in the twentieth. "The task of statesmanship has always been the re-definition of these rights in terms of a changing and growing social order," he announced to the Commonwealth Club. In short, the rights men need to be relieved of their necessitousness are not defined by nature but by men, and therefore are subject to constant "re-definition" by new generations of men. The contemporary term "entitlement" conveys something of these redefined rights: an entitlement is something we are entitled to, not as a natural right but as a positive right, as the result of a legislative enactment that creates an implied contract between the government and present and future generations. But this is a kind of contract that is embarrassingly dependent on having an economy vigorous enough to pay for all the entitlements, while somehow remaining productive.

This is, however, a necessary implication of Roosevelt's famous declaration "that the only thing we have to fear is fear itself." There is nothing to fear *but* fear, and fear can now be eliminated or at least reduced by ensuring that people's necessities are taken care of. The federal government will protect our lives and liberties, see to it that our health care and housing are adequate, oversee our education, mandate our old age insurance, even compensate us for accidents, unemployment, and, lately, past discrimination against our race or sex. With our lives and liberties taken care of by government, we are free to pursue happiness any way we see it, to choose our "values" and construct our "lifestyle" based upon the somewhat contradictory grounds of our "right to privacy" and our "freedom of expression," which also must be guaranteed by the government. Thus government becomes the realm of necessity, privacy the realm of true individual freedom. But what becomes of freedom in the old and honorable sense of self-government? The Framers understood freedom in this sense to be a way of connecting the public and private realms: that a nation could be self-governing, its citizens had first to govern themselves, to rule their own passions and appetites. But the effect of the New Deal has been to make this connection increasingly problematic. To put it uncharitably, the Democratic Party has been devoted to necessitous men for fifty years—an endlessly futile mission, because the hazards of old age, unemployment, bad education, and the like have not been eliminated, but at best only mildly palliated. But the palliation is no comfort to generations who have been promised a transformed human condition, so that the separate constituencies of the party have rightly grown increasingly froward. At bottom, the party has been unable to articulate any grounds for human freedom other than the promised conquest of necessity, a goal that is so far from having been realized in 1932 that even today it can be promised only in the dim and distant future—at the end of history, as the Marxists would say.

Of course the Democrats *can* claim that their policies have saved the nation from another Depression. The Wagner Act, public works programs, Social Security, deficit spending, the Tennessee Valley Authority, all can be understood as parts of a larger plan to prevent depressions by stimulating consumption or increasing aggregate demand: by building inflation or inflationary safeguards into the economy. It was hoped that the constantly rising standard of living generated by these measures would enable the constantly rising costs of the economic Bill of Rights to be paid. In the event, it has not worked out, the costs of entitlement programs launched in the New Deal and of new ones added since having soared. But Roosevelt's genius was to so build these programs into the American economy and government as to make their roll-back virtually impossible, inasmuch as reducing an entitlement is tantamount to breaking the contract made between government and the people. The inertia of these programs therefore drives the government to extend its taxing, regulating, and spending authority more and more deeply into society, at the expense of citizens' pocketbooks but also of their right and duty of self-government. Hence the peculiar rites that Reagan and other Republicans must perform every time the issue of, say, Social Security comes up. Reagan must pledge his allegiance to Social Security as if it were the Flag. And that is the result of F.D.R.'s statesmanship, of the lingering but still powerful sense that the Republicans are an illegitimate party—whether of Tories, economic royalists, or fascists—bent on destroying the equal economic rights of the people. In this elaborate show, Republicans are cast as the party-poopers: the people who try to cure inflation by balancing the budget and creating recessions. This is only further proof that they are not true-believers in "economic rights."

Yet Social Security and other entitlement programs are not part of the Constitution, nor are they inalienable rights; they depend ultimately upon the "plenty" that is created by an "industrial and agricultural mechanism" that "can produce enough and to spare" (to borrow again from the Commonwealth Club Address). Roosevelt's depreciation of the need for new production could not survive his own Administration, but it has never been fully repudiated by his Party. Democrats often deprecate wealth as if it were merely a reward of luck or a token of the rich man's adroit exploitation of the poor. Sometimes, of course, it *is*; but many Democrats insist on making these cases the rule, and talent and virtue as sources of wealth the exception. They speak of the "greedy" and the "needy," as if there were no one in between. Thus the effort to banish necessitousness only ends up by making men more necessitous and less free. Against this background, the real contribution of Reagonomics and supply-side economics may consist in emphasizing that talent, virtue, and hard work are goods, that they are forms of human excellence that exhibit the possibility and character of freedom within a realm of necessity that ordains but does not determine human life.

The Reagan Revolution?

There are, then, some signs that the Republicans are marshaling their forces for a realignment; but these troops must have a moral and political cause to fight for if they are not to remain halfhearted and ineffective. It seems clear that a realignment is impossible so long as both parties conceive of the nature of politics as a pursuit of the social conditions that will make freedom meaningful by making necessity a thing of the past. A liberal regime, a regime that embodies and ennobles human freedom, cannot maintain its freedom if it does not recognize in man a will independent of society, of environment, of entitlements; a will that is independent because man has a nature that is independent of history. The scramble to see which party can spend more for Social Security or for other "economic rights" not only raids the Treasury but deprives the country of any chance of a political realignment, which is to say of any chance of a return to political responsibility. For no permanent (as things go in politics) majority can be sustained so long as political loyalty is held hostage to changing economic fortune. What is worse, freedom itself cannot be long sustained if it has no higher source of dignity than the promise of economic prosperity, for then it too can be bought and sold as an ordinary commodity. This is not to say that a liberal regime should not have a concern for economic prosperity, or that a stable middle class is not necessary for democratic government. These were traditionally understood as tasks that statesmanship set itself to solve. As such, they were means to the end of a certain quality of life, of a certain way of life with characteristic virtues and excellences. By contrast, today these goals are increasingly seen as *ends* in whose terms rightness and excellence must themselves be defined.

This decline in responsibility is visible not only in the loss of control over the federal budget but in the growing strength of the independent vote and the declining vigor of the party system. Though often attributed to the advent of television and direct mail political techniques, the latter phenomena have as least as much to do with the increasingly popular notion that the good citi-zen—the intelligent voter—is or ought to be independent, free to choose the man and not the party—a notion that is certainly encouraged by the media's, and especially television's, contempt for politicians and political parties. The belief that the most respectable voters are independents reflects the Wilsonian view that the people ought to choose "leaders" around whom the strong or responsible party system should be organized—that is, men proper for the times because they know or think they know how to lead the people to the next stage in history's advance. Citizens should therefore be free to select, de-pending on the times, either leaders (of more or less personal parties) who stand for slow adjustment and consolidation, or leaders who boldly sound the trumpet of advance. Voters should not have to make a lasting choice of party that will affect and condition all their future choices. The old doctrine of American party loyalty, of course, never presumed that voters who were stead-fast members of one party might not vote for a manifestly superior candidate of the other party; but this was thought to be an exception to the rule of party loyalty and identification. The new doctrine of voter independence transforms this exception into the rule, on the premise that parties should not be orga-nized around a fixed set of principles and a tradition anchoring them to the American past, which would allow citizens to vote for a party's slate of can-didates on the general understanding that they knew what the candidates stood for. Instead, parties should be organized around leaders, who are them-selves distinguished by their sense of the nation's state of development. As be-tween two leaders' "visions" of the future, there is of course no way to tell who is correct until history discloses the answer. We cannot be sure that progress or order will be the rule of the day until the day arrives. Hence voters must be free to switch back and forth at will to meet the demands of the new day. When parties stood in some sense for abstract principles, it was possible to find in the debate between them an argument that reason could, at least theoretically, decide. But when parties stand for their leaders' views of the future, there is no way for voters to decide rationally between them; they must instead rely on their imaginations or on temperamental judgments (optimism, pessimism) and emotions (hope, fear), balanced by the ability to shift their votes quickly if things do not work out.

Depending on their leadership, the parties themselves are capable of chang-ing character quickly. At one point the Republicans may be the party of prog-ress—as both Wilson and Roosevelt seemed to admit, for instance, of the Re-publicans under Lincoln—and at another point the party of order. What we see today is an attempt by the Republicans to reassume the mantle of progress, and to paint the Democrats as the short-sighted, backward-looking party of order. The difficulty, however, is that after Progressivism and the New Deal, the character of the party system organized around progress is known. The moment of full self-consciousness has come. We know that the dispute be-tween the parties is not over ultimate principles, as the participants thought in all realignments prior to the New Deal. Today's dispute concerns simply the pace of progress: which party is in a better position to move the nation along, historically speaking. Or, rather, that is what the partisans of the New Deal realignment and of the progressive view of politics devoutly hope is true. There are stirrings within the Republican Party suggesting otherwise—suggesting that before the Party lays claim to the mantle of progress it will insist upon raising the question, What is progress? That is a dangerous question precisely because it can lead to a search for principles whose validity is not decided by history, to principles that are themselves standards by which progress must be defined, to principles familiar to the Framers that could serve as the grounds of a genuine realignment questioning the legacy of the New Deal.

Within the current debate over the federal budget and a simplified, flat tax system, there are indications of a Republican desire to find a ground of political responsibility that rejects the Progressive faith in high and redistributive taxation, in inflation, and in history. The proper and prudent expansion of this debate will show that there is a way to unite supply-siders, the religious Right, enemies of quotas and affirmative action—and the majority of American citizens—within the Republican Party. That way cannot be spelled out in detail, inasmuch as it, like all political things, depends upon contingencies, many unforeseen and some unforeseeable; but it would begin by affirming that it was the Progressive and New Deal divorce of freedom and necessity, really of freedom and nature, that created both subjective morality ("values," "lifestyle," etc.) and the excesses of the Welfare State, intent on conquering necessity and redistributing wealth. In meeting these contingencies, the guiding principle in general would be that American government can be limited again only by rediscovering and restoring its foundations in the constitutional morality of the American Founding. For it is only in the light of those great truths of human nature—the rights and laws "of nature and of nature's God"—that individuals can be asked to require enough of themselves to be content with demanding less of government. In the light and by the love of such old truths, a new majority party and all of American politics may be born again.

Incumbency and Nonpartisanship in The Congressional Elections

Peter W. Schramm

It is beyond dispute that Ronald Reagan defeated Walter Mondale with ease in the presidential contest. That the President won by one of the greatest landslides in American history is hardly disputable. It is no exaggeration to state that the Democratic Party was repudiated in the presidential election of 1984. It is also clear that the Democratic Party was not repudiated in the Congressional elections. In fact, it can be argued legitimately that the Democratic Party was victorious in the Congressional elections. How this happened, and what may account for this disjunction between the two majorities in American politics is the purpose of this essay.

In the 1984 elections the Republicans gained 14 seats in the House and lost two in the Senate. In the 99th Congress there are 253 Democrats and 182 Republicans in the House, and 47 Democrats and 53 Republicans in the Senate. The Republicans have ten fewer seats in the House than they had at the start of the 97th Congress, but fourteen more than in the 98th Congress. In the Senate the Republicans hold the same number of seats that they had after their remarkable victory in 1980, when they took control of the Senate for the first time in twenty-six years.

Republican partisans argued that the Republican gains in the House are respectable looked at from the point of view of a President winning a second term. When Richard Nixon won re-election in 1972, the Republicans won 12 House seats. In 1956, when Eisenhower handily defeated Adlai Stevenson for the second time the Republicans lost three House seats. When Franklin Roosevelt won an unprecedented fourth term in 1944, the Democrats won 24 seats, but in 1940 they won only seven, and in 1936 they won only nine. It is not clear how many new House members have to be elected in order for realignment, as traditionally understood, to take place. But still, 1984 was the first time in a Republican presidential victory since World War II in which the GOP couldn't elect at least 190 members.

Given the great Republican fund raising efforts in 1983-84, the logistical and campaign support for their House candidates, the fact that first class candidates were not hard to find since the prospects were promising, the so called Republican victory in the House was not particularly impressive. Without the great renewal in party interest and support for candidates, the GOP did almost as well in 1972. The Reagan White House was openly critical of Nixon's lack of inclination to give support to the party, but they did not do much better. It is interesting to note that former President Nixon predicted, months before the 1984 election, exactly how many House seats the GOP would win.

Was There a Mandate Out There?

Considering the president's great national victory it was not surprising that Democrats immediately after the election fixed the attention of the media, if not the American people, on their apparent victory in the Congressional elections. The argument over the meaning of the election became as important as the election itself, if not more so. Which election, the one for the executive, or the one for the legislative branch, truly represented the American people? In a way it was assumed tacitly that the two elections represented different majorities in American politics. But which one really represented the majority? This discussion took the following form.

House speaker Tip O'Neill assured the American people immediately after the election that "There is no mandate out there." He was supported by a finely tuned chorus of both Democratic politicians and their epigones, the so-called value free academicians and the poll takers. The battle lines for the meaning of the election were drawn, and the war began for the minds of the people, if no longer—at least temporarily—for their votes. The *New York Times*, for example, quickly concluded, based upon sound scientific reasoning (opinion polling), that "Poll finds Reagan failed to obtain policy mandate." That the president won a landslide election in taking 49 states (and just missing Minnesota by a few thousand votes) no one could deny. But why did he win so mightily? The reply was predictable: He is a very popular man. He was liked as a person, and as a man. As journalist Mark Shields wrote during the campaign, Reagan is one of the most well-liked presidents in twenty years: "One reason for this is that Ronald Reagan is a man publicly free of self-pity; he doesn't spend time telling us what a tough, thankless job he has and how lonely and burdensome are the duties of the chief executive." The President likes riding horses, and he wears non-designer work clothes, and looks comfortable because he is comfortable. Although he smiles easily, and likes telling jokes, he is a strong and tenacious man. He obviously thinks well of himself and does not doubt his capacities. That he seems plain and simple, if not ordinary, is an asset with the American people who in recent times have been accused of not being able to govern themselves. Reagan's person is proof that they can. It is also true that he does not ask much from the people in the way of sacrifice; in fact, he tells them to do what is natural, to consider their self interest in the context of what is right.

That many commentators and politicians have tried strenuously to point out what they think are deficiencies in the man—that he does not like to work long hours, that he is bored by detail, that his honesty verges on simplicity—seems to have no effect on the people's affection for the President. They reply with much common sense that the man is paid for his judgement and not for immersing himself in details. The American voters see Reagan as a sound reflection of themselves. And they like him because they like themselves, despite recent onslaughts on their character and capacities.

Theodore Lowi has said that Reagan's victory "was a personal triumph—broad, nationwide, but shallow. The majority was large but weak." Lowi asserts, without proving, that "the thinness of his popular base" shows that his election was not a victory of a "conservative majority but of a Reagan majority." He finds the explanation of a "charismatic, personal presidency" the most useful.

Although most commentators and Democratic politicians took this approach, some, like Morton Kondrake, warned the Democrats that it is a mistake to call Reagan's victory "personal" because the party will not understand the deep seated mistrust in which it is placed by the American people, and will have a tendency to assume, to its disadvantage in the long run, that everything will be fine once Reagan leaves the political scene. These are the same people who assume that the Democrats will win at least 40 House seats in 1986, and take back the Senate. The Democrats who claim that as a result of the "victory" in the Congressional elections their party is doing well on the local level, Mark Shields dubs the "Norman Vincent Peale Democrats." It is these people who make the argument that the American people vote Republican because they are mean spirited and vengeful. When Walter Mondale made similar arguments, they were not well received. But not all Democrats take this view. Senator Dale Bumpers, a Democrat from Arkansas who has been winning statewide elections for years (including the votes of white males) has said: "Americans, male as well as female, are not meaner than a one eyed water moccasin. People do not want to be polarized. And we cannot blame our political failures on the voters."

Tip O'Neill's argument has to do with the impression he has been cultivating ever since 1980, and most powerfully since 1982. He stands as the politician, by virtue of holding the most important office in the House of Representatives, who is in closest proximity to the American people's wants, needs and opinions. The House of Representatives is now the only part of the government that most clearly expresses the will of the people. Since the people voted for the President because they liked him personally, it follows that they did not do so because they favored his often reactionary and dangerous policies. Therefore, they voted for a Democratic majority in the House to watch over the President. Rep. Tony Coelho, Democratic Congressional Campaign Committee Chairman, said it most clearly: "The people gave him a personal victory. But they let us keep effective control of the House to counteract his extremism." Richard Reeves agrees: "The President was rewarded for the tasks accomplished, and, at the same time, he was being cautioned not to go much further than the people, not to push beyond the limits of national consensus."

Is this a sufficient explanation of the disjunction between the majorities? Does this explain why the President and Congressmen are elected on a different basis? In attempting to understand this problem we will focus on two characteristics of Congressional races: their nonpartisan character and the difficulty of defeating incumbents.

Nonpartisanship

The discussion of nonpartisanship may be divided into two parts. First, the President did not, until the last few days of the campaign, appeal to the voters as a Republican, nor did he ask voters to vote Republican. This was in contrast to his strategy in 1980. Second, very few Democratic Congressional candidates attached themselves to the head of their national ticket. In fact, most of them went to great lengths to disassociate themselves from the candidacy of Walter Mondale and emphasized their service to their constituents.

In 1980 Ronald Reagan campaigned openly as a Republican. He campaigned not only against President Carter, but against a Democratic Congress as well. He made full use of a perfect opportunity. "Throw the rascals out" was the public theme of the campaign. In some ways the GOP campaign was directed as much against Tip O'Neill as it was against Jimmy Carter. And it worked. In 1980 the voters responded by electing a Republican Senate and adding 33 House seats to the Republican column. It was as much of a party election as Americans have seen in decades. It is not surprising that talk of party resuscitation and realignment was common, although this understanding was muted after the 1982 GOP losses in the House. By 1984, Reagan was running on his record. He had pledged to cut taxes, increase defense spending, and in general cut the size of the federal government. He had a Republican Senate to work with and a very active Republican party in the House who supported him—surprisingly in the light of recent executive-legislative relations—almost unanimously in his major policies. In fact he worked well with Congressional leaders of both parties. In short, he was fundamentally successful during his first two years in office, and exercised a serious role as the leader of the party. To see more clearly how truly successful he was, and how revolutionary, one needs only to compare him with Jimmy Carter, who was unable to work with a Congress dominated by his own party. Of course the Democrats, mostly as a reaction to Reagan's thrusts, had to respond in a manner to which they had not yet become accustomed: They had to stand against those policies they thought were mischievous, while trying to hold those elements within the party which were inclined to side with the President on specific issues.

At first sight it seems odd that Reagan did not make a strictly partisan appeal. After all, he is very much of a party man. Ever since his entry into political life, from 1964 on, he has immersed himself in the business of the GOP. Aside from supporting Goldwater in 1964, and being a two-term Governor of California, he spent many years, before becoming President, helping GOP candidates around the nation, not only using these occasions to campaign, but also using the party for his own purposes, as Nixon did. It is in part because of this, and his successful policies, as well as general popularity, that Reagan was not challenged in the primaries. He had wholehearted party support. One has only to reflect on recent political history to see the significance of this. We have to turn our eyes back to 1956 to find a sitting president who was not opposed in primaries. In 1968, Johnson was opposed and bested in several primaries by opponents from both the liberal and conservative wings of the party. In 1972 Nixon was opposed from both wings of the GOP; Ford could only with great difficulty turn back the challenge of Reagan in 1976; and Carter had the serious opposition of a Kennedy in 1980.

Of course, Reagan's lack of emphasis on Republicans may be easier to understand by noting one powerful fact: Despite recent gains in registration, the Republican Party is still the minority party in the nation. Since 1932 the Republicans have consistently been the minority party, being outnumbered by the Democrats, during some periods, by almost two to one. A high was reached in 1964 when the Democratic plurality was 27%, but by 1984 the plurality had dropped down to just below 10%. Consequently, it has always been important for Republicans to appeal to the independent voters, as well as disaffected Democrats. When they have not been able to do so, as in 1964, they lost by impressive margins.

Before his first debate with Walter Mondale, President Reagan called on the voters to elect "our team" to Congress. He asked support from "young Americans, independents and rank-and-file Democrats." The President, even before his first debate, rarely used the word Republican in his appeals. Many Republican strategists at the time said that the President was hoping to identify GOP candidates with himself rather than with the party. Reagan made over sixty television commercials for candidates. Many observers said that it was far from clear that Reagan would make an all out personal effort on behalf of Republican Congressional candidates in tough election fights because many of his advisors feared that it may cause him to lose some of his immense popularity, and, after all, they were trying to elect a president. Everything else had to be secondary. They wanted a broad based support for his re-election victory and they feared that the more entangled he got in local affairs, the more he appealed to voters as Republicans, the less broadly based his victory might become. For almost twenty years now the Republicans have been concerned, perhaps too concerned, with the fact that they have to regain legitimacy through massive victories on the presidential level, even at the risk of not making a good showing in the race for other offices. This concern with a broad based victory became a matter of major concern after the first debate when all around him panicked (no matter that the debate was a debacle in large part because his advisors insisted that he appear to be the master of detail) and from then on, to within just a few days of the election, when it became clear to even his closest advisors that he would win handsomely with broadly based support, the Republican Congressional candidates were largely neglected.

The congressional party was disappointed, to say the least, that Reagan did not support the GOP's Congressional candidates. One example will prove the point. Norm Murdock an early Reagan supporter, a co-chairman of his 1980 campaign in Ohio, a Republican county commissioner from the Cincinnati area, was giving the incumbent Democrat Thomas Luken (2nd District) a serious challenge. On October 28, 1984, the *Los Angeles Times* reported:

> Reagan, speaking to more than 10,000 flag-waving supporters in the nation's third most popular Republican city, pledged not to raise taxes, extolled the importance of family and religion—and had even gone so far as to praise Democratic Sen. John Glenn of Ohio as "an authentic American hero." But he did not say anything about Murdock, who was sitting expectantly on the platform near him.

After the first debate the prospects were dimmed for major Republican gains in the House. Democratic party activists were buoyed, and the President was advised to concentrate even more on his own re-election. Representative Tony Coelho was led to declare that the big winners in the first debate were members of his own party who were running for Congress. Some of Mondale's advisors stated that Reagan's poor performance was worth fifteen to twenty House seats. It put enough doubt in people's minds that they would go ahead and vote for some Democratic candidates. And they declared that some Republican candidates, like Senator Charles Percy of Illinois, would now surely lose, because they were so dependent on Reagan's coattails. Edward J. Rollins had said before the election that "If we don't gain Republican seats in Congress, the Reagan Revolution is over." GOP party strategists were hoping that by mid-October the President would have such a commanding lead that he would be able to spend a great deal more time than otherwise expected on marginal congressional races. This did not turn out to be the case.

Democrats Disassociate from Mondale

It is perhaps useful to recall that Democratic candidates for the House (and some even for the Senate) began disengaging themselves from the top of the ticket, as it used to be called, back in 1972. Although this happened less in 1976 (and the Democrats did not gain a seat in the Senate and won only two House seats), in 1980 it became necessary for Democratic candidates to separate themselves from the Carter Presidency. They were not very successful in doing so, in part because the Republicans would not allow it. Reagan ran as much against Tip O'Neill as against Jimmy Carter in 1980—although still not against the Democratic Party simply.

In 1984 Democratic candidates had a serious problem. Their presidential candidate was not an outsider, but the quintessential party man and the Vice President in the previous Democratic administration. He was the first candidate since the start of the reform era who was not simply a reform candidate, as McGovern and Carter had been. Disassociation from such a candidate was more difficult, and even seemed more improper. Nevertheless Democratic congressional candidates showed great creativity. Some were able to be out of town, visiting relatives, or even checking their poultry farms in the northern part of the state, when Mondale was in town. Others were even more imaginative. During the election the story went around that Democratic candidates were in the business of building large wooden platforms for visits from Mondale so that, on the one hand, the candidate could later say—if necessary or useful—that he had indeed shared the same platform with the party leader, but at the same time, the platform being large enough, he could be off to the side and out of the camera range, to make sure he was not seen with Mondale.

Indeed, Democratic candidates for the House, and local offices, did spend a great deal of time and money emphasizing their differences with the top of the ticket. Very few, for example, publicly supported a tax increase. What they tried to do is exemplified by Representative James R. Jones' remark when asked how he was running his campaign. "I always try to bring it down to me—I'm the issue." That is, the question was whether or not Jones was doing a good job. And the best measurement of this was whether or not he was doing what Congressmen are now expected mainly to do: serve their constituents. Partisanship was to be avoided at all costs, because it could lead to defeat. Of course, it helped that the voters thought that times were good, and it was inevitable that some of the responsibility for that would rub off on Democratic members of the House.

It wasn't only the moderate or conservative Democrats who were disassociating themselves from the "San Francisco Democrats," as Jeanne Kirkpatrick called them, but many liberals as well. It was not to their advantage to emphasize their views on the principled differences there may have been between the parties, or to show their support, for example, of the Democratic party platform. In New York's 2nd District, for example, Tom Downey, one of the most liberal Democrats in the House, narrowly defeated a political unknown named Paul Aniboli. The pre-election polls showed that most voters were confused about Downey's positions and were not aware of his liberalism, and some even believed him to be a conservative. Downey took advantage of this and sent a mailer to voters in which he included a photograph of himself with the President, and asked voters to "Return Tom Downey to Congress where he can continue to work with President Reagan."

This emphasis on a connection—however tenuous—between the Democratic candidate and the President was not uncommon. The most immoderate claim in this regard came from Democratic Congressman Jerry Patterson of California's 38th district. Less than one week before the election, the Santa Anna *Register* published a graph showing the voting records of both Patterson and Republican challenger Bob Dornan (who had been a Congressman until 1982 from another district). The graph transposed the two candidates' votes on President Reagan's 1981 tax cut program, a 1982 measure to require a balanced federal budget, and a 1982 measure denying federal funds for court ordered busing. In fact Dornan had voted for all three, and Patterson had opposed them. Patterson, who had been accused by Dornan of being a liberal and opposing some of the President's most important initiatives, immediately took the graph (but not the text of the story, which had stated his view correctly) and had it reproduced as a mailer to voters. He mailed the graph in an envelope that read: "Facts don't lie—read what the *Register* had to say!" He did this despite the fact that three days prior the *Register* had published a new graph and apologized for the error. Dornan rightly accused Patterson of "a deliberate act of deception." Patterson's gambit did not work. He lost to Dornan, the only incumbent Congressman in California to go down in defeat.

Incumbents Win

Although all of the House's 435 seats were up for election, only 27 representatives failed to run for re-election. Of the 408 incumbents who ran for another term, 392 were re-elected. Of the 16 incumbents that were defeated, 13 were Democrats, and three were Republicans. As a result, the freshman class of Congressmen for the 99th Congress was the smallest in decades. Not only were 96% of the incumbents re-elected, but their margin of victory was substantial. Almost 80% won by 60 percent or more, and about 43% won by 70 percent or more. Only 30 of the incumbents (7.3%) won in districts that can be fairly identified as competitive—in the 50-55% range. In 1982, in comparison, 49% of the House races could be called competitive.

Sixty-six of the House races were settled before the election itself. Of these only 13 were held by Republicans, while 53 were held by Democrats. Of the 27 open seats, the Republicans won a majority. Thirteen of these seats had been previously held by Democrats. That is a net gain of four seats. Since the GOP won ten seats by defeating incumbent Democrats, they gained a total of 14 seats. Also, the vast majority of the victorious Republicans won their seats by handsome margins. Almost 80% of the Republican incumbents increased their margin of victory over 1982. Of the 29 incumbents winning in the 50-55% range, only five were Republicans. Whereas only about 40% of the Democratic incumbents increased their margin of victory in 1984. In general it may be said that several heretofore safe Democratic seats became more competitive in 1984, this despite the fact that there were more Democratic incumbents allowed to run without opposition (53) in 1984 than in 1980 or 1982 (41 in both years).

The Republicans made their most impressive gains in the South, the last bastion of Democratic strength. In Texas, despite the fact that nine Democratic Congressman ran unopposed, the Republicans gained five seats. The GOP now controls ten of 27 House seats. Ten years ago they controlled only three in Texas. A number of the switched seats in Texas were due to the ability of the Republican candidates to attach incumbent Democrats—even those with relatively conservative voting records, such as Jack Hightower and Bill Patman—to the more liberal national ticket. The three Republican gains in North Carolina, like the five gains in Texas, were helped by the high voter turnout in large measure due to bitterly fought races for the U.S. Senate. The three incumbent Democrats who lost in North Carolina all had relatively small numbers of black voters in their districts, and two of the Democratic victors won by slim margins.

Theodore Lowi has said that the "ideological cores of the two parties are a great deal more distinct and farther apart than at any time before." Yet he also says that "Despite its landslide proportions, the election of 1984 does not qualify as such a critical realignment, because the Republican victory failed to penetrate local and state electoral patterns. In truth the voters now prefer specialization to realignment." What is this specialization the voters prefer? The simple answer is that the voters prefer, at least on the local and Congressional levels, to look at politicians less as Republicans and Democrats, than as those who are in office and those who are not in office. This division in the mind of the voter is a significant one. The sitting Congressman is no longer a party man, at least not in the way that he has traditionally been understood. He is most meaningfully characterized as being part of the federal government, part of the large federal bureaucracy. He is the one who can get things done for you. His many offices are efficiently organized, and very well staffed. No letter, no inquiry, no complaint goes unanswered. Everything is organized around the needs of the constituents. Of course, the more powerful and the larger an organized interest is within the district, the quicker its needs will be serviced. One may cynically assume that all this is done because the Congressman is smart enough to realize that he is always campaigning and that there is no better way of doing so than by meeting the needs of his constituents. But it is more than that. The Representative understands his role as provider for the constituents to be in perfect harmony with his need to get re-elected, because even if a large number of the citizens in this district may in principle be in favor of cutting back some of the programs that they are trying to take advantage of, they find it more difficult to vote against their self interest. They will speak against those programs that may not be of direct advantage to them, but the ones that are seen to be in their self interest, they are going to view with favor. These are programs that belong to them. After all, they have been taught by over a generation of interest group liberalism that this is the proper use of public funds. They are in favor of supporting, and even enacting, those programs they find to their advantage. This is what Tip O'Neill means when he says that "All politics is local."

On the other hand, they are perfectly capable, notwithstanding the apparent contradiction to criticize the top of the Democratic ticket for tailoring the campaign to the "special interest groups." Since they sense a problem with this approach, voters are not in favor of doing this in principle. And the national campaign is one of principle between two competing views of what the public interest is; it is not merely a question of self interest, or dependence on federal largesse. So when Walter Mondale runs a presidential race in terms that are very similar to a Congressional race, the voters take offense. This is what voter specialization means.

Because of this unnatural logic, many incumbent Congressmen are able to ignore an important aspect of public opinion as it manifests itself in national issues. They can get away with it almost all of the time because a large proportion of the voters have not yet seen the disharmony of principles behind the two majorities. It should not be surprising then that Congressmen are first seen by voters as nonpartisan tools of their self interest, and only second as representing the different principles their parties stand for on the national level. The representative who wants to get re-elected can get away with ignoring the principled issues—the public opinion that shows up in the presidential balloting—because he can still offer great benefits to his constituents who have been habituated to an ever greater expansion of the public sector over the last fifty years. Now that the public sector is no longer expanding, their inclination to guard "what is their own" becomes even more fierce.

How long this state of affairs is going to last is an open question. But there may be signs showing that it will not last much longer. The fact that the Republicans won a majority of the open seats is not insignificant. Where there is true competition among candidates based on principle, where the self interest of the voter is not as manifest, the citizens will be more likely to cast their votes on other grounds than simple advantage.

The Senate Races

Although United States Senators may be accused, from time to time, of having a narrow view of their duties, more often their politics are squarely within the national framework of American politics. In fact, it is not unusual for a senator to be justly accused of ignoring his home state in favor of some powerful and honorable committee assignment which leaves him little time to look after the affairs of his constituents. This is an accusation often heard with regard to those senators who seem to be out of touch with the opinions of the folks back home. Well known personalities, from J. William Fulbright to Frank Church, attest to the truth of this proposition. Unless there is a dramatic turn of events, as in 1980 when the Republicans, having defeated nine Democratic Senators, won control of the Senate for the first time since 1954, Senate races are a finely mixed compound of both national politics (the conservatives versus the liberals), personality, and state interest.

It is fair to say that both sides were disappointed by the 1984 Senate election results. The Republicans had hoped to gain a few seats, while the Democrats had greater hopes of taking back the upper house. In fact what happened was entirely predictable. The Democrats retained 13 of the 14 seats they had occupied, but failed to pick up a number of Republican seats they had considered shaky. Perhaps their greatest disappointment was their inability to oust Jesse Helms of North Carolina. Helms's contest with Governor James B. Hunt, Jr., was the most expensive of the election year, with over $22 million being spent. Helms had surprised everyone because he did not tone down his conservatism, was quite aggressive on the campaign trail, and went so far as to ask for the votes of black voters of the state on his own terms. That is, he appealed to them as a conservative, and even unabashedly so. He was rewarded by winning over 52% of the vote, as well as over 13% of the Black vote.

The outcome in Kentucky was also not expected for the Democrats, where Walter Huddleston barely lost to a county judge named Mitch McConnell. The latter stressed Huddleston's liberal record, and association with the national Democratic ticket, as well as the Senator's poor record of attendance. McConnell referred to Huddleston as the "shadow Senator." Ronald Reagan carried the state by almost 60%, and that could not have hurt the Republican challenger, especially since he attached himself closely with Reagan.

That Republican Roger W. Jepsen of Iowa lost was hardly a surprise to his party. Even Republicans had a difficult time defending his competence. Paul Simon, a five-term member of the House, barely defeated three-term Illinois Republican veteran Charles Percy. He accused Simon throughout the race of being an "ultra liberal." It should not be surprising that the voters had some difficulty with such criticism, considering its source. Simon has the reputation for being a thoughtful and careful man who, in his own words, had "practical answers to practical problems." Percy's loss may be another example of the political dangers one encounters when one too well enjoys the honors that Washington has to bestow.

The Democrats were not as successful as they had hoped in the Senate races of 1984, but although disappointed they have not lost hope. They like to point out that in 1986 the Republicans must defend 22 of the 34 Senate seats then at stake, including 16 seats held by freshmen, many of whom, they like to say, rode in on Reagan's coattails at the beginning of the new regime. Perhaps this prospect will force the Republicans to think more in terms of party advantage and true realignment.

The 1984 Election:
Entitlements Versus Opportunity

Harvey C. Mansfield, Jr.

It is no exception to the contingency of human things that events can occur as expected: this happens so as to lull us for the next surprise. "A good election for poll takers," said one headline of Reagan's lopsided victory. His 18-percentage point margin was exactly predicted by Gallup and roughly approximated by others in a 10 to 25 point range of misses. Once again it was confirmed that science can give mathematical expression to our expectations in politics. But the expected result was also a welcome sign that the American polity was healthy enough to re-elect a president in whom few—and those more his supporters than his opponents—could have been disappointed. A people's ability to express gratitude to its leaders is more than a measure of political stability; it is one end of political stability and when exercised is the most ennobling act of popular sovereignty.

A triumph for President Reagan was not, however, a triumph for the Republican party, and therefore was not entirely a triumph for President Reagan. Republicans suffered a net loss of two seats in the Senate and gained only 14 in the House of Representatives, a result comparable to the elections of 1956 and 1972, when popular Republican presidents (Eisenhower and Nixon) won easy victories for a second term but did not improve the status of their party from minority to majority. It is the habit of Americans to maintain over long periods of time a majority and a minority party, a two-party system that does not alternate victories but keeps a dominant majority and a long-suffering minority in national politics (relieved by local dominances of the national minority in many places). Many had wondered whether a party realignment would reverse the majority and minority parties at a stroke, as happened in the so-called "critical elections" of 1800, 1860 and 1932.

Obviously a party realignment of this kind did not take place. Instead, there were incremental changes favorable to the Republicans portending a future realignment, together with the continued, perhaps intensified division for now between a Republican presidency and a Democratic House of Representatives. I shall first discuss the changes and then consider the stability of incumbents in an aspect less wholesome than as deserving objects of gratitude.

A Personal Victory?

It has been said that the election came out as one would expect with a personally popular president in time of prosperity: thus no realignment and no

277

mandate for Reagan's policies. The people voted out of self-interest mixed with a small measure of gratitude, since the most attentive self-interest looks to the immediate future rather than the present or past. This explanation tells why the incumbent won, but not why the incumbent is Reagan nor how the Democrats might dislodge him apart from waiting for recession. It also does not say whether prosperity was luck or success, or what it consists in: a job, a slightly higher income, or a feeling that things in general are going well. In this skeptical vein Speaker O'Neill, the Democratic leader in the House of Representatives, claimed not unreasonably, if somewhat inconsistently, that the President had no mandate but that the Democratic House had been re-elected to serve as watchdog. He meant that the forces in conflict had not been changed, so that Reagan had no new justification for advance, and he no duty to retreat.

That the result was merely a personal victory for Reagan, or an incumbent's victory in prosperity, however, cannot be maintained. Even in the House the Republicans won 19 of 28 open seats, doing well where incumbency was not a factor. And the Democrats may have held their net loss to 14 by raising their expenditures in closely contested races to an average slightly exceeding the Republicans. This money came from PACs (Political Action Committees), some of them unions but most of them business groups, impressed with the power of incumbency, who confirm once again Machiavelli's view that money goes to power, not power to money. The total popular vote for the House was almost exactly equal, as compared to a slender margin of 51.4 percent for the Democrats in 1980. But because of gerrymandering the Democrats got 253 House seats for their half, the Republicans only 182 for theirs. Moreover, in elections to state legislatures Republicans continued to make gains from their low point in 1974 when they controlled only 17 of 99 state legislative chambers (Nebraska has a unicameral legislature whose members are officially nonpartisan); they now control 32 after a net gain of 4. The most impressive change was in the South, where conservative voters are increasingly turning Republican on the state level. Control of state legislatures is important in national politics because they (with much clumsy interference from the courts) reapportion congressional districts every ten years.

Yet the legislative branch remains Democratic, apart from the Senate, which the Republicans will not find easy to hold in 1986. It is in the presidency that realignment seems already to have occurred. The Republicans have such an advantage in presidential elections from the West and the South that they have only to fight on even terms in the Midwest, while conceding the Northeast, to win easily. They have won four out of the last five elections, three of them by margins designated with the semiofficial metaphor "landslide" (hardly flattering to democratic choice); and the Democrats have won only once, narrowly, with a Southerner. Complementing this decisive fact is evidence from exit polls that the Democrats are losing more of their traditional strength in the South and among blue-collar workers, and that the youth vote (aged 18-24) went Republican for the first time, voting for Reagan 48 to 41 percent and calling themselves Republicans over Democrats 40 to 34 percent. This group is said to lead the trend. First-time voters of whatever age went for Reagan by 60 to 39 percent; new registrations helped Republicans more than Democrats.

Moreover, Republicans have the new ideas, the ruling ideas and the dominant strategy. Gary Hart ran for the Democratic nomination with the slogan, "new ideas," but in fact his proposals for military and tax reform were modulations of Republican issues and in attempting to put a distance between the Democrats and blacks and unions, he was struggling to do what Republicans have done easily. The ruling ideas in American politics now are Republican: the reduction of government regulation and social programs, strong defense, Reaganomics favoring savers and investors, and hopeful patriotism. The Democrats, once the progressive party, have no progressive measure in view that they wish to promote; so they defend the progressive measures they once enacted, now known as "entitlements," and now regarded as progressive only in their uncontrolled cost. Their main issue in the campaign was the budget deficit, an issue handed them by Reagan, which they eagerly and foolishly clasped to heart as if it were not the concern they had ridiculed for many years. For the dominant strategy since 1981 in American politics has been Reagan's. His decision to cut taxes before cutting spending, indeed while increasing military spending, put Democrats on the defensive by forcing them to choose between cutting their own programs or raising taxes to pay for them. "Progress" as progressives have defined it is out of the question; it has been replaced by "opportunity," which does not call for new expense and promises a better life with less government. The Republicans, once known as reactionaries, are no longer so called: they do not demand a return to the past and they do not merely react to others. Reagan did not accomplish this reversal with his 1981 tax cut, but he made the new situation clear to all in that impressive stroke, so that he and his party could profit from it. His strategy was so simple—both obvious and easy—that its effectiveness and his prudence continue to be underestimated. It was not merely Reagan's luck that his opponent began his campaign with a proud, self-congratulatory promise to raise taxes.

The Party of the Sad

The campaign was vapid and lackluster. It was sustained by a succession of media-events such as the "age issue," each of several days' duration, in which the attention of voters seemed not to penetrate to the substance, such as whether Reagan is too old to be President again, but remained on the media-surface as people wondered how the age issue would affect the campaign. Wondering about the campaign is not the same as holding a campaign, however. The media-news, with its boring self-preoccupation and its constant worrying over news management and the lack-of-issues issue, helped to prevent actual news from occurring. Keen reporters allowed many seconds of exposure to the two candidates on the nightly TV news as material for their own reflection on that day's latest twist. Reagan had a surpassing advantage over Mondale in the knack of conveying his message with a few words, a shrug, and a smile through the doltish, moralistic truculence of the reporters. His campaign was designed to the last detail to use this advantage, as was Mondale's to minimize it; for in the media everything is calculated with a view to chance superiority in the use of the media. This is not to say that either Reagan or Mondale did well in the two debates. Mondale won the first one because Reagan did less well than expected, and Reagan won the second by meeting the new, lower standard set by his first performance. Neither candidate in the debates came within sight of the command that urbanity and wit afford to men of the first rank in such a situation, yet neither managed to achieve the power and dignity of simple sincerity, which is nature's compensating resource for second-raters. The campaign was not governed through the media, but nothing was omitted in the attempt to do so, whether in the media or by the candidates. One does not know whether to be more impressed by the limitations on human calculation or by the strength of the human desire to calculate.

Reagan did not run as a Republican, joining his record and his program to the revival of the Republican Party; rather, he presented himself as a former Democrat, still a man of the people but one who, like many others now, had seen the error of his party's ways. He evoked the memory of Roosevelt, Truman and Kennedy, presidents of a size and style no longer seen today—among Democrats. Mondale, in his gracious concession speech on election night, said he was thinking of "the poor, the unemployed, the elderly, the handicapped, the helpless and the sad." The sad! And indeed the Democrats at their convention had stopped playing their old standard, "Happy Days Are Here Again" (celebrating the end of Prohibition in 1933), only to have it picked up by the Republicans at their convention. Mondale's concern for the sad was for those who had nothing to be sad about; it was the same group that had suffered malaise during the Carter administration (in his most notorious speech, Carter spoke of a "malaise" in the American people) and alienation in the 1960s. Reagan harked back to the cheerfulness of earlier Democratic presidents, and skillfully imputed to them in their graves a renewed joy at the defeat of their programs and their party. His audiences were supplied with American flags for all, and they cheered for Reagan as Americans had cheered for their Olympic winners earlier in the summer, with pardonable excess arising from relief of the demand for self-doubt.

Reagan, as is his wont, did not ask for any sacrifice, nor propose any noble goal. In particular, he made sure not to be outpromised by the Democrats in maintaining social security payments. He referred to the "Reagan Revolution" whose purpose is to get the government off our backs, but never called it such, lest it seem to require effort. "Leadership that works" was his slogan, and he did not mean the kind of work from which one sweats, either for himself or the people. His kind of idealism makes idealism easy, even *seem* easy, since the message is not merely that good will is enough—which is the false ease of liberal idealism—but that good *humor* will suffice. If only government will cease its incompetent interference, individuals will take over their own responsibilities with a smile. While the Democrats, usually the happy party, tried to screw their faces into frowns at the deficit, Reagan did not worry and did not ask Americans to worry. But his insouciance was denied by his quickness to reassure the elderly regarding social security. Similarly, in foreign policy he had one easy success in Grenada to boast of, and another undamaging defeat in Lebanon he was quick enough to get out of—the extrication from defeat in a way more impressive than the management of success. He showed he had learned the lesson of Vietnam, that the American people want quick victory or a quick way out; and he has said nothing about the need for patience and perseverance in foreign policy. He has allowed people to think that an arms build-up will lead without difficulty to arms control, and he has not spoken of the stubborn qualities of vigilance that a free people needs to keep itself on guard.[1] Although he has rightly stressed the evil of communism, he has not stressed its menace. The trouble in all this easy hopefulness is that it encourages the American people to believe they can have it both ways: both government payments and release from government regulation in domestic policy, both reduced commitment and heightened security in foreign policy—and therefore, both Democrats and Republicans. Reagan's failure to demand anything of the American people may have improved his own chances for re-election, but by reducing the size of the task, it softened the argument for voting for his party. Why give up the apparent benefits of the Democrats' established programs if the new policies require no sacrifice? Why then replace Democrats with Republicans?

Reagan's decision to run his campaign on his record rather than his program was meant to take full advantage of his incumbency, but it also handed a like advantage to the Democrats in Congress. The temptation to adopt this tactic must have been very strong. Among the chances of the human events we call "elections" few opportunities to defeat one's opponent can have seemed so certain as Reagan's to defeat Mondale by running on his record. Reagan's record, though satisfying to most, and impressive to all, was by no means unassailable—but it was almost unassailable by the Democrats. In domestic policy they had been left with the deficit issue, as explained above. In foreign policy they faced a nation at peace not only with others but with itself, glad to be rid of the Iranian humiliation which it remembered and blamed on the last Democratic administration. Reagan's defeat in Lebanon, which he prevented from becoming a humiliation, could be successfully exploited only from the right, by criticizing the military inefficiency that was shown. An attack from the left would have seemed to endorse that weakness and would have reminded voters of American weakness under the Democrats.

---

1. Reagan did give two notable speeches earlier in the year on the American soldiers who died in Normandy in 1944 and in Lebanon in 1983.

Again, it should not be believed that because Reagan campaigned on his record, he was merely riding on his personality and the country's prosperity as opposed to the issues in a program. Performance is an issue as much as promises are issues, and Reagan's record was judged favorably not simply because it worked or because Americans liked him, but because he persuaded them to judge him by his new standard. With his winning ways he got them to accept his interpretation of his record, and to understand prosperity as opportunity. Nonetheless his "mandate," in the sense of what he can reasonably claim to have put across in the campaign, was confined to an endorsement of what he had done in his first term and a repudiation of what Mondale might have done in his.

The Ferraro Factor

After suffering with outsider candidates like McGovern and Carter, who depended on populist forces hostile to the traditional interest of the party, the Democrats nominated the insider Mondale, former Senator, Vice President under Carter, and candidate of the AFL-CIO, which had supported him, contrary to its usual practice, in the primaries. But though the insider played to win and kept shifting his appeal toward the center, he proved to have no substance except that lent by the outsiders, the McGovern wing of the party. This was strikingly revealed in his choice of Geraldine Ferraro as running mate. Mondale decided to make his choice for vice president before the Democratic convention, after his own nomination was assured. He held a series of well-publicized meetings, by invitation to his home in Minnesota, with vice presidential possibilities, meetings designed in the mode of the insider to recognize and reassure the various parts of the traditional Democratic majority. But doing this publicly created pressure on him to decide, so as to show he was not indecisive, as had been alleged; and it allowed outsider groups, particularly the National Organization for Women, to lobby for their candidates. Soon Mondale was forced to decide, and, since he had made a point of a new way of deciding, he could not easily conclude with an obvious, traditional choice such as a Southerner. So he picked the first woman ever to be on the presidential ticket of a major party. She had been recommended by Speaker O'Neill, insider *par excellence*, and as Italian, Catholic New Yorker, in a blue-collar constituency (though herself, it turned out, very well off), she balanced the ticket in time-honored fashion. But as woman, the candidate of NOW, she represented the outsiders from the 1960s. Above all else, she was an "affirmative action" choice who would never have been considered if she had not been a woman. A three-term Congresswoman with unwavering allegiance to the Speaker, she had never been mentioned as a presidential candidate; and the vice president is someone who might become president. In the event, despite difficulties arising from her own and her husband's finances, she proved to be a formidable character. Not all women liked her; some of them recoiled from her demonstration in a woman of the qualities necessary to succeed in politics. But as a means of recovering the Democratic majority, she was a failure because she was an immediate reminder of a policy, affirmative action, which has been rending that majority apart. Once, in denying (incompletely) that she was overshadowing Mondale, she reminded her audience that whenever they saw her as candidate, "immediately they harken back to the person who made that possible, which is Walter Mondale." And so it was all for nought: according to one exit poll, New York Italian-American Catholic women went for Reagan, 54 to 46 percent.

Thus Mondale let the South go to the Republicans without holding the Democrats' traditional strength among blue-collar workers. His only profit in this move was the Jewish vote, which went 32 percent for Reagan in 1984, as against 39 percent in 1980. Jews were antagonized by Reagan's wooing of Christian conservatives, by which he helped himself win the South, and they swallowed both their fear of Jesse Jackson and their dislike of affirmative action quotas to support Mondale. Blacks went 90 percent for Mondale, and provided one-fourth of his vote. They had been mobilized for the election by Jesse Jackson's candidacy for the Democratic nomination, to which they rallied in near unanimity despite Jackson's far-left politics and his attraction to tyrants such as Arafat, Qaddafi, and Castro. Mondale gladly accepted blacks' votes while taking his foreign policy toward the center and speaking frequently of a strong America. At the end he did his best to raise fears for the American people's "entitlements," with mixed results as we have seen. He did himself no good against Reagan, but he probably helped the cause of the Democrats in Congress.

The Presidential and the Congressional Parties

If we step back from the result of the election and the campaign, we must revise our first impression because the gratitude displayed by the American people to its leaders was not so much ennobling as indiscriminate. Although a democratic election may provide an opportunity for, even a duty of gratitude, such as the British election of 1945, it is more typically an assertion of choice in which the health of a democratic constitution may be judged more by the robustness of the voters than by their deference to doctors. From this election suspicion arises that the American people, by returning both the Republican President and the Democratic House, were trying to have it both ways rather than to make a choice. Discussing the British constitution in its period of separated powers, Montesquieu spoke of the two parties (he meant the court and country parties) that gather around the two visible powers, legislative and executive. In America now, the two parties are legislative and executive, and obviously many people belong to both. This condition is not necessarily deplorable, as in America it is considered that passage of the executive's program in the legislature is a task to be achieved, and not, as in Britain, a normal consequence of a party majority in the House of Commons. In America the task has usually been made easier, though not easy, by the existence of one clear majority party in both the legislature and the executive owing its primacy to a great victory in one critical election whose principles it repeats and whose partners it rallies in following elections. The question, then, of the American people's ability to choose comes down to its ability to live under the last critical election or make a new one. From recent presidential elections it is clear that Americans cannot continue in the choice they made in 1932 for a Democratic majority, but from the Congressional results it is apparent that they have not yet chosen to be Republicans. Perhaps we are headed for a realignment without a critical election, a "rolling realignment." In the meantime the resistance to this realignment seems to me mainly deplorable.

At present the American constitutional structure of separated powers nourishes a party of progress in the Presidency and a party of order in the Congress. But the "progress" is incoherent and the "order" is largely corrupt. And the fault, I believe, lies not in the U.S. Constitution, but in a general departure from the Constitution of which Republicans are uncognizant and Democrats uncaring.

Consider first the Democrats, the party of order entrenched in Congress. There it lives by the devices of constituency service, nonpartisan in themselves, yet instrumental to the getting of—not favors or rights, but "entitlements"— under the broad Welfare State legislation for which this party was responsible. At present, its legislative initiatives in domestic policy consist of generally successful attempts to expand this legislation marginally and to make it more costly. It cannot pass a budget under its own Budget Reform Act (1974), and it appropriates money under emergency procedures now becoming routine, while allowing the deficit to grow and blaming the President (who seems irritatingly unconcerned). A multitude of subcommittees encourages media-display by their chairmen with the immediate object of gaining respect for their own assiduity and rectitude. Their farther goal, the formal cause of the party of order, is incumbency. It must be admitted that the emoluments of incumbency, for example a large and growing staff, are less important than the professional dedication to the needs of the people which such emoluments support. Incumbency for the sake of entitlements: that is the Democratic party today.

Entitlements Versus Opportunity

A liberal constitution, in its most general principle, exists to protect the rights of the people and to advance the public good. How did these rights come to be redefined as entitlements and the public good understood as the collection of entitlements? In the narrow sense an "entitlement" is a budget item that cannot be touched because the law awards it without reference to the number who claim it and thus without reference to cost. But the term has escaped into political philosophy and settled into American political practice. There it challenges the distinction, essential to liberal constitutionalism, between the rights the government exists to protect and the exercise of those rights by private individuals, or between state and society. For an entitlement is a right whose exercise is guaranteed to a certain degree by the government— a right that is therefore exercised to that degree by the government. An equal right to seek a job, for example, becomes an entitlement to a job or rather to the proceeds of a job, which the government performs as it were instead of the worker. In this way government spreads into society, looking for more private activities to equalize and, with decreasing reluctance, to exercise itself instead of, yet on behalf of, those it wishes to benefit. Thus it grows unchecked by the liberal understanding that constitutional government must be limited in scope and in methods, because the defenders of liberalism, the followers of Locke and Mill, have surrendered to the criticisms made by Marx and Nietzsche of the essential liberal distinction. The main obstacle to the growth of entitlements has been popular suspicion and opposition, applauded by a few conservatives, which have been more faithful to liberalism than have liberal intellectuals.

The manifest, utter failure of the social programs establishing entitlements has been ably summarized in Charles Murray's recent book, *Losing Ground: American Social Policy 1950-1980*. He shows that the progress achieved in the 1950s by the poor and by blacks in consequence of equalizing opportunity was slowed and even reversed because of Democratic legislation in the 1960s that turned rights into entitlements. "Popular wisdom"—in truth, liberal opinion—opposing this legislation on the grounds that it would make its beneficiaries dependents of the government has been proved correct, and the sophisticated dismissal of this proven wrong. But the political and constitutional consequences of welfare dependency have not been followed out, and the society of entitlements that makes dependents of all has not been seen in its full extent. Not only the poor, but others as well, become dependent on their entitlements—blacks on affirmative action, workers on social security, farmers on subsidies, the middle class on student loans, and the rich on tax shelters. Indeed, the present tax code epitomizes the situation in its high rate, from which its many loopholes seem to offer relief but in fact lead to more dependency. A people so fragmented by its dependencies has difficulty in seeing itself as a whole and thus in making a choice as a people. Its various dependent groups can hardly be gathered in an active majority because self-restraint in any particular group for the sake of such a majority would make no apparent difference in the sum of entitlements and would bring no discernible benefit to it or to any other group.

Dependency thus reaches beyond private lives into politics, as each group votes to protect its own entitlements. These are the "special interests" for which the Democrats have become known. Such interests are "special" not because they seek out new profit for themselves, which is characteristic of private groups in liberal society, but because they want to secure the advantages government is protecting for them. No group in America now is more victimized by this sort of dependency than blacks are by the policy of affirmative action. Their pattern of voting, not to mention the rhetoric of their leaders, shows that they regard themselves as dependent on government for their well-being, indeed even for their freedom. Whereas blacks have almost no representation in the presidential party, they are (as their leaders claim) the soul of the congressional party because in the policy of affirmative action they have what all other elements of that party seek to have. But precisely in this position blacks call attention to themselves as *the* special interest and thereby suffer from a new ill-will that is not racism but is sometimes mixed or confused with racism.

In foreign policy the Democratic party encourages the belief that the American people have an entitlement to peace. For the right, proclaimed in the Declaration of Independence, of a people to assume a "separate and equal" station among the powers of the earth is no longer understood as a right of self-defense and of self-development but instead as an entitlement to peace and prosperity that government has the duty to guarantee. Since this task has not been accomplished by the United Nations, it falls to the U.S. government; and because the president can take only preliminary or temporary measures, Congress must pass a law; and because that law can reach offenders only within America, the main enemy of peace comes to seem the lawlessness of one's own country. The War Powers Resolution of 1973 has thus been the cornerstone of the congressional party's foreign policy, the war powers controlled therein being those belonging to the U.S. military. "Human rights" in their entitlement understanding are rights the U.S. government has a duty to guarantee anywhere, regardless of the feelings or actions of the peoples involved; so it is not surprising that among these rights, the right of consent by which a people exercises its other rights on its own, is almost never mentioned. The nuclear freeze, a kind of law proposed on behalf of humanity, is another item in the extension of legal entitlements into international relations. It has been promoted by Democratic intellectuals who also accuse Ronald Reagan of simplistic thinking in foreign affairs.

If all this sounds like the talk of yet another ill-tempered critic of the Welfare State, let it be remarked at least that my principal objection is to its political and constitutional effects, to which other critics, especially the Republicans, are not sufficiently attentive. Despite the difficulty mentioned above of gathering a majority against entitlements, the Republicans have done so, though as yet only in the presidential party. That majority has a rather abstract character, since it is not yet clear whether its elements are willing to surrender their separate entitlements by electing a Republican Congress; so far they have passed up three opportunities to do so in 1980, 1982 and 1984. The passage of a flat tax in the next Congress would be an encouraging sign, because this would require an alienation of every group's favorite loopholes in exchange for a better and more equal general incentive. At the moment, however, the desire of Americans to check their Republican president with a Democratic House cannot be interpreted as suggesting the virtue of moderation.

The Republicans have become the party of progress understood as "opportunity," a word used constantly in Reagan's campaign. Opportunity is more naturally suited to, and better symbolized by the president, who has the power and duty to act on his own and has arrived at the office by a route that could almost never be described as an entitlement. America is a land of opportunity because anyone can become president (and anyone sometimes has): the single example of the top political office, or a few examples of successful businessmen, scientists, or inventors, suffuse the less attractive opportunities, some of which can be called such only with sarcasm, which are open to the many, with a glow of success. Even those Americans who have little take satisfaction in the opportunity to have had more, and for their children to have more. Yet despite the central role of politics in making opportunity a viable democratic principle, most Republicans have seen opportunity in terms of incentive, as economic. The Democrats assert that this libertarian view is selfish, to which Republicans can reply that theirs is also the party of traditional or conservative values, or patriotism, family and religion. Republicans, then, have two objections to the society of entitlements: one arising from libertarianism that it stifles incentives, another centered in the Moral Majority that it is morally corrupt. Both are true, in my opinion, but the Republican problem is to reconcile them.

Libertarianism seeks to take the government off our backs and promises to put nothing in its place, neither conscience nor responsibility. It can be quickly described as the belief that a system of self-government does not require any self in the system to govern himself. It speaks of incentives but does not say toward what, except in the meaningless or all too easily understood phrase, maximization of utility. It does not appreciate that individuality cannot be assumed but must be achieved, that human beings come to the dignity of individuality by taking on the responsibilities of family and citizenship. The Moral Majority, on the other hand, is concerned above all with the souls of Americans, but it has difficulty in finding a universal definition of the healthy individual soul suitable for a free, secular society. Whereas the libertarians try to minimize every influence of the state in society, the Moral Majority seems to want to abolish the distinction between state and society. It confuses persuasion with conversion, and it asks for public school prayer with arguments that would justify far more mixing of church and state. Or it clumsily adopts the language of rights used by its opponents, for example the "rights of the unborn" in the abortion debate. These are two glancing blows at the society of entitlements which do not strike its head and its heart. Its head is full of clever theories which have been substituted for liberal constitutionalism, and its heart is sick with the dependency and irresponsibility of the entitled. What we need is comprehensive reflection on the nature, and the ways and means, of self-government. But this can begin from the wisdom in the Constitution and its practices.

Appendix

The Presidential Vote in Social Groups, 1984 and 1980

Percent of 1984 total		1984		1980		
		Reagan	Mondale	Reagan	Carter	Anderson
	Party					
38	Democrats	26	73	26	67	6
26	Independents	63	35	55	30	12
35	Republicans	92	7	86	9	4
	Sex and marital status					
47	Men	61	37	55	36	7
53	Women	57	42	47	45	7
68	Married	63	37	Not available		
32	Not married	51	47	Not available		
	Age					
24	18–29	58	41	43	44	11
34	30–44	58	42	54	36	8
23	45–59	60	39	55	39	5
19	60 and older	63	36	54	41	4
8	First-time voter	60	39	Not available		
	Occupation					
30	Professional/manager	62	37	57	32	9
13	White-collar	59	40	50	41	8
14	Blue-collar	53	46	47	46	5
3	Unemployed	31	68	39	51	8
21	Use computer home/job	62	37	Not available		
26	Union household	45	53	43	48	6
	Income*					
15	Under $12,500	46	53	42	51	6
27	$12,500–$24,999	57	42	44	46	8
21	$25,000–$34,999	59	40	52	39	7
18	$35,000–$50,000	67	32	59	32	8
13	Over $50,000	68	31	63	26	9
	Education					
8	Less than high school	50	49	46	51	2
30	High school graduate	60	39	51	43	4
30	Some college	60	38	55	35	7
29	College graduate	59	40	52	35	11

Percent of 1984 total		1984		1980		
		Reagan	Mondale	Reagan	Carter	Anderson
	Race and ethnic group					
86	White	66	34	55	36	7
10	Black	9	90	11	85	3
3	Hispanic	33	65	33	59	6
	Religion					
51	White Protestant	73	26	63	31	6
26	Catholic	55	44	49	42	7
3	Jewish	32	66	39	45	15
15	White Born-again Christian	80	20	63	33	3
	Region					
24	East	52	47	47	42	9
28	Midwest	61	38	51	40	7
29	South	63	36	52	44	3
18	West	59	40	53	34	10
	Community size					
12	Large cities	36	62	35	54	8
55	Suburbs-small cities	57	42	53	37	8
33	Rural and towns	69	29	54	39	5

*Family income categories in 1980: under $10,000, $10,000–$14,999, $15,000–$24,999, $25,000–$50,000, and over $50,000.

Sources: The New York Times/CBS News poll; *New York Times*, 8 November 1984.

Senate Election Results by State, 1984

	Vote Total	Percent
Alabama		
Howell Heflin (D)*	860,535	63
Albert Lee Smith, Jr. (R)	498,508	36
Alaska		
Ted Stevens (R)*	146,919	71
John E. Havelock (D)	58,804	29
Arkansas		
David Pryor (D)*	502,341	58
Ed Bethune (R)	373,615	42
Colorado		
William L. Armstrong (R)*	833,821	64
Nancy Dick (D)	449,327	35
Delaware		
Joseph R. Biden, Jr. (D)*	147,831	60
John M. Burris (R)	98,101	40
Georgia		
Sam Nunn (D)*	1,344,104	80
Jon Michael Hicks (R)	337,196	20
Idaho		
James A. McClure (R)*	293,193	72
Peter M. Busch (D)	105,591	26
Illinois		
Paul Simon (D)	2,397,165	51
Charles H. Percy (R)*	2,308,039	49
Iowa		
Tom Harkin (D)	716,883	56
Roger W. Jepsen (R)*	564,381	44
Kansas		
Nancy Landon Kassebaum (R)*	757,402	77
James R. Maher (D)	211,664	22
Kentucky		
Mitch McConnell (R)	644,990	50
Walter D. Huddleston (D)*	639,721	50
Louisiana		
J. Bennett Johnston (D)*	X	X
Maine		
William S. Cohen (R)*	404,414	74
Elizabeth H. Mitchell (D)	142,626	26
Massachusetts		
John F. Kerry (D)	1,393,150	55
Raymond Shamie (R)	1,136,913	45

	Vote Total	Percent
Michigan		
Carl Levin (D)*	1,915,831	52
Jack Lousma (R)	1,745,302	47
Minnesota		
Rudy Boschwitz (I-R)*	1,199,926	58
Joan Anderson Growe (DFL)	852,844	41
Mississippi		
Thad Cochran (R)*	580,314	61
William F. Winter (D)	371,926	39
Montana		
Max Baucus (D)*	215,704	57
Chuck Cozzens (R)	154,308	41
Nebraska		
J. James Exon (D)*	332,217	53
Nancy Hoch (R)	307,147	47
New Hampshire		
Gordon J. Humphrey (R)*	225,828	59
Norman E. D'Amours (D)	157,447	41
New Jersey		
Bill Bradley (D)*	1,986,644	64
Mary V. Mochary (R)	1,080,096	35
New Mexico		
Pete V. Domenici (R)*	361,371	72
Judith A. Pratt (D)	141,253	28
North Carolina		
Jesse Helms (R)*	1,156,768	52
James B. Hunt, Jr. (D)	1,070,488	48
Oklahoma		
David L. Boren (D)*	906,131	76
Will E. Crozier (R)	280,638	23
Oregon		
Mark O. Hatfield (R)*	808,152	66
Margie Hendriksen (D)	406,122	34
Rhode Island		
Claiborne Pell (D)*	286,780	73
Barbara Leonard (R)	108,492	27
South Carolina		
Strom Thurmond (R)*	644,815	67
Melvin Purvis, Jr. (D)	306,982	32
South Dakota		
Larry Pressler (R)*	235,176	74
George V. Cunningham (D)	80,537	26

	Vote Total	Percent
Tennesseee		
Albert Gore, Jr. (D)	1,000,607	61
Victor Ashe (R)	557,016	34
Texas		
Phil Gramm (R)	3,116,348	59
Lloyd Doggett (D)	2,202,557	41
Virginia		
John W. Warner (R)*	1,406,194	70
Edythe C. Harrison (D)	601,142	30
Wyoming		
Alan K. Simpson (R)*	146,373	78
Victor A. Ryan (D)	40,525	22

* indicates incumbents
X denotes candidate without major-party opposition
DFL Democratic-Farmer-Labor Party
I-R Independent Republican Pary
Source: *Congressional Quarterly*

The 1984 Presidential Vote

State	Electoral Vote Rep.	Electoral Vote Dem.	Electoral Vote Other	Total Vote	Republican	Democratic	Other	Plurality	Total Vote Rep.	Total Vote Dem.	Major Vote Rep.	Major Vote Dem.
Alabama	9			1,441,713	872,849	551,899	16,965	320,950 R	60.5%	38.3%	61.3%	38.7%
Alaska	3			207,605	138,377	62,007	7,221	76,370 R	66.7%	29.9%	69.1%	30.9%
Arizona	7			1,025,897	681,416	333,854	10,627	347,562 R	66.4%	32.5%	67.1%	32.9%
Arkansas	6			884,406	534,774	338,646	10,986	196,128 R	60.5%	38.3%	61.2%	38.8%
California	47			9,505,423	5,467,009	3,922,519	115,895	1,544,490 R	57.5%	41.3%	58.2%	41.8%
Colorado	8			1,295,380	821,817	454,975	18,588	366,842 R	63.4%	35.1%	64.4%	35.6%
Connecticut	8			1,466,900	890,877	569,597	6,426	321,280 R	60.7%	38.8%	61.0%	39.0%
Delaware	3			254,572	152,190	101,656	726	50,534 R	59.8%	39.9%	60.0%	40.0%
Florida	21			4,180,051	2,730,350	1,448,816	885	1,281,534 R	65.3%	34.7%	65.3%	34.7%
Georgia	12			1,776,120	1,068,722	706,628	770	362,094 R	60.2%	39.8%	60.2%	39.8%
Hawaii	4			335,846	185,050	147,154	3,642	37,896 R	55.1%	43.8%	55.7%	44.3%
Idaho	4			411,144	297,523	108,510	5,111	189,013 R	72.4%	26.4%	73.3%	26.7%
Illinois	24			4,819,088	2,707,103	2,086,499	25,486	620,604 R	56.2%	43.3%	56.5%	43.5%
Indiana	12			2,233,069	1,377,230	841,481	14,358	535,749 R	61.7%	37.7%	62.1%	37.9%
Iowa	8			1,319,805	703,088	605,620	11,097	97,468 R	53.3%	45.9%	53.7%	46.3%
Kansas	7			1,021,991	677,296	333,149	11,546	344,147 R	66.3%	32.6%	67.0%	33.0%
Kentucky	9			1,369,345	821,702	539,539	8,104	282,163 R	60.0%	39.4%	60.4%	39.6%
Louisiana	10			1,706,822	1,037,299	651,586	17,937	385,713 R	60.8%	38.2%	61.4%	38.6%
Maine	4			553,144	336,500	214,515	2,129	121,985 R	60.8%	38.8%	61.1%	38.9%
Maryland	10			1,675,873	879,918	787,935	8,020	91,983 R	52.5%	47.0%	52.8%	47.2%
Massachusetts	13			2,559,453	1,310,936	1,239,606	8,911	71,330 R	51.2%	48.4%	51.4%	48.6%
Michigan	20			3,801,658	2,251,571	1,529,638	20,449	721,933 R	59.2%	40.2%	59.5%	40.5%
Minnesota		10		2,084,449	1,032,603	1,036,364	15,482	3,761 D	49.5%	49.7%	49.9%	50.1%
Mississippi	7			941,104	582,377	352,192	6,535	230,185 R	61.9%	37.4%	62.3%	37.7%
Missouri	11			2,122,783	1,274,188	848,583	12	425,605 R	60.0%	40.0%	60.0%	40.0%

State	EV									
Montana	4	384,377	232,450	146,742	5,185	85,708 R	60.5%	38.2%	61.3%	38.7%
Nebraska	5	652,090	460,054	187,866	4,170	272,188 R	70.6%	28.8%	71.0%	29.0%
Nevada	4	286,667	188,770	91,655	6,242	97,115 R	65.8%	32.0%	67.3%	32.7%
New Hampshire	4	389,066	267,051	120,395	1,620	146,656 R	68.6%	30.9%	68.9%	31.1%
New Jersey	16	3,217,862	1,933,630	1,261,323	22,909	672,307 R	60.1%	39.2%	60.5%	39.5%
New Mexico	5	514,370	307,101	201,769	5,500	105,332 R	59.7%	39.2%	60.3%	39.7%
New York	36	6,806,810	3,664,763	3,119,609	22,438	545,154 R	53.8%	45.8%	54.0%	46.0%
North Carolina	13	2,175,361	1,346,481	824,287	4,593	522,194 R	61.9%	37.9%	62.0%	38.0%
North Dakota	3	308,971	200,336	104,429	4,206	95,907 R	64.8%	33.8%	65.7%	34.3%
Ohio	23	4,547,619	2,678,560	1,825,440	43,619	853,120 R	58.9%	40.1%	59.5%	40.5%
Oklahoma	8	1,255,676	861,530	385,080	9,066	476,450 R	68.6%	30.7%	69.1%	30.9%
Oregon	7	1,226,527	685,700	536,479	4,348	149,221 R	55.9%	43.7%	56.1%	43.9%
Pennsylvania	25	4,844,903	2,584,323	2,228,131	32,449	356,192 R	53.3%	46.0%	53.7%	46.3%
Rhode Island	4	410,492	212,080	197,106	1,306	14,974 R	51.7%	48.0%	51.8%	48.2%
South Carolina	8	968,529	615,539	344,459	8,531	271,080 R	63.6%	35.6%	64.1%	35.9%
South Dakota	3	317,867	200,267	116,113	1,487	84,154 R	63.0%	36.5%	63.3%	36.7%
Tennessee	11	1,711,994	990,212	711,714	10,068	278,498 R	57.8%	41.6%	58.2%	41.8%
Texas	29	5,397,571	3,433,428	1,949,276	14,867	1,484,152 R	63.6%	36.1%	63.8%	36.2%
Utah	5	629,656	469,105	155,369	5,182	313,736 R	74.5%	24.7%	75.1%	24.9%
Vermont	3	234,561	135,865	95,730	2,966	40,135 R	57.9%	40.8%	58.7%	41.3%
Virginia	12	2,146,635	1,337,078	796,250	13,307	540,828 R	62.3%	37.1%	62.7%	37.3%
Washington	10	1,883,910	1,051,670	807,352	24,888	244,318 R	55.8%	42.9%	56.6%	43.4%
West Virginia	6	735,742	405,483	328,125	2,134	77,358 R	55.1%	44.6%	55.3%	44.7%
Wisconsin	11	2,211,689	1,198,584	995,740	17,365	202,844 R	54.2%	45.0%	54.6%	45.4%
Wyoming	3	188,968	133,241	53,370	2,357	79,871 R	70.5%	28.2%	71.4%	28.6%
Dist. of Col.	3	211,288	29,009	180,408	1,871	151,399 D	13.7%	85.4%	13.9%	86.1%
United States	525 / 13 / —	92,652,842	54,455,075	37,577,185	620,582	16,877,890 R	58.8%	40.6%	59.2%	40.8%

Source: Richard M. Scammon and Alice V. McGillivray, eds., *American Votes 16* (*Congressional Quarterly*, 1985).

Contributors

Patrick J. Garrity is Adjunct Teaching Professor of National Security Affairs, Naval Postgraduate School. His views are not necessarily those of the Department of the Navy, or any other U. S. Government Agency.

Thomas B. Silver is President of Public Research, Syndicated and author of *Coolidge and the Historians.*

Glen E. Thurow is Associate Professor of Politics, University of Dallas. He is the Author of *Abraham Lincoln and American Political Religion.*

Douglas A. Jeffrey is a Ph.D. Candidate in the Department of Politics, University of Dallas and a former Publius Fellow.

Dennis Teti is Research Director, House Republican Conference Committee.

Dennis J. Mahoney is Assistant Professor of Political Science, California State College, San Bernadino and is Assistant Editor of the *Encyclopedia of the American Constitution.*

John Adams Wettergreen is Professor of Political Science at San Jose State University.

Thomas F. Payne is Associate Professor of Political Science, Hillsdale College, and has contributed to *Justice and War in the Nuclear Age.*

Josiah Lee Auspitz is Director of the Program in Public Philosophy of the Sabre Foundation.

John Marini is Assistant Professor of Political Science at the University of Dallas.

Steven Hayward is Editor of Public Research, Syndicated, and Editor of *Inland Business.*

Ken Masugi is a Resident Fellow at The Claremont Institute for the Study of Statesmanship and Political Philosophy, and Editor of *The Claremont Review of Books.*

Charles R. Kesler is Assistant Professor of Political Science at Claremont McKenna College, and Associate Director of the Salvatori Center.

Peter W. Schramm is the Director of International Education with the U.S. Department of Education.

Harvey C. Mansfield, Jr. is Professor of Government, Harvard University. He is the translator of Machievelli's *Prince.* This essay is reprinted with permission from *Government and Opposition: A Journal of Comparative Politics,* Volume XX, No. I, Winter 1985.

Index

ABC News, 94
Abortion Issue, 58, 78, 97, 115, 118, 125, 128, 256, 287
Adamany, David, 191, 203, 205, 208
Adams, William C., 218
Affirmative Action, 51, 66, 97, 224, 225, 226, 232, 233, 236, 241, 242, 251, 264, 282, 283, 285, 286
Afghanistan, 5, 31
AFL-CIO, 86, 89, 117, 147, 282
Age Issue, 17, 81-82, 219-220, 279
Agriculture, 61, 102, 112
Alabama, 43, 115
Alexander, Herbert, 194, 200, 203
Allen, Richard, 8
American Conservatism and the American Founding, 236n.5
American Society of Newspaper Editors, 214
Americans for Democratic Action, 85
Anderson, John, 100
Andrews, Mark, 217
Andropov, Yuri, 78
Aniboli, Paul, 271
Angola, 6
Arafat, Yassir, 283
Aristotle, 223, 224
Arizona, 106
Arkansas, 43
Arms Control, 4, 6, 79, 97
Asian Vote, 45, 224, 238-239
Askew, Reuben, 15, 46, 49
Atlantic Alliance, 3

B-1 Bomber, 9, 17, 30
B-52 Bomber, 7
Babbit, Bruce, 106, 107
Baker, Howard, 91, 251
Baker, James, 8, 87, 119
Baker v. Carr, 178
Balanced Budget, 25, 30, 76, 123, 254, 264
Baltimore Sun, 214
Bancroft, George, 212
Banfield, Edward C., 218, 254

Barker, Lucius, 90
Barzini, Luigi, 212
Beijing, 87
Beirut, 10, 21, 76
Bentsen, Lloyd, 49, 87
Bird, Rose, 26
Black, Hugo L., 187
Black Vote, 40, 45, 47-49, 70, 93, 104, 108, 111, 115, 116, 124, 125, 224, 241, 283, 286
Brezhnev, Leonid, 78
Brokaw, Tom, 216
Brown, Jerry, 26, 126
Brown, Willie, 26
Bryan, William Jennings, 102
Bryce, James, 212
Buckley v. Valeo, 183, 199, 209
Budget Process, 67-68, 96, 264
Budget Reform Act, 67, 284
Bull Moose Party, 168 passim
Bumpers, Dale, 267
Bureaucracy, 69, 70, 102, 107, 185, 188, 192, 224, 227, 242, 258, 273
Burns, James MacGregor, 32-33
Burt, Richard, 8
Busby, Horace, 89
Bush, George, 79, 87, 88, 127, 128

C-5A Cargo Plane, 17
Caddell, Pat, 96
Calhoun, John C., 134 ff
California, 26, 31, 49, 74, 82, 83, 86, 120, 126
Campaign Finance Reform, 147, 154, 183-210 passim
Campaign Strategy, 109-132 passim
Canarse: *The Jews and Italians of Brooklyn Against Liberalism,* 235
Capaldi, Nicholas, 283
Carter, Jimmy, 3-12 passim, 15-17, 22-47 passim, 58, 75-97 passim, 114-127 passim, 200-201, 254, 270, 280
Catholicism, 39, 50, 78, 97
Caucus, 40, 73, 143, 146, 150, 164
CBS News, 94, 218

Ceasar, James, 187-188
Central America, 10, 14, 19-20, 47, 51, 69, 129
Chamberlain, Neville, 3
Cheney, Richard B., 191
Chernenko, Andrei, 78-79
Chile, 20
Church, Frank, 274
Churchill, Winston, 30, 34, 54, 233
CIA, 20, 87
Civil Rights, 38, 51, 57, 84, 97, 115, 140, 214, 227, 232
Civil Rights Act, 118
Civil Rights Commission, 97
Clamor at the Gates: The New American Immigration, 237 n.6
Claremont Review of Books, 238
Coelho, Tony, 92, 204, 267
Cold War, 4, 12
Collins, Martha Lane, 49
Commentary, 220
Committee on the Present Danger, 23
Congress: Keystone of the Washington Establishment, 69
Congressional Elections, 69, 83-84, 103-105,108, 130, 184-185, 189-191, 193, 204-205, 217, 245-246, 265-276 passim, 277-279, 283-284
Connecticut, 43, 100
Constitution, U.S., 67, 68, 106, 109, 134, 257, 284
Contras, 19
Conyers, John, 241
Coolidge, Calvin, 60, 61, 66, 170-177
Cousins v. Wigoda, 145
Cranston, Alan, 11-12, 126
Crime (Law and Order), 85-86, 118
Cuba, 5, 14, 19-20, 31
Cuomo, Mario, 226

Darwin, Charles, 66, 257
Deadlock of Democracy, 31-32, 67, 70, 107
Deadly Gambits, 8
Dearborn Independent, 172
Debates, Candidate, 55, 56, 79-82, 220, 270
Declaration of Independence, 133, 134, 231, 252, 257
Deficit, Budget, 28, 29, 76, 79, 123
Delaware, 100
Dellums, Ronald, 241

Democratic Congressional Campaign Committee, 92
Democratic Farm-Labor Party, 84
Democratic National Committee, 75, 125, 153
Demographics, 86, 89-108 passim
Derian, Patricia, 4
Detente, 4, 13
Deterrence, 4, 12, 18-19, 63, 64
District of Columbia, 25, 84
Dole, Robert, 58, 61
Donovan, Raymond, 83
Dornan, Bob, 271-272
Downey, Tom, 271
Dutton, Fred, 89

Eagleburger, Lawrence, 8
Economy (in general), 16, 25-36 passim, 51-52, 76, 96, 98, 99-101, 112, 129, 221
Edsall, Thomas B., 204
Education, 64-65
Eisenhower, Dwight D., 76, 113, 119, 134, 265, 277
El Salvador, 14, 19-20, 47, 48
Electoral College, 83-84, 103, 109-110, 112, 153-156, 157-160, 162-163, 168-182
The Emerging Republican Majority, 237n
Entitlement, 75, 93, 260, 279, 283, 284, 285, 287
Environment Issue, 79, 97
Equal Employment Opportunity Commission, 97
Equal Rights Amendment, 58, 128
The Ethnic Factor: How America's Minorities Decide Elections, 240n
Ethnic Voters, 105-106, 223-244 passim
Europe, 6, 10, 14, 57

F-14 Airplane, 17
Faction, 106-107, 136, 138
Fairness Commission, 45, 46, 51
Farrakhan, Louis, 48, 239
The Fate of the Earth, 11
Federal Budget and Impoundment Control Act (see Budget Reform Act of 1974)
Federal Corrupt Practices Act, 194
Federal Election Campaign Act, 154, 167, 183, 189, 196, 197-203
Federal Election Commission, 183, 199
Federal Reserve Board, 27, 35
Federalism, 64-65, 137, 157, 158

Federalist Papers, 136, 187
  Number 10: 136, 223, 228
  Number 14: 223, 228, 242
  Number 37: 228
  Number 51: 92, 106, 107
Feinstein, Dianne, 86
Feminism, 50, 86
Ferraro, Geraldine, 18, 38-39, 49-52, 74, 75, 77, 78, 85-86 124-125, 128, 282-283
Financial Disclosure, 77, 125
Fiorina, Morris, 69
Firefighters Local Union v. Stotts, 232
First Amendment, 64
Florida, 43, 44
Ford, Gerald, 4-5, 55, 58, 76, 77, 80, 87, 118-119, 200, 252-253, 269
Ford, Henry, 172
Founding Fathers, 57, 68, 106, 107, 187, 255, 257
Frémont, John C., 55
Fulbright, J. William, 274
Fuller, Tony, 235
The Future of American Politics, 235

Gallup Poll, 94, 96, 277
Geneva, 12, 18
Georgia, 43, 115
Georgia Mafia, 85
Gilder, George, 254
Gillet, Frederick H., 172-173
Gingrich, Newt, 58
Glazer, Nathan, 237n
Glenn, John, 15, 46, 49, 146
Goldman, Peter, 235
Goldwater, Barry, 35, 86-87, 90, 117, 118, 127, 268
Goodman, Ellen, 216
Great Britain, 3, 8, 54
Great Depression, 26
Great Society, 26, 28, 36, 56, 57, 85, 185
Grenada, 17, 281
Gromyko, Andrei, 10, 79
Guatemala, 20
Gun Control, 118

Haig, Alexander, 8
Haiti, 20
Harding, Warren G., 169
Harrier Airplane, 17
Harris, Louis, 94-97
Hart, Gary, 12-16, 19, 23, 39, 42-51, 75, 121-122, 137, 146, 279

Hatfield, Mark, 217
Hayek, Friedrich, 254
Heard, Alexander, 194, 196
Helms, Jesse, 274
Henry, William A. III, 214, 235
Hightower, Jack, 272
Hilles, Charles D., 171
Himmelfarb, Milton, 236
Hiroshima, 238
Hispanic Voters, 45, 70, 104-105, 237-238
Hitler, Adolf, 18
Hollings, Ernest, 15, 46, 49
Homestead Act, 111
Homosexuality, 217
Honduras, 14, 47
Hoover, Herbert, 61,138-139
House of Commons, 54, 284
Huddleston, Walter, 275
Human Rights (foreign policy), 4, 63, 65, 286
Humphrey, Hubert, 37, 39, 84, 85, 113, 254
Hunt, James B., 41, 274
Hunt Commission, 43, 44, 51, 86, 142 passim

ICBM, 6-7, 10
Ikle, Fred, 8
Illinois, 43, 44, 106
Imperial Presidency, 67
Indiana, 43, 44, 100
Inflation, 27, 58, 76, 113, 261
Iowa, 42, 44, 45, 102
Iran, 5, 12, 21
Irish Voters, 105, 235
Israel, 13-14
Italian Voters, 78, 97-98, 105, 124, 235
Item Veto, 68

Jackson, Andrew, 110, 112, 212, 254
Jackson, Brooks, 204
Jackson, Henry, 15, 45
Jackson, Jesse, 14-15, 23, 39, 43-51, 90, 91, 116, 122, 125, 137, 164, 224-228, 283
Jacobson, Gary, 190, 192, 194, 200, 208
Jaffa, Harry V., 236n.5
Jefferson, Thomas, 32, 33, 64, 91, 250, 256, 257
Jepsen, Roger W., 275
Jesse Jackson and the Politics of Race, 233
Jesse Jackson: The Man, The Movement, The Myth, 233

Jewish Voters, 97, 235-237, 283
Johnson, Hiram, 169
Johnson, Lyndon B., 37, 55, 76, 77, 85, 140, 269
Joint Center for Economic Studies, 90
Jones, James R., 271
Jordan, Hamilton, 85
Journalism/Journalists, 80-81, 93-94, 95, 138, 211-223 passim, 279-280
Judiciary (Courts), 64, 65, 68, 145-146, 215, 232, 258

Kemp, Jack, 58, 63, 67
Kennedy, Edward, 17, 41, 42, 117, 240
Kennedy, John F., 17-18, 31-32, 76, 79-80, 124, 125
Kennedy, Robert F., 141
Kentucky, 49
King, Martin Luther, Jr., 15, 48, 57, 234
Kirk, Paul, 108
Kirkpatrick, Jeanne, 8
Kirwin, Michael, 192
Kissinger, Henry, 4, 8
Kissinger Commission, 14
Kondrake, Morton, 267
Korean War, 7
Kramer, Michael S., 240n
Kristol, Irving, 254
Ku Klux Klan, 172, 176

Lance, Bert, 75, 125
Landess, Thomas, 233 in 3
Landon, Alf, 25
Leadership Issue, 51, 77-82, 280
League of Women Voters, 80
Lebanon, 10, 14, 21, 76, 281
LeMay Curtis, 19
Levy, Mark, 240n
Lewis, Drew, 60, 70
Libya, 6
Lichter, Linda, 225
Lincoln, Abraham, 57, 60-71 passim, 91, 111, 133-135, 165, 228-229, 257
Lippmann, Walter, 231
Lodge, Henry Cabot, 170
Loeffler, Tom, 59
Long, Huey, 117
Los Angeles Times, 95-97, 213-219 passim
Lott, Trent, 60
Lowi, Theodore, 267, 273
Lubell, Samuel, 235
Luken, Thomas, 270

Machiavelli, Nicolo, 278
Madison, James, 32, 33, 228
Maine, 43
Malbin, Michael, 183, 184, 196, 205
Malcom, Andrew H., 211
Manatt, Charles, 75, 125, 126
Marx, Karl, 18
Marxism-Leninism, 63
Maryland, 100, 101
Massachusetts, 43, 87, 100
Mathias, Charles, 217
Mayer, George H., 176
McCarthy, Eugene, 201
McConnell, Mitch, 275
McFarlane, Robert, 8
McGovern, George, 11-12, 14, 37, 38, 40, 42, 47, 89, 116, 117, 122, 126, 270, 282
McGovern-Fraser Commission, 138, 142
Meany, George, 117
Medicare, 28
Meese, Edwin, 64, 82, 83, 225
Merola, Mario, 83
Michigan, 43, 127
Middle East, 3, 21, 47
Mikulski Commission, 138, 145
Mineta, Norman, 239
Minnesota, 43, 75, 82, 84, 101, 282
Minuteman Missile, 7, 17
"Misery Index", 76, 77
Modern Age, 215
Monetary Policy, 27, 30, 31, 35
Moral Majority, 287
Mount Olympus, 73
Moyers, Bill, 216
Mozambique, 6
Murdock, Norm, 269
Murray, Charles, 218, 285
Mutual Assured Destruction, 63, 64, 83
MX Missile, 9, 26, 50

Nagasaki, 238
Nation of Islam, 48
National Public Radio, 94
The National Republican, 173-175
National Security, 3-24 passim, 63, 82-83
National Security Council, 7, 87
National Women's Political Caucus, 86
NATO, 7, 9, 12, 17
NBC News, 218
New Deal, 26, 32, 34, 37, 47, 56-62 passim, 67, 70, 102, 111, 112, 114, 118, 120, 121, 123, 124, 188

The New Freedom, 57, 108, 258
New Frontier, 36
New Hampshire, 42-46
New Jersey, 49
New Nationalism, 108
The New Republic, 214, 227-231
New Right, 117-119
New York, 14, 43, 48, 112, 127
New York Times, 211, 213, 217, 220, 226, 233, 266
New York Times-CBS Poll, 94, 241, 245
Newsweek, 42
Newton, Isaac, 257
Nicaragua, 6, 19-20, 47, 48
Nitze, Paul, 8
Nixon, Richard, 4, 14, 17-19, 38, 67, 76, 77, 79, 80, 84, 93, 96, 113, 117, 133, 188, 197-199, 265, 268, 269, 277
North Carolina, 41, 108, 272
North Dakota, 102
National Organization for Women, 46, 51, 74, 75, 77, 86, 89, 108, 282
Nuclear Freeze, 11, 18, 46, 50

Ohio, 43
Olympics, 73-74, 76, 114, 211
Office of Management and Budget, 10, 75, 125
O'Neill, Thomas P. (Tip), 25, 26, 86, 90, 106, 117, 266, 267, 268, 273, 278, 282
Oregon, 120
Orwell, George, 66
Overacker, Louise, 195

Party Rules, 37, 39-45 passim, 76, 133-182 passim
Patman, Bill, 272
Patterson, Jerry, 271, 272
Pennsylvania, 43, 100, 112, 127
People's Republic of China, 10, 87
Percy, Charles, 106, 275
Perle, Richard, 8
Perry, James, 219
Pershing II Missile, 9
Persian Gulf, 14, 51
Philadelphia Inquirer, 220
Phillips, Howard, 217
Phillips, Kevin, 89, 237n, 246
Pipes, Richard, 7
Platform (general), 53-54, 121, 222
  Democratic
    1976, 50

1980, 4, 50
1984, 50, 90, 122-123, 247
Republican
  1976, 55
  1980, 3, 7, 64
  1984, 53-72 passim, 246-247
Platform Committee, 50-51
Podhoretz, Norman, 254
Political Action Committees, 126, 184, 189-190, 205-206, 278
Polls, Public Opinion, 16, 89-108 passim, 166-167, 212, 213, 224, 277
Polsby, Nelson, 206
Populism, 67, 102
Poseidon, 17
Pragmatists (GOP Faction), 8, 10, 20, 23, 58-71 passim, 86-87, 119
Presidential Campaign Fund Act, 195-197
Primary Elections, 39, 40, 42-45, 53, 73, 117, 124, 140-141, 144-145, 147, 148-149, 150, 151, 162, 200, 282
Progressivism, 259
Public Opinion (Magazine), 218, 225
Puerto Rico, 43
PUSH, 240

The Quest for the Presidency 1984, 235
Quinn, Richard, 233n

Rabkin, Jeremy, 226-227, 233
Rainbow Coalition, 48, 108, 226-228
Rather, Dan, 216
Rawls, John, 207-208
The Real Majority, 235
Realignment, 30, 34, 53, 70, 84, 90, 91, 111-114, 129-131, 133, 167, 189, 218, 245-264 passim, 277-278, 284
Reeves, Richard, 267
Religion, 39, 64, 78, 97, 113, 223, 287
Republican National Committee, 87, 137, 150, 181, 202
Reynolds, Barbara, 233n
Reynolds, William Bradford, 225
Rhode Island, 43
Rieder, Jonathan, 235
Ripon Society, 179
Robinson, Michael J., 218
Rockefeller, Nelson, 57
Rogers, Will, 138
Rollins, Edward J., 270
Roosevelt, Franklin D., 17, 25, 34, 57, 67, 69, 91, 111, 112, 113, 114, 118, 122, 124, 226, 248-252, 265

Roosevelt, Theodore, 108, 169 passim, 195
Roper Poll, 94, 96
Rostow, Eugene, 8
Rothman-Lichter Poll, 212

Sakharov, Andrei, 239
SALT II, 3, 6-9
Sanford, Terry, 143
Santa Ana *Register,* 271-272
Scammon, Richard, 235
Scheer, Robert, 11, 215
Schell, Jonathan, 11
Schlafly, Phyllis, 128
Schlesinger, Arthur, Jr., 90, 102, 216
Schneider, William, 213, 236n
School Prayer Issue, 64, 97, 115, 118, 287
Schorr, Alvin, 216
Schultz, George, 8
Scott v. Sanford, 232
Screen Actor's Guild, 86
Strategic Defense Initiative, 10, 18, 22, 63, 83
Sears, John, 89
Shields, Mark, 266
Shogan, Robert, 221
Sierra Club, 79
Silent Majority, 67
Simon, Paul, 106, 275
Skerry, Peter, 237n
Slavery, 62, 63, 65, 111, 112, 134-135, 228
Smith, William French, 226
Scowcroft Commission, 9
Social Security, 28, 61, 70, 106, 112, 261
Socialism, 57, 62
Somoza, 15
South Africa, 20
South Carolina, 15
South Yemen, 6
Soviet Union, 3-14, 17-20, 22-23, 31, 48, 51, 63, 74, 78, 79, 97
Sowell, Thomas, 218
Stafford, Robert, 217
START, 9-10, 12
States' Rights, 65, 161
Steiger, William, 179
Stein, Jacob, 82, 83
Steinem, Gloria, 50
Stevenson, Adlai, III, 265
Super-Delegates, 41, 43, 44, 45
Super-Tuesday, 43
Supply Side Economics, 58, 60, 96, 97

Supreme Court, 64, 65, 118

Taft, William Howard, 168
Taiwan, 10
Tammany Hall, 112
Tax Increase, 26, 29, 58-59, 75, 79, 123, 128, 129, 247
Tennessee, 43
Terrorism, 21, 76
Texas, 49, 87, 108, 120, 272
A Theory of Justice, 207
Third Parties, 115, 117-118
Third World, 5-7, 14-15, 48
Time (Magazine), 212
Tocqueville, Alexis de, 65, 206, 212, 256
Truman, Harry, 17, 34, 122

United Nations, 18-20, 79
Uncommitted Voters, 21
Unemployment, 76-77, 100, 101, 112
USA Today, 94

Van Buren, Martin, 136, 166
Vietnam War, 4-8, 11-16, 20, 22-23, 33, 37, 39, 115, 116, 129
Viguerie, Richard, 217
Virginia, 112
Visions of America, 235
Volcker, Paul, 27, 30, 31, 35
Voodoo Economics, 87, 127
Voting Rights Act, 57, 97, 118

Wagner Act, 261
Wall Street Journal, 91, 106, 204, 219
Wallace, George, 115, 118, 142, 145
War Powers Resolution, 67, 286
Warner, John, 63
Washington (state), 120
Washington, Booker T., 230
Washington Post, 8, 94, 204, 212, 213, 220
Watergate, 8, 67, 76, 87, 93, 96, 183, 188, 193 passim
Wattenberg, Ben, 235
Weaver, Paul H., 220
Weicker, Lowell, 58, 217
Weinberger, Caspar, 10
West Virginia, 39
Western Europe, 3, 9-10, 12-13
Whigs, 110, 112
Wildavsky, Aaron, 206
Williams, Walter, 218
Wilson, James Q., 140

Wilson, Woodrow, 56, 57, 108, 168, 256-260
"Wimp" Issue, 17, 49-50
Winograd Commission, 138, 145
Wisconsin, 43, 60, 61
World War I, 112
World War II, 7, 31, 54, 69, 78, 86, 113
Wright, Skelly, 207-209

Yarborough, Ralph, 87
Young, Andrew, 4
Young, Coleman, 240
"Yuppies", 47, 147

Zaccaro, John, 77